CONCISE GUIDE TO ENTREPRENEURSHIP, TECHNOLOGY AND INNOVATION

ELGAR CONCISE GUIDES

Each Elgar Concise Guide provides an accessible and engaging overview of the key research within a specific field.

With each entry written by a key thinker in their field, these books will prove invaluable to students and scholars seeking an introduction to key topics and theories and will guide the reader towards more advanced literature. Encyclopedic in scope, *Elgar Concise Guides* will be an ideal jumping-off point for any researcher seeking the fundamentals of a subject.

Concise Guide to Entrepreneurship, Technology and Innovation

Edited by

David B. Audretsch

Distinguished Professor and Ameritech Chair of Economic Development, Indiana University, USA

Christopher S. Hayter

Assistant Professor, Center for Organization Research and Design, School of Public Affairs, Arizona State University, USA

Albert N. Link

Virginia Batte Phillips Distinguished Professor, University of North Carolina at Greensboro, USA

ELGAR CONCISE GUIDES

Edward Elgar
PUBLISHING

Cheltenham, UK • Northampton, MA, USA

Published by
Edward Elgar Publishing Limited
The Lypiatts
15 Lansdown Road
Cheltenham
Glos GL50 2JA
UK

Edward Elgar Publishing, Inc.
William Pratt House
9 Dewey Court
Northampton
Massachusetts 01060
USA

Reprinted 2016

A catalogue record for this book
is available from the British Library

Library of Congress Control Number: 2015940675

This book is available electronically in the **Elgar**online
Business subject collection
DOI 10.4337/9781783474202

ISBN 978 1 78347 418 9 (cased)
ISBN 978 1 78347 420 2 (eBook)

Typeset by Servis Filmsetting Ltd, Stockport, Cheshire
Printed and bound in Great Britain by T.J. International Ltd, Padstow

Contents

v

Figures and Tables

Contributors

David B. Audretsch is a Distinguished Professor and Ameritech Chair of Economic Development at Indiana University, where he also serves as Director of the Institute for Development Strategies. He also is an Honorary Professor of Industrial Economics and Entrepreneurship at the WHU-Otto Beisheim School of Management in Germany, Honorary Professor at the Friedrich Schiller University of Jena in Germany and Research Fellow of the Centre for Economic Policy Research in London. He co-edits *Small Business Economics: An Entrepreneurship Journal*. Email: daudrets@indiana.edu.

Craig Boardman is Associate Professor in the John Glenn School of Public Affairs at the Ohio State University. He is also the Associate Director of the Battelle Center for Science & Technology Policy. Email: craig.boardman@gmail.com.

Barry Bozeman is Arizona Centennial Professor of Technology Policy and Public Management and Director of the Center for Organization Research and Design at Arizona State University. His research focuses on science and technology policy, including research collaboration, innovation studies, research evaluation and technology transfer. Email: bbozeman@asu.edu.

Samantha R. Bradley is an economist in RTI International's Food and Nutrition Policy Research Program. Her work includes conducting analyses of food policy issues, primarily by analyzing economic, survey response and scanner data. She specializes in applications of econometrics, and is also experienced in managing databases and conducting literature reviews. Email: sbradley@rti.org.

Andrew Burke is the Dean of Trinity Business School and the Chair of Business Studies at Trinity College, Dublin. Previously, he was the Bettany Chair and the founding Director of the Bettany Centre for Entrepreneurship at Cranfield School of Management. He was also a Board Member of Cranfield Ventures Limited – Cranfield University's tech transfer unit. His research is focused on entrepreneurial performance; particularly relating to economics, strategic and financial determinants. Email: andrew.burke@tcd.ie.

Uwe Cantner is Professor of Economics at the Friedrich Schiller University Jena (Germany) and at the University of Southern Denmark in Odense. His research is devoted to economics of innovation and entrepreneurship, evolutionary economics, industrial economics and behavioral economics. Among others he was President of the International Joseph A. Schumpeter Society from 2012 to 2014; he has served as Managing Editor of the *Journal of Evolutionary Economics* since 2002. Email: uwe.cantner@uni-jena.de.

Mark Casson is Professor of Economics and Director of the Centre for Institutional Performance at the University of Reading. His recent books include *Entrepreneurship: Theory, Networks, History* (2010) and *The Entrepreneur in History* (with Catherine Casson, 2013). He also publishes on international business and business and economic history. Email: m.c.casson@reading.ac.uk.

Stefano Cazzago is a Doctoral Student in Management at the Lundquist College of Business, University of Oregon. His primary research interests include social networks and innovation, with a focus on interorganizational networks from an ego perspective. His current research explores the effects of social networks on innovation. Email: stefanoc@uoregon.edu.

James A. Cunningham is a Professor of Strategic Management at Newcastle Business School at Northumbria University in the United Kingdom. His main research interests focus on scientists as principal investigators, scientific entrepreneurship, university technology transfer and entrepreneurial universities. Email: james.cunningham@northumbria.ac.uk.

Per Davidsson is Professor of Entrepreneurship at Queensland University of Technology and the Jönköping International Business School. Recognized as a leading scholar on business startups and small firm growth, he is past Chair of the Entrepreneurship Division of the Academy of Management and Field Editor of the *Journal of Business Venturing*. Email: per.davidsson@qut.edu.au.

Marc Deloof is Professor of Finance at the University of Antwerp. While he has a broad interest in the fields of corporate finance and corporate governance, his research focuses on entrepreneurial and small business finance and financial history. Email: marc.deloof@uantwerpen.be.

Alfredo De Massis is a tenured Full Professor who holds the Chair in Entrepreneurship and Family Business at Lancaster University Management School (UK) and is Director of the School's Centre for Family Business. He currently serves as Chairman of the European Leadership Council of the Global STEP Project for Family Enterprising and his research has been published widely in leading academic and professional journals and books. Email: a.demassis@lancaster.ac.uk.

Denise Dunlap is an Assistant Professor of International Business and Strategic Management at Northeastern University's D'Amore McKim School of Business. She is an interdisciplinary scholar in the areas of innovation, entrepreneurship and international business whose work is well-recognized in practitioner contexts and scholarly journals. Her main research focuses on how global knowledge sourcing practices in developed countries and emerging markets matter for innovation. Email: d.dunlap@neu.edu.

Will Geoghegan is an Assistant Professor in the Management Department of Syracuse University's Martin J. Whitman School of Management. He received his PhD from National University of Ireland, Galway and his research interests pertain to strategic management, innovation, innovation systems, technology transfer and entrepreneurship. Email: wjgeoghe@syr.edu.

Vivek Ghosal is Professor at the School of Economics at Georgia Institute of Technology. His current research interests include: firm strategy and innovation; impact of environmental regulations on business strategy, innovation and firm reorganization; and firms' decision-making under uncertainty. He holds visiting professorships at the European Business School (Germany) and joint OECD-Korea Development Institute School of Public Policy and Management (South Korea). Email: vivekghosal@gatech.edu.

Jürgen Hanssens holds a Master's degree in Business Administration (specialization: corporate finance) from Ghent University. He is currently a PhD Researcher at Ghent University. His research focuses on entrepreneurial finance. Email: Jurgen.Hanssens@ugent.be.

Christopher S. Hayter is an Assistant Professor at the Arizona State University School of Public Affairs where he focuses on entrepreneurship, technology policy and the organization of higher education and science. He is affiliated with the Center for Organization Research and Design and the Center for Science, Technology, and Environmental Policy Studies, and has more than 15 years of experience as a policy practitioner. Email: christopher.s.hayter@gmail.com.

Monika Herzig is a Senior Lecturer in Arts Administration at Indiana University, the author of *David Baker – A Legacy in Music* and an active touring and recording jazz artist with numerous recordings to her credit. Her research focuses on jazz as a creative and living art form. More information and sound samples at www.monikaherzig.com. Email: mherzig@ indiana.edu.

Andrew Kao is a Graduate Student Affiliate at the Center for Organization Research and Design. His research interest sits at the intersection of science and technology policy and organization theory, specifically in university research centers' organizational strategies, technology transfer mechanism and interactive relations among laboratories from different sectors (government, private and university). Email: akao2@asu.edu.

Martin Kenney is a Professor in the Department of Human and Community Development and a Senior Project Director at the Berkeley Roundtable on the International Economy. He is an Editor at *Research Policy* and for a Stanford University Press book series on innovation in the global economy. He is currently a Visiting Researcher at ETLA, the Research Institute for the Finnish Economy. Email: mfkenney@ucdavis.edu.

Donald F. Kuratko is the Jack M. Gill Distinguished Chair of Entrepreneurship; Professor of Entrepreneurship; Executive and Academic Director of the Johnson Center for Entrepreneurship & Innovation, Kelley School of Business, Indiana University Bloomington. His research focuses on entrepreneurship and corporate entrepreneurship with 180 journal articles and 30 books, including one of the leading entrepreneurship books, *Entrepreneurship: Theory, Process, Practice*, 9th edn (2014). Email: dkuratko@indiana.edu.

Hans Landström is Professor in Entrepreneurship at Lund University, Sweden. He is co-founder of two research centers on entrepreneurship and innovation at Lund University: CIRCLE and the Sten K. Johnson Centre for Entrepreneurship. His research interests include entrepreneurial finance, venture capital and business angels, entrepreneurial learning and the history of entrepreneurship research. Email: hans.landstrom@fek.lu.se.

Erik E. Lehmann is a Full Professor of Management and Organization at Augsburg University, Germany and Director of the Master Program Global Business Management, and Applied Professor at Indiana University, Bloomington. His research is focused on the links between governance structures in family and entrepreneurial firms and regional knowledge spillover theory. He serves as an Associate Editor of *Small Business Economics*. His work has been published in leading academic journals including *The Review of Finance, Research Policy, Entrepreneurship Theory and Practice, Journal of Economic Behavior & Organization* and *Journal of Technology Transfer*, among others. Email: erik.lehmann@ wiwi.uni-augsburg.de.

Dennis Patrick Leyden is Associate Professor of Economics at the University of North Carolina at Greensboro. His research focuses on entrepreneurship in both the public and private sector, and on the role and behavior of universities in furthering such entrepreneurial activity and its impact on innovation and economic development. Email: dpleyden@ uncg.edu.

Albert N. Link is the Virginia Batte Phillips Distinguished Professor at the University of North Carolina at Greensboro. His research focuses on technology and innovation policy, academic entrepreneurship, public sector entrepreneurship and the economics of R&D. He is also the Editor-in-Chief of the *Journal of Technology Transfer*. From 2007 to 2012, he served as the US Representative to the United Nations Economic Commission for Europe (Co-vice-chairperson of Team of Specialists on Innovation and Competitiveness Policies Initiative) in Geneva. Email: anlink@uncg. edu.

Xiaohui Liu is Professor of International Business and Strategy at the School of Business and Economics, Loughborough University. Her main research interests include knowledge spillovers, human mobility, innovation and the internationalization strategies of firms from emerging economies. She has published widely and is Senior Editor of *Management and Organization Review* and Advisory Editor of *Research Policy*. Email: X.liu2@lboro.ac.uk.

Sophie Manigart is Full Professor at Ghent University and Partner at Vlerick Business School. Her research deals with both the demand for and the supply of entrepreneurial finance (including venture capital and business angel funding). She is Associate Editor of *Entrepreneurship Theory and Practice*. She is also Non-executive Director of Business Angel Network Vlaanderen and Gimv (quoted private equity firm). Email: sophie.manigart@vlerick.com.

Gideon D. Markman is a Professor at Colorado State University who studies competitive dynamics, market entry, entrepreneurship and innovation. He is an Associate Editor of the *Academy of Management Perspectives* and he serves on the editorial board of several journals, including *Journal of Management Studies*, *Strategic Entrepreneurship Journal*, and *Journal of Management*. He founded the Sustainability, Ethics, and Entrepreneurship Conference, which is supported by the Kauffman Foundation. His research appears in diverse journals: *Academy of Management Review*, *Strategic Management Journal*, *Academy of Management Journal*, *Journal of Applied Psychology*, *Journal of Management*, *Journal of Management*

Studies, *Journal of Business Venturing*, and *Academy of Management Perspectives*. Email: gid.markman@gmail.com.

Heike Mayer is Professor of Economic Geography in the Institute of Geography and Co-director of the Center for Regional Economic Development at the University of Bern in Switzerland. She is also Adjunct Professor in the Urban Affairs and Planning program at Virginia Tech in the United States. Her primary area of research is in local and regional economic development with a particular focus on entrepreneurship and innovation dynamics. Email: mayer@giub.unibe.ch.

Michael H. Morris holds the James W. Walter Clinical Eminent Scholar Chair at the University of Florida. A pioneer in curricular innovation, he launched the first department and first school of entrepreneurship at major research universities. He has published 11 books and more than 150 articles, book chapters and other scholarly publications. His current research focuses on emergence in entrepreneurship. Email: michael.morris@warrington.ufl.edu.

Andrew J. Nelson is Associate Professor of Management; Academic Director of the Lundquist Center for Entrepreneurship; and Bramsen Faculty Fellow in Innovation, Entrepreneurship and Sustainability at the University of Oregon. His research investigates the origins and evolution of new science- and technology-based fields, with an emphasis on how organizational and occupational contexts shape commercialization processes. Email: ajnelson@uoregon.edu.

Conor O'Kane is a Senior Lecturer in Strategic Management at the University of Otago in New Zealand. His current research interests focus on the changing role-identity of scientists, technology transfer offices and the entrepreneurial university at the micro-foundation of the triple helix. Email: conor.okane@otago.ac.nz.

Damien Organ is a Postdoctoral Researcher at University College Cork (Ireland). His PhD research explored the micro-institutional dynamics of university-based entrepreneurship, focusing on the role of context in constraining and enabling entrepreneurial cognition and behavior. His current research explores the cognitive functioning of nascent entrepreneurial teams. Email: Damien.organ@ucc.ie.

Simon Parker is Director of the Entrepreneurship Research Center at Ivey. He researches the economics of entrepreneurship, and is an Associate Editor at the *Journal of Business Venturing* and the *Journal of Economics and Management Strategy*. He is also an active case writer, having published ten case studies to date. Email: sparker@ivey.uwo.ca.

G. Tyge Payne is the Jerry S. Rawls Professor of Strategic Management at Texas Tech University in Lubbock, Texas. An award-winning scholar, he has published widely on such topics as configurations, firm-level entrepreneurship, organizational ethics, multi-level methods, social capital and temporality. He currently serves as an Associate Editor for *Family Business Review*. Email: tyge.payne@ttu.edu.

Markus Perkmann is Associate Professor in the Business School at Imperial College London. His research interests include the business of science, university–industry relations and academic entrepreneurship. He has published numerous articles in journals including *Organization Science*, *Research Policy* and *Economic Geography*, and serves as an Associate Editor of *Innovation: Management, Policy & Practice*. He holds a PhD in Sociology from Lancaster University, and is a Management Practices Fellow of the Advanced Institute of Management Research. Email: m.perkmann@imperial.ac.uk.

Lois S. Peters is Associate Professor, Enterprise Management and Organization Area Coordinator and Director Technology Commercialization and Entrepreneurship Program at the Lally School of Management at Rensselaer Polytechnic Institute. Since 1995 she has been studying breakthrough innovation in collaboration with faculty at RPI, Babson and the Industrial Research Institute an association of the chief technology officers of Fortune 1000 companies. She is co-author of *Radical Innovation: How Mature Companies Can Outsmart Upstarts*, Harvard Business Press, 2000 and *Grabbing Lightning: Building Capability for Breakthrough Innovation*, Jossey Bass, 2008. Currently she is co-authoring her third book on this subject area, *Institutionalizing a Breakthrough Innovation Capability through Talent Selection and Development*, Stanford University Press. Email: peterl@rpi.edu.

Phillip H. Phan is Professor at the Johns Hopkins University Carey Business School and Core Faculty at the Johns Hopkins Medicine Armstrong Institute for Patient Safety and Quality. He researches the management of technological innovation. He is Co-editor of the *Academy of Management Perspectives* and Associate Editor for the *Journal of Family Business Strategy*, *Journal of Technology Transfer*, and *Journal of Financial Stability*. Email: pphan@jhu.edu.

Eko Agus Prasetio is a PhD student at the Faculty of Economics and Business Administration, FSU Jena, Germany. Prior to his studies, he had more than ten years of professional experience in innovation and R&D manufacturing. He gained his MBA from Nyenrode University,

Netherlands and his Bachelor's degree from ITB, Indonesia. Email: eko. prasetio@uni-jena.de.

Jacob H. Rooksby is Assistant Professor of Law at Duquesne University School of Law in Pittsburgh. His research interests concern intellectual property law and policy issues in higher education. Email: rooksbyj@duq. edu.

Gordon E. Shockley, PhD, is Associate Professor of Social Entrepreneurship at Arizona State University. His teaching and research interests concentrate on building the field of non-market entrepreneurship as well as contributing to public policy modeling and the politics, economics, and sociology of the arts and humanities. He recently co-edited *Non-market Entrepreneurship: Interdisciplinary Approaches* with Peter Frank and Roger Stough (Edward Elgar). Email: Gordon. Shockley@asu.edu.

Thomas Standaert holds a degree in Business Engineering (Ghent University). He is a Research Assistant at Ghent University pursuing a doctoral dissertation on government intervention in venture capital markets. Email: ThomasB.Standaert@ugent.be.

Anthony Talarico is a Research Assistant at Arizona State University. His work primarily focuses on the societal impact of entrepreneurship in its commercial, social and policy-based forms. In addition to his entrepreneurial research, he strategizes alternative funding models for nonprofit organizations designed to create venture capital for scaling operations. Email: atalaric@asu.edu.

Roy Thurik is Professor of Economics and Entrepreneurship at Erasmus University Rotterdam and Professor of Entrepreneurship at the Free University of Amsterdam. He is Scientific Advisor at Panteia in Zoetermeer, the Netherlands. He is Directeur de la Recherche at the Montpellier Business School in France. He is a Research Fellow at two renowned Dutch research schools: the Tinbergen Institute for Economic Sciences and the Erasmus Research Institute for Management. He is a member of the IZA Institute for the Study of Labor. Email: thurik@ese. eur.nl.

Tom Vanacker is Assistant Professor at Ghent University and Research Fellow at the Vlerick Business School. He was Visiting Scholar at the Carlson School of Management and the Wharton School. His research focuses on entrepreneurial finance and crosses the traditional boundaries between the disciplines of entrepreneurship, management and finance. Email: tomr.vanacker@ugent.be.

Silvio Vismara, PhD, is Associate Professor of Corporate Finance at the University of Bergamo, Italy. His research activity is in entrepreneurial finance and covers mainly public equity in the form of initial public offerings and crowdfunding. Silvio is Associate Editor of *Small Business Economics* and co-founder of the CISAlpino Institute for Comparative Studies in Europe. Email: silvio.vismara@unibg.it.

Nicholas S. Vonortas is Professor of Economics and International Affairs at The George Washington University. He joined the Department of Economics and the Center for International Science and Technology Policy (Elliott School of International Affairs) in 1990. During 2001–2012, he served as the Director of both the Center and of the graduate program in International Science and Technology Policy. He is also an Editor of the journal *Science and Public Policy*. Email: vonortas@gwu.edu.

Joel West is Professor of Innovation and Entrepreneurship at the Keck Graduate Institute of Applied Life Sciences. His research focuses on innovation communities, ecosystems and networks, and includes co-editing *Open Innovation: Researching a New Paradigm and New Frontiers in Open Innovation*. He has co-founded startups in the software and pharmaceutical industries. Email: kgi@joelwest.org.

Paul Westhead is Professor of Entrepreneurship at Durham University Business School, Durham University. Email: paul.westhead@durham. ac.uk.

Katharine Wirsching is a Research Assistant at Augsburg University. Her research is focused on governance structures and innovation behavior in family firms. Her research has been published in the *Journal of Business Economics* and in edited volumes with Edward Elgar and Springer. Email: Katharine.wirsching@wiwi.uni-augsburg.de.

Mike Wright is Professor of Entrepreneurship at Imperial College, Visiting Professor at University of Ghent, Director of the Center for Management Buy-out Research, Associate Director of the Enterprise Research Center and an Editor of *Strategic Entrepreneurship Journal*. He has honorary doctorates from the Universities of Ghent and Derby, is an Academician of the Academy of Social Sciences and was formerly Chair of the Academy of Management Entrepreneurship Division. Email: mike.wright@ imperial.ac.uk.

1 Introduction

A generation ago, entrepreneurship was a topic that was barely on the radar screen of economics and business. Al and David never came across the word, let alone studied it as graduate students in the 1970s; and they were both students of industrial organization, the subfield of economics specializing in the analysis of firms and industries! It was not as if scholars had never heard of or come across the terms "entrepreneur" or "entrepreneurship." The eminent scholar, Joseph Schumpeter (1911, 1942) made sure of that. With his penetrating and vivid depiction and analysis of both the entrepreneur as well as the entrepreneurial process, Schumpeter made a compelling case explaining why the process of creative destruction triggers innovation and, ultimately, economic growth and development.

Perhaps sated by the post-World War II economic boom, however, the entrepreneur, along with Schumpeter, remained something of the forgotten man of economics. Rather, as the MIT scholar Alfred Chandler (1977, 1990) painstakingly documented, it was the massive economies bestowed from both size and scale that drove competitiveness, productivity and prosperity.

It took a major economic downturn in the 1970s, marking the end of the seemingly unending prosperity that followed World War II, to waken scholars out of intellectual slumber and (re-)discover that entrepreneurship matters.

How and why entrepreneurship matters became vividly clear by the 1990s. Most scholars and thought leaders in business and public policy were poised for an inevitable economic decline of the United States, which seemed unable to compete against their Japanese counterparts in the traditional manufacturing industries, such as steel and automobiles. Through what many perceived to be unfair industrial policies, Japanese companies were able to attain scale and scope, while improving product quality, at a magnitude unthinkable to their American counterparts, who ultimately were constrained by antitrust laws and government regulations. A dream team of scholars spanning a broad range of academic fields and disciplines, the MIT Commission on Industrial Productivity, warned in their highly influential book, *Made in America: Regaining the Productive Edge* (Dertouzos et al., 1990), that unless the United States could match the scale and scope of its Japanese counterparts in industries such as automobiles and steel, a prolonged economic decline was all but inevitable.

Regaining the productive edge is exactly what transpired in the United States in the 1990s as Stiglitz (2004) made clear in his highly celebrated book *The Roaring Nineties: A New History of the World's Most Prosperous Decade*. But it did not come about the way that the MIT Commission on

1

Industrial Productivity had imagined. The American automobile and steel industries never again regained their postwar prominence and dominance. Rather, the unexpected surge that triggered "the most prosperous decade" (Stiglitz, 2004), came instead from a very unexpected direction: the entrepreneur. As entirely new industries – such as software, biotechnology and information technologies – were created by bold entrepreneurs such as Steven Jobs and Bill Gates, scholars along with leaders in government and industry began to take entrepreneurship – and its role in economic dynamism – more seriously.

In the past two decades a considerable body of knowledge has been created by the generation of scholars answering the call to better understand entrepreneurship – and its relationship to technology and innovation. The purpose of this volume is to provide a concise and coherent overview about some of the most salient insights that have been gleaned from state-of-the-art research about entrepreneurs and entrepreneurship. In compiling this volume we have included some of the world's leading scholars on the subject. Taken together, these concise essays provide a compelling picture about the individuals who have emerged to the forefront of the contemporary economy: entrepreneurs.

DAVID B. AUDRETSCH, CHRISTOPHER S. HAYTER AND ALBERT N. LINK

References

Chandler, A. (1977), *The Visible Hand: The Managerial Revolution in American Business*, Cambridge, MA: Belknap Press.

Chandler, A. (1990), *Scale and Scope: The Dynamics of Industrial Capitalism*, Cambridge, MA: Harvard University Press.

Dertouzos, M.L., Lester, R.K. and Solow, R.M. (1990), *Made in America: Regaining the Productive Edge*, Cambridge, MA: MIT Press.

Schumpeter, J. (1911), *Theorie der wirtschaftlichen Entwicklung. Eine Untersuchung über Unternehmergewinn, Kapital, Kredit, Zins und den Konjunkturzyklus*, Berlin: Duncker und Humblot, English translation (1934), *The Theory of Economic Development*, trans. Redvers Opie, Cambridge, MA: Harvard University Press.

Schumpeter, J. (1942), *Capitalism, Socialism and Democracy*, New York: Harper and Brothers.

Stiglitz, J.E. (2004), *The Roaring Nineties: A New History of the World's Most Prosperous Decade*, W.W. Norton and Company.

2   Academic Entrepreneurship

Introduction

In our efforts to find the unifying threads of entrepreneurial endeavour, we students of the pioneering spirit long contemplate the nature of those choices that carry men and women down unfamiliar roads. The motivations that drive departures from the norm, that lead entrepreneurial individuals to seek out novelty and adventure in their life's work and experiences loom large in the narratives we construct. Yet in truth, we do not celebrate these pioneers for their divergent dispositions alone, nor for their willingness to bear the risks such precarious ventures entail. It is the creative power of this temperament that captures our imagination. To forge new pathways is but one dimension of the entrepreneurial story. What lasts – and what truly matters in the end – is where those pathways lead.

Perhaps it is this dimension of academic entrepreneurship that has so captivated both scholarly and policy audiences over the course of recent decades. The implications of entrepreneurship in the academy go beyond the outcomes of the individual stories themselves. Entrepreneurship in this environment transforms the very nature of the relationship between science, the university and society. What academic entrepreneurs vividly illustrate is that the true nature of the entrepreneur is not entirely represented within the spirit of exploration, nor in bold individualism or opportunism. The pioneering entrepreneur is a creative and transformative force. These figures serve to broaden the scope of our experience and understanding through the novel courses of action they undertake, shifting outwards the boundaries of what was once thought reasonable or possible. It is in this manner that the creative power of entrepreneurship in the university is most keenly felt. Academic entrepreneurs reshape not just the boundaries of technology and markets, but also our common understanding of who and what the academic is.

Between the widely divergent popular conceptions of academic and industrial work, these individuals construct new links that are of profound importance for our modern knowledge-driven societies. It is this unique characteristic of their actions that will guide our discussion of the academic entrepreneur in the pages that follow. We will explore how – rather than simply diverging from well-worn pathways and pursuing those that are novel – university-based entrepreneurs serve as builders of byways between the two. As pioneers of science, they strive to push back the boundaries of the unknown and find answers to the mysteries of their research disciplines, but as pioneers of understanding they cut new paths through the institutions of society itself.

This chapter describes how these individuals lay the basis for the

3

alignment and integration of the traditionally distinct roles of the academic and the entrepreneur. It will consider both the significance of the university as the context for entrepreneurial action, and the cognitive infrastructure that at the individual level underpins the broader emergence of an entrepreneurial culture in this environment. The story of the academic entrepreneur is the story of how the novel pathways of research and commerce intersect to create new understanding of the academic's role in our society. It is the story of how roads converge.

Entrepreneurial revolutions in the university
Our starting point in discussing the pioneering nature of academic entrepreneurship must be the university itself. Recent decades have seen a dramatic re-conceptualisation of the economic role of the university as an institution. 'Knowledge,' Drucker stated in 1969, 'has become productive' (1969: 266). Accordingly, the belief that advances in scientific theory are a critical source of innovation, and therefore of economic and social progress, has become ever more prominent in the modern age (Powell and Snellman, 2004). The rise of this paradigm has caused the university to be increasingly regarded as the major engine for economic growth within advanced, knowledge-intensive economies (Etzkowitz and Leydesdorff, 2000).

Within this perspective, it is academic research itself that carries the seeds of future economic and social development (Etzkowitz and Leydesdorff, 1997). And it is by innovatively deploying its research capabilities, thereby cultivating the conditions of economic success, that the university embraces its 'third mission' of economic development (Clark, 1998; Etzkowitz and Leydesdorff, 2000). Primarily, the university is expected to recognise and create economic opportunities, and is therefore required to adopt at both the aggregate and individual level an entrepreneurial attitude towards the conduct of its research activities (Clark, 1998; Kirby, 2005; Guerrero et al., 2014). Given the quite fundamental nature of this institutional transformation then, a process of considerable internal transformation is also required. As Etzkowitz (2003: 109) states, the 'inner logic' of academic work itself must change.

While this shift in the inner logic of the university as an institution is a regarded as a critical element of the broader transformation of the university's societal role, it is also recognised that the foundations of this phenomenon are largely unknown (Bercovitz and Feldman, 2008; Jain et al., 2009; D'Este and Perkmann, 2011; Guerrero and Urbano, 2012). Such changes in the underlying logic of institutions require attendant changes in the powerful belief systems that provide substance and meaning to the working lives of those within them. This logic describes for individuals in institutions (such as the university) the ends that they collectively work towards, and the means through which those ends should be pursued (Thornton and Ocasio, 2008).

Understanding institutional transformation therefore demands an understanding of how changes in these means or ends arise. The nature of these micro-level dynamics, however, remains a troublesome conundrum for those who research entrepreneurship in the university. In the absence of explanatory frameworks at this level, the proliferation of entrepreneurial intent so integral to the entrepreneurial university is only partially understood (O'Shea et al., 2007; Guerrero and Urbano, 2012; Organ and Cunningham, 2014). The implications of this gap in our understanding are especially significant when one considers the importance of the academic role itself within this broader process of cultural transformation.

The nature of institutional roles
Roles shape behavioural boundaries for individuals, and define the meaning and legitimacy of the behaviour that they daily undertake. As such, the institutionally reinforced characterisation of roles has significant consequences for the values, the activities, and the choices of the individuals who occupy them (Thornton and Ocasio, 2008). Jain et al. (2009: 923), exploring the question of role modification in this context, underline the importance of this principle in stating that 'the concept of role identity is integral to the manner in which individuals interpret and act in work situations, providing normative support and cognitive focus regarding what constitutes appropriate behaviours and outputs within one's chosen profession'. As changes in values, activities and choices must underpin the emergence of entrepreneurial universities then, our understanding of the broader transformation of the university as an institution hinges on our understanding of how individual academics come to differently interpret the academic role itself (Organ and Cunningham, 2014).

More importantly, it requires us to explore how individuals in this unique context connect the seemingly divergent routes of academia and entrepreneurship with one another. To do so, is to seek answers to critical questions about the evolving nature of universities, and to – in the end – construct a psychologically richer account of how entrepreneurship itself emerges (Jain et al., 2009; Lam, 2011). It is in the context of these challenges that we consider the socially transformative nature of academic entrepreneurship as an institutional role. Entrepreneurship in the context of the academic role represents more than a unique personal journey, it underpins the proliferation of an entirely new understanding of the means through which academics may pursue the traditional ends of their profession.

Reframing the academic role: resolving contradictions through actions

So far, we have considered two key principles in the story of university-based entrepreneurship. The first is that the institutional revolution from which the entrepreneurial university emerges itself requires a quieter revolution within the university, a process of internal transformation whereby the underlying logic of the university is aligned with the demands of the entrepreneurial mission. The second is that the micro-foundations of this transformation are to be found in the individual academic's interpretation of the meaning and purpose of their role. How the seemingly divergent routes of academic research and commercial entrepreneurship are reconnected is the key to understanding the recasting of the role of science in our society.

Organ and Cunningham (2014) point to a powerful mechanism deeply embedded in the cultural and cognitive structures of social institutions, which provides a new way of understanding this process. This mechanism is the *role frame*. Institutions provide for individuals' shared mental frameworks within which the meaning of behaviour is constructed. It is within a common understanding of the role of a doctor, a fireman or a nurse that their actions make sense to us. We ascribe certain values or functions to these roles, and it is from attendance to these values that the social legitimacy of those roles arises. It is also the shared nature of these role frames that makes their extension or reconstruction a difficult process (Garud et al., 2007). This in turn gives rise to what we think of as institutional persistence. These mental frames give a form of stability to a role, accommodating a degree of variability, but also clearly marking the role's boundaries (Turner, 1990). In this way, certain activities are rendered *illegitimate* within certain social positions (Zucker, 1977).

Exploring the power of the role frame mechanism in constraining or enabling the emergence of an entrepreneurial culture, Organ and Cunningham (2014) uncovered a surprising way in which it shaped the desirability of entrepreneurial behaviour for academic researchers. To conduct their study, they investigated and compared two universities. One university was an established entrepreneurial university with a longstanding record of strong entrepreneurial outputs, and the other university was very much in the early stages of its adaptation to the entrepreneurial mission. The manner in which the prevailing academic role frame in either case shaped the legitimacy of entrepreneurial behaviour gives us new insight into the transformative nature of academic entrepreneurship.

Building on sociological theories of role change, Organ and Cunningham (2014) found that two critical dimensions of social roles were the key to understanding the power of institutional frames in this environment. The first was the *functional* dimension, which relates to the core social purpose of the role in question. The second, was the *representational* dimension, which relates to the image and sentiment associated with the role. 'Nurses care for the sick', for example, is a functional value of nursing as a social role. On the other hand, 'nurses are compassionate', is a statement of the representational value we associate with this role. What this study discovered was that academic entrepreneurship changed the collective framing of entrepreneurial behaviour by fundamentally altering its *meaning* along these two dimensions.

In the early-stage entrepreneurial university, the idea of entrepreneurial behaviour was beset with concerns about the functional and representational challenges it would entail. Fear about its implications for the traditional role of teaching or the independence of the academic scholar abounded. But in the established entrepreneurial university, perspectives were quite different. The evidence provided by academic entrepreneurs in that context had produced an entirely new interpretive frame for entrepreneurial action. Rather than undermining the traditional teaching role, academics saw entrepreneurship as a means of bringing the classroom closer to the real world through the professor's experiences. And far from threatening the independence of academic scholarship, the revenues generated by entrepreneurial activities were seen as a means of enhancing it in a way that would otherwise not be possible. What entrepreneurial academics had achieved through their endeavours in this university was the *resolution of institutional contradictions* between the traditional logic of the university, and the logic of the entrepreneurial mission.

Conclusion – the converging roads of academia and entrepreneurship

What Organ and Cunningham's (2014) study reveals is the manner in which academic entrepreneurs act not only as entrepreneurs in the sense more popularly understood, but that they also act as *institutional entrepreneurs*. Through their pioneering ventures beyond the walls of the university and into the marketplace, they provide evidence for their fellows that reframes the means-ends assumptions that once prevailed. Far from threatening the core values of the university and the academic role, they recast our common understanding of how the traditional ends of teaching, scholarship and public service may be advanced through these novel entrepreneurial behaviours.

They reveal the roads of research and entrepreneurship to be not divergent and irreconcilable, but as intertwined courses through which long-standing values can be served in both the industrial *and* academic domains. In so doing, these pioneers remind us that the essence of entrepreneurship is found in the broadening of the scope of what was once regarded as possible. These figures reframe our understanding of what must and must not be, and in redrawing the boundaries of science's social role, entrepreneurs in the academy find new territories for all of us that follow to explore.

DAMIEN ORGAN

References

Bercovitz, J. and Feldman, M. (2008), Academic entrepreneurs: organizational change at the individual level, *Organization Science*, **19**(1), 69–89.

Clark, B. (1998), *Creating Entrepreneurial Universities: Organisational Pathways of Transformation*, Surrey: IAU Press.

D'Este, P. and Perkmann, M. (2011), Why do academics engage with industry? The entrepreneurial university and individual motivations, *Journal of Technology Transfer*, **36**(3), 316–339.

Drucker, P.F. (1969), *The Age of Discontinuity: Guidelines to Our Changing Society*, New York: Harper and Row.

Etzkowitz, H. (2003), Research groups as 'quasi-firms': the invention of the entrepreneurial university, *Research Policy*, **32**(1), 109–121.

Etzkowitz, H. and Leydesdorff, L. (1997), *Universities and the Global Knowledge Economy: A Triple-helix of University–Industry–Government Relations*, London: Cassell Academic.

Etzkowitz, H. and Leydesdorff, L. (2000), The dynamics of innovation: from national systems to a triple helix of university–industry–government relations, *Research Policy*, **29**(2), 109–123.

Garud, R., Hardy, C. and Maguire, S. (2007), Institutional entrepreneurship as embedded agency: an introduction to the special issue, *Organization Studies*, **28**(7), 957–969.

Guerrero, M. and Urbano, D. (2012), The development of an entrepreneurial university, *Journal of Technology Transfer*, **37**(1), 43–74.

Guerrero, M., Urbano, D., Cunningham, J. and Organ, D. (2014), Entrepreneurial universities in two European regions: a case study comparison, *Journal of Technology Transfer*, **39**(3), 415–434.

Jain, S., George, G. and Maltarich, M. (2009), Academics or entrepreneurs? Investigating role identity modification of university scientists involved in commercialization activity, *Research Policy*, **38**(6), 922–935.

Kirby, D.A. (2005), Creating entrepreneurial universities in the UK: applying entrepreneurship theory to practice, *Journal of Technology Transfer*, **31**(5), 599–603.

Lam, A. (2011), What motivates academic scientists to engage in research commercialization: 'gold', 'ribbon' or 'puzzle'?, *Research Policy*, **40**(10), 1354–1368.

Organ, D. and Cunningham, J. (2014), *Role Frame Dynamics and the Proliferation of Entrepreneurial Propensity in the University Context*, paper presented at the Technology Transfer Society Conference, Johns Hopkins University, Baltimore, 23–24 October.

O'Shea, R.P., Allen, T.J., Morse, K.P., O'Gorman, C. and Roche, F. (2007), Delineating the anatomy of an entrepreneurial university: the Massachusetts Institute of Technology experience, *R&D Management*, **37**(1), 1–16.

Powell, W.W. and Snellman, K. (2004), The knowledge economy, *Annual Review of Sociology*, **30**, 199–220.

Thornton, P.H. and Ocasio, W. (2008), Institutional logics, in R. Greenwood, C. Oliver, K. Sahlin and R. Suddaby (eds), *The Sage Handbook of Organizational Institutionalism*, London: Sage, pp. 99–129.

Turner, R.H. (1990), Role change, *Annual Review of Sociology*, **16**, 87–110.

Zucker, L.G. (1977), The role of institutionalization in cultural persistence, *American Sociological Review*, **42**, 726–743.

3 Backdoor Entrepreneurship

Introduction

Scientists at research universities, as well as those who work for public and private enterprises where basic and applied research are important, produce breakthrough technologies that, if commercialized appropriately, can yield substantial returns. In a university context, for example, basic research is predominantly funded by the US government, much of whose $150 billion R&D budget is channeled through universities (Litan and Mitchell, 2010). The fact that a significant portion of a university research budget comes from taxpayer money means that it is even more vital that these innovations disseminate into the marketplace and generate the greatest benefits for society. Unfortunately, the market for innovation – particularly where research universities can play a critical role – is suboptimal due to severe informational, contracting, and management problems (Hochberg et al., 2014; Markman et al., 2009). Indeed, years of research on the topic of technology commercialization shows that many university-developed inventions could reach the marketplace much faster and have a wider societal impact than they do now (Litan and Mitchell, 2010).

This chapter brings greater awareness to the fact that some scientists siphon off substantial economic value from certain discoveries that they make while working in research institutions – whether these are nonprofit universities, government laboratories or hospitals, and even for-profit enterprises. To remain within reasonable bounds, however, this chapter focuses on research universities in the US. The chapter concludes by featuring alternative views and modality for scientists to get their discoveries to the market without undermining their employment status.

The challenge

University–industry relations, the commercialization of intellectual property (IP) from university labs to markets and industries, and the topic of *backdoor entrepreneurship* – when scientists bypass their institutions and sell, license or build a venture based on their inventions – represent an important subject, because IP-related inventions harness funding for higher education, research and development, and for accelerating economic growth. However, a challenge technology licensing offices (TLOs) face is that licensing and commercialization of technology require two critical conditions: first, scientists must report the development of discoveries to their respective TLOs, and second, scientists must support the licensing process; for example, by helping licensees to validate and advance the commercial utility of initial discoveries. Naturally, successful technology commercialization depends on a well-run TLO, but even the best managed

TLO would not produce high returns unless it engages and motivates scientists' goodwill and vigorous cooperation (Markman et al., 2009).

The critical role that scientists play, and more importantly, the powerful position they hold in the conception of science-based discoveries and then in the commercialization process give scientists ample leverage over their institutions. For instance, TLO personnel in many universities revealed that certain scientists disclose only some, but not all, of the discoveries they make (Jensen and Thursby, 2001; Jensen et al., 2003; Markman et al., 2008; Thursby et al., 2001). Interestingly, even scientists themselves acknowledge that they sometime sidestep their employment contracts and engage in *informal* means of technology commercialization (Link et al., 2007; Siegel et al., 2003).[1]

Of course, some scientists are unengaged vis-à-vis their TLOs because they are unaware of the commercial value that is embedded inside their invention whereas others – because commercializing inventions is a complicated and time-consuming process – are simply disinclined to divert effort away from their research (Markman et al., 2008). The area to which this chapter is directing attention, however, is to the population of scientists who elect to collaborate privately and independently with firms or to quietly use their inventions to either start or continue to build their own ventures. As discussed below, the main support for the existence of backdoor entrepreneurship is the growing evidence that a sizeable portion of 'private' and/or 'informal' commercialization takes place in plain sight, yet outside universities and TLO infrastructure.

A study of National Cancer Institute grant recipients shows that almost 30 percent of scientists assigned one or more of their patents solely to an outside firm (Audretsch et al., 2006). Evidence of backdoor entrepreneurship can also be inferred from research showing that 26 percent of patents that list faculty as 'inventors' were assigned solely to firms, and about a third of those patents were held by ventures in which the inventing scientists were principals (Thursby et al., 2009). A survey of almost 20 percent of all US faculty in Carnegie I and II research universities reveals that of the 682 scientists who used IP to start a business, almost 25 percent had not disclosed all of their discoveries to their university (Fini et al., 2010). And Thursby and Thursby (2011) report that 30 percent of university scientists are inventors on patents that were assigned to firms.

In an effort to better quantify the extent of backdoor entrepreneurship, Markman and his colleagues (2008) examined the patenting activities of 23,394 scientists working in a randomly selected sample of 54 research universities in the US. Their research shows, for example, that 42 percent of the scientists who invent patents circumvent their institutions at least once, and that more than 33 percent of patents that originated in university labs were appropriated privately or informally. Interestingly, the 33 percent of patents that were assigned to firms attracted a significantly larger number of citations, indicating that backdoor entrepreneurship is quite systemic; it is certainly not random. Markman and his colleagues also show that heightened entrepreneurial activities on a university campus and bureaucratic TLOs are often associated with an increase in circumventing activity. University status also plays a critical role in the assignment of patents; the greater the reputation of a university, the more likely scientists are to comply and patent through their university.

Taken as a whole, this line of research shows that backdoor entrepreneurship is quite prevalent. It is important to recognize, however, that although scientists violate their employment contract when they circumvent their institutions, their inventions do reach the markets and benefit society.

A complementing lab-to-market path?

The Bayh-Dole Act (1980) granted universities the rights to the IP that comes from inventions made with federal funding, and today almost every US research university has a TLO to organize its commercialization activities. Centralizing all licensing activities and commercialization capabilities through the TLOs gave immediate benefits, particularly streamlined operations and economies of scale. Some TLOs, primarily in prestigious universities and in research institutions that are 'early-movers' into the commercialization arena, are clearly doing a great job; they work well with their scientists and they bring substantial technical capabilities and business acumen to augment and accelerate the commercialization process. But the centralized TLO model is not without limitations. First, a TLO exhibits a monopsony power, so once an invention is rejected a scientist has very little recourse – for example, abandoning the invention or seeking a special variance to go it alone. Second, when a TLO is short-staffed, bureaucratic, technologically incompetent or lacking suitable ties with industry, scientists are unlikely to support formal commercialization effort. The reality is that despite decades of experience, many TLOs are not doing as well as they could.

In a provocative article, Litan and Mitchell (2010) challenged the centralized TLO model and invited policymakers to amend the Bayh-Dole Act so as to allow scientists to select their own licensing agent – university-affiliated or not (e.g., think how we select other service providers such as lawyers, accountants and physicians). According to Litan and Mitchell (2010), an open and competitive market for technology licensing would not change the legal status of the invention per se, or how royalties or license fees are divided between employees and institutions. Even if a university eliminated its TLO altogether, it would continue to earn licensing revenues (minus the fees that an outside TLO charged). But like other open markets, it would speed up the commercialization of new technologies, thus benefiting consumers more rapidly. An open market might also motivate university TLOs to differentiate, specialize and collaborate with outsiders who hold complementing capabilities.

If the studies we cited are correct, and universities do not wish to experiment with alternative modalities for transferring their inventions to the marketplace, they should at least be tinkering with some aspects of their technology transfer protocols and commercialization policies. For instance, to motivate a wider engagement where scientists actively advance technology transfer efforts, universities may need to shift the royalty distribution formula in favor of scientists.[2] While universities are clearly interested in sponsored research and patenting and licensing opportunities, they should also place a high priority on supporting startup formation and industry engagement, especially in promotion and tenure decisions. These are only a few examples of the changes universities will need to undertake to motivate more invention disclosures and greater engagement in formal university technology transfer.

Conclusions

To prevent valuable ideas from languishing on shelves of university (and for-profit enterprises) and to turn backdoor entrepreneurship into formal entrepreneurship, it is critical that universities adopt and apply policies that (a) support and promote scientists who develop new technologies; and (b) facilitate and accelerate technology commercialization, so the world can benefit from the new products – some of which are life-changing and life-saving (Litan and Mitchell, 2010).

GIDEON D. MARKMAN

Notes

1. Informal technology transfer and commercialization may take many forms, including knowledge transfer, joint publications with industry scientists, and even consulting (Link et al., 2007). This essay focuses primarily on the informal commercialization of IP that reaches the market through the 'back door.'
2. This is also true of research grants, where many universities pass less than 50 percent of the total funds to the faculty member who got the grant in the first place.

References

Audretsch, D., Aldridge, T. and Oettl, A. (2006), *The Knowledge Filter and Economic Growth: The Role of Scientist Entrepreneurship*, Ewing Marion Kauffman Foundation Large Research Projects Research Paper Series, Kansas City.
Fini, R., Lacetera, N. and Shane, S. (2010), Inside or outside the IP system? Business creation in academia, *Research Policy*, **39**, 1060–1069.

Hochberg, Y.V., Serrano, C.J. and Ziedonis, R.H. (2014), *Patent Collateral, Investor Commitment, and the Market for Venture Lending*, NBER Working Papers 20587.

Jensen, R. and Thursby, M. (2001), Proofs and prototypes for sale: the licensing of university inventions, *American Economic Review*, **91**, 240–259.

Jensen, R., Thursby, J. and Thursby, M. (2003), Disclosure and licensing of university inventions: 'the best we can do with the s**t we get to work with', *International Journal of Industrial Organization*, **21**, 1271–1300.

Link, A., Siegel, D. and Bozeman, B. (2007), An empirical analysis of the propensity of academics to engage in informal university technology transfer, *Industrial and Corporate Change*, **16**, 641–655.

Litan, R.E. and Mitchell, L. (2010), Removing the technology licensing obstacle, *Harvard Business Review*, **88**(1/2), 41–57.

Markman, G.D., Gianiodis, P.T. and Phan, P.H. (2008), Full-time faculty or part-time entrepreneurs, *IEEE Transactions on Engineering Management*, **55**(1), 29–36.

Markman, G.D., Gianiodis, P.T. and Phan, P.H. (2009), Supply-side innovation and technology commercialization, *Journal of Management Studies*, **46**(4), 625–649.

Siegel, D., Waldman, D. and Link, A. (2003), Asses sing the impact of organizational practices on the relative productivity of university technology transfer offices: an exploratory study, *Research Policy*, **32**, 27–48.

Thursby, J. and Thursby, M. (2011), Faculty participation in licensing: implications for research, *Research Policy*, **40**, 20–29.

Thursby, J., Fuller, A. and Thursby, M. (2009), US faculty patenting, inside and outside the university, *Research Policy*, **38**, 14–25.

Thursby, J., Jensen, R. and Thursby, M. (2001), Objectives, characteristics and outcomes of university licensing: a survey of major US universities, *Journal of Technology Transfer*, **26**, 59–72.

4   Bootstrapping Finance

Introduction

New and innovative ventures experience a 'liability of newness' (Stinchcombe, 1965; Aldrich and Auster, 1986), which indicates that entrepreneurs experience both external and internal barriers to start and grow their ventures. Particularly, many entrepreneurs face great challenges in obtaining capital to successfully manage their venture. In many cases the problem has been related to the entrepreneurs' effort to raise capital from external financiers such as banks, business angels, venture capitalists, etc.

In this chapter, I elaborate on 'bootstrapping finance,' which is seen as the use of methods to meet the need for resources without relying on external finance, i.e., borrowing money or raising equity (Winborg and Landström, 2000). Some authors add some qualifying dimensions to this definition, such as (a) cost aspects, i.e., the methods used should secure resources at relatively low or no costs (e.g., Winborg, 2007, 2009; Vanacker and Sels, 2009), for example, using personal savings and private credit cards in the venture, using 'free' or low-cost labor from relatives and friends, prepayments by customers, facilities that are acquired with little or no costs, share resources together with other ventures, etc. will all be methods that will lower the costs for the resources acquired. Some authors also add (b) a creative element to the definition of bootstrapping methods (e.g., Freear et al., 1995; Harrison et al., 2004, Vanacker et al., 2010). A creative example of resource acquisition in a new venture could be retrieved from Starr and MacMillan (1990: 81), in which they describe the American entrepreneur that started a men's clothing import business and needed to establish credibility with his Manhattan buyers. He identified a friend that had moved into new offices on Fifth Avenue. They had extra office space and the entrepreneur persuaded his friend to rent him a piece of the office for a low price but also persuaded his friend to give him a telephone line that was answered by their receptionist, he received permission to use their conference room, etc. The arrangement not only enabled the entrepreneur to save money but also gave him access to resources that he could never have afforded as a new venture. In this case, cooptation is a key of bootstrapping methods in which participants consciously and willingly allowed the entrepreneur to coopt resources at below market price in order to gain legitimacy and use underutilized resources.

Bootstrapping finance: what do we know?
The first to use the concept 'financial bootstrapping' was Amar Bhide in his article 'Bootstrap finance: the art of start-ups' in *Harvard Business Review* (1992). In the article, Bhide argued that the belief in a 'big money' model of entrepreneurship is prevailing. Books and entrepreneurship courses often emphasize fundraising from venture capitalists and business angels, but the 'big-money' model has often very little in common with the traditional start-up ventures. Bhide's empirical study of 100 companies on the 1989 Inc. 500 list of the fastest growing companies in the US showed that most ventures started with very small amounts of money, and more than 80 percent of the ventures were financed through the founders' personal savings, credit cards, second mortgages, etc. Thus, 'bootstrapping' played an important role in the start-up process, and Bhide also argued that 'bootstrappers' need a different mindset and approach – the principles and practices imported from the corporate world will not be helpful in this respect.

Since this pioneering contribution, research on bootstrapping finance has evolved. However, since our knowledge is in an early stage, most research has been based on empirical studies and research is not particularly theory-driven. Contemporary knowledge on bootstrapping finance can be divided into three main areas: the use of bootstrapping finance, factors influencing the use of bootstrapping and the effects of 'bootstrapping' (performance).

The use of bootstrapping finance
First, bootstrapping finance seems to be an important financial instrument in new ventures. For example, Gartner et al. (2008), based on the PSED study in the US, showed that as many as 94.6 percent of the entrepreneurs were using personal funds for their ventures and in more than one third of the ventures, personal contributions were their only source of finance. In the study by Harrison et al. (2004), 95 percent of the ventures were engaged in at least some bootstrapping activities. Second, the use of boot-strapping seems to be context-dependent in the sense that bootstrapping finance seems to be more or less used in different countries, for example, dependent on the industrial structure, the growth orientation of the ventures and alternative financial sources available. Third, human and social capital appears to be substitutable for financial capital. Entrepreneurs with a strong background experience and extensive network may be able to start ventures that survive and thrive with less financial capital than less experienced entrepreneurs with less extensive networks (Chandler and Hanks, 1998; Seghers et al., 2012).

When it comes to the use of bootstrapping methods, Winborg and Landström (2000; see also Vanacker and Sels, 2009; Ebben, 2009) identified a couple of broad categories of bootstrapping methods that have received a lot of support and shown to be valid in different contexts (e.g., Carter and Van Auken, 2005; Vassolo et al., 2005; Jones and Jaywarna, 2010): (a) owner financing methods (e.g., use of manager's credit card, loan from relatives and friends, withholding manager's salary, and relatives working in non-market salary), (b) minimizing investments (e.g., in inventory, employees, etc.), (c) minimizing account receivables (e.g., using different kinds of cash management techniques), (d) delaying payment (e.g., lease equipment, and delay payment to suppliers), (e) government subsidies (e.g., subsidies from different governmental agencies), (f) joint usage of resources (e.g., borrow equipment from others, coordinate purchase with others, and barter instead of buying) and (g) customer-related methods (e.g., tapping resources from customers, prepayment of prototypes, etc.).

Factors influencing the use of bootstrapping
What factors influence the use of bootstrapping methods? Why are some ventures and entrepreneurs using bootstrapping to a higher extent than others?

The motives for using bootstrapping methods have been discussed in several studies. It could be argued that financially constrained ventures will use bootstrapping methods to a higher extent than other ventures, because there are no (or few) external financial alternatives available

(Winborg and Landström, 2000). Especially, it has been shown that financially constrained ventures are likely to use customer-related and delaying payment as a 'quick-fix' for cash flow problems (Ebben, 2009; Vanacker et al., 2010). On the other hand, there is research showing that bootstrapping methods are not exclusively used as a response to lack of financial alternatives. The use of bootstrapping could be a deliberate choice, not used by routine but as an explicit motive. The lack of capital, i.e., bootstrapping as a last resort, is one of the motives, but there are several other motives for using bootstrapping, such as lower costs, saving time and reducing risks (Winborg, 2005, 2009).

There seem also to be differences depending on gender. For example, male entrepreneurs choose self-funded methods and share bootstrapping methods more frequently than females, which may be explained by greater earning power in the venture and more extensive networks. Females exploit customer-based bootstrapping more regularly than males, i.e., they have a stronger tendency to manage their business through relationships among stakeholders (Neeley and Van Auken, 2009). It seems also that the use of bootstrapping methods vary by stage in women-led ventures. Emergent ventures are significantly more likely to use bootstrapping methods that reduce labor costs rather than focusing on the rapid development of product and business. Rapid growing ventures are likely to focus on minimizing capital by reducing operational costs (Brush et al., 2006).

In a similar way, small firms use bootstrapping more than larger firms. For larger firms, the usage of bootstrapping methods is highly concentrated to a few bootstrapping methods, especially using exploitation of relationships along the value chain, i.e., customers and suppliers relationships, whereas small firms focuses on cost-reducing bootstrapping (Harrison et al., 2004).

When it comes to the use of bootstrapping methods in technology-based ventures there seems not to be a significant difference between technology-based and non-technology-based ventures when it comes to the general use of bootstrapping finance. However, bootstrapping methods that improve the cash flow of the venture are significantly higher ranked in technology-based firms, and in non-technology-based firms are more concerned with bootstrapping methods that facilitate the delay of payment (Van Auken, 2005).

The effects of 'bootstrapping' (performance)
Will the use of bootstrapping methods contribute to higher growth in the ventures, or maybe the opposite?

Several studies have tried to understand the effects, or performance, of the use of bootstrapping methods. However, from the studies conducted so far it is very difficult to draw any clear conclusions and the results are contradictory as the studies have used different dependent variables and the samples of firms have been very different from one study to another (Vassolo et al., 2005; Ebben, 2009; Vanacker and Sels, 2009). What can be said is that different bootstrapping methods might have different effects on performance, for example, it can be assumed that 'joint-utilization methods' will keep the employment costs low and not contribute to employment growth in a venture (Helleboogh and Laveren, 2008). It could also be assumed that the use of bootstrapping methods will have different effects depending on the firm's situation; for example, when there are high growth aspirations in the firm, the use of several bootstrapping methods may hamper the growth in the venture such as the use of bootstrapping methods that involve business partners (Vanacker et al., 2010).

Conclusions
The main conclusion to be drawn is that our knowledge on bootstrapping resources is fragmented and the results are in many cases contradictory. At best we can say that bootstrapping is an important instrument for entrepreneurs to acquire resources in new ventures. However, the use of bootstrapping seems to be context-dependent in the sense that the behavior varies from country to country, from region to region, depending on factors such as alternative financial possibilities (financial market) and differences in the industrial structure (sector dominance).

There is still a debate with regard to the motives of using bootstrapping resources. In many cases, bootstrapping seems to be a solution for financial constraints and high risks of the ventures (e.g., young ventures and technology-based firms) and when the environment is perceived as hostile, but there seems also to be a group of entrepreneurs that in a more proactive way are using bootstrapping resources in order to gain control over necessary resources.

Studies on the consequences and performance of ventures using bootstrapping methods often use different dependent variables, and in cases where comparisons between studies can be made, the results are contradictory. The conclusion is that it is not possible to generally say that bootstrapping will enhance or inhibit growth in new ventures – we need to analyze the contributions of different bootstrapping modes (or particular methods) for venture growth and performance.

Along with this conclusion I offer advice for practice:

1. As an entrepreneur you should not start to think in terms of applying for external capital. Instead, use your creativity and find new ways of acquiring the resources necessary in your venture.

2. Bootstrapping is an approach that is convenient and an easily obtainable approach, i.e., bootstrapping does not require a business plan or collaterals, and it stimulates a 'lean' mindset and 'resourceful' solutions.

3. However, be aware that (a) bootstrapping may hamper a quick launch of your ventures and the potential growth of the venture, and (b) there are seldom such things as a 'free lunch'; for example, if you are using your social network in your venture, there is often a time for payback.

HANS LANDSTRÖM

References

Aldrich, H. and Auster, E.R. (1986), Even dwarfs started small: liabilities of age and size and their strategic implications, *Research in Organizational Behavior*, **8**, 165–198.

Bhide, A. (1992), Bootstrap finance: the art of start-ups, *Harvard Business Review*, **70**(6), 109–117.

Brush, C.G., Carter, N.M., Gatewood, E.J., Greene, P.G. and Hart, M.M. (2006), The use of bootstrapping by women entrepreneurs in positioning for growth, *Venture Capital*, **8**(1), 15–31.

Carter, R.B. and Van Auken, H. (2005), Bootstrap financing and owners' perceptions of their business constraints and opportunities, *Entrepreneurship and Regional Development*, **17**, 129–144.

Chandler, G.N. and Hanks, S.H. (1998), An examination of the substitutability of founders' human and financial capital in emerging business ventures, *Journal of Business Venturing*, **13**, 353–369.

Ebben, J.J. (2009), Bootstrapping and the financial condition of small firms, *International Journal of Entrepreneurial Behaviour and Research*, **15**(4), 346–363.

Freear, J., Sohl, J.E. and Wetzel, W.E. (1995), Who bankrolls software entrepreneurs, *Frontiers of Entrepreneurship Research*, 394–406.

Gartner, W.B., Fried, C.J. and Alexander, J.C. (2008), *Financing the Emerging Business through Monitored and Unmonitored Sources of Funding*, paper presented at the Babson College Entrepreneurship Research Conference, University of North Carolina at Chapel Hill, NC, June.

Harrison, R.T., Mason, C.M. and Girling, P. (2004), Financial bootstrapping and venture development in the software industry, *Entrepreneurship and Regional Development*, **16**, 307–333.

Helleboogh, D. and Laveren, E. (2008), *Financial Bootstrapping Use in New Ventures and the Impact on Venture Growth*, paper presented at the XXII RENT Conference, Covilhã, Portugal, November.

Jones, O. and Jayawarna, D. (2010), Resourcing new businesses: social networks, bootstrapping and firm performance, *Venture Capital*, **12**(2), 127–152.

Neeley, L. and Van Auken, H. (2009), The relationship between owner characteristics and use of bootstrap financing methods, *Journal of Small Business and Entrepreneurship*, **22**(4), 399–412.

Seghers, A., Manigart, S. and Vanacker, T. (2012), The impact of human and social capital on entrepreneurs' knowledge of financial alternatives, *Journal of Small Business Management*, **50**(1), 63–86.

Starr, J.A. and MacMillan, I.C. (1990), Resource cooptation via social contracting: resource acquisition strategies for new ventures, *Strategic Management Journal*, **11**, 79–92.

Stinchcombe, A. (1965), Organizations and social structure, in J.G. March (ed.), *Handbook of Organizations*, Chicago: Rand-McNally, pp. 142–193.

Vanacker, T. and Sels, L. (2009), *Bootstrapping Strategies and Entrepreneurial Growth: A*

Longitudinal Study, paper presented at the Babson College Entrepreneurship Research Conference, Babson College, Wellesley, MA, June.

Vanacker, T., Manigart, S., Meuleman, M. and Sels, L. (2010), *Bootstrapping and Startup Development: The Role of Cash Flow Problems and Growth Ambitions*, paper presented at the Academy of Management Meeting, Montreal, Canada, August.

Van Auken, H. (2005), Differences in the usage of bootstrapping financing among technology-based versus nontechnology-based firms, *Journal of Small Business Management*, **43**(1), 93–103.

Vassolo, R.S., Weisz, N. and Muñiz, M. (2005), *How Do Argentine Firms Finance Innovation and Growth? An Examination of Financial Bootstrapping Practices*, Working Paper, IAE Universidad Austral, Buenos Aires, Argentine.

Winborg, J. (2005), *Motives for Using Financial Bootstrapping of New Businesses*, paper presented at the XIX RENT Conference, Naples, Italy, November.

Winborg, J. (2007), *The Role of Financial Bootstrapping Mentality for Handling Liability of Newness*, paper presented at the Babson College Entrepreneurship Research Conference, Madrid, Spain, June.

Winborg, J. (2009), Use of financial bootstrapping in new businesses: a question of last resort? *Venture Capital*, **11**(1), 71–83.

Winborg, J. and Landström, H. (2000), Financial bootstrapping in small businesses: examining small business managers' resource acquisition behaviors, *Journal of Business Venturing*, **16**, 235–254.

5 Culture and Innovation

Introduction

All of the contributions in this volume are united by a conviction that innovation and entrepreneurship underpin economic growth and competitiveness. This chapter addresses the critical influence of culture on these activities.

Cultural anthropologists and sociologists were among the first scholars to elaborate on the role and influence of culture. Edward Tylor, the so-called 'father of anthropology,' defined culture as 'that complex whole which includes knowledge, belief, art, law, morals, custom and any other capabilities acquired (learned) . . . as a member of society' (1873/1920: 1). More recent work emphasizes culture as 'a way of thinking or interacting that is shared among a group of people' (Nanda and Warms, 2010), as a 'core set of attitudes and practices that are shared by the members of a collective entity' (Tellis et al., 2009), and as 'some combination of artifacts . . ., values and beliefs, and underlying assumptions that . . . members share about appropriate behavior' (Detert et al., 2000; see also Hofstede, 2003; Smircich, 1983).

This recent work also has moved beyond a focus on societal or national cultures to consider culture among a variety of collectives, including organizations (e.g., Pettigrew, 1979: Schein, 1992), regions (e.g., Cooke, et al., 1997; Saxenian, 1994), and industries (e.g., Chatman and Jehn, 1994; Gertler, 2004). In this chapter, we consider the relationship between innovation and culture through these different lenses. We then offer several thoughts on future research directions.

National culture

Hofstede (1980) has offered a highly influential conceptualization of national culture in which nations may be distinguished from one another on the basis of their citizens' inclinations with regards to *individualism*; *power distance* or inequalities; *masculinity*; and *uncertainty avoidance*. Hofstede and Bond (1988) later added a fifth dimension – the Confucian dynamic, or long- versus short-term orientation – to this framework (see also House et al., 2004). Of course, these dimensions of national culture interact with features such as religion, geography and politics (Freeman, 2002; Landes, 1999; Tellis et al., 2009; Weber, 1905/2002).

In turn, a number of studies link national culture to the entrepreneurial orientation of particular individuals and to innovation more generally. For example, Shane (1993) found that lack of power distance, individualism and, especially, uncertainty acceptance are closely associated with rates of innovation (see also Mueller and Thomas, 2001; Lee and Peterson, 2001). A follow-on to Shane's (1993) study finds that the way in which people approach innovation more generally – for instance, by working with those in authority or by relying on 'champions' – also depends on aspects of culture (Shane et al., 1995).

Other work, however, cautions that these effects depend on the aspect of innovation in question. For instance, Nakata and Sivakumar (1996) distinguish between the initiation and implementation stages of innovation and they argue that different positions on a given cultural dimension may be useful towards different stages. Thus, high individualism can be useful for developing new ideas, while low individualism (or collectivism) can be useful towards improving these ideas, as with product quality circles. Similarly, low risk-aversion can help to initiate projects, while high risk-aversion may help to ensure that these projects are successful. Thus, this work suggests that favored dimensions of national culture may depend on the innovation context.

Regional culture

Other scholars focus on the link between innovation and regional culture. Dating to Marshall (1919), economists have argued that the 'secrets of industry are in the air,' noting the economic reasons why firms cluster in a region (see also Porter, 1998). Regional culture scholars, however, argue that cultural factors, too, shape regional character. One of the most influential studies in this vein is Saxenian's (1994) comparison of Silicon Valley and Boston's Route 128. Saxenian emphasizes that Silicon Valley's culture is accepting of both failure and frequent job shifts. In turn, this culture supports informal networks of exchange and collaborations between firms, which undergird Silicon Valley's entrepreneurial dynamism (see also Asheim and Gertler, 2005).

Silicon Valley's culture, specifically, has motivated a number of studies (e.g., Kenney, 2000; Rogers and Larsen, 1984). Yet scholars have studied the link between innovation and culture in other regions, too. For instance, Keeble and colleagues (1999) describe how Cambridge, England has a regional culture of trust and collaboration that underpins the innovation success of businesses in the region. Russo (2010) describes how shared values around environmental sustainability led innovative organizations to cluster in Portland, Oregon. Thus, these studies, and others, highlight how innovative activity and aspects of regional culture can be mutually reinforcing.

Industry and professional cultures

Regions, of course, differ in their dominant industries and professions, too (Gertler, 2004). In turn, these industries and professions also have distinct cultures. Saxenian's (1994) work, for example, tied Silicon Valley's regional culture to the high-growth semiconductor industry. By contrast, other research demonstrates that firms in low-growth industries have cultures that emphasize different values and practices. By extension, regions dominated by these industries may likewise have different regional cultures (Chatman and Jehn, 1994; Wilkins and Ouchi, 1983).

Different industries also attract unique professions, which also have their own cultures. For example, Menzel et al. (2007) argue that the engineering profession has a culture of problem-solving that ties engineers to innovation. Similarly, Brown and Ulijn (2004) contrast the professional cultures of engineers and marketers, tying them to an emphasis on technological invention versus customers respectively (see also Kunda, 1992; Van Maanen and Barley, 1984).

Nelson and Irwin (2014) offer another perspective, linking an occupation's identity – which is closely tied to its culture – to its engagement in innovation activities. Investigating the case of librarians and internet search, they find that librarians' occupational identity limited their ability to recognize innovation potential around search engines, despite librarians' professional expertise in information organization and retrieval. Studies such as these remain the exception, however, and very little work has explored the links between professional culture and innovation.

Organizational culture

Finally, scholars have offered considerable attention to organizational culture (see, e.g., Denison, 1996; Detert et al., 2000; Hatch, 1993; Martin, 2002; O'Reilly et al., 1991; Pettigrew, 1979; Schein, 1992). The underlying premise of these studies is that organizational culture matters to a wide range of behaviors, including innovation. Nelson (2014) offers a stark demonstration of how organizational culture can shape innovation. Employing a pseudo-natural experiment in which the same team pursues development of the same technology in a university and then in a startup, he shows how these different organizational cultures lead the same individuals to engage in very different innovation behaviors.

Scholars have identified a number of features of 'innovative' organizational cultures. For example, Tellis et al. (2009) identify three firm attitudes – (1) willingness to cannibalize assets; (2) future orientation; and (3) tolerance for risk – and three firm practices – (1) empowerment of product champions; (2) establishment of incentives for enterprise; and (3) creation and maintenance of internal markets – that can drive innovation.

Similarly, Jassawalla and Sashittal (2002) conclude that innovative organizational cultures are marked by four guiding values or beliefs – (1) an encouragement of initiative, creativity and risk-taking; (2) trust; (3) treating everyone as an insider with early involvement; and (4) embracing change – and by three behaviors – (1) participants voice a clear sense of control; (2) participants collaborate; and (3) participants are willing to be vulnerable.

Studying Japanese companies, Deshpandé and colleagues (1993) highlight two key features of innovative corporate cultures: competitiveness and entrepreneurship. Meanwhile, Sutton (2002) emphasizes that innovative cultures defy conventional wisdom and he offers a series of 'weird ideas' to further an innovative culture, such as: hire people who do not necessarily 'fit in'; reward success *and* failure, but punish inaction; encourage people to ignore and defy one another; and forget the past, especially past successes. Sutton (2007) also emphasizes that creative cultures do not have 'assholes.'

At the same time, scholars caution that some organizational culture initiatives can be harmful. Specifically, disingenuous nods to culture – for example, paying it only 'lip service' – can backfire and damage innovation efforts (Ahmed, 1998; Khazanchi et al., 2007). More pointedly, Kunda (1992) offers a deeper critique, arguing that organizational culture initiatives that are ostensibly aimed at promulgating creativity can be a form of corporate control that limits employees' behaviors and aspirations.

Discussion

A great deal of work explores the relationship between innovation and various dimensions of culture. Collectively, this work highlights how culture does, indeed, matter to innovation. Moreover, many of the celebrated features of culture are consistent across levels of analysis. For instance, whether the level of analysis is the country, region, industry or organization, a culture that tolerates risk appears to be associated with innovation.

Of course, there is still much value in considering different levels of analysis, for three reasons. First, such comparisons can reveal understudied areas within or across different levels of analysis, such as the relative lack of attention to occupational culture and, within studies of national culture, the relative lack of attention to culture outside of the US, Europe and Asia.

Second, a comparative approach enables a consideration of the relative importance of different aspects of culture and of changes over time. For example, several scholars argue that globalization has reduced the importance of the nation-state and that national cultures are increasingly homogenous (Drori et al., 2006; Ohmae, 1990; Tellis et al., 2009). In turn, this work suggests a greater role for other dimensions of culture.

Finally, consideration of different kinds and levels of culture underscores the interactions between them. For example, it is difficult to understand Silicon Valley (regional culture) independent of the engineering culture that drives it (professional culture) and independent of the US culture in which it exists (national culture). In turn, what is particularly interesting, and worthy of much more research, is the extent to which these different kinds of culture reinforce or conflict with one another.

The fact that 'culture matters' also raises questions as to how to develop a culture for innovation. Here, too, levels of analysis are important. For example, individuals may have far more leeway and ability to shape culture within an organization than they do to shape regional or national culture. Thus, there is no shortage of advice on how to develop a strong organizational culture. (Nonetheless, even attempts to change organizational culture typically meet with failure and/or result in unintended consequences; March, 1981; Pfeffer, 1992.) By contrast, as Starr (1995: 382) wrote in his review of Saxenian's book on regional culture: 'Investing in technology centers is relatively easy; creating a regional economic culture of trust, collaborative relationships, and open communication is a more elusive target.' Similarly, innovation-minded efforts to shape a national culture can be far more challenging than other national initiatives, such as increasing research funding or developing industrial infrastructure (Shane, 1993).

Complicating matters further is the fact that culture is but one influence on innovation and entrepreneurship. Human capital, organizational capital, social capital, natural capital and a host of other factors also shape innovation (Byers et al., 2015; Covin and Slevin, 1991). Further research is needed, however, to understand the relationship between these elements and various dimensions of culture.

Finally, the keen reader will note that we largely have sidestepped the definition and conceptualization of innovation itself. Yet surely the kind of innovation in question is central to understanding the role of culture in shaping it. For example, innovations dependent on tacit knowledge may rely on cultures that facilitate the sharing of such knowledge (e.g., cultures higher in trust), while innovations based on codified knowledge may not. In other words, despite considerable research on culture and innovation – and a clear consensus that culture matters – much work remains to be done.

ANDREW J. NELSON AND STEFANO CAZZAGO

References

Ahmed, P.K. (1998), Culture and climate for innovation, *European Journal of Innovation Management*, **1**(1), 30–43.

Asheim, B. and Gertler, M. (2005), The geography of innovation, in J. Fagerberg and D. Mowery (eds), *The Oxford Handbook of Innovation*, Oxford: Oxford University Press, pp. 291–317.

Brown, T. and Ulijn, J. (2004), Innovation, entrepreneurship and culture: a matter of interaction between technology, progress and economic growth? An introduction, in T. Brown and J. Ulijn (eds), *Innovation, Entrepreneurship and Culture: The Interaction between Technology, Progress and Economic Growth*, Northampton, MA: Edward Elgar Publishing.

Byers, T., Dorf, R. and Nelson, A.J. (2015), *Technology Ventures: From Idea to Enterprise*, 4th edn, New York: McGraw-Hill.

Chatman, J.A. and Jehn, K.A. (1994), Assessing the relationship between industry characteristics and organizational culture: how different can you be? *Academy of Management Journal*, **37**(3), 522–553.

Cooke, P., Gomez Uranga, M. and Etxebarria, G. (1997), Regional innovation systems: institutional and organisational dimensions, *Research Policy*, **26**(4), 475–491.

Covin, J.G. and Slevin, D.P. (1991), A conceptual model of entrepreneurship as firm behavior, *Entrepreneurship Theory and Practice*, **16**(1), 7–25.

Denison, D.R. (1996), What is the difference between organizational culture and organizational climate? A native's point of view on a decade of paradigm wars, *Academy of Management Review*, **21**(3), 619–654.

Deshpandé, R., Farley, J.U. and Webster, F.E. (1993), Corporate culture, customer orientation, and innovativeness in Japanese firms: a quadrad analysis, *The Journal of Marketing*, **57**(1), 23–37.

Detert, J.R., Schroeder, R.G. and Mauriel, J.J. (2000), A framework for linking culture and improvement initiatives in organizations, *Academy of Management Review*, **25**(4), 850–863.

Drori, G.S., Meyer, J.W. and Hwang, H. (2006), *Globalization and Organization: World Society and Organizational Change*, Oxford: Oxford University Press.

Freeman, C. (2002), Continental, national and sub-national innovation systems – complementarity and economic growth, *Research Policy*, **31**(2), 191–211.

Gertler, M. (2004), *Manufacturing Culture: The Institutional Geography of Industrial Practice*, Oxford: Oxford University Press.

Hatch, M.J. (1993), The dynamics of organizational culture, *Academy of Management Review*, **18**(4), 657–693.

Hofstede, G. (1980), *Culture's Consequences: International Differences in Work-Related Values*, Beverly Hills, CA: Sage Publications.

Hofstede, G. (2003), What is culture? A reply to Baskerville, *Accounting, Organizations and Society*, **28**(7), 811–813.

Hofstede, G. and Bond, M.H. (1988), The Confucius connection: from cultural roots to economic growth, *Organizational Dynamics*, **16**(4), 5–21.

House, R., Hanges, P., Javidan, M., Dorfman, P. and Gupta, V. (2004), *Culture, Leadership and Organizations: The GLOBE Study of 62 Societies*, Thousand Oaks, CA: Sage Publications.

Jassawalla, A.R. and Sashittal, H.C. (2002), Cultures that support product-innovation processes, *The Academy of Management Executive*, **16**(3), 42–54.

Keeble, D., Lawson, C., Moore, B. and Wilkinson, F. (1999), Collective learning processes, networking and 'institutional thickness' in the Cambridge region, *Regional Studies*, **33**(4), 319–332.

Kenney, M. (ed.) (2000), *Understanding Silicon Valley: The Anatomy of an Entrepreneurial Region*, Stanford: Stanford University Press.

Khazanchi, S., Lewis, M.W. and Boyer, K.K. (2007), Innovation-supportive culture: the impact of organizational values on process innovation, *Journal of Operations Management*, **25**(4), 871–884.

Kunda, G. (1992), *Engineering Culture: Control and Commitment in a High-Tech Corporation*, Philadelphia: Temple University Press.

Landes, D.S. (1999), *The Wealth and Poverty of Nations: Why Some Are So Rich and Some So Poor*, New York: W.W. Norton & Company.

Lee, S.M. and Peterson, S.J. (2001), Culture, entrepreneurial orientation, and global competitiveness, *Journal of World Business*, **35**(4), 401–416.

March, J.G. (1981), Footnotes to organizational change, *Administrative Science Quarterly*, **26**(4), 563–577.

Marshall, A. (1919), *Industry and Trade*, London: Macmillan.

Martin, J. (2002), *Organizational Culture: Mapping the Terrain*, Thousand Oaks, CA: Sage Publications.

Menzel, H.C., Aaltio, I. and Ulijn, J.M. (2007), On the way to creativity: engineers as intrapreneurs in organizations', *Technovation*, **27**(12), 732–743.

Mueller, S.L. and Thomas, A.S. (2001), Culture and entrepreneurial potential: a nine-country study of locus of control and innovativeness, *Journal of Business Venturing*, **16**(1), 51–75.

Nakata, C. and Sivakumar, K. (1996), National culture and new product development: an integrative review, *The Journal of Marketing*, **60**(1), 61–72.

Nanda, S. and Warms, R. (2010), *Cultural Anthropology*, 10th edn, Boston: Cengage.

Nelson, A.J. (2014), From the ivory tower to the startup garage: how organizational context shapes commercialization processes, *Research Policy*, **43**(7), 1144–1156.

Nelson, A.J. and Irwin, J. (2014), 'Defining what we do – all over again': occupational identity, technological change, and the librarian-internet search relationship, *Academy of Management Journal*, **57**(3), 892–928.

Ohmae, K. (1990), *The Borderless World*, New York: Harper.

O'Reilly, C.A., Chatman, J. and Caldwell, D.F. (1991), People and organizational culture: a profile comparison approach to assessing person-organization fit, *Academy of Management Journal*, **34**(3), 487–516.

Pettigrew, A.M. (1979), On studying organizational cultures, *Administrative Science Quarterly*, **24**(4), 570–581.

Pfeffer, J. (1992), *Managing with Power: Politics and Influence in Organizations*, Cambridge, MA: Harvard Business Press.

Porter, M.E. (1998), Clusters and the new economics of competition, *Harvard Business Review*, **76**(6), 77–90.

Rogers, E.M. and Larsen, J.K. (1984), *Silicon Valley Fever: Growth of High-Technology Culture*, New York: Basic Books.

Russo, M. (2010), *Companies on a Mission: Entrepreneurial Strategies for Growing Sustainably, Responsibly, and Profitably*, Stanford: Stanford University Press.

Saxenian, A. (1994), *Regional Advantage: Culture and Competition in Silicon Valley and Route 128*, Cambridge, MA: Harvard University Press.

Schein, E. (1992), *Organizational Culture and Leadership*, San Francisco, CA: Wiley.

Shane, S. (1993), Cultural influences on national rates of innovation, *Journal of Business Venturing*, **8**(1), 59–73.

Shane, S., Venkataraman, S. and MacMillan, I. (1995), Cultural differences in innovation championing strategies, *Journal of Management*, **21**(5), 931–952.

Smircich, L. (1983), Concepts of culture and organizational analysis, *Administrative Science Quarterly*, **28**(3), 339–358.

Starr, P. (1995), Review of Annalee Saxenian, regional advantage, *Contemporary Sociology*, **24**(3), 381–382.

Sutton, R.I. (2002), *Weird Ideas that Work: 11½ Practices for Promoting, Managing, and Sustaining Innovation*, New York: Simon and Schuster.

Sutton, R.I. (2007), *The No Asshole Rule: Building a Civilized Workplace and Surviving One That Isn't*, New York: Warner Business Books.

Tellis, G.J., Prabhu, J.C. and Chandy, R.K. (2009), Radical innovation across nations: the preeminence of corporate culture, *Journal of Marketing*, **73**(1), 3–23.

Tylor, E. (1873/1920), *Primitive Culture*, New York: G.P. Putnam's Sons.

Van Maanen, J. and Barley, S.R. (1984), Occupational communities: culture and control in organizations, *Research in Organizational Behavior* **6**, 287.

Weber, M. (1905/2002), *The Protestant Ethic and the Spirit of Capitalism*, New York: Penguin Classics.

Wilkins, A.L. and Ouchi, W.G. (1983), Efficient cultures: exploring the relationship between culture and organizational performance, *Administrative Science Quarterly*, **28**(3), 468–481.

6 Determinants of Entrepreneurship: The quest for the entrepreneurial gene

Introduction

Research on the determinants of entrepreneurship has a long history (Parker, 2009). The most recent and promising approaches include the investigation of biological determinants, such as genes, hormones and brain activity measures (electroencephalography or magnetic resonance imaging). The present chapter reviews several recent endeavors to connect genes to proxies of entrepreneurship, in particular self-employment. It should be read as an overview of the shortcomings and potential of two research methods: candidate gene studies and genome-wide association (GWA) studies.[1]

There are two popular views on what makes an entrepreneur. The first is that anyone can learn the necessary skills, provided they dedicate sufficient time and effort. The second view is that people are either born with the right personality and skills or they are not, and developing these traits is impossible. Which of these two views – the nurture or the nature hypothesis – is true, or the interplay between the two, has far-reaching implications for individual behavior and economic policies. Evidence suggests that inherited qualities play a role in occupational choice, with recent scientific advances showing different pathways through which genes can influence entrepreneurial behavior. The current view in this debate concludes that neither nurture nor nature alone are responsible for behavioral outcomes such as entrepreneurial choice. Rather, it is a complex interplay of both.

Self-employed parents may transfer relevant skills and a familiarity with entrepreneurial behavior to their children. Alternatively, inherited characteristics that can affect the tendency to become an entrepreneur may also explain the observed intergenerational effects. Examples of such characteristics include preferences for risk-seeking, altruism in dictator games, job satisfaction, vocational interests, work values, novelty-seeking, gambling, general cognitive ability and intelligence, educational attainment and overconfidence. Moreover, several twin studies suggest a genetic influence on the propensity to become self-employed (Nicolaou et al., 2008a, 2008b; Nicolaou and Shane, 2009; Zhang et al., 2009). In these studies, the heritability of proxies for entrepreneurship is consistently estimated to be in the range of 40 to 60 percent.

Entrepreneurship – which is proxied by self-employment in the present chapter – has been the target of attempts to identify specific genetic polymorphisms underlying its heritable variation. These attempts have been unsuccessful so far because the candidate gene studies were not replicable, while genome-wide association studies did not have sufficient sample sizes for genetic discovery, and the available proxy for entrepreneurship (i.e., self-employment) is too broad. In this chapter, the results of both the candidate gene and the genome-wide association approach are presented. These two approaches make it possible to find individual genetic variants associated with entrepreneurship, and complement other methods that consider (scaled) combinations of genetic variants simultaneously, such as twin studies and genomic-relatedness-matrix restricted maximum likelihood (GREML) studies (Benjamin et al., 2012).

Before presenting the dos and don'ts of the quest for the entrepreneurial gene, it is important to note that, in contrast to popular views, a genetic influence would not imply determinism or the irrelevance of the environment or free will; a genetic influence only implies a shift in an individual's probability of exhibiting a behavior, such as the tendency to become self-employed.

Basic genetic concepts

When a trait is heritable, it is, in principle, possible to locate the sites in the human genome that influence it. The human genome consists of all of the genetic information in human cells and is composed of 23 chromosomal pairs; half of the chromosomes are inherited from the mother and half from the father. These chromosomes 'package' DNA molecules and encode the genetic information along two DNA strands. A DNA strand is a polymer of nucleotides. Each nucleotide is a building block containing a base, which can be adenine (A), cytosine (C), guanine (G) or thymine (T); thus, there are four distinct nucleotides. DNA is structured as a double helix, where two DNA strands are held together by weak hydrogen bonds. Hydrogen bonding occurs between the bases of opposing nucleotides along the two strands: adenine always binds to thymine, and cytosine always binds to guanine. Consequently, two DNA strands of a DNA duplex have complementary sequences, and the sequence of one DNA strand can easily be inferred if the DNA sequence of its complementary strand is already known. DNA sequences are usually described by writing the sequence of the bases for only one strand. For example, an individual may have inherited the AA nucleotides for one particular position on a pair of chromosomes (i.e., a genotype). This inheritance would imply that the individual inherited an A base from the paternal chromosome and an A base from the maternal one. Another individual may have inherited the AG nucleotides at the same position, i.e., a different base from each of the two parents, while a third may have inherited both GG nucleotides from each parent. Alternative bases in a nucleotide at the same physical locus are called alleles. A DNA sequence on one position of the genome that exhibits at least a 1 percent variation between members of a species is called a single nucleotide polymorphism (SNP). The minor allele frequency (MAF) refers to the frequency of the less common allele of a SNP in a population.

Almost all human DNA is identical from person to person. To date, geneticists have identified 27 million SNPs among humans, while the entire human genome consists of some three billion nucleotides. These SNPs and other types of genomic variation are what make humans different from each other. The total number and locations of SNP markers that need to be genotyped to detect an association between common genetic variants and an outcome of interest (a phenotype of an individual) were identified by the HapMap project (International HapMap Consortium, 2005).

Until recently, genotyping was performed with arrays of 550,000 SNPs that, after data cleaning, deliver information about the specific alleles for approximately 500,000 SNPs. Although these arrays already give a high-resolution image of the human genome, the newest generation microarrays allow researchers to array two to 12 million markers per sample, including comprehensive coverage of both common and rare variants.

Candidate gene studies and genome-wide association studies

When the DNA of a sufficient number of individuals has been genotyped, their genotypes for certain SNPs can be associated with an outcome of interest, such as the presence of a disease, an IQ score, or the employment status of an individual. For a binary outcome such as entrepreneurship (with $y = 1$ for the individual being an entrepreneur, and $y = 0$ otherwise), we can test for an association by conducting a logistic regression for each SNP. When 500,000 SNPs are available for statistical analyses, 500,000 logistic regressions must be conducted.

The question is whether it is really necessary to test each SNP for association, or whether the analysis can be limited to a subset of SNPs. This choice is, in essence, the difference between candidate gene studies and genome-wide association (GWA) studies. Candidate gene studies hypothesize the relation between certain genes and the outcome of interest (phenotype). Only the hypothesized SNPs are tested for an association. GWA studies are hypothesis-free: no association between certain genes and a particular phenotype is hypothesized, and therefore, all available SNPs are tested. Hence, the GWA study is an exploratory method that does not rely on prior hypotheses.

As the number of independent statistical tests increases, so does the problem of multiple testing. By pure chance, a number of SNPs will show significant associations, even if there is no actual relationship between the

SNPs and the phenotype. For example, assume that we analyze 500,000 SNPs where none are truly associated with the phenotype, i.e., the statistical null hypothesis of no association between the SNP and the outcome is correct. If we adopt a 1 percent significance level for hypothesis testing, performing 500,000 tests should yield 5,000 incorrect rejections of the null hypothesis (i.e., false positives).

Following this reasoning, the number of false positives could be reduced by testing only a small set of SNPs instead of all available genotyped SNPs. The question is, however, whether selecting a limited set of SNPs and, consequently, testing a limited number of hypotheses is appropriate. Current knowledge of DNA does not enable us to predict which genes and how many are associated with entrepreneurship nor how strong their association is. For example, we know that approximately 70 percent of all genes are expressed in the brain and that brain function influences behavior. Thus, it is very possible to derive a seemingly plausible hypothesis for practically every gene (and therefore every SNP), and each of these hypotheses may sound credible for different reasons.

As a consequence, empirical research that focuses on a small subset of these hypotheses, such as candidate gene studies, is forced to make arbitrary choices regarding these hypotheses. A large number of false positive results can be expected if the statistical confidence intervals are not appropriately adjusted to reflect the total number of plausible hypotheses (Ioannidis, 2005) and if researchers yield to publication bias sentiments. Such adjustments are typically missing in candidate gene studies because researchers only point to their 'theory' as a justification for focusing on a small number of candidates. As a result, most findings of candidate gene studies are not replicable, while replication in an independent study dramatically lowers the chance of a false positive. Examples of replication failure in the social sciences include genetic loci associated with personality traits, behavior in dictator games and harm avoidance. For instance, Israel et al. (2009) report an association between a variant of the OXTR gene and the dictator game, which Apicella et al. (2010) failed to replicate. Vormfelde et al. (2006) report an association between a variant in the serotonin transporter gene and anxiety-related traits such as harm avoidance, which Lang et al. (2004) failed to replicate. Ioannidis (2005) showed that the pre-study probability of a genetic association being true is generally extremely low, and consequently, the post-study probability is also low.

To keep the false positive rate at an acceptably low level, stringent significance tests must be used to compensate for multiple testing. Even if researchers do not test all SNPs for an association, correcting for the existence of these alternative hypotheses is imperative. For individuals of

European descent, the consensus is to account for one million independent tests. Based on this number, the often used so-called Bonferroni correction proposes a significance level of 5×10^{-8} to obtain a family-wise significance level of 5 percent (the probability of making one or more type I errors among all hypotheses while performing multiple testing). This significance level is often referred to as 'genome-wide significance,' and only SNPs that pass this threshold are considered to be true positives (Beauchamp et al., 2010). This also makes clear that very large sample sizes are needed in GWA studies to discover true associations.

Non-replication of a candidate gene study

In a recent paper, Nicolaou et al. (2011) reported a significant association between a SNP in the dopamine receptor D3 (*DRD3*) gene and the tendency to be an entrepreneur in a group of 1,335 British subjects. In this candidate gene study, SNPs in a set of nine genes were tested for an association with the tendency to be an entrepreneur, resulting in a single significant association. The set of candidate genes consisted of five dopamine receptor genes associated with novelty- or sensation-seeking and four genes associated with attention deficit hyperactivity disorder (ADHD). These specific genes were selected based on the observation that sensation-seeking and ADHD are more common among entrepreneurs. The authors claimed that this is the first evidence of an association between variants of a specific gene and entrepreneurship.

As argued above, the appropriate significance threshold in candidate gene studies should be 5×10^{-8}. The reported association by Nicolaou et al. (2011) has a *p*-value of 0.0002, much higher than the genome-wide significance level. To evaluate this result, Van der Loos et al. (2011) tried to replicate their findings by performing an association analysis of the 18 SNPs reported in Nicolaou et al. (2011), including the significant association between a SNP in the *DRD3* gene and entrepreneurship, in three much larger independent groups of Dutch subjects from the Rotterdam Study (Hofman et al., 2009).

The Rotterdam Study (RS) consists of three cohorts: 5,974 participants in RS-I have been successfully genotyped, 2,129 in RS-II and 2,030 in RS-III. Because the type of array differs between the candidate gene study and the replication study, not all 18 reported SNPs were readily available in the Rotterdam Study cohorts. Therefore, these SNPs from the available genotype data were imputed using MACH (Li et al., 2009).

Van der Loos et al. (2011) constructed a binary variable indicating whether a subject (i) had never been self-employed or (ii) had been self-employed at least once during his/her complete working life (RS-I) or in his/her current or last occupation (RS-II and RS-III). For RS-I, the individuals with an incomplete working life history and the individuals who had never had a job were excluded, except those who were self-employed at least once. The rationale for this exclusion is that incomplete work life histories could 'contaminate' the control group with people who were self-employed at least once. Complete SNP and self-employment data were available for 5,374 subjects (531 cases, 4,843 controls) in RS-I, 2,066 subjects (197 cases, 1,869 controls) in RS-II, and 1,925 subjects (209 cases, 1,716 controls) in RS-III. The measure of entrepreneurship in Van der Loos et al. (2011) is equivalent to the definition used by Nicolaou et al. (2011), i.e., 'Have you ever started a business in your working life?' This equivalence was confirmed by a correlation coefficient of 0.87 between the two proxies for self-employment and starting a new business (Nicolaou et al., 2008a).

An association analysis was performed by Van der Loos et al. (2011) for each SNP by logistic regression (Li et al. 2009). For each SNP, two models were estimated: Model 1, which includes the SNP as an independent variable, and Model 2, which controls for sex and possible population stratification by including the first four principal components of the genotypic covariance-variance matrix. For RS-III, a dummy for age (>=50) was included in the latter model. Because Van der Loos et al. (2011) were replicating previously reported associations, it was appropriate to correct only for the number of SNPs that are replicated. The Bonferroni correction results in a significance level of 0.0028 (0.05/18 tests), which corresponds to a significance level of 0.05 for all tests. This level is much higher than the genome-wide significance level of 5×10^{-8}. The full estimation results are given in Van der Loos et al. (2011): none of the SNPs are even remotely significant in both models.

The estimation results for RS-I require additional explanation. Nicolaou et al. (2011) reported a significant association between a certain SNP in the *DRD3* gene and the tendency to be an entrepreneur. This SNP was not significantly associated in RS-I at the chosen significance level of 0.0028. Moreover, the negative coefficient suggests the opposite association, which demonstrates that the original finding was probably a false positive.

Further inspection of the results indicates that three SNPs within the *DRD3* gene survive the Bonferroni-corrected significance level of 0.0028. However, the direction of the associations is opposite to the associations reported in the original candidate gene study. Although the hypothesis that the *DRD3* gene is associated with entrepreneurship cannot be rejected based on these results, they do not support the effect of the G allele of the SNP reported by Nicolaou et al. (2011).

Discussion of non-replication

There are several shortcomings in the candidate gene studies, exemplified in Nicolaou et al. (2011), that lead to the skepticism that a reported association is a false positive and that all of the results in this area so far should also be interpreted with care. These shortcomings are lessons learned from the era of candidate gene studies, usually pursued with ill-defined markers across genes, small samples and/or lacking replication. The fact that the reported associations cannot be replicated underlines several arguments.

First, there is the suspicion that the selection of candidates, although seemingly sound, is largely arbitrary. This selection consists of genes previously thought to be associated with novelty- or sensation-seeking and ADHD, characteristics that are hypothesized to be more common among entrepreneurs. However, there are many other candidate genes, such as the serotonin 2A and 1B transporters (*HTR2A* and *HTR2B*), dopamine and serotonin transporters (*SLC6A3*, *SLC6A4*), dopamine beta-hydroxylase (*DBH*), monoamine oxidase B (*MAOB*), and genes associated with testosterone levels. Furthermore, the majority of genes are related to either brain function or to the expression of proteins in the brain and could therefore be candidates. Hence, there may be hundreds of thousands of potential candidate loci. This large number of potential genes makes the candidate gene approach, at present, unfeasible for the study of complex behaviors such as entrepreneurship.

Second, the selection criteria of SNPs within the chosen candidate genes are confined to the coding regions. A complete overview of the selected SNPs is lacking, although Nicolaou et al. (2011) report that the SNPs from the coding regions of the nine candidate genes were selected. SNPs in regulatory non-coding regions are not considered, although these could have substantial effects on a given phenotype. For an overview, see www. genome.gov/gwastudies.

Third, the hypothesis that dopamine receptor genes are associated with novelty- or sensation-seeking is based on mixed evidence from small-scale studies that could not always be replicated. For example, one study reported a significant association between a variant of the *DRD4* gene and novelty-seeking, but this association could not be replicated by a different study. A recent meta-analysis concludes that the *DRD4* gene may be associated with measures of novelty-seeking and impulsivity, but significant evidence of publication bias was found (Munafo et al., 2008).

Therefore, unfortunately, the candidate gene study of Nicolaou et al. (2011) should be interpreted with care because it does not sufficiently adjust for multiple testing. Even the significance level of 0.0028 used in the replication study is potentially too liberal. The reported association from Nicolaou et al. (2011) is likely to be a false positive and, hence, not a serious candidate for replication studies.

A genome-wide association study

In Van der Loos et al. (2013), self-employment (having started, owned and managed a business) is used as a proxy for entrepreneurship. A meta-analysis of GWA studies of self-employment was performed using 16 studies to identify genetic variants that are robustly associated with self-employment. Together, these studies were composed of 50,627 participants of European ancestry who are part of the Gentrepreneur Consortium. This study is the first large-scale effort to identify common genetic variants that are associated with an economic variable. A second study is Rietveld et al. (2013), which analyzed educational attainment.

Theoretical and empirical evidence from entrepreneurship research suggests that there are differences between males and females with respect to the types of businesses they start. These differences also extend to individuals' motivations, goals and resources (Verheul et al., 2012) and exist because women face different – and often more – barriers to entrepreneurship than men (Verheul and Thurik, 2001). Therefore, both pooled and sex-stratified analyses were performed.

The discovery stage of this study did not identify any genome-wide significant associations: there are no common SNPs for self-employment with moderate to large effect sizes. Gene-based tests for approximately 17,700 genes, including several candidate genes for entrepreneurship that have been previously suggested in the literature (Shane, 2010), did not reveal any significant associations. A SNP that is located in the *DRD3* gene and was identified by Nicolaou et al. (2011) did not correlate with the tendency to be an entrepreneur. Lastly, 58 SNPs in the discovery stage with a *p*-value below 10^{-5} (a threshold that was predefined in the analysis plan) were tested in a replication sample of 3,271 individuals, but none were replicated.

As the heritability of entrepreneurship is consistently measured between 40 and 60 percent (Nicolaou et al., 2008a; Zhang et al., 2009; Van der Loos et al., 2010), a plausible interpretation of these results is that the molecular genetic architecture of self-employment is highly polygenic: there are hundreds or maybe thousands of genetic variants that individually have a small effect, which together explain a substantial proportion of the heritability. Additionally, a complex interplay between genes and the environment may play a role. Finally, the possibility cannot be ruled out that rare genetic variants or other currently unknown and unmeasured variants that are insufficiently correlated with the SNPs have large effects on an individual's tendency to be self-employed. However, if these genetic variants are rare, they would not contribute a great deal to the population-based variance in self-employment, and large samples would be required to identify these variants.

The results of Van der Loos et al. (2010) are similar to those that have been reported for biologically more proximate human traits, such as height, and diseases, such as schizophrenia, for which a polygenic molecular genetic architecture has also been suggested. One implication of this similarity is that with sufficiently large sample sizes, SNPs that are associated with self-employment can, in principle, be discovered, as has been the case for height (Wood et al., 2014). A discovery sample of approximately 50,000 individuals is apparently still too small for a meta-analysis of GWA studies on a biologically distal, complex, and relatively rare human behavior such as self-employment. Moreover, self-employment is a fuzzy phenotype, having different meanings in different environments, i.e., cohorts. Lastly, there is the possibility of gene-environment interactions (the interplay between nature and nurture), which would make it even more difficult to identify the effects of individual SNPs in a GWA study that pools results from very different cohorts and environments.

Conclusion

Twin study estimates show that part of the variance in the propensity to engage in entrepreneurship can be explained by genetic variation. Hence, in principle, it should be possible to find the genetic loci that influence this propensity. In this chapter, it is argued that GWA studies are the best scientific approach given our current knowledge of DNA. There are several reasons: first, theories for selecting SNPs for candidate gene approaches are typically weak and arbitrary and, therefore, not convincing. Second, GWA studies make clear the need to correct for multiple testing. The non-replication of the candidate gene study illustrates this argument.

Therefore, large-scale GWA studies are the best method to conduct research in the 'quest for the entrepreneurial gene.' However, a discovery sample from Van der Loos et al. (2013) of approximately 50,000 individuals was apparently still too small for a meta-analysis of GWA studies on a biologically distal, complex, and relatively rare human behavior such as self-employment. A potential opportunity for future research includes performing GWA studies on endophenotypes such as risk preferences, confidence, and independence. The effect sizes of individual SNPs on these endophenotypes may be larger because of their greater biological proximity. However, these variables are difficult to measure reliably and are not (yet) available in many genotyped samples. An alternative may be to use less noisy proxies for entrepreneurship than just a measurement of self-employment, such as serial self-employment or successful business ownership. Finally, very large datasets (some say that at least 200,000 individuals are needed) may uncover the molecular architecture of entrepreneurship, even when the measurement is self-employment.

Scholars in the social sciences widely adopted the so-called standard social science model, which assumes that the mind is a cognitive device shaped by culture and socialization only. The model implies that variation in economic outcomes, such as human decisions, is the result of nurture (the environment) rather than nature or the interplay of nurture and nature. The quest for the entrepreneurial gene is one of the first initiatives to introduce biology into the realm of economic outcomes.

Why is the role of genetics in explaining entrepreneurship interesting? Koellinger et al. (2010) give various reasons. The first is simple curiosity. Genetics can help find the origins of individual differences and how they shape behaviors. Second, genetic differences across populations may be identified that will help explain aggregate economic outcomes, such as the share of nascent entrepreneurship. Third, knowledge of the genetics of economic behavior may improve our understanding of the boundaries of economic policies: a poor fit between genetic predisposition and occupational choice may result in an inferior performance. The rapid progress in the field of genetics, the advent of the so-called bio-banks with their extensive datasets and the limited progress in the traditional approaches of the determinants of entrepreneurship point toward a bright future for the quest for the entrepreneurial gene.

ROY THURIK

Note

1. The present chapter on entrepreneurship and genes would not have been possible without the following persons: Patrick Groenen, Albert Hofman, Philipp Koellinger, Matthijs van der Loos, Niels Rietveld, Fernando Rivadeneira, Frank van Rooij, André Uitterlinden and many others. I thank them for letting me use jointly written texts. I will refrain from burdening the below text with constantly citing the four publications on which it is based: Koellinger et al. (2010), Van der Loos et al. (2011, 2013) and Rietveld and Van der Loos (2012).

References

Apicella, C., Cesarini, D., Johanneson, M., Dawes, C., Lichtenstein, P., Wallace, B., Beauchamp, J. and Westberg, L. (2010), No association between oxytocin receptor (OXTR) gene polymorphisms and experimentally elicited social preferences, *PLoS ONE*, **5**(6), e11153.

Beauchamp, J.P., Cesarini, D., Johannesson, M., van der Loos, M.J.H.M., Koellinger, P.D., Groenen, P.J.F., Fowler, J.H., Rosenquist, J.N., Thurik, A.R. and Christakis, N.A. (2011), Molecular genetics and economics, *Journal of Economic Perspectives*, **25**, 57–82.

Benjamin, D.J., Cesarini, D., van der Loos, M.J.H.M., Dawes, C.T., Koellinger, P.D., Magnusson, P.K.E., Chabris, C.F., Conley, D., Laibson, D., Johannesson, M. and

Visscher, P.M. (2012), The genetic architecture of economic and political preferences. *Proceedings of the National Academy of Sciences of the United States of America*, **109**(21), 8026–8031.

Hofman, A., Breteler, M.M.B., van Duijn, C.M., Janssen, H.L.A., Krestin, G.P., Kuipers, E.J., Stricker, B.H.C., Tiemeier, H., Uitterlinden, A.G., Vingerling, J.R. and Witteman, J.C.M. (2009), The Rotterdam Study: 2010 objectives and design update, *European Journal of Epidemiology*, **24**, 553–572.

International HapMap Consortium (2005), A haplotype map of the human genome, *Nature*, **437**, 1299–1320.

Ioannidis, J.P.A. (2005), Why most published research findings are false, *PLoS Medicine*, **2**(8), e124.

Israel, S., Lerer, E., Shalev, I., Uzefovsky, F., Reibold, M., Laiba, E., Bachner-Melman, R., Maril, A., Bornstein, G., Knafo, A. and Ebstein, R.P. (2009), The oxytocin receptor (OXTR) contributes to prosocial fund allocations in the dictator game and the social value orientations task, *PLoS ONE*, **4**(5), e5535.

Koellinger, P.D., Van der Loos, M.J.H.M., Groenen, P.J.F., Thurik, A.R., Rivadeneira, F., van Rooij, F.J.A, Uitterlinden, A.G. and Hofman, A. (2010), Genome-wide association studies in economics and entrepreneurship research: promises and limitations, *Small Business Economics*, **35**, 1–18.

Lang, U.E., Bajbouj, M., Wernicke, C., Rommelspacher, H., Danker-Hopfe, H. and Gallinat, J. (2004), No association of a functional polymorphism in the serotonin transporter gene promoter and anxiety-related personality traits, *Neuropsychobiology*, **49**, 182–184.

Li, Y., Willer, C.J., Sanna, S. and Abecasis, G.R. (2009), Genotype imputation, *Annual Review of Genomics and Human Genetics*, **10**, 387–406.

Munafo, M.R., Yalcin, B., Willis-Owen, S.A. and Flint, J. (2008), Association of the dopamine D4 receptor (DRD4) gene and approach-related personality traits: meta-analysis and new data, *Biological Psychiatry*, **63**, 197–206.

Nicolaou, N. and Shane, S. (2009), Can genetic factors influence the likelihood of engaging in entrepreneurial activity? *Journal of Business Venturing*, **24**, 1–22.

Nicolaou, N., Shane, S., Cherkas, L., Hunkin, J. and Spector, T.D. (2008a), Is the tendency to engage in entrepreneurship genetic?, *Management Science*, **54**, 167–179.

Nicolaou, N., Shane, S., Cherkas, L. and Spector, T.D. (2008b), The influence of sensation seeking in the heritability of entrepreneurship, *Strategic Entrepreneurship Journal*, **2**, 7–21.

Nicolaou, N., Shane, S., Adi, G., Mangino, M. and Harris, J. (2011), A polymorphism associated with entrepreneurship: evidence from dopamine receptor candidate genes, *Small Business Economics*, **36**, 151–155.

Parker, S.C. (2009), *The Economics of Entrepreneurship*, Cambridge: Cambridge University Press.

Rietveld, C.A. and Van der Loos, M.J.H.M. (2012), The quest for the entrepreneurial gene: the importance of study design. *Medium Econometrische Toepassingen* **19**(1), 14–21.

Rietveld, C.A. et al. (2013), GWAS of 126,559 individuals identifies genetic variants associated with educational attainment, *Science*, **340**(6139), 1467–1471.

Shane, S. (2010), *Born Entrepreneurs, Born Leaders: How Your Genes Affect Your Work Life*, New York: Oxford University Press.

Van der Loos, M.J.H.M., Koellinger, P.D., Groenen, P.J.F. and Thurik, A.R. (2010), Genome-wide association studies and the genetics of entrepreneurship, *European Journal of Epidemiology*, **25**, 1–3.

Van der Loos, M.J.H.M., Koellinger, P.D., Groenen, P.J., Rietveld, C.A., Rivadeneira, F., van Rooij, F.J.A, Uitterlinden, A.G., Hofman, A. and Thurik, A.R. (2011), Candidate gene studies and the quest for the entrepreneurial gene, *Small Business Economics*, **37**, 269–275.

Van der Loos, M.L.H.M. et al. (2013), The molecular genetic architecture of self-employment, *PLOS One*, **8**(4).

Verheul, I. and Thurik, A.R. (2001), Start-up capital: does gender matter? *Small Business Economics*, **16**: 329–346.

Verheul, I., Thurik, R., Grilo, I. and van der Zwan, P. (2012), Explaining preferences and actual involvement in self-employment: gender and the entrepreneurial personality, *Journal of Economic Psychology*, **33**, 325–341.

Vormfelde, S.V., Hoell, I., Tzvetkov, M., Jamrozinski, K., Sehrt, D., Brockmöller, J. and Leibing, E. (2006), Anxiety- and novelty seeking-related personality traits and serotonin transporter gene polymorphisms, *Journal of Psychiatric Research*, **40**, 568–576.

Wood, A.R. et al. (2014), Defining the role of common variation in the genomic and biological architecture of adult human height, *Nature Genetics*, **46**, 1173–1186.

Zhang, Z., Zyphur, M.J., Narayanan, J., Arvey, R.D., Chaturvedi, S., Avolio, B.J., Lichtenstein, P. and Larsson, G. (2009), The genetic basis of entrepreneurship: effects of gender and personality, *Organizational Behavior and Human Decision Processes*, **110**, 93–107.

7 Disruptive Technology

Introduction

The discussion of the intensity of innovations has tradition with pairs such as 'incremental versus radical innovations' or 'changes along a trajectory versus paradigm changes.' The concept of a disruptive technology contributes to this discussion by focusing on a certain type of an in the end radical innovation.

The term 'disruptive technology' was popularized by Christensen (1997) in his seminal book entitled *The Innovator's Dilemma*. There disruptive technologies are described as (1) providing value quite different from concurrent mainstream technologies and (2) showing initially a comparatively lower performance along those dimensions that are most important to mainstream technology's customers. The term 'disruptive innovation' was used in a later publication to extend the scope of disruptive technologies not only to technological products but also to process and business model innovations (Christensen and Raynor, 2003). In Figure 7.1, Christensen describes the important aspect of a technology's changing performance over time (measured on the abscissa), identifies the trajectories of (the established technology by the bold line and the disruptive technology by the scattered line) product performance (measured on the ordinate) supplied by firms and demanded by (high- and low-end) customers for different technologies and market segments, and shows that technology disruptions occur when these trajectories intersect.

Whereas so-called 'sustaining' innovations are simply innovations that follow and feed a current paradigm of competition and technological progression expected in a given market, 'disruptive' innovations challenge a current paradigm of competition expected in a given market segment and develop towards new dimensions of innovation (Mount, 2012; Kassicieh

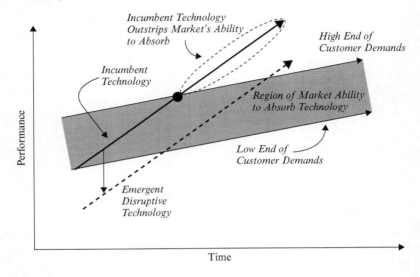

Source: Krikos (2011)

Figure 7.1   The disruptive technology model

et al., 2002, Kostoff et al., 2004; Walsh, 2004). Hence, disruptive innovations create new, low value markets and initiate their further growth by steadily modifying the underlying value proposition expected by mainstream customers (Mount, 2012). Contrary to sustained innovations a changed market and/or a changed business model are characterizing disruptive innovation.

Govindarajan and Kopalle highlight Canon as a case in point:

> Canon's introduction of slower but inexpensive tabletop photocopiers in the late 1970s relative to Xerox's high-speed big copiers is an example of disruptive innovation. The tabletop copiers were rapidly accepted by small businesses and individuals who appreciated the convenience and price despite poor resolution. At the time of their introduction, the mainstream market (larger companies) still preferred the large copiers because of speed, resolution, collation, etc. However, over time, further developments in small copiers have allowed Canon to improve quality, speed, and features and offer them at the price point that is sufficient to satisfy the needs of mainstream market.
>
> (Govindarajan and Kopalle, 2006b: 15)

The definition and scope of disruptive innovation triggered a controversial discussion (e.g., Adner, 2002; Danneels, 2004; Govindarajan and Kopalle, 2006b; Markides, 1998; Sood and Tellis, 2011; Paap and Katz, 2004) by which some authors support Christensen but propose a slightly different view. Adner (2002) complements the idea that decreasing marginal utility as the reason for consumers to switch from sustaining to disruptive innovation. Govindarajan and Kopalle (2006b) challenge Christensen's low performance/low price concept and suggest an innovation measure to include high-end as well as low-end disruption; consequently disruptive innovation can also show up as low performance/high price combination as in the case of the cellular phone compared to the landline phone.

Further discussion on disruptive innovation attempts to clarify some potential misunderstandings. First, disruption needs to be considered a relative phenomenon (Christensen and Raynor, 2003). For Dell, the initiative to sell computers over the internet is a sustaining innovation since they began selling computers via their previous business model, namely by telephone or by mail. This has not been the case for IBM, HP and Compaq, for whom the new way of selling over the internet was disruptive to their previous retailer based model (Christensen and Raynor, 2003). Second, disruptive innovation does neither necessarily cause incumbents to be replaced by entrants (Yu and Hang, 2009), nor does it require a disruptor to be a startup. For incumbents there is room to survive by focusing activities on the most demanding but least price-sensitive customers (Schmidt and Druehl, 2008). And there is the possibility for incumbents to become smart disruptors, on the basis of accumulated transformational experience from the past (King and Tucci, 2002). Third, disruptive innovation is not the same as destructive innovation (Yu and Hang, 2009). Technological innovations characterized by high performance/low price (contrary disruptive innovations' low performance/low price) directly invade the mainstream market and cause destructive effects there. The SiGe-chip, a communication chip developed by IBM, characterized by a four times higher switching speed, that reduced power requirements significantly and at low-cost production is a case in point. It had destructive impacts on its competitors and became a mainstream technology for wireless communication but it is not a disruptive innovation (Yu and Hang, 2009).

The theory of disruptive technology

Christensen (1997) explains the emergence of a disruptive innovation as the results of two dynamics, a steady invasion of the disruptive technology from a niche in the main market on the one hand and a performance overshooting of the mainstream technology on the other. In the beginning, a product based on a potential disruptive technology serves a niche market with customers valuing its non-standard (ancillary) and low performance attributes. Further development raises that disruptive technology's performance on relevant mainstream attributes to a level that attracts mainstream customers. Despite these improvements, the performance of the disruptive technology still lacks behind the performance offered by the established mainstream technology. On the side of the mainstream technology improvements are also accomplished; however, there the performance achieved may exceed or 'overshoot' a level for which mainstream customers are willing to pay (see Figure 7.1). The market disruption occurs when the new product displaces the mainstream product in the mainstream market. Christensen documented these technologies and market dynamics in numerous contexts such as hard disk drives, steel mills, earth-moving equipment and motor controls.

Besides the performance overshoot, market disruption requires asymmetric incentives between incumbents offering established products based on mainstream technology and new entrants offering products with disruptive technology. Contrary to sustaining innovations that are concerned with improving performance along established metrics that customers in the mainstream market already value (Christensen and Overdorf, 2000) disruptive innovations do not reinforce these established dimensions (Christensen, 1997). As a result, incumbent performance-oriented firms have very little incentive to invest in disruptive innovation with apparently unattractive technological opportunities (Danneels, 2004; Hüsig et al., 2005) and intensify their investments towards sustaining innovation (Hüsig et al., 2005). The new entrants invest into new dimensions at a lower level of performance and attempt to conquer the mainstream market via customers at the lower end of preferences.

For this fundamental process of disruptive innovation/technology to work, the core building blocks of preference structure, demand structure, innovation dynamics and market structure as well as their interactions are relevant.

The *structure of consumer preferences* that exist within competitive market and market segments and their spread from low-end to high-end are at the core of disruptive innovation processes (Mount, 2012). They directly influence an innovation's potential to invade new markets. Disruptive innovations are initially introduced in low-end and peripheral market segments and compete there with the mainstream; further improvements in the disruptive innovations allow satisfying more and more high-end demand requirements of mainstream customers; the invasion of the mainstream market proceeds that way step by step (Christensen and Bower, 1996). For this process to work out, the structure of mainstream customer preferences between markets and market segments is decisive (Hüsig et al., 2005). According to Adner (2002) to enable disruptive dynamics this structure has to be characterized by *preference overlap and preference asymmetry*. Preference overlap refers to the extent to which performance improvement in one markets segment is also valued in another market segment (Adner, 2002, 2004) – if that is not the case, the market segment and the mainstream market are not in competition and invasion from the former into the latter is unlikely. Preference asymmetry refers to the degree to which one of these two markets is better equipped to invade the other. Without asymmetry invasion of the market segment into the mainstream is unlikely (Adner, 2002, 2004).

Next to preferences a certain *distribution of demand* is required covering the attributes' range from high-end to low-end (see Figure 7.1); with an established technology that is more oriented towards high-end and a potentially disruptive technology that is more oriented towards low-end attributes, the mainstream and the competitive market segment are defined. In these markets, firms engage in *innovation activities* that lead to an upgrading of the functional attributes (product improvement) and/or a reduction of production costs (process improvement) (Adner, 2002). Such technological developments shape the respective technological trajectories (see Figure 7.1) and thereby influence the degree by which upstream or downstream market segments will be invaded (Mount, 2012). Sustaining improvements in the mainstream technology that surpass the high-end demand thresholds are subject to diminishing marginal utility. The higher marginal utility derived from the additional performance of the disruptive innovation eventually shifts competitive advantage to the new technology, thus causing disruption (Adner, 2002; Keller and Hüsig, 2009).

It is the *market structure*, in terms of the size, distribution and segmentation of consumers in different adopter categories that determines the intensity by which disruption takes place (Danneels, 2004). Since low customers show the lowest willingness to pay for sustained innovations in the established technology, they will be the first recipients of the disruptive innovations, which therefore will invade the mainstream market from the low-end (Hüsig et al, 2005) (see Figure 7.1).

Empirical research on disruptive innovations
Empirical research on disruptive innovation has been oriented towards the validity of the concept, measuring issues and actors involved.

Testing the validity of the disruptive innovation concept, Sood and Tellis (2011) investigated seven markets covering 36 technologies in a period of 50 years. They distinguish technology and firm disruption as follows: technology disruption occurs when the new technology crosses the performance of the dominant technology on the primary dimension of performance, whereas firm disruption occurs when the market share of a firm whose products use new technology exceeds the market share of the largest firm whose products use dominant technology. Their analyses show that many aspects of the theory of disruption in which entrants invading from the lower end of the market cause disruption are exaggerated and account for only a small fraction of all cases. Only 8 percent of all technology disruptions and 25 percent of all firm disruptions were caused by entrants using a lower attack. In case the term 'disruptive technology' is attributed to technologies invading via lower attack, their results show that although 47 percent of all technologies adopt that method, only 16 percent (14 percent) of all technologies cause technology disruption (firm disruption). More in line with the extant theory, Sood and Tellis (2011), however, conclude that the hazard of disruption by low-priced new technology is indeed higher.

With respect to measuring disruptive innovation, Govindarajan and Kopalle (2006a) suggest a scale for disruptiveness. To test the reliability and validity, they report on an empirical study focusing on the strategic business unit (SBU) level and based on data from 38 Fortune 500 corporations, involving 330 senior executives as respondents. In their subsequent work, Govindarajan and Kopalle (2006b) argue about the usefulness of measuring the disruptiveness of innovation ex-post to make an ex-ante prediction about the type of firms that may be better able to develop disruptive innovations. This work meant to answer the critics from Danneels (2004) regarding the predictive value of disruptive innovation theory.

Finally, looking at the type of actors managing disruptive innovations empirical research has highlighted the issue of collaboration (Chesbrough and Crowther, 2006; Paap and Katz, 2004). Here spin-offs, alliances and acquisitions show to be comparatively better suited to pushing disruptive innovations – looked at for corresponding points at different stages of innovation (Claude-Gaudillat and Quelin, 2006). Case studies by Macher and Richman (2004) find that IBM, Kodak and HP have adopted either form of collaborations to create disruptive innovations.

Conclusions

Following a review on disruptive innovation by Yu and Hang (2009) there are new areas of research that could be pursued.

From an organizational perspective, disruptive innovations could take advantage of the collaboration between incumbents and startups. Interesting here are the differences between collaborations pursuing sustained versus disruptive innovations in terms of the motivation for the collaboration, the factors incumbents and startups should consider when making decisions, and the different types of collaborative arrangements.

Since focusing only on mainstream markets will be detrimental to disruptive innovations, from a marketing perspective the question of how to find emerging markets and understand their unmet needs will be of paramount interest for developing disruptive innovation. From a technology perspective, it might be important to integrate the literature in technology forecasting in order to identify technologies that may render an enabling role for disruptive innovations.

In existing literature, the influence of network externalities and increasing return to adoption in the development dynamics of disruptive innovation has received very limited coverage and needs to be further investigated. Network effects created lock-ins and barriers for new technology to enter the market (Arthur, 1989). Disruptive innovation might be able to overcome the lock-in by attacking from niche and low-end market segment, while developing compatibility to the existing network.

UWE CANTNER AND EKO AGUS PRASETIO

References

Adner, R. (2002), When are technologies disruptive? A demand-based view of the emergence of competition, *Strategic Management Journal*, **23**(8), 667–688.

Adner, R. (2004), A demand-based perspective on technology life cycles, *Advances in Strategic Management*, **21**, 25–53.

Arthur, W.B. (1989), Competing technologies, increasing returns and lock-in by historical events, *The Economic Journal*, **99**(394), 116–131.

Chesbrough, H. and Crowther, A.K. (2006), Beyond high tech: early adopters of open innovation in other industries, *R&D Management*, **36**(3), 229–236.

Christensen, C.M. (1997), *The Innovator's Dilemma: When New Technologies Cause Great Firms to Fail*, Boston, MA: Harvard Business School Press.

Christensen, C.M. and Bower, J.L. (1996), Customer power, strategic investment, and the failure of leading firms, *Strategic Management Journal*, **17**, 197–218.

Christensen, C.M. and Overdorf, M. (2000), Meeting the challenge of disruptive change, *Harvard Business Review*, **78**(2), 66–76.

Christensen, C.M. and Raynor, M.E. (2003), *The Innovator's Solution: Creating and Sustaining Successful Growth*, Boston, MA: Harvard Business School Press.

Claude-Gaudillat, V. and Quelin, B.V. (2006), Innovation, new market and governance choices of entry: the internet brokerage market case, *Industry and Innovation*, **13**(2), 173–187.

Danneels, E. (2004), Disruptive technology reconsidered: a critique and research agenda, *Journal of Product Innovation Management*, **21**(4), 246–258.

Govindarajan, V. and Kopalle, P.K. (2006a), Disruptiveness of innovations: measurement and an assessment of reliability and validity, *Strategic Management Journal*, **27**(2), 189–199.

Govindarajan, V. and Kopalle, P.K. (2006b), The usefulness of measuring disruptiveness of innovations ex-post in making ex-ante predictions, *Journal of Product Innovation Management*, **23**, 12–18.

Hüsig, S., Hipp, C. and Dowling, M. (2005), Analyzing the disruptive potential: the case of wireless local area network and mobile communications network companies, *R&D Management*, **35**(1), 17–35.

Kassicieh, S.K., Walsh, S.T., Cummings, J.C., McWhorter, P.J., Romig, A.D. and Williams, W.D. (2002), Factors differentiating the commercialization of disruptive and sustaining technologies, *Engineering Management*, **49**, 375–387.

Keller, A. and Hüsig, S. (2009), Ex ante identification of disruptive innovations in the software industry applied to web applications: the case of Microsoft's vs. Google's office applications, *Technological Forecasting and Social Change*, **76**, 1044–1054.

King, A.A. and Tucci, C.L. (2002), Incumbent entry into new market niches: the role of experience and managerial choice in the creation of dynamic capabilities, *Management Science*, **48**(2), 171–186.

Kostoff, R.N., Boylan, R. and Simons, G.R. (2004), Disruptive technology roadmaps, *Technological Forecasting and Social Change*, **71**, 141–159.

Krikos, A. (2011), Cloud computing as disruptive technology, *Cloudbook*, **2**(2), 1–5.

Macher, J.T. and Richman, B.D. (2004), Organizational responses to discontinuous innovation: a case study approach, *International Journal of Innovation Management*, **8**(1), 87–114.

Markides, C. (1998), Strategic innovation in established companies, *Sloan Management Review*, **39**(3), 31–42.

Mount, P.M. (2012), *The Mechanisms that Drive Disruptive Innovation*, PhD dissertation, University of York.

Paap, J. and Katz, R. (2004), Anticipating disruptive innovation, *Research Technology Management*, **47**(5), 13–22.

Schmidt, G.M. and Druehl, C.T. (2008), When is a disruption innovation disruptive? *Journal of Product Innovation Management*, **25**, 347–369.

Sood, A. and Tellis, G.J. (2011), Demystifying disruption: a new model for understanding and predicting disruptive technologies, *Marketing Science*, **30**, 339–354.

Walsh, S.T. (2004), Roadmapping a disruptive technology: a case study: the emerging microsystem and top-down nanosystems industry, *Technological Forecasting and Social Change*, **71**, 161–185.

Yu, D. and Hang, C.C. (2009), A reflective review of disruptive innovation theory, *International Journal of Management Reviews*, **12**(4), 435–452.

8 Education, Entrepreneurship and the Unreasonable

Introduction

The emergence of entrepreneurship education within universities over the past 30 years has been unprecedented (Greene and Rice, 2007; Hills, 1988; Kuratko, 2005; Neck and Greene, 2011). Contemporary academic programs include formal degree programs at the undergraduate and graduate levels (i.e., entrepreneurship majors, minors, concentrations, certificates, Master's degrees and PhD programs), a curriculum with 20 or more courses, a portfolio of co-curricular programming and a mix of community engagement initiatives (Katz, 2003; Morris et al., 2013a). From a handful of programs three decades ago, today there are more than 3,000 institutions offering entrepreneurship programs (Katz, 2003). The growth has been unabated, and is likely to continue in the years to come.

In this chapter, we examine key patterns in the emergence of these programs within colleges and universities. It is argued that, as both the supply of and demand for entrepreneurship education have increased, a number of serious gaps persist in our understanding of how to best design and deliver these programs. Especially critical is the core content that is taught. Three perspectives are provided on the nature of this content, with emphasis placed on the need to focus on entrepreneurial competencies and the entrepreneurial mindset. When teaching entrepreneurship, it is suggested that educators strike a balance between encouraging unreasonable thinking and acting, on the one hand, and introducing rigor, structure and discipline, on the other hand. The roles of deliberate practice and experiential learning in entrepreneurship pedagogy are highlighted. We close with a look to the future.

Emergence of entrepreneurship education

A synopsis of how entrepreneurship education has emerged can be found in Table 8.1. Here, we see dramatic change as a formal discipline has taken shape, a considerable volume of high-quality research has appeared, and diverse and innovative programs of study have been established. Entrepreneurship's position has been institutionalized as university structures have been modified to include not only centers of entrepreneurship, but academic co-departments (e.g., management and entrepreneurship), departments and schools. Universities are employing dedicated, tenure-track faculty in entrepreneurship, and these faculty members are able to pursue career tracks in entrepreneurship and enjoy significant professional mobility. Meanwhile, the scope of these programs has extended across the campus, into the community and across the globe. The programs are introducing novel approaches to staffing, funding, and economic

Table 8.1   Emergence of entrepreneurship education

◆ Relative emphasis: sidelight ➔ sub-area ➔ area ➔ major discipline
◆ Curriculum: courses ➔ structured curriculum ➔ undergraduate degrees ➔ graduate degrees
◆ Structure: based in existing academic unit ➔ based in center or institute ➔ creation of co-department of entrepreneurship ➔ creation of separate departments and schools of entrepreneurship
◆ Funding model: cost center ➔ revenue center ➔ profit center
◆ Outreach: campus-based events ➔community and campus events ➔ integration of curriculum and outreach
◆ Assurance of learning: course evaluations ➔ venture metrics ➔ competencies ➔ integrative model
◆ Faculty: adjuncts ➔ shared faculty ➔ dedicated faculty ➔ joint appointments
◆ Research: little scholarly activity ➔ core faculty publishing ➔ stimulation of interdisciplinary research agendas
◆ Focal market: business school ➔ local community ➔ campus ➔ region ➔ nation/globe
◆ Purpose: fill a gap ➔ develop area of study ➔ empower students and create ventures ➔ transform campuses and communities
◆ Philosophy: help students learn about venture creation ➔ create ventures ➔ think and act entrepreneurially

---

Source: Adapted from Morris et al. (2013a)

engagement with the society (Morris et al., 2013a). In the process, they are often able to generate significant resources for universities. And in some cases, they are playing a central role in a movement toward establishing the 'entrepreneurial university' (Clark, 2004; Gibb and Hannon, 2006).

It could be argued that this growth and expansion has exposed tens of thousands of students to entrepreneurial possibilities, given young entrepreneurs a set of tools and concepts that can enhance their likelihood of success, and encouraged the development of ecosystems to support an entrepreneurial community, while fostering (an unclear level of) startup activity. Yet, the case could also be made that the emergence of entrepreneurship education has occurred so rapidly that it has outpaced our understanding of what should be taught by entrepreneurship educators, how it should be taught and how outcomes should be assessed.

Persistent gaps in our understanding of entrepreneurship education
A gap exists between a growing demand for and supply of entrepreneurship education and our understanding regarding how best to design and deliver these educational programs. Gaps continue to exist in key areas, including:

- defining the field's core content or substance;
- the structure and flow of an entrepreneurship degree program;
- teaching techniques that are most effective under varying conditions;
- best practices in classroom innovation;
- the relative effectiveness of differing educational delivery mechanisms;
- implications of different learning approaches;
- appropriate learning outcomes and standards; and
- assurance of learning measures when it comes to entrepreneurship.

There is little sign these gaps are receiving the kind of attention that will result in their elimination. While scholarly research in entrepreneurship has been greatly expanded, the volume of substantive research focused on issues in education and pedagogy has been limited (Katz, 2003). Similarly, few attempts have been made to document effective and ineffective practices in the classroom, or measure the relationship between course or program design and delivery approaches and tangible outcomes from entrepreneurship programs (Solomon et al., 2002).

It is also possible that these gaps will get greater. Entrepreneurship education is not static. It represents a moving target, with continuous additions to both the depth and breadth of the content of the discipline (DeTienne and Chandler, 2004). Meanwhile, entrepreneurship programs are emerging as innovation platforms (Honig, 2004). They are continually spinning off a fascinating array of new courses, pedagogies, student support programs and outreach initiatives. Further, new learning platforms, technologies and vehicles are appearing for enhancing how entrepreneurship can be taught. In addition, the student audience for entrepreneurship education is not only growing in size, but it is becoming more diverse as reflected in the age, gender, life stage, ethnicity, professional background, motives and contexts of those wishing to better understand entrepreneurship in all of its manifestations.

What we teach when we teach entrepreneurship
In reflecting on whether entrepreneurship can be taught, Peter Drucker (1985: 144) explains, 'The entrepreneurial mystique? It's not magic, it's not mysterious, and it has nothing to do with the genes. It's a discipline. And,

like any discipline, it can be learned.' Support for this view comes from a ten-year literature review of entrepreneurship education that reported, 'Most of the empirical studies surveyed indicated that entrepreneurship can be taught, or at least encouraged, by entrepreneurship education' (Gorman et al., 1997: 63).

Part of the challenge in establishing what is taught in the entrepreneurship classroom concerns who is doing the teaching and where the teaching is taking place. Courses today are being taught by full-time dedicated faculty members (some with degrees in entrepreneurship and some with degrees in other disciplines), faculty who primarily teach in other disciplines but find themselves teaching an entrepreneurship course, professors of practice and adjunct faculty who have strong commercial backgrounds, and others. This tendency alone can lead to wide differences in knowledge, beliefs and attitudes regarding what should be taught. Courses are taught both inside and outside business schools, which can also influence content.

The focus of entrepreneurship education would seem to include three general areas of emphasis, as summarized in Table 8.2. The first area might be labeled 'business basics', or how the different functional areas

Table 8.2   What we teach when we teach entrepreneurship

Business basics	Entrepreneurship basics	Entrepreneurial mindset/ competencies
Setting up the books	Entrepreneurship defined	Opportunity alertness
How to sell	Entrepreneurial process	Risk mitigation
Hiring of staff	Characteristics of entrepreneurs	Resource leveraging
Forms of enterprise	Types of entrepreneurs	Conveying a compelling vision
Cash flow management	Contexts for entrepreneurship	Value innovation
Formulating strategy	Innovative business models	Passion
Market analysis	Entrepreneurial cognition	Persistence and tenacity
Setting up operations	Nature of opportunity	Creative problem-solving
Pricing	Opportunity discovery/ creation	Guerrilla behavior
Promotion and advertising	Seed and venture capital	Optimism
Financial statements	Lean start-up	Learning from failure
Franchising	Entrepreneurial orientation	Implementing change
Management control	Entrepreneurship and society	Adaptation
Cost analysis	Exit strategies	Resilience
Protecting intellectual property	Ethical challenges in entrepreneurship	Creative problem-solving
		Building and using networks

of business apply in an early stage venture context. Approached as business basics, one might question the extent to which entrepreneurship represents a unique discipline with its own defined content, as opposed to a field of study that relies on teaching borrowed content from such fields as management, psychology, sociology, anthropology, physics and ecology. The second area of focus might be termed 'entrepreneurship basics', where core content from the emerging discipline is emphasized. Examples of topical issues here would include the entrepreneurial process, innovative business models, lean start-ups, entrepreneurial orientation, and entrepreneurial cognition, among others. The third focal area is the entrepreneurial mindset and its associated mix of entrepreneurial competencies. Here, educators focus on helping students develop their abilities in such areas as opportunity recognition and assessment, conveying a compelling vision, leveraging resources, mitigating risks, and engaging in guerrilla behavior (Morris et al., 2013b).

Arguably, the greatest promise lies within columns two and three in Table 8.2. Business schools already teach business basics, effectively eliminating the need for this type of entrepreneurship education. Approached as business basics, new ventures simply represent another context for managerial action, as opposed to a distinct discipline with a unique subject matter. The real promise of entrepreneurship education is in its potential to promulgate the entrepreneurial mindset and facilitate entrepreneurial action.

Teaching reason and the unreasonable

Entrepreneurship education must involve more than the mechanics of business start-up. The core precept guiding our pedagogical approaches should be the idea that entrepreneurship is disruptive. As Morris, Kuratko and Cornwall (2013: 3) explain, 'entrepreneurship educators are the promoters of dreams, agents of change, facilitators of opportunity, generators of empowerment and promulgators of revolution – whether through our research, teaching or outreach, this is our sacred role.' Yet, as we teach students to challenge assumptions, think in bold innovative terms, identify and leverage resources, and persist in creatively overcoming obstacles, we must also teach them to approach entrepreneurial action from a perspective of structure, rigor, logic and realism. In this sense then, entrepreneurship education represents the confluence of unreasonable thinking and discipline.

Accordingly, educators are engaged in a balancing act. They must provide the tools and perspectives that enable students to think in bigger terms and challenge them to imagine truly novel value propositions that lead customers, create markets and transform the competitive landscape. Yet they must be vigilant in teaching and applying the frameworks and principles that bring rigor, logic and realism to student thinking and acting.

Achievement of this balance can be facilitated by pedagogical approaches built around three pillars: content-based education, competency-based education and experientially-based education. With regard to content, there is a rich and growing knowledge base surrounding the entrepreneurial process and the requirements for entrepreneurial action available for educators (column two in Table 8.2). Yet, available teaching resources, including textbooks, tend to emphasize business basics (column one in Table 8.2). In terms of competencies, Morris and colleagues (2013b) have generated a set of 13 core entrepreneurial competencies, together with guidance in how to teach and measure progress on each of them (see also DeTienne and Chandler, 2004; Fiet, 2001). Finally, a larger percentage (perhaps as much as 60 percent) of the education program should center on experiential learning, or what Neck, Greene and Brush (2014) label 'deliberate practice.' While typically approached as 'learning by doing,' the educator is creating and using experiences that address four questions:

- What do I want the student to do?
- What do I want the student to see?
- What do I want the student to think?
- What do I want the student to feel?

More than just case studies or business plans, the experiential dimension of education places students into their discomfort zones, forces them to think and act under conditions of ambiguity, introduces vexing obstacles, includes real elements of risk and rewards tenacity, adaptation and creative problem-solving (see also Solomon et al., 2002). Building on the work of Kolb and Kolb (2005), Schindehutte (2007) stresses the importance of having a portfolio of experiential approaches that reflect different student learning styles.

Conclusion

With a history of dramatic growth and expansion, entrepreneurship education suffers from growing pains as fundamental gaps have emerged in our understanding of what works in the structuring, design and delivery of educational programs. Yet, entrepreneurship programs may be uniquely positioned to transform higher education. Unfettered by a long academic history, entrepreneurship educators operate with a largely blank canvas. Where established disciplines operate with assumptions, traditions, rules and politics that can produce inertia and rigidity, entrepreneurship as a discipline has yet to develop such obstacles. As a result, in coming years entrepreneurship educators are poised to shed new light on inter-disciplinary approaches to teaching, uncover entirely new methods for experiential learning and the design of curricula around experiences, and create new ways for universities to engage society and connect such engagement to the learning process. Achieving this potential requires that faculty members see themselves 'academic entrepreneurs,' recognizing and exploiting new opportunities for learning, taking calculated risks, leveraging resources and pioneering innovation within and outside the classroom.

MICHAEL H. MORRIS

References

Clark, B.R. (2004), Delineating the character of the entrepreneurial university, *Higher Education Policy*, **17**(4), 355–370.

DeTienne, D.R. and Chandler, G.N. (2004), The role of gender in opportunity identification, *Entrepreneurship Theory and Practice*, **31**(3), 365–386.

Drucker, P.F. (1985), *Innovation and Entrepreneurship*, New York: Harper and Row.

Fiet, J.O. (2001), The pedagogical side of entrepreneurship theory, *Journal of Business Venturing*, **16**(2), 101–117.

Gibb, A. and Hannon, P. (2006), Towards the entrepreneurial university, *International Journal of Entrepreneurship Education*, **4**(1), 73–110.

Gorman, G., Hanlon, D. and King, W. (1997), Some research perspectives on entrepreneurship education, enterprise education, and education for small business management: a ten-year literature review, *International Small Business Journal*, **15**, 56–77.

Greene, P.G. and Rice, M.P. (2007), *Entrepreneurship Education*, Cheltenham, UK and Northampton, MA: Edward Elgar Publishing.

Hills, G.E. (1988), Variations in university entrepreneurship education: an empirical study of an evolving field, *Journal of Business Venturing*, **3**, 109–122.

Honig, B. (2004), Entrepreneurship education: toward a model of contingency-based business planning, *Academy of Management Learning & Education*, **3**(3), 258–273.

Katz, J.A. (2003), The chronology and intellectual trajectory of American entrepreneurship education, *Journal of Business Venturing*, **18**(2), 283–300.

Kolb, A.Y. and Kolb, D.A. (2005), Learning styles and learning spaces: enhancing experiential learning in higher education, *Academy of Management Learning and Education*, **4**(2), 193–212.

Kuratko, D.F. (2005), The emergence of entrepreneurship education: development, trends, challenges, *Entrepreneurship Theory and Practice*, **29**(3), 577–598.

Morris, M.H., Kuratko, D.F. and Cornwall, J.R. (2013a), *Entrepreneurship Programs and the Modern University*, Cheltenham, UK and Northampton, MA: Edward Elgar Publishing.

Morris, M.H., Webb, J.W., Fu, J. and Singhal, S. (2013b), A competency-based perspective on entrepreneurship education: conceptual and empirical insights, *Journal of Small Business Management*, **51**(3), 352–369.

Neck, H.M. and Greene, P.G. (2011), Entrepreneurship education: known worlds and new frontiers, *Journal of Small Business Management*, **49**(1), 55–70.

Neck, H., Greene, P. and Brush, C. (2014), Practice-based entrepreneurship education using actionable theory, in M.H. Morris (ed.), *Annals of Entrepreneurship Education and Pedagogy*, Cheltenham, UK and Northampton, MA: Edward Elgar Publishing.

Schindehutte, M. (2007), *Play to Learn and Learn to Play*, working paper, Syracuse University.

Solomon, G.T., Duffy, S. and Tarabishy, A. (2002), The state of entrepreneurship education in the United States: a nationwide survey and analysis, *International Journal of Entrepreneurship Education*, **1**(1), 65–86.

9   Engineering Research Centers

Introduction

Over the past three decades, there has been a dramatic shift in US science and technology policy; such a shift has occurred in the public investment of university research funding and emerging institutional designs. Specifically, the science community has witnessed the transition from discipline-based, principal investigator (PI)-oriented, university research to a new interdisciplinary, block grant, industry-oriented research center – generally described as cooperative research centers (CRC). This new model encourages university researchers to work with industry and to work beyond the strictures of academic disciplines. The belief is that these CRCs have the capacity required to address complex social and scientific challenges (NAE, 1984; NSF, 1984; Bozeman and Boardman, 2004; Committee on Science, Engineering and Public Policy, 1996).

Nowadays, there are several different types of CRCs operating in the US universities, and about a third of academic scientists and engineers are affiliated at least with one CRC (Bozeman and Boardman, 2004). Among these university research center programs, the Engineering Research Centers (ERCs) program of the National Science Foundation (NSF) is considered to be one of the most influential programs that pioneers the practice of CRCs. ERCs are university-based research and education centers. These centers bring together multidisciplinary teams of university scientists to interact with firms in research and education. Many – although not all – of the ERCs address technological problems facing industry, as industrial workforce needs. While the ERC program was not the first research center program initiated by NSF, it was the first large-scale such program involving major expenditures and extensive industrial participation and emphasis on integration of research and education.

While initially controversial, the ERC program has come to be viewed as a major success and has been emulated by other government research agencies and in other nations' National Innovation Systems. The perceived early success of the ERCs led NSF officials to establish structurally similar programs, ones of similar size and scope, including the Science and Technology Centers (STCs), Materials Research Science and Engineering Centers (MRSECs) and Supercomputing Centers. In addition, the ERC program also prompts other federal agencies such as DoD, NIH and NASA to invest in these types of CRCs. Several US state governments have created their own 'Centers of Excellence' programs largely modeled on the ERC design. In short, the CRC design is ubiquitous and the characteristic government approach to addressing scientific and technological challenges and opportunities has changed remarkably during the more than 30 years since the inception of the ERC program.

Historical background of the NSF ERC program

The ERC program was a policy response to the 'competitiveness crisis' facing the United States' manufacturing industries during the 1980s. At the time, US corporations such as Xerox, Westinghouse and General Electric were losing their international market due in part to Japanese industrial competitors. In 1984, the Office of Science and Technology Policy of the White House asked the National Academy of Science to assemble a panel of experts to address this problem (Mayfield, 1987). The panel experts published their report in 1985 detailing their diagnoses of the crisis and recommended that the NSF establish an interdisciplinary centers program for engineering research to solve these challenges (NAE, 1984). The report noted that the primary problem causing US firms to lose their competitiveness was the disconnection between industries and universities.

As the panel report noted, the education functions of the university system were carried out by the academics in largely partitioned academic structures dominated by traditional disciplinary boundaries. This design usually provided no role for interaction with industry. The result, at least in the view of some observers (Bozeman and Boardman, 2004), was that students were not adequately trained for the team-based, interdisciplinary engineering required for industrial practice. In short, any improvement in the competitiveness of the US economy required a closer connection between universities' educational and research 'products' and industry's needs (NRC, 1986).

To address these problems, the NSF, under the leadership of NSF director and National Science Board director Eric Bloch, established the ERC program with the goal of reforming the engineering research and education system in US universities. The ERCs are designed to bridge the gap between industrial and academic research, with emphasis on interdisciplinary problems and providing a more hands-on education for engineering students (NSF, 1996). Most ERCs work closely with industry. On the one hand, ERC members regularly interact with industry partners to ensure that their researches are relevant to the needs of the engineering practitioners. On the other, students receive practical guidance from the industrial scientists. NSF expects that the interdisciplinary research conducted at the ERCs will enhance the innovative capacity of industries. It was expected that the education experience the ERCs provided would better prepare students to practice engineering, as well as transform the culture of higher education. With these expectations, NSF established its first six ERCs in 1986 with a $10 million budget. This initial investment has over time led to

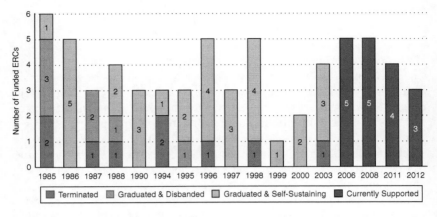

Note: Status of ERCs by year. Retrieved October 26, 2014, from http://erc-assoc.org/content/status-ercs-year.

Figure 9.1   Current ERC program status

a much more extensive set of ERCs. The NSF has established a total of 64 ERCs over the past 30 years, with 20 operating presently with $62 million support from the NSF (see Figure 9.1). Currently, the ERC program represents around 22 percent of the NSF funding for center programs. According to the latest NSF budget, the ERC program also received $144 million support from its industry partners in addition to the NSF funding. With these resources, the total participants of the current ERC program include 814 academic institutions, 1,833 non-academic organizations (industry firms, state and other federal agencies) and close to 5,000 personnel (faculty, students and industry researchers) associated with ERCs (see Table 9.1).

Evaluation imperative
Inasmuch as the ERC program has for many years been quite popular among policymakers, university administrators and scientists, it is easy to forget the early criticisms and controversies when the program was established. When created, it was widely feared that the ERC program would threaten the NSF historical focus on basic research. Related, the program seemed to challenge the traditional paradigm of peer-reviewed, investigator-initiated basic science research. From the founding of the NSF in the early 1950s until the ERC program began in 1985, almost all awards were made through grants to universities acting as fiduciaries for principal investigators. The ethos was simple and compelling: that

Table 9.1   Engineering Research Centers program data, 1994–2013

Year	# of ERCs	ERC funding	NSF center funding	Institutions	Partners	Leverages	Participants
1994	18	51.25	186.12	18	416	96.4	3,370
1995	21	51	189	100	590	96	4,648
1996	21	52	192	100	687	111	9,384
1997	19	48	190	20	700	131	10,123
1998	21	53	212	21	600	107	9,000
1999	18	57	232	126	505	111	8,700
2000	20	55	240	147	439	100	10,482
2001	19	63	238	147	515	140	3,634
2002	16	61	254	383	522	86	3,622
2003	16	66	250	471	448	53	9,828
2004	19	66	261	373	433	72	7,810
2005	19	62	236	280	482	72	8,310
2006	19	60	252	228	425	89	10,803
2007	15	47	234	494	455	181	4,647
2008	15	53	258	432	455	100	4,302
2009	15	61	277	423	534	101	4,089
2010	15	49	281	369	263	85	3,583
2011	18	59	297	472	299	101	2,720
2012	20	70	289	621	252	125	3,964
2013	20	62	282	814	355	144	4,919

Note: ERC funding and NSF center funding denote dollars in millions. Institutions: all academic institutions participated in activities at the centers. Partners: total number of non-academic participants, including industry, states, and federal agencies, at centers. Leverages: funding for centers from sources other than NSF. Participants: the total number of people who utilize center facilities; not just persons directly supported by NSF.

Source: Extracted from NSF (2014)

the NSF should support the best research as defined by scientific experts themselves without interference from others. Therefore, when the NSF shifted from the traditional research grants to a more centralized cooperative research agreement contracting vehicle used for the ERC program, critics suggested that ERCs were distracting from the NSF mission and at the expense of basic research (Bozeman and Boardman, 2004).

The criticisms of the ERC program reflect the conflicted paradigms in the federal agencies and universities, the tensions between the belief that US scientific and technological achievements are based on the support of individual science research, and the alternative mode of cooperative research centers (Lee, 1996). While the NSF acknowledged that the creation of ERCs should not jeopardize the support for basic research (NAE,

1985), the NSF budget from 1984 to 1990 suggests that the support for the ERC program has grown faster than the support for individual-investigator research, which implies that the initial concerns for ERCs have some merit, at least if one accepts the premises of those arguments (NAE, 1989). Nearly three decades since the ERC achieved that which could not have been achieved through individual grants.

Evaluation efforts and barriers
The main goal of the ERC program is to improve engineering research so that US engineers will be better prepared to contribute to engineering practice and to assist US industry in becoming more competitive in global markets (NAE, 1984). The NSF mandated that every ERC should have three main characteristics. First, ERCs should conduct interdisciplinary research of importance to industry. Second, ERCs should encourage industry collaborations and technology transfer. Third, ERCs should design education components attuned to the needs of industry. Therefore, the comparison between the ERC program and individual grants should be judged by their effectiveness in achieving these criteria.

During the early phase of the ERC program, the NSF commissioned the National Academy of Engineering (NAE) to create evaluation metrics for ERCs (NAE, 1986). In 1988 and 1989, the NSF also asked the NAE to assess ERC program effectiveness (NAE, 1988a, 1988b, 1989); and the US Congress requested the Government Accountability Office to examine ERC effectiveness (US Government Accountability Office, 1988). There is only limited performance data to draw any definitive conclusion since the program had just initiated, but all the reports agree that the ERC program is achieving its purposes. In particular, the NAE panel concluded that the mission of connecting academic engineering research and education to engineering practice couldn't be accomplished through the traditional avenues of academic research alone (NAE, 1989).

It is important to note that these earlier evaluations were focused mainly on the ERC program's industrial interaction, since its performance on engineering research and education required a longer time to observe. After the ERC program had become fully developed, the NSF conducted a series of assessment studies of the impact of ERCs, including impacts on local economies (SRI, 2008), industry interaction (Roessner et al., 2004), university culture (Ailes et al., 2001), and education (Parker, 1997).

By 2007, ERCs had produced 1,430 inventions, 524 patents, 1,886 licenses and 113 spinoff firms with more than 1,300 employees. In addition, the NSF budget breakout suggests that ERCs demonstrate, by comparison with other NSF center programs, the best capacity to attract outside industrial funding and the highest participant number per dollar spent. However, these studies do not consider whether the traditional mechanism for academic research can achieve similar results with similar resources. In addition, there are several problems constructing the proper instruments to distinguish the ERC-enabled results from others. First, the majority of ERC scientists and engineers are supported by multiple funding sources, which often include individual grants. Second, ERC participants are engaged with multiple collaborators. Third, ERC students reside in their own academic department and receive education and training in a specific discipline. Therefore, to determine whether the ERC program is more effective than traditional academic practice in engineering research and education is extremely difficult as ERCs rely entirely on the traditional academic departments for the preponderance of students' formal training. Further, the ERC program is intended to enhance the capacity for engineering research and education, yet most measures of impacts examine the results in terms of the execution of activities not impacts. Finally, it is still not clear whether the ERC model is sustainable without federal base support. The ERC program was set up with a 'sunset clause,' expecting that centers would be self-supporting and that NSF support would be withdrawn after a few years. As centers have hit their sunset year, some have vanished, some have been sustained for short periods and others have flourished. However, in some cases, the centers flourish due to university support that could have emerged absent the ERC startup funds. Recent NSF studies suggest that it is difficult for ERCs to maintain their operations characteristics without NSF funding. Few ERCs have found they could rely chiefly on industry funds.

Discussion

After reviewing the development of the ERC program and its current status, it seems safe to assume that if the NSF had not established the ERC program decades ago, the extensive interaction between US universities and industries would not be as prevalent as it is today. The more important question is whether these interactions among universities and industries are sustainable or desirable. To answer this question, we need to shift away from a focus on outputs, and understand the process of knowledge creation. If ERCs are to serve as an engineering workforce pipeline, the evaluation of their effectiveness should be determined by the growth of human capital capacity.

What is missing from the current research is a study on scientific careers of students working in university research centers. Understanding student-related outcomes in terms of skills, knowledge and their social capital is crucial to evaluations of research activities. Current literature shows that the primary motivations and benefits for industrial firms to participate in ERCs is the access to the students (Feller et al., 2002), yet studies also suggest that firms are reluctant to invest resources in education activities. In addition, the recent studies show that ERCs with strong industry involvement often discontinue education components once the NSF phased out their funding support. On the one hand, students that participated in ERCs are perceived as having education advantages; they are exposed to multidisciplinary, hands-on experiences and contacts with industry. On the other, industry could also deflect students' research topics in ways that could, in the long run, prove less than optimal.

In short, the gap in our knowledge is a lack of understanding of the career and research lifecycle effects of ERCs. It would not be easy to make these determinations but it seems desirable and possible. For example, a panel study comparing ERC student participants with a quite similar pool of students not participating in ERCs could prove quite valuable. We expect that the results would, indeed, show an effect, especially among graduate students. Our own research (e.g., Bozeman and Boardman, 2013) on CRCs shows that graduate students working in these centers more often pursue careers in industry and that the ERCs are instrumental to these choices. But to what effect? We need better understanding of the career trajectories and achievements of ERC students, and the extent to which these outcomes can be attributed to ERC experience and training.

ANDREW KAO AND BARRY BOZEMAN

References

Ailes, C.P., Feller, I. and Coward, H.R. (2001), *The Impact of Engineering Research Centers on Institutional and Cultural Change in Participating Universities: Final Report*, Washington, DC: National Science Foundation, Engineering Education and Centers Division.

Bozeman, B. and Boardman, C. (2004), The NSF Engineering Research Centers and the university–industry research revolution: a brief history featuring an interview with Erich Bloch, *The Journal of Technology Transfer*, **29**(3–4), 365–375.

Bozeman, B. and Boardman, C. (2013), Academic faculty in university research centers: neither capitalism's slaves nor teaching fugitives, *The Journal of Higher Education*, **84**(1), 88–120.

Committee on Science, Engineering and Public Policy (1996), *An Assessment of the National Science Foundation's Science and Technology Centers Program*, Washington, DC: National Academy of Sciences, National Academy of Engineering, Institute of Medicine.

Feller, I., Ailes, C.P. and Roessner, J.D. (2002), Impacts of research universities on technological innovation in industry: evidence from engineering research centers, *Research Policy*, **31**(3), 457–474.

Lee, Y.S. (1996), 'Technology transfer' and the research university: a search for the boundaries of university–industry collaboration, *Research Policy*, **25**(6), 843–863.

Mayfield, L.G. (1987), NSF's Engineering Research Center Program: how it developed, *Engineering Education*, **78**(2), 130–132.

NAE (1984), *Guidelines for Engineering Research Centers*, Washington, DC: National Academy of Engineering.

NAE (1985), *New Directions for Engineering Research Centers in the National Science Foundation*, Washington, DC: National Academy of Engineering.

NAE (1986), *Evaluation of the Engineering Research Centers*, Washington, DC: National Academy of Engineering.

NAE (1988a), *The Engineering Research Centers and Their Evaluation*, Washington, DC: National Academy Press, http://books.google.com/books?id=czgrAAAAYAAJ.

NAE (1988b), *Assessment of the Engineering Research Centers' Selection Process*, Washington, DC: National Academy Press, http://books.google.com/books?id=KDgrAAAAYAAJ.

NAE (1989), *Assessment of the National Science Foundation's Engineering Research Centers Program*, Washington, DC: National Academy of Engineering.

NRC (1986), *The New Engineering Research Centers: Purposes, Goals, and Expectations*, Washington, DC: National Academies Press.

NRC (1987), *The Engineering Research Centers: Leaders in Change*, Washington, DC: National Research Council.

NRC (1988), *The Engineering Research Centers and Their Evaluation*, Washington, DC: National Academies Press.

NSF (1984), *Development of University–Industry Cooperative Research Centers: Historical Profiles*, Washington, DC: National Science Foundation.

NSF (1996), *Engineering Research Centers: A Partnership for Competitiveness*, Arlington, VA: National Science Foundation.

NSF (2014), *FY1995 – FY2014 Budget Request to Congress*, www.nsf.gov/about/budget.

Parker, L. (1997), *The Engineering Research Centers Program: An Assessment of Benefits and Outcomes*, Arlington, VA: National Science Foundation.

Roessner, J.D., Cheney, D.W. and Coward, H.R. (2004), *Impact on Industry of Interactions with Engineering Research Centers: Repeat Study: Summary Report*, Washington, DC: SRI International, http://erc-assoc.org/sites/default/files/studies_reports/Impact%20on%20Industry%20of%20ERC%20Interactions_SRI_12-04.pdf.

SRI (2008), *National and Regional Economic Impacts of Engineering Research Centers: A Pilot Study*, Engineering Education and Center Division, National Science Foundation, http://csted.sri.com/projects/national-and-regional-economic-impacts-engineering-research-centers-pilot-study.

US Government Accountability Office (1988), *Engineering Research Centers: NSF Program Management and Industry Sponsorship*, Publication No. RCED-88-177.

10 Entrepreneurial Buyouts

Introduction

In recent years, buyouts have become an important way to facilitate entrepreneurship through a change in the ownership of existing businesses. In general, these buyouts involve the creation of a new independent entity in which ownership is concentrated in the hands of management and private equity (PE) firms, if present, and increased leverage secured against the firm's assets and future cash flows provided by banks. PE firms become active investors, taking board seats and specifying contractual restrictions on the behaviour of management that include detailed reporting requirements (for more details on the practical aspects of buyouts, see Gilligan and Wright, 2014). The first wave of these buyouts occurred in the 1980s, with a second major wave between the late 1990s and 2008 (Wright et al., 2000b).

Forms of buyouts

Buyouts can take several forms. A *leveraged buyout* (LBO) or investor-led buyout (IBO) typically involves a publicly quoted corporation or a large division of a group, which is acquired by a specialist PE firm. The PE firm will typically either retain existing management to run the company or bring in new management. Incumbent management may or may not receive a direct equity stake or may receive stock options.

A *management buyout* (MBO) usually involves the acquisition of a divested division of a larger group or of a private family-owned firm by a new company in which the existing management takes a substantial proportion of the equity. MBOs typically involve a small group of senior managers as equity-holders. Increasingly, in many smaller transactions, the acquisition is likely to be funded by bank borrowings as the business is not large enough to be attractive to PE firms.

A *management buyin* (MBI) involves a buyout-type transaction where the leading members of the management team are outsiders. Although superficially similar to MBOs, MBIs carry greater risks as incoming management do not have benefits of insider knowledge regarding the operation of the business. Hybrid buyin/management buyouts (so-called BIMBOs) can benefit from the entrepreneurial expertise of outside managers and the intimate internal knowledge of incumbent management.

Buyouts as a managerial strategy

Buyouts have been widely associated with refocusing the strategic activities of underperforming listed corporations, but the majority of buyouts by number involve divisions of larger groups and privately held family firms. Increasingly, secondary buyouts are an important feature of the buyout market, involving the sale by the initial PE investor of its equity to a new incoming PE firm, re-leveraging of the business and often an increase in managerial equity stakes.

The traditional agency theory perspective proposes that the buyout governance structure attenuates the agency costs associated with the listed firm. Managers' significant equity stake following buyout was held to encourage them to behave like residual claimants, while PE firms have a financial incentive to monitor firm performance, and the high leverage bonds managers to make interest payments using cash that would otherwise be used to make non-value-maximizing investments. Much of the expected benefits of these buyouts were generated by improvements in efficiency or by revitalizing the firm through catch-up investment (Wright et al., 2000a). In large, integrated, diverse organizations, bureaucratic measures may be adopted to try to ensure performance. These measures may restrict experimentation and constrain innovative activity. These problems may be eased after the buyout. Instead of following headquarters' controls – designed to optimize the goals of the diversified parent company, but which block innovation and investment – the buyout creates discretionary power for the new management team to decide what is best for the business.

There may also be opportunities for buyouts where pre-ownership agency problems are not significant. The strategic entrepreneurial perspective on buyouts emphasizes that PE firms not only provide finance and monitoring functions, but also provide complementary resources and capabilities to those in the buyout target. A strategic entrepreneurship perspective complements an agency approach in helping explain value creation through the exploitation of entrepreneurial opportunities and the provision of resources and capabilities by the PE firm to realize those opportunities that previously have been neglected, particularly if the firm had been a division in a bureaucratic structure.

In addition, management with an entrepreneurial cognition or mindset, who adopt heuristic-based decision-making, that is decision-making based on rules of thumb, may be able to pursue entrepreneurial opportunities that they had discovered, but which could not previously be pursued within a larger group. For example, entrepreneurial buyouts may emerge in technology-based industries where the parent company did not have the capability to manage, or understand, the technology, but where divisional management do. These entrepreneurial buyouts require management with superior and idiosyncratic skills to process limited and incomplete information on new opportunities, rather than managers who respond well to close monitoring to prevent them not putting in the full effort to meet shareholders' interests.

Studies of management's motivation for buying out show that they place great emphasis on being able to develop entrepreneurial opportunities that they were prevented from doing under the previous owners. For example, the clothing retailer Kohl's was divested from the BAT conglomerate, enabling the management buying the company to introduce many innovations including new store design and transforming the business into a hybrid discounter/department store.

Entrepreneurial owner-managers may have the skills and incentives to pursue strategic innovations but, as a new venture, little control may have been exercised over management even when the firm has grown sufficiently to achieve an initial public offering (IPO). When a firm in such circumstances encounters financial difficulties, a buyout opportunity may arise to introduce necessary governance mechanisms, which will allow the innovative opportunities to continue to be exploited, but in a better controlled way. These entrepreneurial buyouts are labelled *busted tech buyouts*. For example, the publicly listed disk drive company Seagate Technology was taken private to enable the company to restructure and develop new innovative products away from the short-term demands of the stock market. Within two years, the company returned to the stock market, and a year later was named the number one company for innovation and enterprise in disk drives.

A buyout may be a means of ensuring survival of a family firm through the injection of entrepreneurial management (Howorth et al., 2004). Non-family managers acquiring the business may bring the ability to discover and exploit growth opportunities that may have been previously resisted by former family firm owners who may have been more interested in family lifestyle agendas, rather than agendas focused on improving efficiency and profitability. In some cases, where dominant family owners have not developed strong second-tier management, a pool of managerial talent located outside the family firm may be required to purchase the family firm in an MBI and take advantage of entrepreneurial opportunities that were being missed.

Secondary buyouts provide a means to continue the buyout organizational form with a different set of investors. The increased managerial equity stakes and loosened controls by private equity firms, or the introduction of more skilled PE firms with the ability to add value to the business, typical in this kind of buyout, may in principle facilitate improved performance through pursuit of growth opportunities beyond efficiency improvements in the first buyout.

Evidence indicates increases in corporate entrepreneurship, including new product development, better use of research and development, and increased patent citations following buyouts. However, the entrepreneurial opportunities may vary depending on the vendor source of the buyout. Divisional buyouts have significantly greater growth than family or secondary buyouts (Meuleman et al., 2009), suggesting that the constraints of the previous ownership regime were greater for divisional buyouts. Positive effects of secondary buyouts on firms' operating cash flows seem to be achieved through expansions, not by running the firms more efficiently. However, secondary buyouts between specialized PE firms perform better than those conducted between other PE firms (Alperovych et al., 2013). Majority private equity backed buyouts significantly increase entrepreneurial management practices but increased debt negatively affects entrepreneurial management (Bruining et al., 2013).

Conclusions

In sum, entrepreneurial buyouts represent an important segment of the wider buyout market, with important effects on performance that were not possible under the previous ownership regime.

MIKE WRIGHT

References

Alperovych, Y., Amess, K. and Wright, M. (2013), Private equity firm experience and buyout vendor source: what is their impact on efficiency? *European Journal of Operational Research*, **228**, 601–611.

Bruining, H., Wervaal, E. and Wright, M. (2013), How does private equity ownership affect entrepreneurial management in management buyouts, *Small Business Economics*, **40**, 591–605.

Gilligan, J. and Wright, M. (2014), *Private Equity Demystified*, 3rd edn, London: ICAEW.

Howorth, C., Westhead, P. and Wright, M. (2004), Buyouts, information asymmetry and the family management dyad, *Journal of Business Venturing*, **19**(4), 509–534.

Meuleman, M., Amess, K., Wright, M. and Scholes, L. (2009), Agency, strategic entrepreneurship and the performance of private equity backed buyouts, *Entrepreneurship Theory and Practice*, **33**(1), 213–239.

Wright, M., Hoskisson, R., Busenitz, L. and Dial, J. (2000a), Entrepreneurial growth through privatization: the upside of management buyouts, *Academy of Management Review*, **25**(3), 591–601.

Wright, M., Robbie, K., Chiplin, B. and Albrighton, M. (2000b), The development of an organizational innovation: management buyouts in the UK, 1980–97, *Business History*, **42**(4), 137–184.

11 Entrepreneurial Networks

Introduction

Since seminal works such as Burt (1982), Granovettor (1985), Bourdieu (1986) and Coleman (1988), there has been increasing recognition that social relationships are important to business outcomes (Payne et al., 2011). In the entrepreneurship literature, social relationships have been examined in relation to creativity, intentions to create a new venture, innovation, family business enterprise, venture financing, among others (Hoang and Antonicic, 2003; Gedajlovic et al., 2013). Overall, there is rising recognition that entrepreneurship – the processes of identifying, pursuing and exploiting opportunities – is socially situated and that networks and social capital reside at the very heart of entrepreneurship (Gedajlovic et al., 2013).

Social networks and social capital represent closely connected perspectives, yet tend to focus on different aspects of social relationships. The networks literature aims more at understanding the emergent and complex structures of relationships between actors (e.g., patterns of relationships, number/strength of ties), including individuals or collectives such as groups, organizations or communities. The social capital literature, on the other hand, focuses on the resources (e.g., trust, goodwill and information) embedded within and derived from networks of relationships. Hence, social capital – commonly defined as the 'sum of actual and potential resources embedded within, available through, and derived from the network of relationships possessed by individuals or social units' (Nahapiet and Ghoshal, 1998: 243) – is generally considered as the outcome or return on investments in social relationships (Lin, 2001).

While the basic connection between networks and social capital seems relatively straightforward, the reality is much more complex. Consider, for example, the difficulty associated with understanding *what* resources flow through a network, *how* and *through which* actors the resources flow, and the *speed, quality* and *consistency* with which the resources flow to a focal actor (i.e., individual or collective). As one might expect, there is an ongoing problem with conceptual and empirical ambiguity with regard to the nature of network relationships and the resources that the network endows upon an actor. Further, application to multiple levels of analysis (e.g., individuals, groups, organizations) and accounting for temporality (i.e., change over time) tends to complicate matters all the more. The remainder of this chapter discusses these issues more fully in an effort to inform readers about the current state and future of research on entrepreneurial networks.

Key areas of research
Payne and colleagues (2011) developed a four-quadrant typology that is useful for understanding the various studies of entrepreneurial networks. On one axis of the typology, studies are classified based on levels of analysis – either individual-level or collective-level. On the other axis, studies are classified according to the general source of social capital – either internal or external locus of activity. Respectively, this delineation aligns with the bonding/network closure (Coleman, 1988) and bridging/structural holes (Burt, 1982) views of social capital, which have been historically regarded as contrasting but are now commonly viewed as complementary (Lin, 2001). The four resulting quadrants are:

1. Individual/Internal
2. Collective/Internal
3. Individual/External
4. Collective/External

As exemplified below, entrepreneurship research occurs in all four quadrants, demonstrating the broad appeal and applicability of networks and social capital perspectives.

Studies classified as Individual/Internal generally examine how individuals derive resources from social collectives (e.g., family or ethnic groups) to facilitate entrepreneurial activity (e.g., starting a venture). For example, Kalnins and Chung (2006) study how immigrant entrepreneurs access resources from their ethnic community to create ventures. Studies classified as Collective/Internal, however, tend to examine how internal relationships influence collective entrepreneurial outcomes such as survival (e.g., Fischer and Pollock, 2004) and venture financing (e.g., Stam and Elfring, 2008). Also, family business is a key topic of inquiry in this quadrant. Family business studies tend to demonstrate how family members – a collective within an organization – can impact outcomes such as knowledge-sharing, job satisfaction and performance (e.g., Carr et al., 2011).

The Individual/External quadrant is arguably the most developed, because entrepreneurship scholars are often concerned with how individuals utilize external connections to identify, pursue and exploit opportunities. More specifically, studies often examine the linkage between entrepreneurship and external, weak ties – with bankers, trade and political organizations, government agencies and others – because such connections provide access to non-redundant information, suppliers, customers, etc. (e.g., Davidsson and Honig, 2003). However, strong tie conceptualizations of external social capital were also utilized to examine trust, norms and reciprocity in a somewhat oppositional way to weak tie arguments. Indeed, research has started to explore more temporal perspectives regarding how some social relationships lead to other types over time, as well as how diverse benefits are gained from various relationships (e.g., Jack, 2005).

Collective/External studies commonly examine how external relationships are critical to the development and performance of entrepreneurial ventures. Specifically, research in this quadrant shows the importance of utilizing external relationships to overcome liabilities of newness, such as through gaining access to financial resources (e.g., Fischer and Pollock, 2004). Also, this research illustrates the importance of external relationships to corporate entrepreneurship and innovation. For example, findings suggest social interaction and the development of trust between organizations fosters resource exchange and improves innovation (Tsai and Ghoshal, 1998).

Conclusions

Gedajlovic and colleagues (2013) suggest that social capital theory should be considered a foundational theory of entrepreneurship. But, despite progress, the field remains in an emerging state. At the very foundation of this research domain, there is an ongoing problem with conceptually and empirically differentiating between network relationships and resulting resources (i.e., social capital) accrued by an actor. For example, studies often use measures of network attributes (e.g., number of network ties, position in the network) as social capital. So while some social capital resources (e.g., amount of information) might be ascribed as an attribute of the network and serve as a reasonable proxy, it is conceptually not the same. Hence, to avoid confusion, careful attention should be given to definitions and measurements.

Network and social capital research could also benefit from applying more longitudinal and multilevel perspectives. In most entrepreneurship research, network attributes are analyzed as predictors of outcomes; rarely are the factors or processes leading to social relationships considered. Further, temporal considerations are rare; there is a need to better understand how networks change over time and what effects change has on opportunity identification, pursuit and exploitation. Also, given the importance of networks and social capital to both individual entrepreneurs and collectives, further integration of these levels is needed. For example, it seems important to understand how individual entrepreneurs utilize their social capital to develop an organization's social capital and vice versa.

As a final issue for consideration, there is growing evidence of the potential negative implications of building and maintaining social relationships – a 'dark side' of social capital. Specifically, as network complexity increases, the likelihood of costly, unproductive or destructive social capital is augmented. Molina-Morales and Martinez-Fernandez (2009: 1019), for instance, find that the 'positive effect of the social capital factors was eroded by making intensive use of them.' Also, Maurer and Ebers (2006) suggest that the continuous adaptation of a network can keep social capital inertia from becoming a liability. Generally, a better understanding of the potential dark side of networks is needed.

In summary, it is hard to imagine any entrepreneurial endeavor that is not, in some way, influenced by social relationships. From nascent activities to corporate innovation, entrepreneurship is embedded in a complex array of social relationships that can increase or, perhaps, decrease the chances of success. Hence, both scholars and practitioners can benefit from a better understanding of the structures, processes and outcomes of entrepreneurial networks and social capital.

G. Tyge Payne

Acknowledgements

Special thanks to Curt B. Moore and Miles A. Zachary for comments on earlier drafts of this chapter.

References

Bourdieu, P. (1986), The forms of capital, in J.G. Richardson (ed.), *Handbook of Theory and Research for the Sociology of Education*, New York: Greenwood, pp. 241–258.

Burt, R.S. (1982), *Toward a Structural Theory of Action*, New York: Academic Press.

Carr, J.C., Cole, M.S., Ring, J.K. and Blettner, D.P. (2011), A measure of variations in internal social capital among family firms, *Entrepreneurship Theory and Practice*, **35**(6), 1207–1227.

Coleman, J.S. (1988), Social capital in the creation of human capital, *American Journal of Sociology*, **94**, S95–S120.

Davidsson, P. and Honig, B. (2003), The role of social and human capital among nascent entrepreneurs, *Journal of Business Venturing*, **18**(3), 301–331.

Fischer, H.M. and Pollock, T.G. (2004), Effects of social capital and power on surviving transformational change: the case of initial public offerings, *Academy of Management Journal*, **47**(4), 463–481.

Gedajlovic, E., Honig, B., Moore, C.B., Payne, G.T. and Wright, M. (2013), Social capital and entrepreneurship: a schema and research agenda, *Entrepreneurship Theory and Practice*, **37**(3), 455–478.

Granovettor, M.S. (1985), Economic action and social structure: the problem of embeddedness, *American Journal of Sociology*, **91**, 481–510.

Hoang, H. and Antonicic, B. (2003), Network-based research in entrepreneurship: a critical review, *Journal of Business Venturing*, **18**(2), 165–187.

Jack, S.L. (2005), The role, use and activation of strong and weak network ties: a qualitative analysis, *Journal of Management Studies*, **42**(6), 1233–1259.

Kalnins, A. and Chung, W. (2006), Social capital, geography, and survival: Gujarati immigrant entrepreneurs in the US lodging industry, *Management Science*, **52**(2), 233–247.

Lin, N. (2001), Building a network theory of social capital, in N. Lin, K.S. Cook and R.S. Burt (eds), *Social Capital: Theory and Research*, New Brunswick, NJ: Transaction Publishers, pp. 3–30.

Maurer, I. and Ebers, M. (2006), Dynamics of social capital and their performance implications: lessons from biotechnology start-ups, *Administrative Science Quarterly*, **51**(2), 262–292.

Molina-Morales, F.X. and Martinez-Fernandez, M.T. (2009), Too much love in the neighborhood can hurt: how an excess of intensity and trust in relationships may produce negative effects on firms, *Strategic Management Journal*, **30**(9), 1013–1023.

Nahapiet, J. and Ghoshal, S. (1998), Social capital, intellectual capital, and the organizational advantage, *Academy of Management Review*, **23**(2), 242–266.

Payne, G.T., Moore, C.B., Griffis, S. and Autry, C. (2011), Multilevel challenges and opportunities in social capital research, *Journal of Management*, **37**(2), 395–403.

Stam, W. and Elfring, T. (2008), Entrepreneurial orientation and new venture performance: the moderating role of intra- and extra-industry social capital, *Academy of Management Journal*, **51**(1), 97–111.

Tsai, W. and Ghoshal, S. (1998), Social capital and value creation: the role of intrafirm networks, *Academy of Management Journal*, **41**(4), 464–476.

12 Entrepreneurial Risk and Uncertainty

Introduction

It is generally accepted that innovation is at the heart of long-term economic growth and prosperity and that innovation occurs through a process that Schumpeter (1950) called 'creative destruction' driven by entrepreneurial action. However, the association of entrepreneurship with risk and uncertainty, while it has intuitive appeal, is more subtle than it might first seem, and scholars have disagreed as to whether risk and uncertainty are essential to an understanding of the entrepreneurial process.

The reason for the disagreement stems from a failure to understand the distinction between risk and uncertainty, and, as Frank Knight (1921) argued in *Risk, Uncertainty, and Profit*, that distinction is crucial to understanding the nature of the entrepreneurial process. Risk may or may not be a factor in the entrepreneurial process. Uncertainty, however, is – by the very nature of the entrepreneurial process – always present for the entrepreneur and something with which the entrepreneur must come to terms with.

Early views[1]

Richard Cantillon (1680–1734), the earliest scholar to use the word 'entrepreneur' in its modern form, saw entrepreneurs as intermediaries in the market process who took upon themselves the risks associated with uncertain demand by paying workers a fixed wage for their work and taking their chances in the marketplace (Cantillon, 1755/1931). To this argument, Nicolas Baudeau (1730–1792) added the concept of the entrepreneur as an innovator, one who invents and applies new techniques or ideas in order to reduce costs and thereby increase profit (Baudeau, 1767/1910). But it was J.H. von Thünen (1783–1850), building on the works of Cantillon and Baudeau, who clarified the nature of entrepreneurial profit and its connection to risk and uncertainty. For von Thünen, entrepreneurial reward was equal to an enterprise's residual profit after subtracting returns to the capitalist, returns to the manager and payments to insure against business losses. Thus, for von Thünen the entrepreneur was neither a capitalist nor a manager; the entrepreneur was an innovator and the one person who accepted risks that were uninsurable (von Thünen, 1863/1960). Unfortunately, Joseph Schumpeter (1883–1950), who followed von Thünen and is rightly extolled for his insights regarding the fundamental role that innovation plays in the entrepreneurial process and the connection of innovation to economic growth, confused the issue by dismissing the notion that the entrepreneur in any fundamental way bears risk (Schumpeter, 1926/1934).[2]

Frank Knight

It was left to Frank Knight (1885–1972) to correct Schumpeter's mistake and reunite the notion of the entrepreneur as innovator with the notion of the entrepreneur as a risk-taker. To accomplish that task, Knight (1921) argued that much of the confusion over the connection of risk with the entrepreneur was attributable to a failure to properly distinguish two very different kinds of risk. On the one hand, risk can signify a quantity capable of being measured, that is, the objective probability that a known event will happen. Because this kind of risk can be shifted from the entrepreneur to another party by an insurance contract, it is not an uncertainty in any meaningful sense. On the other hand, risk can also signify a non-measurable eventuality because all possible outcomes and/or the probabilities of all possible outcomes cannot be specified. Such is the case, for example, for Cantillon's entrepreneur trying to predict consumer demand. Designating the first type of risk, due to measurable uncertainty, as simply 'risk' and the second type of risk, due to unmeasurable uncertainty, as simply 'uncertainty,' Knight argued that it was only uncertainty that was an essential part of the entrepreneur's world. As he summarized cogently in a later work:

> [N]ot all risks necessarily give rise to [entrepreneurial] profit, or loss. Many kinds can be insured against, which eliminates them as factors of uncertainty. . . . The essential point for profit theory is that insofar as it is possible to insure by any method against risk, the cost of carrying it is converted into a constant element of expense, and it ceases to be a cause of profit and loss. The uncertainties which persist as causes of profit are those which are uninsurable because there is no objective measure of the probability of gain or loss. This is true especially of the prediction of demand. It not only cannot be foreseen accurately, but there is no basis for saying that the probability of its being of one sort rather than another is of a certain value – as we can compute the chance that a man will live to a certain age. Situations in regard to which business judgment must be exercised do not repeat themselves with sufficient conformity to type to make possible a computation of probability.
>
> (Knight, 1951: 119–120)

Knightian uncertainty is not easily compartmentalized because it pervades all human decision-making, especially in the realm of innovation where, by the very nature of the innovation process, the entrepreneur confronts circumstances for which there is no ability through logic or prior experience to make the uncertainty of the situation measurable. Yet, it helps establish a boundary (as Cantillon and von Thünen argued) between the manager and the capitalist on the one hand and the entrepreneur on the other. According to Knight, the function of the manager does not in itself imply entrepreneurship, but a manager becomes an entrepreneur when the manager's performance requires that judgment be exercised involving unquantifiable uncertainty; that is, liability to error. Likewise, the entrepreneur may or may not be a capitalist, but whether or not the entrepreneur owns capital, the essence of entrepreneurship is not in the role of capitalist.

An interesting corollary of Knight's theory is that entrepreneurial profit cannot exist without error. Echoing von Thünen's argument, Knight argued that entrepreneurial profit depends on whether an entrepreneur can make productive services yield more than the price fixed upon them by what other people think they can make them yield. Therefore, its magnitude is based on a margin of error in calculation by entrepreneurs as well as non-entrepreneurs who do not force the successful entrepreneurs to pay as much for productive services as those entrepreneurs could be forced to pay. It is this margin of error in judgment that constitutes the only true uncertainty in the workings of the competitive organization, and it is this uncertainty that is borne by the entrepreneur and explains entrepreneurial profit.

Implications

Although the entrepreneurship literature has increasingly come to accept Knight's view that entrepreneurial action takes place under conditions of uncertainty (Papandreou, 1943; Alvarez and Busenitz, 2001; Loasby, 2002; Leyden and Link, 2014), that view is far from universal.[3] For those who take the view that the entrepreneur lives in a world of (quantifiable) risk, it may be reasonable to think of entrepreneurial opportunities as objective phenomena waiting to be discovered, albeit with risk (Kirzner, 1973; Shane, 2003). But under an uncertainty-based view, entrepreneurs do not so much discover profit opportunities as create them. As Alvarez and Barney (2005) note, such creativity is the result of the entrepreneurs' own organizing efforts in the face of uncertainty. However, because the condition of uncertainty may change over time, the bases for organizing entrepreneurial firms are also likely to change. As a result, entrepreneurial (that is, uncertainty-based) firms over time may be transformed into non-entrepreneurial (that is, risk-based) firms once the probability distribution of outcomes associated with uncertain exchanges is learned through experience. Based on this reasoning, Schumpeter's notion of creative destruction can be thought of as including not just the replacement of older firms by newer firms, but also the transformation of entrepreneurial firms into non-entrepreneurial firms over time. Such transformations, which Schumpeter saw as common,[4] imply a continual need for new (or reinvented) firms that, through their decision to be entrepreneurial, enter willingly into a world of uncertainty and creativity.

This argument, however, should not be taken to imply that entrepreneurs do not engage in discovery. As Leyden and Link (2014) argue, the question over whether entrepreneurial behavior is essentially one of discovery or creation is false one. Entrepreneurial behavior in general includes both and can be thought of as an iterative two-step process in which the entrepreneur creates a social network based on subjective expectations about the future effectiveness of that network, chooses (that is, creates the idea of) the innovation to pursue, and then maps out a search process using that social network to discover how to bring the desired innovation to fruition.[5] An entrepreneur's social network is composed of what Granovetter (1973) and Burt (2005) referred to as 'strong ties' (that is, relationships among individuals in a focused organization under the control of the entrepreneur) and 'weak ties' (that is, relationships among a more diffused range of contacts who have a heterogeneous set of knowledge and perspectives). Both types of ties are important, because it is only when both are present that the entrepreneur can generate the social capital (that is, knowledge) that is used to identify and then bring to fruition an innovation through a process of creativity and discovery.

Finally, it should be emphasized that understanding the role that uncertainty plays in the entrepreneurial process means that one cannot think of the entrepreneur's problem as one of assessing alternative prospects objectively and calculating the associated present values of future streams of revenues and costs. Instead, one must think in terms of the entrepreneur's subjective perspectives on the returns to possible future actions. Examples of this perspective can be seen in the knowledge spillover theory of entrepreneurship (Acs et al., 2009; Audretsch and Lehmann, 2005; Braunerhjelm et al., 2010), which argues that small, nascent enterprises engage in a greater level of innovative activity than larger, incumbent firms precisely because they place a higher subjective value on possible innovations, and in Leyden and Link's (2014) argument that the ability of entrepreneurs to garner financial support for innovation projects is constrained by the fact that much of their knowledge regarding their projects is subjective and therefore non-transferable to those who would fund such projects.[6]

Conclusions

While entrepreneurship necessarily involves decision-making without certainty of outcome, the failure to understand the nature of that lack of certainty has hampered the ability to fully understand the entrepreneurial process. Risk properly construed may or may not be an issue for the entrepreneur, but uncertainty is always present and inseparable from the innovation process that defines the entrepreneur. As a result, while entrepreneurs may, and often do, engage in acts of discovery, it is creativity that lies at the heart of what it means to be an entrepreneur. And such creativity if it is to take place implies a need for social networks and a Schumpeterian act of will if the entrepreneur is to take action in the face of a lack of objective knowledge about the future.

DENNIS PATRICK LEYDEN

Notes

1. This section and the next draw heavily on Leyden and Link's (2015) examination of the historical origins of the modern understanding of entrepreneurship.
2. '[O]ur definition [of the entrepreneur] agrees with the usual one on the fundamental point of distinguishing between "entrepreneurs" and "capitalists" irrespective of whether the latter are regarded as owners of money, claims to money, or material goods. . . . It also settles the question whether the ordinary shareholder as such is an entrepreneur, and disposes of the conception of the entrepreneur as risk bearer' (Schumpeter, 1926/1934: 75).
3. Outside the entrepreneurship literature, the confounding of the terms 'risk' and 'uncertainty' is more common than not. See Bolton et al. (2014) for a recent example.
4. '[E]veryone is an entrepreneur only when he actually carries out new combinations, and loses that character as soon as he has built up his business, when he settles down to running it as other people run their businesses' (Schumpeter, 1926/1934). See Knight (1921) for an extended examination of the ways in which a firm may transform uncertainty over time into risk.
5. The notion of a social network is also referred to as the social dimension of context in the entrepreneurial literature (Hoang and Antoncic, 2003; Welter, 2011; Zahra and Wright, 2011) and as creative cognition in the psychology literature (Ward et al., 1999; Shalley and Perry-Smith, 2008).
6. This discussion is based on the premise that what one is concerned with is the entrepreneurial decision-making process going forward, that is, from an ex-ante perspective. Such an approach necessarily must view that decision-making process as taking place under uncertainty and not risk. Whether there is value in looking backwards at the entrepreneurial process after the fact, that is, analyzing entrepreneurial activity from an ex-post perspective and treating the entrepreneurial environment as one of risk rather than uncertainty (hindsight being perfect) is an open question. Current long-run growth theory that includes creative destruction as a driving force essentially takes this perspective (Aghion and Howitt, 1992; Howitt and Aghion, 1998).

References

Acs, Z.J., Braunerhjelm, P., Audretsch, D.B. and Carlsson, B. (2009), The knowledge spillover theory of entrepreneurship, *Small Business Economics*, **32**, 15–30.

Aghion, P. and Howitt, P. (1992), A model of growth through creative destruction, *Econometrica*, **60**, 323–351.

Alvarez, S.A. and Barney, J.B. (2005), How do entrepreneurs organize firms under conditions of uncertainty? *Journal of Management*, **31**, 776–793.

Alvarez, S.A. and Busenitz, L.W. (2001), The entrepreneurship of resource-based theory, *Journal of Management*, **27**, 755–775.

Audretsch, D.B. and Lehmann, E.E. (2005), Does the knowledge spillover theory of entrepreneurship hold for regions? *Research Policy*, **34**, 1191–1202.

Baudeau, N. (1767/1910), *Première Introduction à la Philosophie Économique*, trans. A. Dubois, Paris: P. Geuthner.

Bolton, P., Wang, N. and Yang, J. (2014), *Investment Under Uncertainty and the Value of Real and Financial Flexibility*, www.nber/papers/w20610.

Braunerhjelm, P., Acs, Z.J., Audretsch, D.B. and Carlsson, B. (2010), The missing link: knowledge diffusion and entrepreneurship in endogenous growth, *Small Business Economics*, **34**, 105–125.

Burt, R.S. (2005), *Brokerage and Closure: An Introduction to Social Capital*, Oxford: Oxford University Press.

Cantillon, R. (1755/1931), *Essai sur la Nature du Commerce en Général*, trans. H. Higgs, London: Macmillan.

Granovetter, M.S. (1973), The strength of weak ties, *American Journal of Sociology*, **78**, 1360–1380.

Hoang, H. and Antoncic, B. (2003), Network-based research in entrepreneurship, *Journal of Business Venturing*, **18**, 165–187.

Howitt, P. and Aghion, P. (1998), Capital accumulation and innovation as complementary factors in long-run growth, *Journal of Economic Growth*, **3**, 111–130.

Kirzner, I.M. (1973), *Competition and Entrepreneurship*, Chicago, IL: University of Chicago Press.

Knight, F.H. (1921), *Risk, Uncertainty, and Profit*, Boston, MA: Houghton Mifflin.

Knight, F.H. (1951), *The Economic Organization*, New York: Augustus M. Kelley.

Leyden, D.P. and Link, A.N. (2014), Toward a theory of the entrepreneurial process, *Small Business Economic*, http://dx.doi.org/10.1007/s11187-014-9606-0.

Leyden, D.P. and Link, A.N. (2015), *Public Sector Entrepreneurship: US Technology and Innovation Policy*, New York: Oxford University Press.

Loasby, B.J. (2002), The organizational basis of cognition and the cognitive basis of organization, in M. Augier and J.G. March (eds), *The Economics of Choice, Change and Organization: Essays in Honor of Richard M. Cyert*, Cheltenham: Edward Elgar Publishing, pp. 147–167.

Papandreou, A.G. (1943), *The Location and Scope of the Entrepreneurial Function*, PhD thesis, Harvard University.

Schumpeter, J.A. (1926/1934), *The Theory of Economic Development*, 2nd edn, trans. R. Opie, Cambridge, MA: Harvard University Press.

Schumpeter, J.A. (1950), *Capitalism, Socialism and Democracy*, 3rd edn, New York: Harper and Row.

Shalley, C.E. and Perry-Smith, J.E. (2008), The emergence of team creative cognition: the role of diverse outside ties, sociocognitive network centrality, and team evolution, *Strategic Entrepreneurship Journal*, **2**, 23–41.

Shane, S. (2003), *A General Theory of Entrepreneurship: The Individual-Opportunity Nexus*, Cheltenham: Edward Elgar Publishing.

von Thünen, J.H. (1863/1960), The isolated state in relation to agriculture and political economy, in *The Frontier Wage: The Economic Organization of Free Agents*, trans. B.W. Dempsey, Chicago, IL: Loyola University Press, pp. 187–367.

Ward, T.B., Smith, S.M. and Finke, R.A. (1999), Creative cognition, in J. Sternberg (ed.), *Handbook of Creativity*, New York: Cambridge University Press, pp. 189–212.

Welter, F. (2011), Contextualizing entrepreneurship: conceptual challenges and ways forward, *Entrepreneurship Theory and Practice*, **35**, 165–178.

Zahra, S.A. and Wright, M. (2011), Entrepreneurship's next act, *Academy of Management Perspectives*, **25**, 67–83.

13 The Entrepreneurship Theory Jungle

Introduction

More than 50 years ago, Harold Koontz pointed out a 'management theory jungle' of varying definitions and approaches that were plaguing the field of management. He stated 'all [theories] have essentially the same goals and deal essentially in the same world' (Koontz, 1961: 182). Yet he warned of the 'confused and destructive' effects that the differences cause the field. Twenty years later he revisited his contention, only to be shocked by the increase in theories and approaches to the field (Koontz, 1980). The 'jungle,' according to Koontz, still existed – with nearly double the approaches to management that were identified nearly two decades earlier.

It appears that the emerging field of entrepreneurship research has been confronting a similar 'jungle' in the form of different theories on what constitutes entrepreneurship and the manner in which it is being studied. The field of management worked through its 'jungle' of confusion that was apparent more than 50 years ago, and so too now must the entrepreneurship field work through its own theoretical 'jungle.' The field of management grew to realize that Koontz's jungle was only developing into a multiple-lens perspective through which the field could be studied more effectively (Okhuysen and Bonardi, 2011). With the various and diverse theories being proposed in entrepreneurship research, it may be that combination approaches will be the most valuable approach for the future of this field.

Theory development in entrepreneurship

A *theory of entrepreneurship* is a verifiable and logically coherent formulation of relationships, or underlying principles, that either explains entrepreneurship, predicts entrepreneurial activity or provides normative guidance. It has become increasingly apparent in the new millennium that we need cohesive theories or classifications to better understand this emerging field (Phan, 2004). In the study of contemporary entrepreneurship, one concept recurs: Entrepreneurship is interdisciplinary. It contains various approaches that can increase one's understanding of the field. Thus, we need to recognize the diversity of theories as an emergence of entrepreneurial understanding (Moroz and Hindle, 2012).

While this explanation sounds logical, the domain of entrepreneurship has expanded exponentially in the past three decades, with the theories of entrepreneurship being not only numerous and diverse, but also confusing. Perhaps that is the nature of this emerging field, but it certainly did not begin that way. Years ago, Baumol (1968) lamented the paucity of entrepreneurship theory by protesting the singular view of entrepreneurship within a traditional economic paradigm. However, there is a rich intellectual history of who the entrepreneur is and what he or she does that will allow us to go beyond Baumol's view (Hébert and Link,1989, 2009). In the subsequent years, scholars have responded in force to Baumol's plea by positing what became an avalanche of entrepreneurship theories. The result has been that Baumol's unhappy recognition of a singular theoretical view of the entrepreneur has been replaced by a multitude of diverse and sometimes contradicting theories of entrepreneurship.

Recognition of the importance of entrepreneurship over the past three decades is reflected in an unprecedented amount of attention from scholars and educators. It is important to note the research and educational developments that have occurred in this century. Some of the major themes that characterize recent research about entrepreneurs and new-venture creation can be summarized as follows:

- **Venture financing**, including both venture capital and angel capital financing as well as other innovative financing techniques, emerged in the 1990s with unprecedented strength, fueling entrepreneurship in the twenty-first century (Busenitz et al., 2004).
- **Corporate entrepreneurship** (entrepreneurial actions within large organizations) and the need for entrepreneurial cultures have gained much attention during the past few years (Morris et al., 2011; Ireland et al., 2009).
- **Social entrepreneurship and sustainability** has emerged with unprecedented strength among the new generation of entrepreneurs (Dean and McMullen, 2007; Shepherd and Patzelt, 2011).
- **Entrepreneurial cognition** (examining the great variety among types of entrepreneurs and the methods they have used to achieve success) is a wave of research on the psychological aspects of the entrepreneurial process (Haynie et al., 2010; Grégoire et al., 2011).
- **Women and minority entrepreneurs** have emerged in unprecedented numbers. They appear to face obstacles and difficulties different from those that other entrepreneurs face (de Bruin et al., 2006; DeTienne and Chandler, 2007).
- The **global entrepreneurial movement** is increasing, judging by the enormous growth of interest in entrepreneurship around the world in the past few years (Autio et al., 2011; Coviello et al., 2011).
- **Family businesses** have become a stronger focus of research. The economic and social contributions of entrepreneurs with family businesses have been shown to make immensely disproportionate contributions to job creation, innovation and economic renewal (Morris et al., 2010; Chrisman et al., 2011).
- **Entrepreneurial education** has become one of the hottest topics in business and engineering schools throughout the world. The number of schools teaching an entrepreneurship or similar course has grown from only a few 30 years ago to more than 2,500 at this time (Kuratko, 2005; Neck and Greene, 2011).

Despite such trends, or perhaps because of them, the field of entrepreneurship has evolved in a rather disjointed or seemingly random manner and entrepreneurship has developed as a business discipline by borrowing, building upon and adapting theoretical and conceptual work from such fields as sociology, psychology, anthropology, marketing, management, finance, organizational behavior and engineering. And yet, it would appear that the volume of work attempting to describe, explain and predict aspects of entrepreneurship has grown to a point where we can begin to develop a more complete and integrated picture.

Theories of entrepreneurship have been proposed to explain a broad spectrum of phenomena, ranging from the firm level, such as why small firms exist or why some firms are more innovative or enjoy greater growth than do others (McKelvie and Wiklund, 2010), to the individual level such as why some people choose to start a new business or why some individuals recognize as well as act upon certain opportunities (Mitchell and Shepherd, 2010).

One reaction to these entrepreneurship theories has been to suggest that the field needs to become narrower and more defined in focus (Bull and Willard, 1993). In this manner, only bona fide entrepreneurship theories would explain entrepreneurial phenomena in a way that is not explained by some other field or even academic discipline so that it becomes unique to entrepreneurship scholarship. As Shane and Venkataraman (2000: 217) noted:

> For a field of social science to have usefulness, it must have a conceptual framework that explains and predicts a set of empirical phenomena not explained or predicted by conceptual frameworks already in existence in other fields. What appears to constitute entrepreneurship research today is some aspect of the setting (e.g., small businesses or new firms), rather than a unique conceptual domain.

Accordingly, future theories of entrepreneurship should be focused solely and exclusively on aspects of behavior that involve creating and/or discovering opportunities, as well as evaluating and subsequently exploiting and acting upon those opportunities (Wiklund et al., 2011). By contrast, in this chapter we anticipate a very different future for entrepreneurship theories. We suggest that the call for a narrowing and focus of entrepreneurship theories to a singular view is reminiscent of the state of scholarship that alarmed Baumol (1968) decades ago. Rather, we anticipate new opportunities for entrepreneurship theory that will be based on both expanding the contexts for entrepreneurship as well as a deepening of the existing theoretical approaches. The current chapter identifies the various trends in the entrepreneurship research and offers a multi-lens solution for some organization to the field.

Multi-lens theories in entrepreneurship

A newer strand of entrepreneurship theory has developed as a combination of the numerous theoretical approaches that have emerged from the differing trends. While these theories have produced insightful results over the years, some researchers are using a combination of theoretical lenses to examine particular aspects of the discipline. The reasoning behind this combination approach is that the complexity of studying the phenomenon of entrepreneurship can be far more encompassing than the tools or paradigms of any one discipline (Sorenson and Stuart, 2008; Anderson et al., 2012).

As mentioned in the beginning of this essay, the field of management was plagued by what was termed a 'jungle' of theoretical approaches in the 1960s. However, the result was not a unification of theory but rather a diversification and expansion of theories that produced a 'multiple lens' approach that characterizes the field today. Thus, we are witnessing a similar approach with the entrepreneurship theories based on combinations. As Okhuysen and Bonardi stated in examining the field of management in general:

> More than other 'classical' disciplines in social science, management research uses combinations of ideas or blends of theories to advance new insights and develop novel hypotheses that can ultimately be tested empirically. As a practical field, management deserves attention from a multiple-lens perspective because the phenomena within it can often be explained using different theoretical approaches. And it is perhaps obvious to note that the complexity of management as a setting often requires explanations that are matched in complexity – explanations that can be built from combinations of perspectives to provide answers that are uniquely suited to management.
>
> (Okhuysen and Bonardi, 2011: 6)

Thus, combinations of theories are revealing themselves to be far more effective for researching the issues that arise under the taxonomy of entrepreneurial activity. As an example, when Shepherd (2011) discussed the opportunities with multilevel entrepreneurship research, he demonstrated the value of this research with individual differences in decision policy. He showed that, while there may be commonality in decision policies across a sample, there is likely variance across individuals in their weighting of criteria when making decisions on an entrepreneurial task. For example, DeTienne, Shepherd, and DeCastro (2008) built on escalation of commitment theory and the motivation literature to explain variance in entrepreneurs' decision policies for persisting with a poorly performing firm. Even more specifically, Shepherd showed how using differing theories with moderators to decision policies may help explain variance in decision policies to exploit an opportunity. Some examples included: attitudes toward the different errors arising from making decisions in environments of high uncertainty, as informed by regret theory (Zeelenberg, 1999) and/or norm theory (Zeelenberg et al., 2002); the level of positive affect, negative affect and the combination of the two, as informed by the psychology literature on emotion and cognition (Izard, 2009); the intrinsic motivation to act, as informed by self-determination theory (Ryan and Deci, 2000); the level of prior knowledge, as informed by the Austrian economics (Shane, 2000), opportunity recognition (Grégoire et al., 2010), or entrepreneurial action (McMullen and Shepherd, 2006) literatures.

Conclusion

The theories based on combinations offer a more dynamic view of the phenomenon of entrepreneurship. Much like the 'multiple lens' approach that characterizes general management, the theories based on combinations can delve into some of the particular aspects of entrepreneurship with greater granularity. As Shepherd (2011: 419) stated in regards to entrepreneurial decision-making:

> By theorizing and testing cross-level models of decision making on entrepreneurial tasks, such studies can make a substantial contribution to the entrepreneurship literature. Furthermore, because entrepreneurial tasks are often extreme – high levels of uncertainty, time pressure, stress, and emotions – studies that exploit the above research opportunities can extend the boundaries of current theories and make contributions to the management, decision making, and psychology literatures more generally. Whether it is decision-making research using conjoint analysis or another topic using a different method, there are numerous opportunities for multilevel research to make a substantial contribution to the field of entrepreneurship.

DONALD F. KURATKO, DAVID B. AUDRETSCH AND ALBERT N. LINK

References

Anderson, A.R., Dodd, S.D. and Jack, S.L. (2012), Entrepreneurship as connecting: some implications for theorising and practice, *Management Decision*, **50**(5), 958–971.

Autio, E., George, G. and Alexy, O. (2011), International entrepreneurship and capability development—qualitative evidence and future research direction, *Entrepreneurship Theory & Practice*, **35**(1), 11–37.

Baumol, W. (1968), Entrepreneurship in economic theory, *American Economic Review*, **58**(2), 64–71.

Bull, I. and Willard, G.E. (1993), Towards a theory of entrepreneurship, *Journal of Business Venturing*, **8**(3), 183–195.

Busenitz, L.W., Fiet, J.O. and Moesel, D.D. (2004), Reconsidering the venture capitalists' value-added proposition: an interorganizational learning perspective, *Journal of Business Venturing*, **19**(6), 787–807.

Chrisman, J.J., Chua, J.H. and Steier, L. (2011), Resilience of family firms: an introduction, *Entrepreneurship Theory & Practice*, **35**(6), 1107–1119.

Coviello, N.E., McDougall, P.P. and Oviatt, B.M. (2011), The emergence, advance and future of international entrepreneurship research, *Journal of Business Venturing*, **26**(6), 625–631.

Dean, T.J. and McMullen, J.S. (2007), Toward a theory of sustainable entrepreneurship: reducing environmental degradation through entrepreneurial action, *Journal of Business Venturing*, **22**(1), 50–76.

de Bruin, A., Brush, C.G. and Welter, F. (2006), Towards building cumulative knowledge on women's entrepreneurship, *Entrepreneurship Theory and Practice*, **30**(5), 585–594.

DeTienne, D. and Chandler, G.N. (2007), The role of gender in opportunity identification, *Entrepreneurship Theory and Practice*, **31**(3), 365–386.

DeTienne, D., Shepherd, D.A. and DeCastro, J.O. (2008), The fallacy of 'only the strong survive': the effects of human capital and extrinsic motivation on the persistence decisions of under-performing firms, *Journal of Business Venturing*, **23**, 526–548.

Grégoire, D.A., Barr, P.S. and Shepherd, D.A. (2010), Cognitive processes of opportunity recognition, *Organization Science*, **21**, 413–431.

Grégoire, D.A., Corbett, A.C. and McMullen, J.S. (2011), The cognitive perspective entrepreneurship: an agenda for future research, *Journal of Management Studies*, **48**(6), 1443–1477.

Haynie, J.M., Shepherd, D.A., Mosakowski, E. and Earley, P.C. (2010), A situated meta-cognitive model of the entrepreneurial mindset, *Journal of Business Venturing*, **25**(2), 217–229.

Hébert, R.F. and Link, A.N. (1989), In search of the meaning of entrepreneurship, *Small Business Economics*, **1**(1), 39–49.

Hébert, R.F. and Link, A.N. (2009), *A History of Entrepreneurship*, London: Routledge.

Ireland, R.D., Covin, J.G. and Kuratko, D.F. (2009), Conceptualizing corporate entrepreneurship strategy, *Entrepreneurship Theory & Practice*, **33**(1), 19–46.

Izard, C.E. (2009), Emotion theory and research: highlights, unanswered questions, and emerging issues, *Annual Review of Psychology*, **60**, 1–25.

Koontz, H. (1961), The management theory jungle, *Academy of Management Journal*, **4**(3), 174–188.

Koontz, H. (1980), The management theory jungle revisited, *Academy of Management Review*, **5**(2), 175–187.

Kuratko, D.F. (2005), The emergence of entrepreneurship education: development, trends, challenges, *Entrepreneurship Theory and Practice*, **29**(3), 577–598.

McKelvie, A. and Wiklund, J. (2010), Advancing firm growth research: a focus on growth mode instead of growth rate, *Entrepreneurship Theory & Practice*, **34**(2), 261–268.

McMullen, J. and Shepherd, D.A. (2006), Encouraging consensus-challenging research in universities, *Journal of Management Studies*, **43**, 1643–1669.

Mitchell, J.R. and Shepherd, D.A. (2010), To thine own self be true: images of self, images of opportunity, and entrepreneurial action, *Journal of Business Venturing*, **25**(1), 138–154.

Morris, M.H., Allen, J.A., Kuratko, D.F. and Brannon, D. (2010), Experiencing family business creation: differences between founders, nonfamily managers, and founders of nonfamily firms, *Entrepreneurship Theory & Practice*, **34**(6), 1057–1084.

Morris, M.H., Kuratko, D.F. and Covin, J.G. (2011), *Corporate Entrepreneurship and Innovation*, 3rd edn, Mason, OH: Cengage/South-Western.

Moroz, P.W. and Hindle, K. (2012), Entrepreneurship as a process: toward harmonizing multiple perspectives, *Entrepreneurship Theory & Practice*, **36**(4), 781–818.

Neck, H.M. and Greene, P.G. (2011), Entrepreneurship education: known worlds and new frontiers, *Journal of Small Business Management*, **49**(1), 55–70.

Okhuysen, G. and Bonardi, J.P. (2011), The challenges of building theory by combining lenses, *Academy of Management Review*, **36**(1), 6–11.

Phan, P.H. (2004), Entrepreneurship theory: possibilities and future directions, *Journal of Business Venturing*, **19**(5), 617–620.

Ryan, R.M. and Deci, E.L. (2000), Self-determination theory and the facilitation of intrinsic motivation, social development, and well-being, *American Psychologist*, **55**, 68–78.

Shane, S. (2000), Prior knowledge and the discovery of entrepreneurial opportunities, *Organization Science*, **11**, 448–469.

Shane, S. and Venkataraman, S. (2000), The promise of entrepreneurship as a field of research, *Academy of Management Review*, **25**(1), 217–226.

Shepherd, D.A. (2011), Multilevel entrepreneurship research: opportunities for studying entrepreneurial decision making, *Journal of Management*, **37**(2), 412–420.

Shepherd, D.A. and Patzelt, H. (2011), The new field of sustainable entrepreneurship: studying entrepreneurial action linking 'what is to be sustained' with 'what is to be developed,' *Entrepreneurship Theory & Practice*, **35**(1), 137–163.

Sorenson, O. and Stuart, T.E. (2008), Entrepreneurship: a field of dreams? *Academy of Management Annals*, **2**(1), 517–543.

Wiklund, J., Davidsson, P., Audretsch, D.B. and Karlsson, C. (2011), The future of entrepreneurship research, *Entrepreneurship Theory & Practice*, **35**(1), 1–9.

Zeelenberg, M. (1999), Anticipated regret, expected feedback and behavioral decision making, *Journal of Behavioral Decision Making*, **12**, 93–106.

Zeelenberg, M., van Dijk, E., van den Bos, K. and Pieters, R. (2002), The inaction effect in the psychology of regret, *Journal of Personality and Social Psychology*, **82**, 314–328.

14 Evolution of the Concept of Entrepreneurship

Introduction

In the 1960s there was little public discussion of the entrepreneur. The future of business lay in the large bureaucratic corporation, it was believed; professional management held the key to economic success. Beginning in the 1970s, low-cost, high-quality manufactured imports from Asia flooded into Western markets. Western businesses had become complacent and failed to anticipate the threat. They should have been more entrepreneurial: the scarcity of entrepreneurship drew attention to its value. Michael Porter of the Harvard Business School emphasised the need for business to be aware of competitive threats in his bestseller *Competitive Strategy* (1980). But Porter was mainly concerned with the survival of big business. Others were more concerned with small business.

In the Western recession of the 1970s, many managers and professionals became redundant. Many opted for self-employment; while some switched to other industries, others stayed put. They 'dis-intermediated' their former employers by going directly to the customers they already knew. They cut their own salaries to zero, and worked for free for their own businesses. They became risk-takers, living off uncertain profits rather than a known salary.

Entrepreneurship therefore became identified, in many people's minds, with small firms. This suited government policymakers. 'Enterprise culture' could take people out of unemployment and into self-employment, and thereby reduce the tax bill for benefits. Indeed, if small businesses grew into big businesses then they would contribute taxes and improve the finances of the state. The key was to promote small business startups and encourage high-growth small firms.

Some startups were highly innovative (Acs and Audretsch, 1990). While big firms with large R&D departments continued to develop incremental innovations within existing technological paradigms, startups such as Apple and Microsoft launched more radical innovations, not only shaking up their own sectors but developing products that changed business processes in other sectors too. Radical innovation by small firms was boosted further by the growth of the venture capital market.

Today business students no longer aspire to be faceless 'suits' in giant corporations; they prefer to start their own businesses and create distinctive personal brands. Business school professors have responded by improvising theories of entrepreneurship to cater for this demand. Political slogans are turned into theoretical dogma overnight. 'Entrepreneurs are wealth-creators' began life as a political slogan, designed to win votes from the business community, but it is now presented as if it were a principle derived from economic theory.

Theories of entrepreneurship

As it happens, economists already have a theory of the entrepreneur, with a substantial intellectual pedigree (Hébert and Link, 2009). Unfortunately, however, it is somewhat abstract and conceptual; 'too philosophical' is a common criticism. But it is philosophical because it deals with fundamental questions, such as 'Why do we need entrepreneurs anyway?' The answer to that question is that the world is volatile and unpredictable, and so no one knows for sure what is going to happen next (von Hayek, 1951). Entrepreneurs know better than most people and so it pays to let them take decisions. People who have good judgement will make better decisions than other people, although they will not be right every time. People entrust entrepreneurs to take decisions on their behalf by investing in their firms, as explained below.

But how do entrepreneurs excel at decision-making? Entrepreneurs are good at synthesising information from different sources (Casson, 1982). This allows them to recognise opportunities that other people have missed (Kirzner, 1973). They have the imagination to recognise possibilities that others cannot visualise, and they can see the true potential of possibilities that others have considered and dismissed (Shackle, 1955).

According to Joseph Schumpeter (1934), entrepreneurs also excel at innovation. Schumpeter distinguished five types of innovation: in technology, new products, new export markets, new sources of supply and new organisational forms (his examples included US trusts and German cartels). Modern entrepreneurship literature (Baumol, 1993) emphasises the first two forms of innovation, sometimes to the exclusion of the others. International business studies provides a corrective, however. It highlights new export markets and new sources of supply; historically, both have been important in imperial expansion, from classical Rome to nineteenth-century Europe, and both continue to be important for the emerging industrial economies of today. Organisational innovation also continues to be important, from multidivisional corporations to networks of joint ventures and alliances (Rugman and D'Cruz, 2000).

While Schumpeter emphasised heroic large-scale innovations, such as railways and industrial chemicals, the typical innovation undertaken by an entrepreneur is small and much more mundane. Innovations are usually local rather than global, and their impact is confined to a single sector of the economy. Establishing the first coffee bar in a country town, for example, is an innovation when considered locally, but is simply imitation when considered from a wider perspective. It is therefore a mistake to identify entrepreneurship purely with radical innovations.

It is also a mistake to suppose that innovation is always the right decision for an entrepreneur to make. Although Schumpeter applauded the development of marginalism in nineteenth-century economics, he did not apply marginalist analysis to the innovation decision. Instead he adopted a social psychological approach. He described the entrepreneur as inspired by fantasy, driven by a will to succeed and a need to prove himself superior to others. These were desirable qualities, in Schumpeter's view, because they overcame a psychological barrier to innovation posed by the timidity of ordinary people. This timidity creates a bias against innovation, which is overcome only by willpower.

According to Schumpeter, therefore, the role of the entrepreneur is to innovate, whereas in reality their role is to take the innovation decision. The important thing is not to innovate under all conditions, but simply to take the right decision. There are not only good ideas for new technologies and products; there are also really bad ideas, involving technologies that do not work and products that people do not want. More significantly, perhaps, there are many not-so-bad ideas that are just wasteful: technologies that work but are costly to use, and products that do a job, but not so well as some other product does. Good judgement is not just about recognising the hidden potential of good projects but recognising the hidden snags in bad ones (Casson, 2010).

Schumpeter is also clear that the entrepreneur is not an inventor. The role of the entrepreneur is economic rather than scientific: it is to decide whether to commit resources to the exploitation of an invention – an invention that someone else may have made. To succeed, the entrepreneur must appraise the practical usefulness of the invention, the feasibility of scaling up production and the willingness of customers to pay for the resulting product.

The economic aspects of innovation also highlight the importance of sunk costs (Casson and Wadeson, 2008). The costs of innovation cannot normally be recovered (at least in full) if it fails. A small firm can be bankrupted by a single failure. Sometimes the risks can be laid off (e.g., by hiring rather than buying specialised equipment). In many cases, however, large innovations have to be financed by firms with deep pockets, which manage a portfolio of innovations in order to spread their risks (e.g., modern pharmaceutical firms). Entrepreneurs cannot avoid failure altogether, but they can at least manage risks effectively; as a result they can salvage enough from failure to pursue another innovation. Managing downside risks is crucial to the strategy of the serial entrepreneur (Ucbasaran et al., 2006).

The notion of the entrepreneur as a risk-taker goes back to Richard Cantillon (1755/1931), an Irish economist, probably of Norman descent, who was a notorious speculator and is believed to have faked his own death (Murphy, 1989). Cantillon divided society into two groups, who were linked by a contract that allocated risks between them. Cantillon correctly recognised that production takes time, that consumer products are sold in spot markets and that employees normally receive a fixed wage. Under these conditions, the producer-entrepreneur must contract with workers before they know the price at which the product will be sold. At the time they hire the worker they may not even be sure which particular variety of product should be produced. They therefore hire the worker, then tell him what to produce and agree to pay him whether or not the product sells. As a result, the worker is insured against unexpected changes in the price of the product and the entrepreneur bears all the risk. The quality of the entrepreneur's judgement determines the average profit that he earns. This profit is a compensation for the risks he bears.

Cantillon's analysis precedes the seminal work of Adam Smith (1776/1976). Cantillon analysed the division of labour in society in terms of quality of judgement and attitude to risk, while Smith analysed it in terms of learning by repetition and underlying aptitudes for different kinds of work. Cantillon's approach is surprisingly modern; his points were later restated formally by Simon (1947) and Kihlstrom and Laffont (1979).

How then does one recognise an entrepreneur? Some people claim that the entrepreneur is the owner-manager of a small firm. But successful small firms grow and become large. Did Bill Gates cease to be an entrepreneur when Microsoft became large? Certainly not! It can be difficult, however, to locate the entrepreneur within a large firm. The Chicago economist Frank Knight (1921) argued that the shareholders were the entrepreneurs in a large joint stock company, because it was their money that was at risk. Furthermore, they appointed the directors of the firm who in turn appointed the CEO; therefore the shareholders were ultimately accountable (to themselves) for whatever the CEO decided. This ingenious argument overlooks the fact, however, that CEOs are often the founders and almost always formulate the long-term strategies of their firms. There is another way of looking at this issue (Casson, 2010). Shareholders seeking a good return will want to invest in firms controlled by a successful entrepreneur. Once an entrepreneur has gained a reputation for good decision-making, he will find it easy to expand his business and increase its capital. It will be even easier to expand the firm if he gives the shareholders the freedom to oust him from control should he 'lose his touch'. The entrepreneur must therefore trade off total autonomy against the prospect of cheaper capital, and if he decides on the latter then he will finish up as a Knightian CEO who is accountable to a board; but unlike the Knightian CEO, he will remain the entrepreneur as well until he quits or is ousted.

Another way of looking at large firm entrepreneurship is through the lens of the entrepreneurial team (Foss and Klein, 2012). Before company law reform in the 1850s, almost all large businesses were partnerships, and the partners often pooled their judgement as well as their capital. In modern joint stock firms, judgement is pooled both horizontally and vertically. 'Horizontal' pooling is effected through consultative committees, such as a board of directors, where judgements are based on the balance of opinion rather than the judgement of any single individual. 'Vertical' pooling is achieved by delegation, in which different levels of the organisation decide strategy, tactics and implementation plans. Team entrepreneurship often thrives on interpersonal differences rather than similarities – for example, the 'good guys' in marketing, who like to say 'yes', and the 'bad guys' in finance, who like to say 'no' – rather than on similarities that promote 'group think'. Team members can fall out, however, and so a culture of mutual respect must be promoted.

Conclusions

Considered as an academic discipline, entrepreneurship studies developed slowly until the 1970s, and has really boomed since then. The quality of early work was extremely high, and has stood the test of time well, but the quantity was very low. The best modern work has built on the analytical foundations of the past, which are largely economic; the worst of the literature has been that which tried to create entrepreneurship as a new subject from scratch. The theory of entrepreneurship will doubtless continue to evolve, but the direction of that evolution will depend crucially on the range of evidence that is used to guide theory development (Casson et al., 2006). Since the 1970s there has been a growing body of empirical evidence, from qualitative case studies of individual firms and from panels of small firm data based on surveys or company accounts. Regional studies of small firm clusters have also been common (Acs and Audretsch, 2010). There has, however, been relatively little study of the impact of entrepreneurship over time. It is difficult, for example, to assess how far entrepreneurship policy has affected long-term GDP growth in regional or national economies. While many comparative cross-country studies have been undertaken, most rely on just a single source, notably the Global Entrepreneurship Monitor database.

There is an important body of historical evidence on entrepreneurship that has hardly been used at all (Casson and Casson, 2014). In England, for example, entrepreneurship thrived long before the Industrial Revolution: there are good sources on the business activities of William de la Pole, a fourteenth-century wool merchant and banker to the king (Fryde, 1988), while in the fifteenth century there is good evidence on the business careers of the mayors of London, including the famous Dick Whittington (Thrupp, 1948; Besant and Rice, 1881). Historical comparative studies of entrepreneurship are still in their infancy. Access to a wider range of evidence that tracks entrepreneurship over time is crucial for the continual evolution of entrepreneurship theory.

MARK CASSON

References

Acs, Z. and Audretsch, D.B. (1990), *Innovation and Small Firms*, Cambridge, MA: MIT Press.
Acs, Z. and Audretsch, D.B. (2010), *Handbook of Entrepreneurship Research*, 2nd edn, New York: Springer.
Baumol, W.J. (1993), *Entrepreneurship, Management and the Structure of Pay-Offs*, Cambridge, MA: MIT Press.
Besant, W. and Rice, J. (1881), *Sir Richard Whittington, Lord Mayor of London*, London: M. Ward.
Cantillon, R. (1755/1931), *Essai sur la Nature du Commerce en Generale*, (ed.) Henry Higgs, London: Macmillan for Royal Economic Society.
Casson, M. (1982), *The Entrepreneur: An Economic Theory*, Oxford: Martin Robertson, 2nd edn, 2001, Cheltenham: Edward Elgar Publishing.
Casson, M. (2010), *Entrepreneurship: Theory, Networks, History*, Cheltenham: Edward Elgar Publishing.
Casson, M. and Casson, C. (2014), History of entrepreneurship: medieval origins of a modern phenomenon, *Business History*, **56**(8), 1223–1242.
Casson, M. and Wadeson, N.S. (2008), Entrepreneurship and macroeconomic performance, *Strategic Entrepreneurship Journal*, **1**(3–4), 239–262.
Casson, M., Yeung, B., Basu, A. and Wadeson, N.S. (eds) (2006), *Oxford Handbook of Entrepreneurship*, Oxford: Oxford University Press.
Foss, N.J. and Klein, P.G. (2012), *Organizing Entrepreneurial Judgment: A New Approach to the Firm*, Cambridge: Cambridge University Press.

Fryde, E.B. (1988), *William de la Pole: Merchant and King's Banker*, London: Hambledon Press.

Hébert, R.F. and Link, A.N. (2009), *History of Entrepreneurship*, London: Routledge.

Kihlstrom, R.E. and Laffont, J.-J. (1979), A general equilibrium entrepreneurial theory of firm formation based on risk aversion, *Journal of Political Economy*, **87**(4), 719–748.

Kirzner, I.M. (1973), *Competition and Entrepreneurship*, Chicago: University of Chicago Press.

Knight, F.H. (1921), *Risk, Uncertainty and Profit*, Boston: Houghton Mifflin.

Murphy, A.E. (1989), *Richard Cantillon: Entrepreneur and Economist*, Oxford: Oxford University Press.

Porter, M.E. (1980), *Competitive Strategy*, New York: Free Press.

Rugman, A.M. and D'Cruz, J. (2000), *Multinationals as Flagship Firms: Regional Business Networks*, Oxford: Oxford University Press.

Schumpeter, J. (1934), *The Theory of Economic Development*, trans. R. Opie, Cambridge, MA: Harvard University Press.

Shackle, G.L.S. (1955), *Uncertainty in Economics: And Other Reflections*, Cambridge: Cambridge University Press.

Simon, H.A. (1947), A formal theory of the employment relationship, *Econometrica*, **19**(3), 293–305.

Smith, A. (1776/1976), *An Inquiry into the Nature and Causes of the Wealth of Nations*, London: Oxford University Press.

Thrupp, S. (1948), *The Merchant Class of Medieval London*, Chicago: University of Chicago Press.

Ucbasarn, D., Westhead, P. and Wright, M. (2006), *Habitual Entrepreneurs*, Cheltenham: Edward Elgar Publishing.

von Hayek, F.A. (1951), *Individualism and Economic Order*, London: Routledge.

15 Family Business and Innovation

Introduction

While scholars from different disciplines have amply investigated innovation management, most of the traditional literature focuses on firms where ownership and management are separate, without explicitly taking into account what happens when they are combined.

Unification of ownership and control is typical of family businesses. The involvement of family owners in management endows firms with distinctive incentives, authority structures and accountability norms, resulting in unique resources and capabilities. Different types of controlling owners may have different investment horizons, risk aversion, diversification plans, return aspirations and governance structures that are likely to affect innovation activities and outcomes. For instance, the pursuit of noneconomic goals (Kotlar and De Massis, 2013) may reduce their willingness to undertake collaborative innovation projects (e.g., Kotlar et al., 2013). Moreover, family involvement in ownership, management and governance can result in developing unique resources that can then be leveraged in ways that affect innovation. For example, the unique characteristics of the social capital of family firms can affect their ability to use external knowledge sources during the innovation process or adopt functional structures rather than cross-functional teams to organize the innovation process (De Massis et al., 2015). In addition to strong theoretical reasons, empirical evidence shows that innovation management differs in family and nonfamily firms, leading to different decisions, processes and performance patterns.

Beyond the ubiquity of family firms, which are the most common organizational form with a crucial role in all world economies, understanding innovation behavior in family businesses is important since they increasingly make use of innovation to nurture their competitive advantage and to overcome economic downturns. Companies such as Beretta, Booths, Fiat, Knauf, Salewa and Walmart are just some well-known family businesses that have strongly anchored their competitive advantage in innovation. This indicates a strong need for family owners, managers, scholars and business educators to understand how innovation management practices, strategies and organizational solutions change in the context of family businesses.

This chapter briefly illustrates how innovation is distinctly managed in family firms and discusses the importance of a temporal perspective on family business innovation, drawing largely on the findings of prior studies I conducted to show how family involvement in a business organization affects innovation inputs, activities and outputs (for a review see De Massis et al., 2013).

Effect of family involvement on innovation inputs

Literature on family business innovation is largely consistent in showing that family firms invest less in R&D than nonfamily firms (e.g., Block, 2012). However, due to their long-term orientation, the variability of R&D investments is greater in family firms (Chrisman and Patel, 2012). A notable exception is Asaba's study (2013) showing that family firms tend to invest more than their counterparts when financial factors and environmental uncertainty are controlled. Moreover, Sciascia et al. (2015) show that in small and medium-sized enterprises (SMEs), the relationship between family ownership and R&D intensity is contingent on the way the family invests its wealth. Family ownership is a negative correlate of R&D intensity when family wealth and firm equity overlap is high, implying that the more a family controls firm ownership, the less the SME is inclined to invest in R&D. Conversely, if the portion of family wealth invested in the firm is low, cautious behavior is replaced by a more innovative attitude resulting in higher R&D expenditure.

Effects of family involvement on innovation activities

Through a multiple case study, De Massis, Frattini, Pizzurno and Cassia (2015) analyze how and why the anatomy of the product innovation process differs between family and nonfamily firms. The analysis shows that, due to their distinctive characteristics, family businesses differ with regard to product innovation strategies and organization of the innovation process. For instance, family firms use a functional organization in the innovation process, with high levels of decisional autonomy given to project leaders. Throughout this process, they rely on a higher number of collaborations with universities and public research centers, while the organizational climate is largely informal and unstructured. Conversely, nonfamily firms predominantly establish cross-functional teams to carry out these projects, with limited delegation of decisional authority to project leaders and a highly structured and formalized organizational climate. Kotlar et al. (2013, 2014a, 2014b) offer other examples of studies on how family involvement affects innovation activities.

Effects of family involvement on innovation outputs

The findings on innovation outputs are mixed (De Massis et al., 2013). Some studies show that family involvement is negatively associated with the quantity and quality of patents obtained (e.g., Chin et al., 2009) while others show that family involvement positively affects innovation outputs (e.g., Westhead, 1997).

Some scholars indicate that the distinctive traits of family firms affect their propensity to respond to discontinuous technological changes

(König et al., 2013), suggesting that family governance implies family firms adopt discontinuous technology later than nonfamily firms but implement the decision more rapidly when they do. Chrisman et al. (2015b) extend this work and explain that the heterogeneity of family business goals, governance structures, resources and idiosyncratic situational factors can affect strategic innovation decisions such as the adoption of discontinuous technologies.

Temporal dynamics of innovation in family firms and effect of intra-family succession

Many scholars have emphasized the time-variant nature of family firms and the importance of adopting a temporal perspective to understand family business behavior (Gagné et al., 2014; Sharma et al., 2014). To the best of my knowledge, no study has investigated how family business innovation behavior changes over time. However, De Massis et al. (2014a) show that firm proactiveness, which is closely related to innovation, changes over time in family firms following a horizontal-S pattern. This temporal evolution is due to time-variant family dynamics in terms of goal alignment, trust, altruism and interpersonal contract. Moreover, Kotlar and De Massis (2013) show that goal diversity is more pronounced when an intra-family succession is imminent. Intra-family succession unfreezes the previously stabilized organizational goals, leading individuals to express their goals more fervently and activate social interactions that lead to new stabilizations, similarly to the classic description of disruptive change as freezing-transition-unfreezing. Thus, intra-family succession would act as a catalyst of revolutionary change and innovation. An area ripe for future research is 'transgenerational innovation' and how family business innovation changes over time.

Finally, Chrisman et al. (2015a) propose a framework of how family involvement affects innovation management based on ability (discretion to act) and willingness (disposition to act), two drivers that distinguish family firms (De Massis et al., 2014b). Paradoxically, we argue that family firms have greater ability yet lower willingness to engage in technological innovation, highlighting the importance of distinguishing between these two aspects in future theorizing about family firm innovation.

Conclusions

I recognize that I offer only a brief insight into a very complex area of study, but this essay has provided a good opportunity to concisely inform family business scholars and decision-makers on how the idiosyncratic characteristics of family businesses affect innovation management.

ALFREDO DE MASSIS

References

Asaba, S. (2013), Patient investment of family firms in the Japanese electric machinery industry, *Asia Pacific Journal of Management*, **30**(3), 697–715.

Block, J.H. (2012), R&D investments in family and founder firms: an agency perspective, *Journal of Business Venturing*, **27**(2), 248–265.

Chin, C.L., Chen, Y.J., Kleinman, G. and Lee, P. (2009), Corporate ownership structure and innovation: evidence from Taiwan's electronics industry, *Journal of Accounting, Auditing & Finance*, **24**(1), 145–175.

Chrisman, J.J. and Patel, P.C. (2012), Variations in R&D investments of family and non-family firms: behavioral agency and myopic loss aversion perspectives, *Academy of Management Journal*, **55**(4), 976–997.

Chrisman, J.J., Chua, J.H., De Massis, A., Frattini, F. and Wright, M. (2015a), The ability and willingness paradox in family firm innovation, *Journal of Product Innovation Management*, **32**, 310–318.

Chrisman, J.J., Fang, H., Kotlar, J., and De Massis, A. (2015b), A note on family influence and the adoption of discontinuous technologies in family firms, *Journal of Product Innovation Management*, **32**, 384–388.

De Massis, A., Frattini, F. and Lichtenthaler, U. (2013), Research on technological innovation in family firms: present debates and future directions, *Family Business Review*, **26**(1), 10–31.

De Massis, A., Chirico, F., Kotlar, J. and Naldi, L. (2014a), The temporal evolution of proactiveness in family firms: the horizontal S-curve hypothesis, *Family Business Review*, **27**(1), 35–50.

De Massis, A., Kotlar, J., Chua, J.H. and Chrisman, J.J. (2014b), Ability and willingness as sufficiency conditions for family-oriented particularistic behavior: implications for theory and empirical studies, *Journal of Small Business Management*, **52**(2), 344–364.

De Massis, A., Frattini, F., Pizzurno, E. and Cassia, L. (2015), Product innovation in family versus non-family firms: an exploratory analysis, *Journal of Small Business Management*, **53**(1), 1–36.

Gagné, M., Sharma, P. and De Massis, A. (2014), The study of organizational behavior in family business, *European Journal of Work and Organizational Psychology*, **23**(5), 643–656.

König, A., Kammerlander, N. and Enders, A. (2013), The family innovator's dilemma: how family influence affects the adoption of discontinuous technologies by incumbent firms, *Academy of Management Review*, **38**(3), 418–441.

Kotlar, J. and De Massis, A. (2013), Goal setting in family firms: goal diversity, social interactions, and collective commitment to family-centered goals, *Entrepreneurship Theory & Practice*, **37**(6), 1263–1288.

Kotlar, J., De Massis, A., Frattini, F., Bianchi, M. and Fang, H. (2013), Technology acquisition in family and non-family firms: a longitudinal analysis of Spanish manufacturing firms, *Journal of Product Innovation Management*, **30**(6), 1073–1088.

Kotlar, J., De Massis, A., Fang, H. and Frattini, F. (2014a), Strategic reference points in family firms, *Small Business Economics*, **43**(3), 597–619.

Kotlar, J., Fang, H.C., De Massis, A. and Frattini, F. (2014b), Profitability goals, control goals, and the R&D investment decisions of family and nonfamily firms, *Journal of Product Innovation Management*, **31**(6), 1128–1145.

Sciascia, S., Nordqvist, M., Mazzola, P. and De Massis, A. (2015), Family ownership and R&D intensity in small- and medium-sized firms, *Journal of Product Innovation Management*, **32**(3), 349–360.

Sharma, P., Salvato, C. and Reay, T. (2014), Temporal dimensions of family enterprise research, *Family Business Review*, **27**(1), 10–19.

Westhead, P. (1997), Ambitions, external environment and strategic factor differences between family and non-family companies, *Entrepreneurship & Regional Development*, **9**(2), 127–158.

16 Family Business Entrepreneurship

Introduction

When speaking about family businesses, they are often named the engine of the European economies. To be successful in an increasingly globalized world, academic research has developed a strategic concept for family business firms: entrepreneurial orientation. This concept is discussed in the literature for several reasons. First, almost every family firm starts with its founder, the entrepreneur. Second, friends and family members are often the first and only financier of a new venture and thus involved in the firm. Finally, family firms should behave like entrepreneurial firms, always seeking for opportunities, ideas to realize competitive advantages.

Over the past 20 years, the political and public perception of large and public corporations as the one and only generator for jobs and welfare has changed (Audretsch, 2009). The paradigm in academic research and politics has shifted towards new ventures on the one hand and established family firms on the other. Both types of firms, however, share one idea – the role model of individuals as owners and managers and their entrepreneurial orientation. The following section will point out critically some commonalities and intersections of both research areas. Furthermore, the relevance of different aspects of entrepreneurship for family firm research will be discussed.

Commonality in entrepreneurship and family firms research

The academic literature on family firms addresses the definitional dilemma of family business research in any manner. Until now, the research community has not found a generally accepted definition of the family firm. This, however, is important to contrast characteristics, strategies or performance of family firms with other types of firms, like new ventures or large and public companies. The simplest way, defining a threshold of equity shares owned by an individual, fails to sufficiently describe and capture the nature of a family firm (Audretsch et al., 2013). Thus, several streams in the literature have been established to circumvent the problem of operationalization and measurement. One stream of literature defines the family business by its main components, namely ownership, management and control. According to this literature, a family business is either controlled, managed or both controlled and managed by a group of individuals belonging to at least one family (Anderson and Reeb, 2003; Familienunternehmen, 2014; Maury, 2006). This stream treats the entrepreneurial orientation of family firms by considering different generations. While the first generation is almost always the founder and entrepreneur, the second, third and following generations are, by definition, less entrepreneurial in the sense of the spirit and characteristics of its founder (Audretsch et al., 2013). The second strand of literature follows the essence approach, in that a family firm is characterized by its behavior, vision and mission (for example Chrisman et al., 2005). While this concept captures almost all of what is meant by 'familiness,' it is faced with a measurement problem for quantitative studies.

Both streams on the literature, however, are based on the assumption that the willingness to transfer the business to the next generation is a key characteristic of the family business. And, following Brockhaus (1994), both entrepreneurship researchers as well as academic research in family business have to master the same challenge concerning the definition of their object of interest and consider the strategic orientation beyond the myopic and capital market-driven view. No empirical evidence is truthful without a clear-cut definition of what is meant by a family and how this construct is measured. The results should then be reflected on and discussed within this context.

Entrepreneurial orientation in family firms

Entrepreneurial orientation (EO) is a very popular, fruitful and promising topic in family business research if they are willing to transfer the business to the next generation. Since environment changes over time and such changes are often unforeseen and exogenous, family firms should behave like entrepreneurs to survive. Lumpkin and Dess distinguish entrepreneurship and entrepreneurial orientation in a simple way: 'new entry explains what entrepreneurship consists of, and entrepreneurial orientation describes how new entry is undertaken. [. . .] An EO refers to the processes, practices, and decision-making activities that lead to new entry' (Lumpkin and Dess, 1996: 136, 137). EO is generally described by the following components: the autonomy to promote ideas, the willingness to innovate and take risks, proactiveness as the ability to identify new market or product opportunities, and competitive aggressiveness.

These dimensions are assumed to play a key role in family businesses and that family firms differ in some of these dimensions from other types of firms. In particular, risk-taking and proactiveness are assumed to have a different impact on firm performance (Naldi et al., 2007; Short et al., 2009). It could also be shown that EO is dynamically changing in successful family firms and should thus not be treated as a once-and-forever level (Zellweger and Sieger, 2012). The concluding remark is that entrepreneurial orientation is a relevant and necessary condition for family firms in pursuing their strategy of surviving over generations.

Corporate entrepreneurship in family firms

Entrepreneurial orientation is also discussed in the context of established and large companies regardless of the ownership structure (Zahra, 1991), such as Johnson & Johnson, a publicly listed Forbes 500 Company that yet labels itself as 'a family firm.' Academic researchers in corporate entrepreneurship point out that the large and established companies also have to behave like entrepreneurs to survive in almost global markets. They assume that increased competition leads to shorter product lifecycles and thus a struggle for new ideas, innovations and technologies (Randøy et al., 2009). Corporate entrepreneurship is thus seen as a strategic orientation of family firms to gather the scare resources to compete successfully (Salvato, 2004; Uhlaner et al., 2012). Kellermanns and Eddleston (2006) identify several technological opportunities and how to exploit them in family firms. However, the concept of corporate entrepreneurship and the entrepreneurial orientation seems only to be successful if the family is not only involved within the firm by large ownership stakes but also by an involvement beyond ownership (Hamelin, 2013; Rogoff and Heck, 2003; Sciascia et al., 2012). Again, these findings suggest that future research should strongly focus on the effects of different measures on family firms.

Conclusions

All concepts of 'entrepreneurship,' 'corporate entrepreneurship' and 'entrepreneurial orientation' are promising and fruitful to describe and analyze the strategic orientation of family firms. Empirical research should put effort into solving measurement problems, both for the construct of family firms and different concepts of entrepreneurial orientation. Many open questions could be examined from a similar perspective and theoretical background, and the interrelated research fields, entrepreneurship and family firms can benefit from each other. Today's entrepreneurial firms are the family firms of tomorrow.

ERIK E. LEHMANN AND KATHARINE WIRSCHING

References

Anderson, R.C. and Reeb, D.M. (2003), Founding-family ownership and firm performance: evidence from the S&P 500, *Journal of Finance*, **58**(3), 1301–1328.

Audretsch, D.B. (2009), The entrepreneurial society, *Journal of Technology Transfer*, **34**(3), 245.

Audretsch, D.B., Hülsbeck, M. and Lehmann, E.E. (2013), Families as active monitors of firm performance, *Journal of Family Business Strategy*, **4**(2), 118–130.

Brockhaus, S.R.H. (1994), Entrepreneurship and family business research: comparisons, critique, and lessons, *Entrepreneurship Theory & Practice*, **19**(1), 25–38.

Chrisman, J.J., Chua, J.H. and Sharma, P. (2005), Trends and directions in the development of a strategic management theory of family firm, *Entrepreneurship Theory & Practice*, **29**(5), 555–576.

Familienunternehmen, S. (2014), Daten, Zahlen und Fakten zur volkswirtschaftlichen Bedeutung von Familienunternehmen, www.familienunternehmen.de/de/daten-fakten-zahlen.

Hamelin, A. (2013), Influence of family ownership on small business growth: evidence from French SMEs, *Small Business Economics*, **41**(3), 563–579.

Kellermanns, F.W. and Eddleston, K.A. (2006), Corporate entrepreneurship in family firms: a family perspective, *Entrepreneurship Theory & Practice*, **30**(6), 809–830.

Lumpkin, G.T. and Dess, G.G. (1996), Clarifying the entrepreneurial orientation construct and linking it to performance, *The Academy of Management Review*, **21**(1), 135–172.

Maury, B. (2006), Family ownership and firm performance: empirical evidence from Western European corporations, *Journal of Corporate Finance*, **12**(2), 321–341.

Naldi, L., Nordqvist, M., Sjoberg, K. and Wiklund, J. (2007), Entrepreneurial orientation, risk taking, and performance in family firms, *Family Business Review*, **20**(1), 33–58.

Randøy, T., Dibrell, C. and Craig, J. (2009), Founding family leadership and industry profitability, *Small Business Economics*, **32**(4), 397–407.

Rogoff, E.G. and Heck, R.K.Z. (2003), Evolving research in entrepreneurship and family business: recognizing family as the oxygen that feeds the fire of entrepreneurship, *Journal of Business Venturing*, **18**(5), 559–566.

Salvato, C. (2004), Predictors of entrepreneurship in family firms, *The Journal of Private Equity*, **7**(3), 68–76.

Sciascia, S., Mazzola, P., Astrachan, J. and Pieper, T. (2012), The role of family ownership in international entrepreneurship: exploring nonlinear effects, *Small Business Economics*, **38**(1), 15–31.

Short, J.C., Payne, G.T., Brigham, K.H., Lumpkin, G.T. and Broberg, J.C. (2009), Family firms and entrepreneurial orientation in publicly traded firms: a comparative analysis of the S&P 500, *Family Business Review*, **22**(1), 9–24.

Uhlaner, L., Kellermanns, F., Eddleston, K. and Hoy, F. (2012), The entrepreneuring family: a new paradigm for family business research, *Small Business Economics*, **38**(1), 1–11.

Zahra, S.A. (1991), Predictors and financial outcomes of corporate entrepreneurship: an exploratory study, *Journal of Business Venturing*, **6**(4), 259–285.

Zellweger, T. and Sieger, P. (2012), Entrepreneurial orientation in long-lived family firms, *Small Business Economics*, **38**(1), 67–84.

17 Habitual Entrepreneurs

Introduction

Entrepreneurship is not a single action event because some people have careers in entrepreneurship (Westhead and Wright, 1998). Entrepreneur heterogeneity exists relating to variations in the extent and nature of entrepreneurs' prior business ownership experience (PBOE). Business ownership and a decision-making role within the venture are important dimensions of entrepreneurship. *Novice entrepreneurs* are individuals without PBOE who currently own a stake in an independent firm that is either new or purchased. *Habitual entrepreneurs* hold or have held an ownership stake in two or more firms, at least one of which was established or purchased. Habitual entrepreneurs can be subdivided into serial and portfolio entrepreneurs. *Serial entrepreneurs* have sold/closed at least one firm that they had an ownership stake in, and currently have an ownership stake in a single independent firm. *Portfolio entrepreneurs* currently have ownership stakes in two or more independent firms.

The role of habitual entrepreneurs

A business opportunity can be exploited through new firm formation, purchase of an existing private firm, discovery and creation of new opportunities in existing firms or discovery and creation of opportunities for self-employment. This variety gives rise to a categorization of habitual entrepreneurship by the modes through which it can occur. Table 17.1 shows that habitual entrepreneurs covered by cells 1–5 engage in entrepreneurship sequentially, while those in cells 6–10 engage in concurrent entrepreneurial activities. The entrepreneurs in cells 1 and 6 found a new independent firm, while those in cells 2 and 7 are involved in new firms spun-off from other organizations. Entrepreneurs in cells 3 and 8 have become owners of an established independent firm either as individuals from outside the firm undertaking a straight purchase or a management buyin (MBI), or individuals from inside undertaking a management buyout (MBO). Some buyouts involve founders selling their businesses and subsequently buying them back when the acquirers find themselves unable to generate adequate performance because they do not possess the tacit knowledge of the founder. Further, some buyouts are secondary buyouts where the same management acquires a larger stake in the firm through a financial restructuring associated with initial private equity investors selling their shares. Entrepreneurs in cells 4 and 9 are engaged as corporate entrepreneurs in existing firms, and have not purchased the firm. Entrepreneurs in cells 5 and 10 are self-employed individuals who do not form a specific legal entity.

Table 17.1   Categorization of habitual entrepreneurship

Nature of entrepreneurship			Serial entrepreneurs	Portfolio entrepreneurs
Involving new business(es)		De Novo business Spinoff (including corporate and university spinoffs)	Serial founders (1) Serial spinout entrepreneurs (2)	Portfolio founders (6) Portfolio spinout entrepreneurs (7)
Involving existing business(es)		Purchase (including buyouts/buyins) Corporate entrepreneurship	Serial acquirers (e.g., secondary MBOs/MBIs) (3) Serial corporate entrepreneurs (4)	Portfolio acquirers (e.g., leveraged buildups) (8) Portfolio corporate entrepreneurs (9)
Involving No New Legal Entity		Self-employment	Serial self-employed (5)	Portfolio self-employed (10)

Source: Prepared by the authors

Habitual entrepreneurs have been detected to be highly prevalent in the UK (12–52 percent), US (51–64 percent), Finland (50 percent), Australia (49 percent), Norway (47 percent), Ghana (41 percent), Sweden (30–40 percent) and Malaysia (39 percent). Scholars have also examined the business groups under control of the habitual entrepreneur. Iacobucci (2002) noted that 25 percent of Italian manufacturing firms were members of a business group created by a habitual entrepreneur (or their associated entrepreneurial team). Habitual entrepreneurship may arise in settings where opportunities for growth are restricted, forcing the entrepreneurs to substitute growth of one venture with the creation of multiple firms. The following reasons for habitual entrepreneurship have been identified: tax reasons and to support the first venture established; and desire for independence, autonomy and personal wealth creation. Monetary gain may become less important in subsequent ventures, partly because they do not want to put at risk wealth generated from an earlier successful venture.

Research has evolved from initial 'ground-clearing' descriptive studies of the phenomenon through qualitative studies focused on theory development, to quantitative studies undertaking hypothesis testing. Thorgen and Wincent (2015) detected that habitual entrepreneurs are more likely to report more obsessive passion than novice entrepreneurs. Portfolio entrepreneurs report more harmonious passion than novice entrepreneurs. Further, portfolio entrepreneurs report more harmonious passion than serial entrepreneurs. Serial entrepreneurs report more obsessive passion than novice entrepreneurs.

PBOE provides a signal favourably received by external resource providers. Robson et al. (2013) found that entrepreneurs with longer PBOE and habitual entrepreneurs were less likely to be credit-rationed in Ghana. Mueller et al. (2012) detected that the PBOE signal is favourably received in the UK. University spinoff organizations not located in 'star' universities with habitual entrepreneurs increased their likelihood of obtaining formal venture capital.

Habitual entrepreneurs can accumulate assets (such as skills and networks) (Wiklund and Shepherd, 2008) and liabilities (such as hubris). Novice, serial and portfolio entrepreneurs differ in relation to their attitudes to entrepreneurship (Westhead et al., 2005). Portfolio entrepreneurs are more creative and more innovative than novice entrepreneurs.

Experienced (habitual) entrepreneurs identify more business opportunities than inexperienced (novice) entrepreneurs, in a given time period, and portfolio entrepreneurs identify more business opportunities in a given period than serial entrepreneurs. Ucbasaran et al. (2008) noted that entrepreneurs with up to 15 PBOEs identified significantly more opportunities, and more innovative opportunities. Beyond this point, entrepreneurs may believe that they already have sufficient knowledge and subsequently do not search for additional information, especially in new areas.

Some highly successful entrepreneurs are associated with PBOE 'failure(s),' which represent potentially valuable opportunities for learning, and the revision of expectations (Ucbasaran et al., 2010). A certain amount of prior failures can encourage habitual entrepreneurs to learn from their mistakes, and to subsequently practise what they have learnt. Ucbasaran et al. (2009) detected an inverse U-shaped relationship between the proportion of failed businesses relative to the number of businesses owned by habitual entrepreneurs and the number of opportunities identified in a given period.

Early studies generally assumed that entrepreneurs' PBOE would be associated with superior firm performance outcomes. Birley and Westhead (1993), however, detected that the performance of habitual entrepreneurs in terms of employment generation and wealth creation was not significantly better than that reported by novice entrepreneurs. Conversely, Westhead et al. (2003) found that, on average, businesses owned by portfolio entrepreneurs reported larger absolute sales and employment growth than those owned by novice entrepreneurs. A larger proportion of serial rather than novice entrepreneurs reported that their current profit performance was above average relative to competitors. Habitual entrepreneurs appear significantly more likely to be involved in exporting, with portfolio rather than serial entrepreneurs reporting higher exporting intensities (Robson et al., 2012a). Portfolio entrepreneurs appear more likely than other entrepreneurs to successfully introduce innovations (Robson et al., 2012b). From a policy perspective, if policy goals are to increase the 'quality' of new business startups and maximize investment returns, there is a case to target assistance to habitual entrepreneurs, particularly portfolio entrepreneurs.

Conclusion

In sum, habitual entrepreneurs represent an important part of the entrepreneurial landscape, whose learning and behaviour shaped by PBOE varies according to the nature and extent of that PBOE.

PAUL WESTHEAD AND MIKE WRIGHT

References

Birley, S. and Westhead, P. (1993), A comparison of new businesses established by 'novice' and 'habitual' founders in Great Britain, *International Small Business Journal*, **12**(1), 38–60.

Iacobucci, D. (2002), Explaining business groups started by habitual entrepreneurs in the Italian manufacturing sector, *Entrepreneurship and Regional Development*, **14**(1), 31–47.

Mueller, C., Westhead, P. and Wright, M. (2012), Formal venture capital acquisition: can experienced entrepreneurs compensate for the spatial proximity benefits of 'star universities'?, *Environment and Planning A*, **44**(2), 281–296.

Robson, P., Akuetteh, C., Westhead, P. and Wright, M. (2012a), Export intensity, human capital and business ownership experience, *International Small Business Journal*, **30**(4), 367–387.

Robson, P., Akuetteh, C., Westhead, P. and Wright, M. (2012b), Innovative opportunity pursuit, human capital and business ownership experience in an emerging region: evidence from Ghana, *Small Business Economics*, **39**(3), 603–625.

Robson, P., Akuetteh, C., Westhead, P., Wright, M. and Stone, I. (2013), Credit-rationing and entrepreneurial experience: evidence from a resource deficit context, *Entrepreneurship and Regional Development*, **25**(5–6), 349–370.

Thorgen, S. and Wincent, J. (2015), Passion and habitual entrepreneurship, *International Small Business Journal*, **33**(2), 216–227.

Ucbasaran, D., Westhead, P. and Wright, M. (2008), Opportunity identification and pursuit: does an entrepreneur's human capital matter? *Small Business Economics*, **30**(2), 153–173.

Ucbasaran, D., Westhead, P. and Wright, M. (2009), The extent and nature of opportunity identification by experienced entrepreneurs, *Journal of Business Venturing*, **24**(2), 99–115.

Ucbasaran, D., Westhead, P., Wright, M. and Flores, M. (2010), The nature of entrepreneurial experience, business failure and comparative optimism, *Journal of Business Venturing*, **25**(6), 541–555.

Westhead, P. and Wright, M. (1998), Novice, portfolio and serial founders: are they different?, *Journal of Business Venturing*, **13**(3), 173–204.

Westhead, P., Ucbasaran, D. and Wright, M. (2003), Differences between private firms owned by novice, serial and portfolio entrepreneurs: implications for policy-makers and practitioners, *Regional Studies*, **37**(2), 187–200.

Westhead, P., Ucbasaran, D. and Wright, M. (2005), Experience and cognition: do novice, serial and portfolio entrepreneurs differ?, *International Small Business Journal*, **23**(1), 72–98.

Wiklund, J. and Shepherd, D. (2008), Portfolio entrepreneurship, habitual and novice founders, new entry and mode of organizing, *Entrepreneurship Theory and Practice*, **32**(4), 701–725.

18 Harnessing Radical Innovation

Introduction

Companies are severely challenged when it comes to a sustained disciplined approach to radical or breakthrough innovation. The given wisdom that large mature companies must bow to new firms, especially new high tech startups, for radical innovation (RI) is flawed. Yet the histories of Corning, IBM, GE, Nokia and DSM, as well as others, underscore that companies can remake themselves through RI – but they encounter substantial obstacles. The problems faced include relying too much on individuals, senior management and serendipity (Day, 1994; O'Connor et al., 2008) and combating resistance of the mainstream business (Leifer et al., 2000). The mainframe business of IBM challenged its entry into the PC business, Kodak had robust R&D in the digital domain but its commercialization was squelched by Kodak's film business and Corning faces barriers to commercializing new business creation in areas outside of glass and ceramics. While large companies can launch RI, they just don't know how to do it over and over again as needed and have a hard time building legitimacy for an institutionalized innovation function. In the past, programs set up by large companies to foster repeated high-impact innovation have often been perceived as failures and shut down within four years of initiation. This wastes resources and compromises the future. How does a company go from a paper and rubber company to a cell phone company? Or from a light bulb company to a molecular imaging company? Or from a mining company to a health, nutrition and materials company. The Boston Consulting Group reported that 90 percent of organizations believe innovation is a strategic priority for 2004 and beyond. But 81 percent of the 550 companies surveyed by Loewe and Dominiquini (2006) questioned their innovation effectiveness. Our ongoing research on RI launched in 1995 reveals that innovation effectiveness continues to be a challenge (Leifer et al., 2000; O'Connor et al., 2008; O'Connor and Peters, 2011; Peters et al., 2011).

We think we have some answers for companies in the twenty-first century based on our multidisciplinary, prospective study of RI in large established multinational companies. We claim that organizing sustainable RI programs requires:

1. Developing a spectrum of innovation competencies.
2. Monitoring company innovation capacity.
3. Harmonizing this capacity with investment in innovation competencies.
4. Institutionalizing RI by clarifying roles and responsibilities at different levels of the corporation and identifying suitable career options for innovation experts.
5. Metrics used to evaluate the performance of RI initiatives, that go beyond the value of a specific product or new business created.

We define radical or breakthrough innovation as the ability of an organization to commercialize products and technologies that have (a) high impact on the market in terms of offering wholly new benefits, and (b) high impact on the firm in terms of their ability to spawn whole new lines of business. These are situations that involve high levels of market, resource, technical and organizational uncertainty. In consultation with the Industrial Research Institute (IRI), a professional organization of directors of research, we operationalized these impact levels as projects with the potential to offer either (a) new to the world performance features; (b) significant (e.g., 5–10×) improvement in known features, or (c) significant (e.g., 30–50 percent) reduction in cost.

So what are companies doing wrong? Many think that a 'call to action' from leadership will do it. Some look to investing in small firms as a path to breakthroughs and others make it the responsibility of a small group. Then there are those who engage an organizational development group to foster 'culture' change. None of these is sufficient on its own. All are needed simultaneously, operating as a well-integrated innovation system. There are, however, fundamental practices that need to be undertaken to drive such a system.

The building blocks or competencies (O'Connor et al., 2008) related to these practices are:

- **Discovery**, which involves activities that build skills of imagination and creativity and the ability to link sources of ideas to market and application spaces.
- **Incubation**, which relies on experimentation that will help the organization understand how identified opportunities may play out as businesses.
- **Acceleration**, which requires building a solid foundation for a fledgling business by developing processes and resources for growth and sustainability.
- **Orchestration** requires activities aimed at achieving timely project pacing and learning and shaping innovation strategy.

Orchestration aims to develop and maintain a management system for innovation. The elements of management systems for operational excellence and RI are similar, but the associated practices are different. Orchestrators must align them according to a company's overarching goals and capacity.

If any of the building blocks are missing you run into problems. For example, many companies have a robust process for idea generation but the ideas go nowhere, even the good ones. Most likely such companies do not have a competency in building businesses linked appropriately to the idea-generation activity or they do not take time to test business hypotheses. The punchline is that incubation is missing in most firms today. Let's say, for example, you are a member of corporate R&D for DuPont and, in working in your lab, you discover a certain fiber that emits light 40,0000 times faster than has been previously shown. You tell your boss, who sees its immediate application to display technology in laptops. He tells the appropriate division, they agree to fund the work and off you go. But is anyone asking what else this physical property, this material, might be useful for: medical equipment applications? Automotive applications? Energy savings in consumer electronics? There are myriad opportunities and many potential value propositions to be tested. Together they could generate a whole new platform for DuPont. But alas, no incubation capability, no one to conduct those market experiments. Discovery without incubation under-leverages opportunities.

In addition to falling short in terms of insufficient attention to breakthrough innovation (BI) competencies and their linkages, companies often fail to recognize that BI practices need to be attuned to their innovation capacity. Culture, business environment and attention-begetting things, such as lawsuits, mergers and acquisitions, are features determining capacity, which changes over time. The failure of firms to sustain a disciplined innovation system is often because management overlooks the need to align these programs with innovation capacity or takes steps to reshape it. Capacity sets the stage for how managerial strategies can deploy BI outcomes. This translates to another requirement of orchestration and that goes beyond the activities required to knit competencies together. Orchestration's aim is to organize and deploy BI options toward corporate survival.

If firms don't innovate, given the tempo of today's fast-paced environment, they will not survive. Even in a constrained or weakening economy there are opportunities for innovation. Companies that put in place an innovation system or function will handle environmental turmoil more effectively. The innovation system as we see it is not just around new business creation or new product development. The identified competencies and approach can also lead to innovating around cost, business model innovation or access to key materials or inputs. It can lead to more effective organizational design and performance-improving activities such as readiness for change and adopting new resources and technology (Brix and Peters, 2015a, 2015b). This approach can work for small and medium-sized companies but the target audience is large, established multinational corporations. It informs corporate adapters as well as those firms that are inclined to shape turbulence to their advantage (Hagel et al., 2008).

Conclusions

Our arguments are supported by empirical observation informed by business principles. During the first five years we investigated radical innovation projects (Leifer et al., 2000). During the second five years we studied firms with a strategic intent to put in place a breakthrough innovation program or system (O'Connor et al., 2008). The current phase is on institutionalizing a breakthrough innovation capability through people (O'Connor et al., 2011; Peters et al., 2011).

LOIS S. PETERS

References

Brix, J. and Peters, L.S. (2015a), Exploring an innovation project as a source of change in organization design, *Journal of Organization Design*, **4**(1), 29–43.

Brix, J. and Peters, L.S. (2015b), The performance-improving benefits of a radical innovation initiative, *International Journal of Productivity and Performance Management*, **64**(3), 356–376.

Day, D. (1994), Raising radicals: different processes for championing innovative corporate ventures, *Organization Science*, **5**(2): 149–172.

Hagel, J., Seely Brown, J. and Lang, D. (2008), Shaping strategy in a world of constant disruption, *Harvard Business Review*, **86**(10), 80–89.

Leifer, R., McDermott, C., O'Connor, G.C., Peters, L., Rice, M. and Veryzer, R.W. (2000), *Radical Innovation: How Mature Firms Can Outsmart Upstarts*, Boston: Harvard Business School Press.

Loewe, P. and Dominiquini, J. (2006), Overcoming the barriers to effective innovation, *Strategy and Leadership*, **34**(1), 24–31.

O'Connor, G. and Peters, L.S. (2011), Finding talent for breakthrough innovation, in *Innovation Management*, Raleigh, NC: Center for Innovation Management Studies, NC State University, pp. 8–11.

O'Connor, G., Leifer, R., Paulson, A. and Peters, L. (2008), *Grabbing Lightning: Building a Capability for Breakthrough Innovation*, New York: Jossey-Bass.

Peters, L.S., O'Connor, G., Farrington, T. and Kirk, B. (2011), Institutionalizing innovation competency through people, *Research Technology Management*, **54**(6), 56–59.

19 Impact of Entrepreneurship

Introduction
Entrepreneurship affects individuals, regions and entire economies. For that reason, it has also begun to impact public policy, through a variety of programs designed to maximize its positive – and minimize its negative – effects. This chapter briefly reviews these impacts in turn.

Evidence on the impact of entrepreneurship
The impact of entrepreneurship on individuals can be understood in terms of both financial rewards and non-financial satisfaction. In terms of financial returns, an influential paper by Hamilton (2000), which compared raw earnings data taken from the US Survey of Incomes and Program Participation, found that all but the most successful self-employed respondents seemed to earn less than employees. Hamilton suggested that non-financial rewards such as greater autonomy in self-employment (Benz and Frey, 2004) might explain why people nevertheless chose to become entrepreneurs. However, once one corrects for measurement error, in particular income underreporting by the self-employed, the financial impact of entrepreneurship turns out to be much more favorable than Hamilton estimated. Many recent comparisons now estimate that entrepreneurs earn higher incomes on average than employees (Parker, 2009, ch. 13; Astebro and Chen, 2014).

Turning from flows to stocks, other evidence shows that entrepreneurship is associated with above-average savings and wealth accumulation (Quadrini, 2000). However, it is also true that entrepreneurs earn returns on their business equity that do not compensate them for the greater risk they bear compared with diversified equity investors (Moskowitz and Vissing-Jørgensen, 2002). Hence, entrepreneurship appears to positively impact wealth creation, if not investment returns. Entrepreneurship is also associated with upward social mobility in both the US (Gentry and Hubbard, 2004) and the UK (Frankish et al., 2014). US evidence suggests that entrepreneurship facilitates upward mobility for members of both advantaged and disadvantaged ethnic groups (Bradford, 2003).

Overall, entrepreneurship has been found to positively and substantially impact both job and life satisfaction (Aguilar et al., 2013; Schneck, 2014). This individual non-financial return to entrepreneurship is a remarkably robust finding, which holds across countries and cultures as well as over different periods of time (Parker, 2009: ch. 4). Hence in nonfinancial terms, entrepreneurship overall seems to have a positive impact on individuals' lives, despite the bad experiences of a few unlucky entrepreneurs resulting from overwork, marital breakdown or bankruptcy.

Entrepreneurship also affects regional prosperity. Silicon Valley is a prominent example of a successful entrepreneurial region: startups, innovation and job creation are all jointly observed there (Saxenian, 1994). Regions that depend on the employment provided by a few large firms rather than entrepreneurship are more vulnerable to adverse trends in downsizing, acquisitions and global downturns (Feldman, 2014). High levels of entrepreneurial activity in cities and regions promote further startups later on, reinforcing the geographical concentration of entrepreneurship (Parker, 2005). This turns out to be important, because entrepreneurship appears to stimulate regional employment growth, both directly via new competition and production and also indirectly by challenging incumbent firms to become more efficient and expand by pursuing new growth opportunities (Fritsch, 2013). In summary, both theory and evidence points to a strongly positive impact of entrepreneurship on the evolution of regional rates of employment and income growth.

At the level of the national economy, entrepreneurship seems to drive innovation, productivity and employment growth, and wealth accumulation. Entrepreneurs introduce into the economy a disproportionate number of radical, path-breaking innovations (Baumol, 2004), in contrast to large incumbent firms, which often focus more on incremental process innovations. Viewed from an aggregate perspective, entrepreneurship involves abundant, audacious and ongoing experimentation, most of which does not succeed, but some of which does, creating fantastic social value in the process. Just the four examples of Apple, Amazon, Google and Facebook attest to the massive economic and social impact of successful innovative entrepreneurship.

Through 'creative destruction,' entrepreneurs rewrite the rules of business in numerous industries. That ranges from the mundane (e.g., ordering taxicabs via Uber) to the exotic (travelling to outer space via Space X). Even capital-intensive industries get disrupted by entrepreneurship, as we have seen in telecommunications and are likely to witness soon in the field of energy generation. In the process, entrepreneurs replace less efficient technologies and firms with more productive technologies and business models, which adds up to a sizeable impact on economy-wide productivity. For example, over the long run, the exit of incumbents and the entry of new firms accounts for more than half of productivity growth (Foster et al., 2001). Since productivity drives real wages and prosperity, this provides a direct link between entrepreneurship and economic growth. Another such linkage occurs via knowledge spillovers, through which entrepreneurs commercially exploit knowledge generated by corporate R&D labs or universities, which would otherwise go unused (Audretsch and Lehmann, 2006).

All of these reasons suggest that entrepreneurship should have a positive impact on aggregate incomes. From an empirical standpoint, this is actually a surprisingly hard thesis to test rigorously, and the macro time series evidence that exists on this issue is suggestive but inconclusive (Parker, 2009: ch. 11). There is more of a consensus about the impact of entrepreneurship on the business cycle, which is usually found to be positive and exhibits positive feedback (Parker, 2012; Parker et al., 2012).

The evidence on the impact of entrepreneurship on aggregate wealth accumulation, in contrast, is stronger and more consistent. Entrepreneurs are responsible for a disproportionate share of aggregate US wealth (Gentry and Hubbard, 2004), generating fortunes for themselves and their offspring. Entrepreneurship also seems to increase wealth inequality, however (Meh, 2005).

Conclusions

In view of the positive and substantial impact of entrepreneurship on outcomes in regional and national economies, it is perhaps unsurprising that governments the world over have responded with policy agendas intended to stimulate it. Public policy measures relating to entrepreneurship include loan guarantee schemes to help credit-constrained entrepreneurs access bank loans; employment assistance schemes to encourage welfare recipients to transition into self-employment; and programs designed to screen and develop innovations to attract private venture capital (Parker, 2009: chs. 15–17). Entrepreneurship has therefore had a major impact on public policy, despite unevenness in the successful applications of the policy set tried out to date.

SIMON PARKER

References

Aguilar, A.C., Garcia Munoz, T.M. and Moro-Egido, A.I. (2013), Heterogeneous self-employment and satisfaction in Latin America, *Journal of Economic Psychology*, **39**, 44–61.

Astebro, T. and Chen, J. (2014), The entrepreneurial earnings puzzle: mismeasurement or real? *Journal of Business Venturing*, **29**, 88–105.

Audretsch, D.B. and Lehmann, E. (2006), Location and new venture creation, in S.C. Parker (ed.), *The Life Cycle of Entrepreneurial Ventures*, New York: Springer, pp. 137–160.

Baumol, W.J. (2004), *The Free Market Innovation Machine: Analyzing the Growth Miracle of Capitalism*, Princeton, NJ: Princeton University Press.

Benz, M. and Frey, B.S. (2004), Being independent is a great thing: subjective evaluations of self-employment and hierarchy, *Economica*, **75**, 362–383.

Bradford, W.D. (2003), The wealth dynamics of entrepreneurship for black and white families in the US, *Review of Income & Wealth*, **49**(1), 89–116.

Feldman, M.P. (2014), The character of innovative places: entrepreneurial strategy, economic development and prosperity, *Small Business Economics*, **43**, 9–20.

Foster, L., Haltiwanger, J. and Krizan, C.J. (2001), Aggregate productivity growth: lessons from microeconomic evidence, in C.R. Hulten, E.R. Dean and M.J. Harper (eds),

New Developments in Productivity Analysis, Chicago, IL: University of Chicago Press, pp. 303–372.

Frankish, J.S., Roberts, R.G., Coad, A. and Storey, D.J. (2014), Is entrepreneurship a route out of deprivation? *Regional Studies*, **48**(6), 1090–1107.

Fritsch, M. (2013), New business formation and regional development – a survey and assessment of the evidence, *Foundations and Trends in Entrepreneurship*, **9**, 249–364.

Gentry, W.M. and Hubbard, R.G. (2004), Entrepreneurship and household saving, *BEP Advances in Economic Analysis & Policy*, **4**(1), 1–55.

Hamilton, B.H. (2000), Does entrepreneurship pay? An empirical analysis of the returns to self-employment, *Journal of Political Economy*, **108**, 604–631.

Meh, A.A. (2005), Entrepreneurship, wealth inequality and taxation, *Review of Economic Dynamics*, **8**, 688–719.

Moskowitz, T.J. and Vissing-Jørgensen, A. (2002), The returns to entrepreneurial investment: a private equity premium puzzle? *American Economic Review*, **92**, 745–778.

Parker, S.C. (2005), Explaining regional variations in entrepreneurship as multiple occupational equilibria, *Journal of Regional Science*, **45**, 829–850.

Parker, S.C. (2009), *The Economics of Entrepreneurship*, Cambridge: Cambridge University Press.

Parker, S.C. (2012), Theories of entrepreneurship, innovation and the business cycle, *Journal of Economic Surveys*, **26**(3), 377–394.

Parker, S.C., Congregado, E. and Golpe, A. (2012), Is entrepreneurship a leading or lagging indicator of the business cycle? Evidence from the UK, *International Small Business Journal*, **30**(7), 736–753.

Quadrini, V. (2000), Entrepreneurship, saving, and social mobility, *Review of Economic Dynamics*, **3**, 1–40.

Saxenian, A. (1994), *Regional Advantage: Culture and Competition in Silicon Valley and Route 128*, Cambridge, MA: Harvard University Press.

Schneck, S. (2014), Why the self-employed are happier: evidence from 25 European countries, *Journal of Business Research*, **67**, 1043–1048.

20 Incubators and Accelerators

Introduction

A *business incubator* is an organization designed to accelerate the growth and success of entrepreneurial companies. An incubator brings in an external management team to manage an idea. Depending on vintage and specific objectives, incubators can focus on tasks such as job creation, professional services, training, networking, venture capital financing and utilization of specific technologies. Aerts et al. (2007) highlight how incubators guide starting enterprises through their growth process, and constitute a strong instrument to promote innovation and entrepreneurship. While the Batavia Industrial Center (New York, 1959) was the first US incubator, broader growth of this type of organization did not occur until the 1980s.

The literature identifies several different types of incubators. The university-based incubators, and university-associated business incubators link entrepreneurial talent and skills to specific types of technologies, capital and services. The private business incubators provide any aspect of a wide range of support and services. Lewis et al. (2011) note another type of incubator, the international business incubator, which concentrates on international firms that want to access overseas markets and resources.

As noted by Lewis et al. (2011), the development of *business accelerators* was inspired by the development of the incubators. They note that an accelerator can be either: (a) an advanced stage incubation program that assists relatively mature entrepreneurial firms and may be ready for external financing; or (b) an organization that contains hybrid business incubation programs designed for incubators to enter the market. According to Miller and Bound (2011), accelerators have been driven almost exclusively by private investors, and concentrated in the internet and mobile sectors. They note several key characteristics of accelerators: (a) open and competitive applications process; (b) pre-seed investment, typically in exchange for equity; (c) focus on small teams as opposed to individuals; and (d) limited-duration and intensive mentoring.

Incubators and accelerators share some common features. Wu (2012) notes that there are five principal elements in the value provided by the accelerator for startups: human capital, signaling and credibility, search costs, networking, and venture capital. Miller and Bound (2011) note that in contrast to the incubators, the benefits of the accelerator programs can include angel investors. Cohen (2013) succinctly summarizes the differences between the three concepts, which are noted in Table 20.1.

Table 20.1   Key differences between incubators, accelerators and angel investors

	Incubators	Accelerators	Angel investors
Duration	1–5 years	3 months	Ongoing
Cohorts	No	Yes	No
Business model	Rent; nonprofit	Investment, can also be nonprofit	Investment
Selection	Noncompetitive	Competitive, cyclical	Competitive, ongoing
Venture stage	Early, or late	Early	Early
Education	Ad hoc, human resources, legal	Seminars	None
Mentorship	Minimal, tactical	Intense, by self and others	As needed, by investor
Venture location	Onsite	Onsite	Offsite

Characteristics and evolution

The literature on incubators and accelerators provides considerable details on the characteristics of incubators and accelerators, and how some of these features have evolved over time.

Barbero et al. (2014) note that incubators are quite heterogeneous, and can be of four types: (a) basic research; (b) university; (c) economic development; and (d) private incubator. Bøllingtoft and Ulhøi (2005) note a new incubator model, the networked incubator, which is a hybrid form of the typical incubator, based on territorial synergy, relational symbiosis and economies of scope.

In terms of the similarities and differences in the services provided, Bruneel et al. (2012) find that while all generations offered similar support services, tenants in the older generation of incubators made less use of the service portfolio. They suggest that this is a consequence of slack selection criteria and the absence of clearly defined exit policies among different incubators. Scillitoe and Chakrabarti (2010) highlight variations in counseling and networking interactions across incubators, and how these features impact the incubation process of new ventures. Aernoudt (2004) focuses on the dynamic process of incubation and highlights the importance of close links between incubators and business angel networks.

Historically, the US had attained significant maturity in the development of incubators and accelerators. In examining similarities and differences, Aernoudt (2004) notes that one of the barriers for the development of incubators in Europe was the lack of entrepreneurship and the underdevelopment of seed financing and business angel networks. Often, very different approaches tended to be associated with the incubator concept. Aerts et al. (2007) compare the screening practices between European and US incubators. They find that most incubators do not screen potential tenants on a balanced set of factors, but concentrate either on the characteristics of the tenant's market or the management team. They find that the tenant survival rate is positively related to a more balanced screening profile.

Innovation and entrepreneurship

The objectives of incubators and accelerators, broadly speaking, are to foster entrepreneurship and innovation among SMEs. Numerous studies have examined the effects the incubators and accelerators have on alternative measures of performance. Table 20.2 presents examples of some noteworthy accelerators, along with information on the levels of funding and prominent startups.

Colombo and Delmastro (2002) conclude that science parks are an important element of overall technology strategy and policy. They find

Table 20.2   Accelerator examples

Name	Country (location)	Year	$Total ($average)	Startups	Startups – selected examples
Y Combinator	USA (Silicon Valley)	2005	$4,029.12 (5.81)	694	Dropbox, AirBnb, Strip, Optimizely, Zenefits
TechStars Boulder	USA (Boulder)	2007	$249.48 (3.24)	77	DigitalOcean, Gearbox, SendGrid, Take Comics, FullContact
AngelPad	USA (San Francisco)	2010	$231.21 (2.72)	85	Crittercism, Vungle, Postmates, MoPub, ElasticBox
TechStars Boston	USA (Boston)	2009	$199.67 (2.40)	83	Localytics, Kinvey, EverTrue, GrabCAD, PillPack
500startups	USA (Silicon Valley)	2010	$178.49 (0.74)	240	Club W, Whill, visual.ly, 955dreams, InternMatch
Seedcamp	UK (London)	2007	$130.83 (1.10)	118	Transferwise, Basekit, GrabCad, Profitero, zemanta
DreamIT Ventures	USA (Philadelphia)	2008	$123.22 (1.95)	63	SeatGeek, SCVNGR, Adapt.ly, MindSnacks, Parsely
fbFund	USA (Silicon Valley)	2007	$110.42 (2.45)	45	Life360, Kontagent, Koofers, BarTab, Networked Blogs
Mucker Lab	USA (Santa Monica)	2012	$110.06 (5.79)	19	Surf Air, Retention Science, Lifecrowd, Younity, The Black Tux
RockHealth	USA (San Francisco)	2010	$71.25 (1.45)	49	Omada Health, Kit Check, Mango Health, CellScope, Sano Intelligence
Flashpoint	USA (Atlanta, Geo)	2011	$63.30 (1.66)	38	Ionic Security, Pindrop Security, Springbot, eCommHub, Lucena

Table 20.2 (continued)

Name	Country (location)	Year	$Total ($average)	Startups	Startups – selected examples
LaunchpadLA	USA (Los Angeles)	2009	$61.70 (2.37)	26	Tradesy, Chromatik, ChowNow, Preact, DanceOn
Brandery	USA (Cincinnati)	2010	$60.69 (1.78)	34	FlightCar, Bitcasa, Pingage, RoadTrippers, ChoreMonster
Springboard	UK (London)	2009	$53.97 (2.15)	25	PagerDuty, Hassle.com (prev. Teddle), Birdback, Apiary.io, PlayMob
Portland Incubator Experiment	USA (Portland)	2009	$51.63 (2.34)	22	VendScreen, Cloudability, Orchestrate, Vadio, Little Bird
StartmateLink	Australia (Sydney)	2011	$16.62 (0.79)	21	Scriptrock, Ninja Blocks, Bugcrowd, Bugherd, Happy Inspector
FounderFuelLink	Canada (Montreal)	2011	$11.88 (0.32)	37	ooomf, Notesolution, Seevibes, Playerize, Urbita
ChinacceleratorLink	China (Shanghai)	2010	$10.05 (0.32)	31	OrderWithMe, AYLIEN, Splitforce, Piktochart, Kwestr
Le CampingLink	France (Paris)	2011	$9.95 (0.20)	48	Sketchfab, infinit, docTrackr, Augment, qunb
Rockstart AcceleratorLink	Netherlands (Amsterdam)	2011	$9.94 (0.25)	39	3Dhubs, Wercker, Syndicate Plus, PastBook, Peerby

Note: Year is the start year. $Total ($average) refers to the total (average) funding ($ millions). Startups is total number of startups.

that the: (a) Italian science parks attracted entrepreneurs with better human capital; (b) on-incubator firms had higher growth rates than their off-incubator counterparts and performed better in terms of adoption of advanced technologies, aptitude to participating in international R&D programs and establishment of collaborative arrangements, especially with universities; and (c) they had easier access to public subsidies.

Barbero et al. (2014) find that some types of incubators were more prolific in generating product and process innovations than others. Using data on Helsinki-based incubators, Abetti (2004) finds a positive relationship between incubators and economic growth. Rice (2002) finds that the allocation of the time of the incubator manager, the intensity of intervention, the breadth of co-production and the readiness of the entrepreneur to engage in co-production are important factors affecting the output elasticities related to co-production inputs. Clausen and Rasmussen (2011) find that by acting as open innovation intermediaries, publicly supported incubators were able to transfer knowledge from large firms to society. They argue that most of these activities would not have taken place without the incubators. In contrast to the characteristics-based evidence above, Chen (2009) finds that incubator and venture capital support influenced technology commercialization and the performance of new ventures.

Some studies, however, have questioned the generality of the findings in the literature. Phan et al. (2005) note that there is no systematic framework to assess science parks and incubators, that there is a failure to understand their characteristics as well as that of the companies located on them, and that there is a lack of clarity regarding the performance of science parks. Chan and Lau (2005), using data on technology startups in the Hong Kong Science Park, found that the benefits required by technology founders at different stages of development are varied. As a result, they question the general conclusion that incubators are useful to technology startups.

Role of universities

The evidence suggests a significant role played by various university-based science parks in fostering innovation and entrepreneurship. Table 20.3 notes some of the university-based incubators, and reveals wide variation in the types and number of institutions that form the organization.

In terms of specific evidence, Rothaermel and Thursby (2005a), using data on 79 technology ventures, find evidence of knowledge flows from universities to incubator firms. Their findings suggest that incubator firms' absorptive capacity is an important factor when transforming university knowledge into firm-level competitive advantage. In a related paper, Rothaermel and Thursby (2005b) focus on two types of university linkages to the sponsoring institution: a license obtained from the university

Table 20.3   University-based incubator examples

Name	Country (Location)	Year	Type	Institution(s)
Rice Alliance for Technology and Entrepreneurship	USA (Houston)	2000	UBI	Rice University
SETsquared	UK (Bristol, Southampton, Bath, Guildford, Exeter)	2003	UBI	University of Bath, Bristol, Exeter, Southampton, Surrey
SCUT National University Science Park	China (Guangzhou)	1999	UBI	South China University of Technology
ATP Innovations	Australia (Sydney)	2000	UBI	University of Sydney; University of Technology, Sydney; Australian National University; University of New South Wales
Digital Media Zone	Canada (Toronto)	2010	UBI	Ryerson University
IncubaUC	Chile (Santiago)	2002	UBI	Pontifical Catholic University of Chile
Industry Accelerator and Patent Strategy	Taiwan (Hsinchu City)	2013	UBI	National Chiao Tung University
Encubator	Sweden (Gothenburg)	2001	UBI	Chalmers University of Technology
Instituto Genesis PUC–Rio	Brazil (Rio de Janeiro)	1997	UBI	Pontifical Catholic University of Rio de Janeiro
TEC Edmonton	Canada (Edmonton)	2004	UBI	University of Alberta
INiTS Universitäres Gründerservice Wien	Austria (Vienna)	2002	UBI	Vienna University of Technology, Vienna University "Alma Mater Rudolphina"
DTU Symbion Innovation	Denmark (Copenhagen)	2009	UBI	Technical University of Denmark
Melbourne Accelerator Program	Australia (Melbourne)	2012	UBI	University of Melbourne
HUST Science Park Development Corp.	China (Wuhan)	2001	UBI	Huazhong University of Science and Technology

114

Name	Country (City)	Year	Type	University
Incubatore di Imprese Innovative del Politecnico di Torino (I3P)	Italy (Turin)	1999	UBI	Politecnico di Torino
VentureLab	USA (Atlanta)	2001	UBI	Georgia Institute of Technology
Uppsala Innovation Centre	Sweden (Uppsala)	2004	UBI	Swedish University of Agricultural Sciences; Uppsala University
NDRC	Ireland (Dublin)	2008	UBI	Dublin City University; Dún Laoghaire Institute of Art, Design and Technology; National College of Art and Design; Trinity College Dublin; University College Dublin
Western Research Parks	Canada (Ontario)	1989	UBI	Western University
Chrysalis	Chile (Valparaíso)	2012	UBI	Pontifica Catholic University of Valparaíso
National Chiao Tung University Business Incubation Center	Taiwan (Hsinchu City)	1998	UBI	National Chiao Tung University
iMinds	Belgium (Ghent)	2004	UBI	University of Antwerp; University of Leuven; Ghent University; Vrije Universiteit Brussel
Youngstown Business Incubator	USA (Youngstown)	1995	UABI	Kent State University; University of Akron; Hiram College; Youngstown State University; Case Western Reserve University
H-FARM Ventures	Italy (Roncade)	2005	UABI	Università Ca' Foscari Venezia
TechColumbus	USA (Columbus)	2005	UABI	Ohio State University; Columbus State Community College; Otterbein University; Denison University

Table 20.3 (continued)

Name	Country (Location)	Year	Type	Institution(s)
Montpellier Agglomeration Business & Innovation Centre	France (Paris)	1991	UABI	Montpellier University
Hub China	China (Beijing)	2013	UABI	Capital Normal University; Beijing Technology and Business University; North China University of Technology
Los Angeles Cleantech Incubator	USA (Los Angeles)	2011	UABI	University of Southern California; University of California, Los Angeles; California Institute of Technology; California State University, Northridge
Stiftelsen Chalmers Innovation	Sweden (Gothenburg)	1999	UABI	Chalmers University of Technology
Nanotechnology Incubator	Mexico (Monterrey)	2005	UABI	Instituto de Innovación y Transferencia de Tecnología de Nuevo León
1871	USA (Chicago)	2012	UABI	Northwestern University; University of Chicago; Illinois Institute of Technology; University of Illinois; DePaul University
Nuvolab	Italy (Milan)	2011	UABI	Universita' Cattolica del Sacro Cuore; Scuola Superiore Sant'anna

Note: Year is the start year. The incubators are either: (a) UBI (University Business Incubator); or (b) UABI (University Associated Business Incubator). The information on the institutions involved is mostly from the website of UBI Index (http://ubiindex.com).

and a link to university faculty. They examine whether a university link to the sponsoring institution reduces the probability of new venture failure and, at the same time, retards timely graduation. Their evidence suggests that these effects are more pronounced the stronger the university link. Markman et al. (2005) find that whereas for-profit university technology transfer offices are positively related to new venture formation, traditional university and nonprofit transfer offices are more likely to correlate with the presence of university-based business incubators.

McAdam and McAdam (2008) note the paucity of studies exploring how lifecycle development within high-technology business firms in university science parks can affect how they use the resources and opportunities. Using interviews and surveys of high technology business firms within two university parks, they find that a high-technology firm's propensity to make effective use of the university parks' resources and support increases as the lifecycle stage of the company increases and the small firm searches for independence and autonomy. Lockett and Wright (2005) find that the number of spinout companies created, and the number of spinout companies created with equity investment, are positively associated with expenditure on intellectual property protection, the business development capabilities of technology transfer offices and the royalty regime of the university.

Conclusions

Looking at the big picture, the literature reveals that while incubators and accelerators are widespread and appear to have a positive effect on innovation and entrepreneurship, there are gaps in our understanding of the intricate linkages between the characteristics of the two types of organizations and the performance they deliver. The differences in characteristics occur in these organizations within a country, as well as potentially pronounced differences across countries due to social, cultural and economic issues, and the structure of financial markets. Future research perhaps can concentrate on unraveling these relationships.

VIVEK GHOSAL

References

Abetti, P.A. (2004), Government-supported incubators in the Helsinki region, Finland: infrastructure, results, and best practices, *The Journal of Technology Transfer*, **29**(1), 19–40.

Aernoudt, R. (2004), Incubators: tool for entrepreneurship? *Small Business Economics*, **23**(2), 127–135.

Aerts, K.P., Matthyssens, P. and Vandenbempt, K. (2007), Critical role and screening practices of European business incubators, *Technovation*, **27**(5), 254–267.

Barbero, J.L., Casillas, J.C., Wright, M. and Garcia, A.R. (2014), Do different types of incubators produce different types of innovations? *The Journal of Technology Transfer*, **39**(2), 151–168.

Bøllingtoft, A. and Ulhøi, J.P. (2005), The networked business incubator – leveraging entrepreneurial agency? *Journal of Business Venturing*, **20**(2), 265–290.

Bruneel, J., Ratinho, T., Clarysse, B. and Groen, A. (2012), The evolution of business incubators: comparing demand and supply of business incubation services across different incubator generations, *Technovation*, **32**(2), 110–121.

Chan, K.F. and Lau, T. (2005), Assessing technology incubator programs in the science park: the good, the bad and the ugly, *Technovation*, **25**(10), 1215–1228.

Chen, C. (2009), Technology commercialization, incubator and venture capital, and new venture performance, *Journal of Business Research*, **62**(1), 93–103.

Clausen, T. and Rasmussen, E. (2011), Open innovation policy through intermediaries: the industry incubator program in Norway, *Technology Analysis & Strategic Management*, **23**(1), 75–85.

Cohen, S. (2013), What do accelerators do? Insights from incubators and angels, *Innovations*, **8**(3), 19–25.

Colombo, M.G. and Delmastro, M. (2002), How effective are technology incubators? Evidence from Italy, *Research Policy*, **31**(7), 1103–1122.

Lewis, D.A., Harper-Anderson, E. and Molnar, L.A. (2011), Incubating success: incubation best practices that lead to successful new ventures, Washington, DC: US Department of Commerce, Economic Development Administration.

Lockett, A. and Wright, M. (2005), Resources, capabilities, risk capital and the creation of university spin-out companies, *Research Policy*, **34**(7), 1043–1057.

Markman, G.D., Phan, P.H., Balkin, D.B. and Gianiodis, P.T. (2005), Entrepreneurship and university-based technology transfer, *Journal of Business Venturing*, **20**(2), 241–263.

McAdam, M. and McAdam, R. (2008), High tech start-ups in University Science Park incubators: the relationship between the start-up's lifecycle progression and use of the incubator's resources, *Technovation*, **28**(5), 277–290.

Miller, P. and Bound, K. (2011), *The Startup Factories: The Rise of Accelerator Programs to Support New Technology Ventures*, NESTA discussion paper.

Phan, P.H., Siegel, D.S. and Wright, M. (2005), Science parks and incubators: observations, synthesis and future research, *Journal of Business Venturing*, **20**(2), 165–182.

Rice, M.P. (2002), Co-production of business assistance in business incubators: an exploratory study, *Journal of Business Venturing*, **17**(2), 163–187.

Rothaermel, F.T. and Thursby, M. (2005a), University–incubator firm knowledge flows: assessing their impact on incubator firm performance, *Research Policy*, **34**(3), 305–320.

Rothaermel, F.T. and Thursby, M. (2005b), Incubator firm failure or graduation? The role of university linkages, *Research Policy*, **34**(7), 1076–1090.

Scillitoe, J.L. and Chakrabarti, A.K. (2010), The role of incubator interactions in assisting new ventures, *Technovation*, **30**(3), 155–167.

Wu, A. (2012), Do startup accelerators deliver value? The economics of creating companies, *MIT Entrepreneurship Review*, August 14.

21 Innovating through Licensing

Introduction

Multinational corporations constantly reach outside their boundaries, viewing the world as a global canvas dotted with dispersed pockets of knowledge. Research suggests that multinationals that source such dispersed knowledge – by identifying and accessing diverse competencies, innovative technologies and leading market knowledge – innovate more effectively than their domestic rivals (Doz et al., 2001). Research also has acknowledged that the search for diverse knowledge around the globe is one of the key drivers of foreign direct investment. Traditionally, research has focused on the implications of sourcing knowledge from established local subsidiaries in particular host countries through long-term foreign direct investments (Berry, 2006; Cantwell, 1989; Chung and Alcácer, 2002; Nachum and Zaheer, 2005). Today, multinational corporations increasingly are investing in sourcing knowledge via non-equity modes of international production such as licensing. This trend is affecting a multitude of industries, yet there is probably no better example of the importance and the prevalence of knowledge sourcing of this kind than the global pharmaceutical industry (Mudambi and Hannigan, 2013; United Nations, 2011).

The global pharmaceutical industry generates revenues of more than $800 billion a year and is involved in the discovery, development, manufacturing, marketing and distribution of medical drugs. Intellectual property protection and product testing are two defining attributes of this industry. Since both activities are at earlier stages of the value chain, the industry can be characterized as one that is investment intensive. There is substantial research that goes into drug discovery and development, and firms seek to extract as much revenue from successful drug releases as possible. Intellectual property is therefore a crucial asset to the pharmaceutical industry, and patents remain the primary protection method. However, drug patents have a limited shelf life, and to compete effectively companies either must continue to extract revenue from existing discoveries by finding new applications for old drugs or establish new sources of income from the discovery of new drugs. This is clearly an industry where the increasing cost of drug discovery and the expiration of key patents have forced firms to broaden their repertoire of knowledge-sourcing options in order to maintain robust drug pipelines to ensure stable and consistent growth. A key trend since 1980 has been the proliferation of licensing deals across the world.

A licensing agreement is a contractual arrangement whereby the owner of an intangible asset (the licensor) grants the rights to use the asset to another entity (the licensee) for a specified period and within a specified geographical domain, in exchange for a payment (royalty). Intangible assets in licensing contracts include patents, formulas, designs, copyrights, processes and trademarks. Pharmaceutical firms have realized that early stage drug development is increasingly expensive and fraught with risk. Moreover, complete ownership of the pharmaceutical value chain can be cumbersome and inefficient. The benefits of licensing in this industry include increased financial flexibility, reduced risk in pipeline development, and increased ability to leverage experience in other important areas that benefit from economies of scale, such as marketing, sales and distribution. As pressure continues to increase R&D efficiency, firms are moving to licensing deals as a key strategic alternative. The top ten pharmaceutical companies entered into 12 percent more licensing deals in 2009 than in 2008 (Datamonitor, 2010), and this growth is expected to continue.

As a number of large pharmaceutical companies learn the risks and costs of drug discovery and recognize the impending 'patent cliff' they face, their in-licensing of knowledge is becoming a more prominent strategic activity. Based on a proprietary database of global pharmaceutical firms from 1992 to 2008 (Dunlap, 2014), the percentage of in-licensed patents used by leading firms compared to those created internally varied significantly, ranging from a low of 7 percent to a high of 62 percent. Further analysis shows the outward licensing trends from a global perspective, as seen in Table 21.1. Given the dominant role of US firms within the industry, it is unsurprising to see nearly three-quarters of all patent licensing going to US firms. Indeed, much of the licensing from firms in the US stays in the country. In a similar vein, there is a fair amount of patent licensing within the core cohort of major pharmaceutical nations: the US, Great Britain, Switzerland, Japan and Germany.

Further analysis reveals that, as pharmaceutical products move further along the global value chain, emerging market countries are showing a greater absolute level of licensing activity later in the global value chain. This pattern may be attributed to the levels of risk inherent in the global value chain. Pharmaceutical licenses are complex arrangements that are often structured around contingencies such as regulatory approvals and have unique regional configurations. Early stage deals that occur at one end of the global value chain are positioned as collaborative 'discovery' partnerships, while later stage deals are parceled out as marketing and distribution deals. In early stage deals, where compounds are unknown, there is greater risk of discovery involved, and therefore many of the trading partners are likely to be established pharmaceutical firms from developed countries. An interview with a senior pharmaceutical executive in one of the BRIC countries revealed a measured opinion on later-stage licensing, from the host country's perspective. The executive noted that licensing is not seen as a part of a global strategy, but rather is largely approached as a local marketing and distribution deal. To that point, he concluded that such licensing tends to produce a negligible impact on the innovativeness of firms located in these countries.

Conclusion
To license or not remains a difficult decision since licensing deals are organic agreements with an evolving scope. The data on licensing show that deals have multiple iterations and forms, and they are often

Table 21.1   Patent licensing flows, by country: 1992–2008

Licensor country	Licensing country																	
Count of licensing country	AU	BE	CA	CH	DE	DK	FI	FR	GB	IE	IL	IN	JP	NL	NO	PR	US	Grand total
AU	1		2						3				1				10	17
BB			1															1
BE																	10	10
BM				1					5									6
CA			13			2			9								11	35
CH			1	15				5	1								13	35
CS																	1	1
CY																	2	2
DE				2	27	4		1	4								22	60
DK																	9	9
ES																	2	2
FI					1		10											11
FR	3			7				2	1								12	25
GB				3					15	5							16	39
IE	1			3					2								6	12

121

Table 21.1   (continued)

Licensor country / Count of licensing country	Licensing country																	
	AU	BE	CA	CH	DE	DK	FI	FR	GB	IE	IL	IN	JP	NL	NO	PR	US	Grand total
IL										5	4						1	10
IN												1						1
IT			2														1	3
JP				9	6			1	14				14				93	137
KR																	7	7
LU			2															2
NL				4			2	4						4			1	15
NO									2						1		6	9
PR	1															1		2
SE								1	3								10	14
US	2	4	15	46	27			14	63	2			10	6			562	751
VG								2										2
Grand total	**3**	**5**	**38**	**92**	**61**	**6**	**12**	**30**	**122**	**12**	**4**	**1**	**25**	**10**	**1**	**1**	**795**	**1218**

Source: Dunlap (2014)

122

terminated or extended as new information becomes available to either party. Similarly, as developments arise, such as clinical trial results or shifts in the regulatory environment, the structure of deals may change. Further, the introduction of new indications around a drug or compound can lead to expanded agreements. The fluid nature of licensing deals, both from a structure and a process standpoint, generates multiple data points per deal. Moreover, pharmaceutical licensing data is somewhat elusive. As the consumption of pharmaceuticals grows outside of the Western world, so does the complexity of regulatory compliance, licensing and intellectual property protection. In this regard, some industry watchers, analysts and market researchers construct proprietary databases and reports because data are not publicly available. While such proprietary databases contain some of these data, future researchers are encouraged to track the volume of deals, as well as points of origination and destination to allow for a measurement of deal flow and concentration by corporate dyad and, by implication, country location. Lastly, the way in which licensing impacts a host country remains an important topic of debate and future research for academics and practitioners alike.

DENISE DUNLAP

References

Berry, H. (2006), Leaders, laggards, and the pursuit of foreign knowledge, *Strategic Management Journal*, **27**(2), 151–168.

Cantwell, J. (ed.) (1989), *Technology Innovation and Multinational Corporations*, Oxford: Basil Blackwell.

Chung, W. and Alcácer, J. (2002), Knowledge seeking and location choice of foreign direct investment in the United States, *Management Science*, **48**(12), 1534–1554.

Datamonitor (2010), Creative solutions needed as pharmaceutical in-licensing competition heats-up, http://about.datamonitor.com/media/archives/4097.

Doz, Y.L., Santos, J. and Williamson, P. (eds) (2001), *From Global to Metanational: How Companies Win in the Knowledge Economy*, Cambridge, MA: Harvard Business School Press.

Dunlap, D. (2014), *Database on Pharmaceutical Products from 1992 to 2008*, unpublished database.

Mudambi, R. and Hannigan, T.J. (2013), Licensing, *Oxford Bibliographies*, Oxford: Oxford University Press.

Nachum, L. and Zaheer, S. (2005), The persistence of distance? The impact of technology on MNE motivations for foreign investment, *Strategic Management Journal*, **26**(8), 747–767.

United Nations (ed.) (2011), *World Investment Report on Non-Equity Modes of International Production and Investment*, Geneva: United Nations Publications.

22 Managing Creativity

Introduction

With the rise of the creative economy, the concept and traits of creative personalities have received much attention over the past 60 years. In 1950, J.P. Guilford reframed the scope and amount of creativity research by presenting his 'Structure of Intellect' (SI) theory of creativity as a combination of content, product, and operations. Prior to his famous address to the American Psychological Association, creativity was linked to high intelligence and behaviorism and Freudian psychoanalysis defined artistic creativity as a compensatory neurosis (Sawyer, 2006b: 40–41).

A number of theories evolved and by 1980 personality studies ceased as it became clear that creativity is not a scientific trait, but an idea that varies depending on cultural and historic factors (Sawyer, 2006b: 36). Failure to produce reliable measurements of creativity became obvious. Since then the focus of creativity research has shifted to three general areas: the creative thinker's cognitive processes; the creative personality; and environmental factors that interact and support creative work (Amabile and Kurtzberg, 2000). This essay presents a possible model for managing the factors that influence creative group interaction based on the social structure, history and etiquette that shape the successful outcome of a jazz jam session. Potential jammers enter the process with the expectation of creating a novel product by following certain rules and conventions. Seven prominent factors were identified in this research through interviews, survey results, literature reviews and personal experience as a professional jazz musician that shape the quality of the process and outcome. With examples from a variety of fields, suggestions for implementation in creative group settings were provided.

The jazz jam session: historical and social context

Originally used as a verb, 'jam' indicated cramming as many musicians as possible into one room or possibly the maximum number of ideas into each solo. The term 'jam session' came to denote informal gatherings of musicians from different bands and diverse playing levels allowing for extended playing opportunities away from the demands of their regular jobs. Such sessions may be arranged or arise spontaneously when musicians drop in on each other at practice studios or in public. These relaxed environments were ideal for learning and exploration of new ideas (Berliner, 1994).

During the height of the jam session culture in the 1940s and 1950s, new stylistic developments such as bebop were attributed to the after-hours gatherings at Minton's Playhouse in Harlem. Furthermore, jazz impresario Norman Granz built his commercial empire by pairing musicians in concert settings thus staging a jam session type environment with audiences responding to the explosive energy of the moment (McDonough, 1979: 31). The New York Loft Scene in the 1960s and 1970s continued the tradition of extended after-hours jamming with ample room for musical explorations (Stephenson, 2009).

A set of shared expectations and goals have shaped rules and norms for jam sessions that maintain a social structure and provide the basis for successful interaction. These rules are highly flexible and open for revision depending on the circumstances of any particular jam session, but overall help maintain a degree of stability (Nelson, 1995), enable creative collaboration and reduce individual uncertainty (Bastien and Hostager, 1988: 586). Musical structures include of course the grammar of music theory as well as songs. The chosen songs feature particular patterns of chordal structures and immediately provide information on time, chord progression, chorus length and complexity. Musicians who are familiar with the song may use this information in creating variations on musical themes. Hence, the level of collaborative creativity then directly depends on the skill and knowledge level of all collaborating musicians, with the weakest participant dictating the limits of creative potential. Social structures include behavioral norms and communication codes. Such codes are also referred to as etiquette and usually include visual and verbal cues.

Several social mechanisms and communication tools are typically present to maintain basic etiquette rules. Nelson (1995) identifies three such social mechanisms that help mediate the tension between the need for personal creativity versus the need for cooperation among the participants. First, a designated leader helps facilitate performers and their order of appearances, tunes, and tempos with varying degrees of control. Nelson refers to the second mechanism as 'sanctioning behavior,' consisting of facial expressions, body language, comments or a change in performance level and expression if a participant is in violation of an 'unwritten rule.' Such violations can be calling an unapproved tune, performing at an inappropriate level or other etiquette breaches. Finally, audience response reflects on the social reality of the event. Low response might indicate a low level of cooperation on the bandstand, while active audience responses can move the expression and cooperation of the musicians to a higher level. Other tools include a standard terminology known by the jazz insiders, such as the 'head' referring to the main melody of the tune, or 'trading fours' to a practice of exchanging bars of four between the soloists and the drummer, or 'rhythm changes' as a particular kind of form and harmonic structure. Gestures are used to indicate the next soloist or to end a song, the audience responds with applause or other body language that communicates approval or disapproval, and even the type of tune selected for a newcomer can indicate the expectations of the band. For example, calling a 'simple blues' means taking the level to the lowest denominator as an indication of uncertainty.

It is still not uncommon, however, for competitiveness, jealousy and resentment to hamper cooperative attempts. Most musicians have to pay their dues, meaning they have to prove themselves and show their commitment before being accepted in the jazz community (Berliner, 1994: 52). The social structure of jam sessions can be described as concentric circles around a core of performing musicians clustering together on stage, with the second tier being the musicians waiting to get their turn and the third tier any audience members attempting to look into that inner circle without disturbing the ambience (DeVeaux, 1997: 204).

Seven elements for successful group creativity
The historical and social synopsis of jazz jam sessions above reveals seven facilitating factors for successful group creativity. Extensive interviews, surveys, literature reviews and examples from other fields led to the following suggested list.

1.   Individual competence and knowledge of the field
Limited competence and knowledge of one participant inhibit the creative potential of the whole group. Jazz musicians spend hours every day listening to, imitating, and transcribing jazz icons (Berliner, 1994). Similarly, the Beatles honed their skills in the Hamburg strip club called Indra from 1960 to 1962, where they performed daily for eight hours. The results are legendary (Clydesdale, 2006). Thus, potential for group creativity increases by assembling experienced and competent individuals as well as providing ample time for interaction and communal learning.

2.   Practicing improvisation as the ability to overcome self-consciousness
Participation in a jam session requires taking a series of risks such as entering an unknown group of musicians, using instruments or amps that belong to someone else, possibly playing unfamiliar repertoire, and engaging in improvisation in front of an unfamiliar audience. According to research by Charles Limb and Allan Braun (2008), jazz musicians actually train their brains in this type of risk-taking by extensive deactivation of the prefrontal cortex as they engage in the process of improvisation. In order to increase creative potential, any groups should engage in regular practice of improvisation and taking risks.

3. Establishing a mentoring system and role models

The mentoring aspect of jam sessions historically developed from a need to learn the art form through oral imitation with no written materials available. More established players instructed younger players on the bandstand and functioned as role models. In fact, participants in a survey conducted by the author in 2012 indicated a rating of 4.56 on a five-point scale when asked to rate the importance of participating in jam sessions for aspiring jazz musicians (n = 365). Further evidence is a study on artistic creativity and interpersonal relationships conducted by Dean Keith Simonton (1984) that documented the positive correlation of a large number of diverse models and mentors to a successful artistic career. Thus, availability of role models and more experienced personnel increases the potential of an entrepreneurial unit.

4. Democracy and collaboration

As discussed earlier, the collective product rises and falls with the willingness of each performer to engage in this truly democratic process of trading leadership and supporting roles and contributing towards the common good at every moment during a performance. The innovation labs especially at IDEO, the award-winning global design firm with a focus on a human-centered approach to innovation (see www.ideo.com), operate on similar principles of democracy. The crucial element is the ability and willingness of participants to exchange roles in the group and provide equal opportunity for everyone to step forward as a soloist while everyone else assumes supporting roles.

5. Leaders and sidemen

An experienced performer often takes on a leadership role in a jam session functioning as liaison between the venue management, the house band, the jam session participants and the audience. For a variety of reasons, musicians might not be willing to take on such managerial tasks and rather be what is commonly referred to as 'sidemen.' As such they need to develop musical versatility in order to meet the demands of any musical settings they might get hired for. Gathering the ideal mix of leaders and sidemen was one of the ingredients for the success of Pixar Studios (Catmull, 2014). Leaders Steve Jobs, Ed Catmull, Alby Ray and John Lasseter gathered a team of 'sidemen' to collaborate with and switch off during the jam session in their specific area of expertise. A similar mix is recommended for any entrepreneurial unit.

6. Community support

The segregated black community clustered around Indiana Avenue in Indianapolis during the 1930s and 1940s was small but extremely supportive and full of opportunities. Indiana Avenue was lined with more than 40 clubs hosting nightly jam sessions and the teachers at Crispus Attucks High School believed in and supported the creativity and potential of their students. A host of legendary jazz musicians including Wes Montgomery, Slide Hampton, Freddie Hubbard, J.J. Johnson, David Baker, Larry Ridley and many more were the result of this community investment (Herzig, 2011). Further examples of successful community support include Silicon Valley and the growing number of arts districts where small organizations collaborate in creating strong arts communities with increased economic impact.

7.   Continuous evaluation systems

Immediate feedback shapes the jam session process with facial expressions, body language, comments, cues and common vocabulary, and response to audience feedback. Similarly, recent research on brainstorming techniques confirms that groups who also engage in active debate and critical feedback on ideas beyond traditional brainstorming are able to generate more meaningful results (Feinberg and Nemeth, 2008). Again, Pixar Studios incorporated this system of continuous constructive feedback in their daily meetings of the 'Brain Trust' (eight directors), shortly named 'Daily', where creative issues and progress are discussed in an environment of trust and respect (Linkner, 2011: 106).

Conclusions

Experts in a variety of fields have discussed the metaphor of the improvisational process in jazz for group creativity (Barrett, 1998; Bastien and Hostager, 1988; Dennis and Macaulay, 2003, 2007; Holbrook, 2007; Kao, 1996; Sawyer, 2006a; Weick, 1990). The seven factors discussed above facilitate successful jazz jam sessions and could be management tools for any entrepreneurial group gatherings.

Tina Seelig (2011) proposed a model for creativity and innovation based on the triangle relationship of knowledge, imagination and attitude enhanced by resources, habitats and culture. She calls it the 'Innovation Engine' and admits that mastery is complex but results can be achieved through practice and improvisatory engagement with the components. Similarly to Seelig's model, this analysis suggests the jazz jam session model and its seven factors as a management tool for group creativity. Qualitative and quantitative analysis of the impact of these factors in a variety of group settings may provide further leads and best practices for engaging in the improvisational and creative process.

MONIKA HERZIG

References

Amabile, T. and Kurtzberg, T. (2000), From Guilford to creative synergy: opening the black box of team-level creativity, *Creativity Research Journal*, **13**(3–4), 285–294.

Barrett, F. (1998), Creativity and improvisation in jazz and organizations: implications for organizational learning, *Organization Science*, **9**(5), 605–622.

Bastien, D. and Hostager, T. (1988), Jazz as a process of organizational innovation, *Communication Research*, **15**, 582–602.

Becker, H. (2000), The etiquette of improvisation, *Mind, Culture, and Activity*, **7**, 171–176 and 197–200.

Berliner, P. (1994), *Thinking in Jazz – The Infinite Art of Improvisation*, Chicago, IL: University of Chicago Press.

Berliner, P. (2007), Art Farmer on learning and improvisation, *Jazzforschung/Jazz Research*, **39**, 89–98.

Catmull, E. (2014), *Creativity, Inc.: Overcoming the Unseen Forces that Stand in the Way of True Inspiration*, New York: Random House.

Clydesdale, G. (2006), Creativity and competition: the Beatles, *Creativity Research Journal*, **18**(2), 129–139.

Dennis, N. and Macaulay, M. (2003), Jazz and marketing planning, *Journal of Strategic Marketing*, **11**, 177–185.

Dennis, N. and Macaulay, M. (2007), Miles ahead – using jazz to investigate improvisation and market orientation, *European Journal of Marketing*, **41**(5–6), 608–623.

DeVeaux, S. (1997), *The Birth of Bebop: A Social and Musical History*, Berkeley, CA: University of California Press.

Ericsson, K.A., Krampe, R.T. and Tesch-Romer, C. (1993), The role of deliberate practice in the acquisition of expert performance, *Psychological Review*, **100**(3), 363–406.

Feinberg, M. and Nemeth, C. (2008), *The 'Rules' of Brainstorming: An Impediment to Creativity?*, IRLE Working Paper No. 167-08, http://irle.berkeley.edu/workingpapers/167-08.pdf.

Gioia, T. (1988), *The Imperfect Art. Reflections on Jazz and Modern Culture*, New York: Oxford University Press.

Gladwell, M. (2008), *Outliers. The Story of Success*, New York: Little, Brown, and Company.

Herzig, M. (2011), *David Baker: A Legacy in Music*, Bloomington, IN: Indiana University Press.

Holbrook, M. (2007), Playing the changes on the jazz metaphor: an expanded conceptualization of music-, management-, and marketing-related themes, *Foundations and Trends in Marketing*, **2**(3–4), 185–442.

Jankowiak, J. (1996), Running a jam session, *Down Beat*, **63**(8).

Jeffri, J. (2003), *Changing the Beat: A Study of the Worklife of Jazz Musicians*, NEA Research Report #43.

Kao, J. (1996), *Jamming: The Art and Discipline of Business Creativity*, New York: HarperCollins.

Limb, C. and Braun, A. (2008), Neural substrates of spontaneous musical performance: an fMRI study of jazz improvisation, *PLoS ONE*, **3**(2), e1679.

Linkner, J. (2011), *Disciplined Dreaming: A Proven System to Drive Breakthrough Creativity*, San Francisco, CA: Jossey-Bass.

McDonough, J. (1979), Norman Granz JATP pilot . . ., *Down Beat*, **45**(16), 31–32.

Nelson, L. (1995), The social construction of the jam session, *Jazz Research Papers*, **15**, 95–100.

Sawyer, K. (2006a), Group creativity: musical performance and collaboration, *Psychology of Music*, **34**(2), 148–165.

Sawyer, K. (2006b), *Explaining Creativity – The Science of Human Innovation*, New York: Oxford University Press.

Seelig, T. (2012), *InGenius: A Crash Course on Creativity*, New York: HarperCollins.

Simonton, D.K. (1984), Artistic creativity and interpersonal relationships across and within generations, *Journal of Personality and Social Psychology*, **46**(6), 1273–1286.

Stephenson, S. (2009), *The Jazz Loft Project: Photographs and Tapes of W. Eugene Smith from 821 Sixth Avenue, 1957–1965*, New York: Random House.

Weick, K. (1990), *Managing as Improvisation: Lessons from the World of Jazz*, Aubrey Fisher Memorial Lecture, University of Utah, October 18.

23 Nascent Entrepreneurship

Introduction

Research on nascent entrepreneurship concerns itself with the emergence of new business ventures. The research aims to capture the pre-operational stage, from first idea or action to the point where the process ends either in the establishment of a viable new business or in termination of the startup attempt. Although the label 'nascent entrepreneur' is commonly used, it should be noted that it is really the venture that is nascent. The founder(s) may or may not have prior entrepreneurial experience.

Nascent entrepreneurship research is closely associated with two major research programs orchestrated by Paul Reynolds, the Global Entrepreneurship Monitor (GEM) and the Panel Study of Entrepreneurial Dynamics (PSED) (see Davidsson, 2005; Reynolds, 2005). The former compares early stage entrepreneurial activity across countries whereas the latter (and its international counterparts) follows ongoing startup processes over time. Both research programs mostly rely on carefully developed screening interviews of adult members of randomly sampled households to identify those few who are currently involved in a startup effort (Reynolds, 2009). The research stream has more recently broadened into other methodological approaches (e.g., Black et al., 2010; Corner and Wu, 2012). However, the marker of 'nascent' status remains that the case has moved beyond mere intention, but has not yet become a fully operational business enterprise.

What we have learned

Research on nascent entrepreneurship has grown rapidly. GEM- or PSED-type data has been the basis for well over 200 journal articles (Amorós et al., 2013; Davidsson and Gordon, 2012; Frid, 2013) and Google Scholar counts nearly 6,000 works published in the 2009–2013 period that use the expression 'nascent entrepreneurship,' 'nascent entrepreneur/s,' 'nascent venture/s' or 'nascent firm/s.' Contributions within the research stream have been compiled as well as thoroughly described and reviewed from both content and method angles in several works (e.g., Álvarez et al., 2014; Amorós, et al., 2013; Bergmann et al., 2013; Davidsson, 2006; Davidsson and Gordon, 2012; Davidsson et al., 2011; Gartner and Shaver, 2012; Johnson et al., 2006; Reynolds, 2009; Reynolds et al., 2005; Yang and Aldrich, 2012). These works also provide detailed accounts of the substantive and methodological progress, for which there is no room in this short chapter. In short, the macro-level interest has naturally been in explaining the antecedents and effects of different levels of entrepreneurial activity across countries (e.g., Stel et al., 2005; Wennekers et al., 2005). On the micro level, identifiable sub-streams focus on characteristics of the *individuals* engaging in nascent entrepreneurship; the *process* by which the start-up attempt progresses, and drivers of the *outcomes* achieved (Davidsson et al., 2011).

To fully appreciate the contributions of this research, it is useful to revisit the state of the art of entrepreneurship research in the mid-1990s. The GEM and PSED projects were initiated at that time in part as a response to the under-coverage and non-comparability of data regarding the youngest and smallest businesses in then existing national datasets; the scantiness of information about cases in such datasets; selection bias resulting from excluding startups that fail before becoming operational businesses; hindsight bias and memory decay pertaining to retrospective research designs, and the lack of time separation between assumed causes and effects in cross-sectional data.

Substantively, very little was then known about how the prevalence *and nature* of pre-operational startup attempts vary across countries and over time; what proportion of nascent ventures are started by teams and how these teams are composed; what proportion ever becomes operational businesses; how long that process takes and how it unfolds over time; what resources are required to successfully complete it and where these resources are sourced. The same cannot be said today. Nascent entrepreneurship research has yielded an enormous trove of new insights. Whereas much of this knowledge is tentative and incomplete, there are elements that have arguably become common knowledge among scholars as well as many policymakers and support organizations.

New insights bring new challenges. One such insight is the extreme heterogeneity of any random sample of nascent ventures. Different people try to start different new ventures for a broad range of different reasons. This happens within geographic and industry contexts that are also highly variable. The ventures are unequally developed when first captured and continue the journey at unequal pace. Further, they use different types and amounts of resources. All of this makes it difficult to capture the phenomenon within a coherent theoretical perspective and to arrive at strong, clear generalizations.

One generalization that can be safely made constitutes a second, major challenge: that a random sample of nascent ventures will always be dominated by a 'modest majority' (Davidsson and Gordon, 2012) with limited ambitions, resources and novelty. Although unlikely to ever become significant economic entities in their own right, by their sheer numbers this majority can add up to considerable economic effects.

A third challenge is to obtain information about these emerging ventures from any other source than from the founders themselves. Consequently, there is a risk of common-method bias (Podsakoff et al., 2003).

Researchers are not blind to these challenges and have already applied countermeasures. For example, GEM has gradually introduced a richer set of indicators of early stage entrepreneurial activity, and undertakes comparisons within more homogenous subsets of countries (Xavier et al., 2013). Conceptualizations of what marks the start and the end of a venture creation process have been refined (McMullen and Dimov, 2013; Schoonhoven et al., 2009), leading to finetuning of criteria for capturing eligible cases (Reynolds, 2009) and introduction of more researcher-controlled performance criteria (Reynolds and Curtin, 2009). Individual researchers have addressed temporal heterogeneity by reorganizing the dataset according to the nascent ventures' own development timeline instead of the timing of interview waves (e.g., Delmar and Shane, 2004). Rather than forcing assumptions of radical innovation and high growth ambition onto a more mundane reality, others have adapted their choice of research questions and theoretical lenses to embrace the phenomenon as it actually presents itself (e.g., Kim et al., 2015).

Future challenges
Now that the basic questions about the prevalence and composition of the phenomenon in the general population have been answered, future projects can aim for less heterogeneous and higher-potential samples to study, as required by the research questions and theoretical perspectives driving their research. Some contexts for such sampling (e.g., business incubators) may also allow for capturing data from sources other than the founders. Early capture and longitudinal following of cases can also be applied to internal nascent ventures in established firms. Future projects can also add refinements to conceptualization and operationalization of relevant dependent variables, as well as applying more stage-dependent theorizing of their antecedents (Davidsson, 2012). Although current datasets offer other alternatives, there has been an unfortunate tendency to use survival (continuation) of the nascent venture as a criterion, and to interpret it as an indicator of success (Davidsson and Gordon, 2012). This overlooks the possibility that continuation is ill-informed (DeTienne et al., 2008) or signifies a low intensity effort that is never put to an acid test (Parker and Belghitar, 2006).

The micro-level process sub-stream has arguably yielded some of the most unique contributions compared to other branches of entrepreneurship research (Davidsson and Gordon, 2012). This has largely built on data about the occurrence and timing of a broad set of 'gestation activities,' such as writing a business plan, talking to potential customers, developing a prototype, buying equipment, creating a website, etc. Initially held back by excessive temporal heterogeneity in the ordering of manifest activities (Liao and Welsch, 2008; Liao et al., 2005), researchers have found ways to make progress by focusing on subsets of activities, increasing the level of abstraction, and trying new analysis approaches (Delmar and Shane, 2004; Gordon, 2012; Hak et al., 2013; Lichtenstein et al., 2007). However, the dichotomous and one-off assessment of gestation activities in past projects has been a limitation. Further development of conceptualizations and operationalizations, as well as their alignment, will be needed in order to reach the full potential of this line of research. For example, past research has often relied on Katz and Gartner's (1988) categories (intentionality, resources, boundaries and exchange) without agreeing on which gestation activities belong where. Future projects may wish to start from richer operationalizations of clearer behavioral categories, as well as better-developed theoretical ideas about their likely roles at different stages of the nascent entrepreneurship process.

Conclusions

In summary, research on nascent entrepreneurship has made many fruitful contributions to our understanding of entrepreneurial phenomena and how to study them. Although new issues and challenges have been revealed, they are manageable and they are being addressed. Along with the rapidly growing research on 'entrepreneurial opportunities' (Short et al., 2010), the nascent entrepreneurship stream has helped shift the epicenter of entrepreneurship research towards the very early stages of development of new economic activities. This is arguably where entrepreneurship research can make its most distinct contributions to the broader fields of economic and organizational research.

PER DAVIDSSON

References

Álvarez, C., Urbano, D. and Amorós, J.E. (2014), GEM research: achievements and challenges, *Small Business Economics*, **42**(3), 445–465.

Amorós, J.E., Bosma, N. and Levie, J. (2013), Ten years of Global Entrepreneurship Monitor: accomplishments and prospects, *International Journal of Entrepreneurial Venturing*, **5**(2), 120–152.

Bergmann, H., Mueller, S. and Schrettle, T. (2014), The use of Global Entrepreneurship Monitor data in academic research: a critical inventory and future potentials, *International Journal of Entrepreneurial Venturing*, **6**(3), 242–275.

Black, J.A., Oliver, R.L. and Paris, L.D. (2010), Modeling entrepreneurial action choice: from intent through rhetoric to action, *Advances in Applied Business Strategy*, **12**, 201–233.

Corner, P.D. and Wu, S. (2012), Dynamic capability emergence in the venture creation process, *International Small Business Journal*, **30**(2), 138–160.

Davidsson, P. (2005), Paul Davidson Reynolds: entrepreneurship research innovator, coordinator and disseminator, *Small Business Economics*, **24**(4), 351–358.

Davidsson, P. (2006), Nascent entrepreneurship: empirical studies and developments, *Foundations and Trends in Entrepreneurship*, **2**(1), 1–76.

Davidsson, P. (2012), Engagement, persistence, progress and success as theoretically distinct aspects of business creation processes, in A. Zacharakis, S. Carter, A. Corbett, F. Delmar, L. Edelman, M. Gruber, B. Honig, D. Kelley, J. Kickul, B. Leleux, T. Lumpkin, L. Marino and M. Schindehutte (eds), *Frontiers of Entrepreneurship Research 2011*, vol. 31, Wellesley: Babson College, pp. 307–321.

Davidsson, P. and Gordon, S.R. (2012), Panel studies of new venture creation: a methods-focused review and suggestions for future research, *Small Business Economics*, **39**(4), 853–876.

Davidsson, P., Gordon, S.R. and Bergmann, H. (eds) (2011), *Nascent Entrepreneurship*, Cheltenham, UK and Northampton, MA: Edward Elgar Publishing.

Delmar, F. and Shane, S. (2004), Legitimating first: organizing activities and the survival of new ventures, *Journal of Business Venturing*, **19**(3), 385–410.

DeTienne, D.R., Shepherd, D.A. and De Castro, J.O. (2008), The fallacy of 'only the strong survive': the effects of extrinsic motivation on the persistence decisions for under-performing firms, *Journal of Business Venturing*, **23**(5), 528–546.

Frid, C. (2013), *Publications Based on the Panel study of Entrepreneurial Dynamics*, www. psed.isr.umich.edu/psed/documentation.

Gartner, W.B. and Shaver, K.G. (2012), Nascent entrepreneurship panel studies: progress and challenges, *Small Business Economics*, **39**(3), 659–665.

Gordon, S.R. (2012), *Dimensions of the Venture Creation Process: Amount, Dynamics, and Sequences of Action in Nascent Entrepreneurship*, doctoral dissertation, Queensland University of Technology.

Hak, T., Jaspers, F. and Dul, J. (2013), The analysis of temporally ordered configurations: challenges and solutions, *Research in the Sociology of Organizations*, **38**, 107–127.

Johnson, P.S., Parker, S.C. and Wijbenga, F. (2006), Nascent entrepreneurship research: achievements and opportunities, *Small Business Economics*, **27**(1), 1–4.

Katz, J. and Gartner, W.B. (1988), Properties of emerging organizations, *Academy of Management Review*, **13**(3), 429–441.

Kim, P.H., Longest, K.C. and Lippman, S. (2015), The tortoise versus the hare: progress and business viability differences between conventional and leisure-based founders, *Journal of Business Venturing*, **30**(2), 185–204.

Liao, J. and Welsch, H. (2008), Patterns of venture gestation process: exploring the differences between tech and non-tech nascent entrepreneurs, *The Journal of High Technology Management Research*, **19**(2), 103–113.

Liao, J., Welsch, H. and Tan, W.L. (2005), Venture gestation paths of nascent entrepreneurs: exploring the temporal patterns, *The Journal of High Technology Management Research*, **16**(1), 1–22.

Lichtenstein, B.B., Carter, N.M., Dooley, K.J. and Gartner, W.B. (2007), Complexity dynamics of nascent entrepreneurship, *Journal of Business Venturing*, **22**(2), 236–261.

McMullen, J.S. and Dimov, D. (2013), Time and the entrepreneurial journey: the problems and promise of studying entrepreneurship as a process, *Journal of Management Studies*, **50**(8), 1481–1512.

Parker, S. and Belghitar, Y. (2006), What happens to nascent entrepreneurs? An econometric analysis of the PSED, *Small Business Economics*, **27**(1), 81–101.

Podsakoff, P.M., MacKenzie, S.B., Lee, J.-Y. and Podsakoff, N.P. (2003), Common method biases in behavioral research: a critical review of the literature and recommended remedies, *Journal of Applied Psychology*, **88**(5), 879–903.

Reynolds, P.D. (2005), Understanding business creation: serendipity and scope in two decades of business creation studies, *Small Business Economics*, **24**(4), 359–364.

Reynolds, P.D. (2009), Screening item effects in estimating the prevalence of nascent entrepreneurs, *Small Business Economics*, **33**(2), 151–163.

Reynolds, P.D. and Curtin, R.T. (eds) (2009), *New Firm Creation in the United States: Initial Explorations with the PSED II Data Set*, New York: Springer.

Reynolds, P.D., Bosma, N., Autio, E., Hunt, S., De Bono, N., Servais, I., Lopez-Garcia, P. and Chin, N. (2005), Global Entrepreneurship Monitor: data collection design and implementation 1998–2003, *Small Business Economics*, **24**, 205–231.

Schoonhoven, C.B., Burton, M.D. and Reynolds, P.D. (2009), Reconceiving the gestation window: the consequences of competing definitions of firm conception and birth, in P.D. Reynolds and R.T. Curtin (eds), *New Firm Creation in the United States*, New York: Springer, pp. 219–237.

Short, J.C., Ketchen, D.J., Shook, C.L. and Ireland, R.D. (2010), The concept of 'opportunity' in entrepreneurship research: past accomplishments and future challenges, *Journal of Management*, **36**(1), 40–65.

Stel, A., Carree, M. and Thurik, A.R. (2005), The effect of entrepreneurial activity on national economic growth, *Small Business Economics*, **24**(3), 311–321.

Wennekers, S., Stel, A., Thurik, A.R. and Reynolds, P.D. (2005), Nascent entrepreneurship and the level of economic development, *Small Business Economics*, **24**(3), 293–309.

Xavier, S., Kelley, D., Kew, J., Herrington, M. and Vorderwülbecke, A. (2013), *Global Entrepreneurship Monitor (GEM) 2012 Global Report*, Global Entrepreneurship Research Association, www.gemconsortium.org/docs/2645/gem-2012-global-report.

Yang, T. and Aldrich, H.E. (2012), Out of sight but not out of mind: why failure to account for left truncation biases research on failure rates, *Journal of Business Venturing*, **27**(4), 477–492.

24 Open Innovation

Introduction

In the years since Chesbrough (2003) coined the term, open innovation (OI) has grown to encompass a broad range of mechanisms and phenomena related to knowledge flows that cross firm boundaries. This summary focuses on open innovation in the context of smaller and younger firms, with a particular focus on their entry, commercialization (i.e., path to first revenues) and growth strategies.

Chesbrough (2006) defined open innovation as firms combining internal and external ideas – as well as internal and external paths to market – to accelerate their technology commercialization. In many cases, open innovation means using markets to supplement (or replace) managerial hierarchies for one or more steps of the commercialization process.

The original definition included two main forms of open innovation: the inbound flows of knowledge as firms seek to integrate external sources of innovation, and the outbound flows of knowledge when firms leverage external paths for commercialization. In Chesbrough's firm-centric view, these flows are usually monetized – often through contractual agreements between two organizations – but as Dahlander and Gann (2010) note, such inbound and outbound flows may also occur for non-pecuniary reasons.

A third mode of open innovation is the coupled process that combines inbound and outbound flows (Enkel et al., 2009). Such a coupled process may be found in networks of alliances, working with innovation communities (such as open source software), ecosystem management or in ICT platforms (West, 2014).

While Chesbrough's original focus was the innovation strategies of large multinationals such as IBM and Intel, van de Vrande and her colleagues (2009) were among the first to study OI in the context of Dutch small and medium-sized enterprises (SMEs), finding that medium-sized firms were more likely to engage in open innovation than small ones. Recently Brunswicker and van de Vrande (2014) identified 19 empirical studies on open innovation in SMEs, but only three of these studies focused on young (rather than small) firms.

Inbound open innovation

To date, open innovation researchers have studied inbound OI more than outbound OI. Within inbound OI, research tends to emphasize the use of OI to search for and acquire external innovations (such as crowdsourcing), rather than the integration (let alone commercialization) of such external innovations (West and Bogers, 2014).

A common source of external innovations for new firms is seen in the use of open source software (OSS) by ICT firms. Gruber and Henkel (2006) found that the availability of OSS speeded the entry of new firms into the market, reducing liability of newness and smallness. OSS also makes it easier for small firms to diversify their market offerings (Colombo et al., 2014). Dahlander (2007) found considerable variation among 67 OSS startups in the degree of involvement and control of communities, variation correlated to differences in the role of external technology in a firm's business models.

How does inbound OI impact SME performance? Parida et al. (2012) found that technology scouting and technology sourcing were positively associated with the ability of Swedish SMEs to introduce innovations that were new to the world or new to the firm. Spithoven et al. (2011) found that OI use increased the ability of Belgian SMEs to generate revenue from new products and services – comparable to larger firms.

Outbound open innovation
The outbound OI model was inspired by Teece (1986), and his seminal observation that small and new firms often lack the ability to commercialize their innovations and thus need to partner for manufacturing, distribution, support and other functions.

However, outbound OI is less often used by SMEs than is inbound (e.g., van de Vrande et al. 2009). While this appears to be true for firms more generally, it may be a particular problem for small firms that lack the scale for innovative R&D.

A notable exception is the emergence over the past 30 years of innovative startup biotech firms. Often spun off from a university to commercialize a specific technology, these firms focus on the technology discovery and development while contracting with larger pharma firms for distribution. Bianchi et al. (2011) found learning effects and economies of scope as small Italian pharmaceutical firms out-licensed their discoveries to larger partners.

Coupled and other forms
While the coupled form may encompass dyadic interactions between two organizations (such as an R&D alliance), it is also associated with network and related topologies of value creation strategies by firms (West, 2014).

For many types of innovations, firms must orchestrate a value-creating network to bring their technologies to market and win adoption from customers (Vanhaverbeke and Cloodt, 2006). This often requires collaborating (and using coupled open innovation) with external partners such as communities (Dahlander, 2007) or ecosystems (West, 2014). Lee et al. (2010) found that Korean SMEs were most likely to collaborate with customers and competitors in their value networks, and also to use both as sources for technology innovations.

Firms may also work with third parties who directly provide value to customers, as with ICT platforms. For example, West and Kuk (2014) studied how MakerBot encouraged consumers to donate digital goods to an online community that provided an inventory of designs that could be produced by its 3D printers.

A challenge unique to smaller and younger firms – particularly those without established cash flows – is the ability to orchestrate and shape these external networks or ecosystems to their own advantage. In his study of Symbian Ltd., West (2014) concluded that the startup software firm's use of corporate venture capital to finance its growth limited its freedom to support independent software vendors, including creating an app store to help them bring their products to market.

The future of open innovation in SMEs
Going forward, new firms in new industries will continue to experiment with different forms and degrees of openness in their innovation strategies, including their control of external communities (Dahlander, 2007), other network forms (West, 2014) and the complementarities between open and proprietary strategies (West and Kuk, 2014). An under-researched topic – for SMEs (Vanhaverbeke et al., 2014) and open innovation more broadly (West and Bogers, 2014) – is linking firms' open innovation strategies back to their business models, as originally advocated by Chesbrough (2003).

Finally, while open innovation needs a greater understanding of how and why managers implement open innovation, this is particularly true for SMEs (Brunswicker and van de Vrande, 2014). In the context of new and small firms, it's impossible to ignore the unique strategic role of founder-managers – and thus the impact of their personal history, attitudes and behaviors upon a firm's open innovations strategy (Vanhaverbeke et al., 2014). We see some hint of this in the role of founder beliefs in studies of startups enabled by open source software (Gruber and Henkel, 2006) and hardware (West and Kuk, 2014). However, more systematic research is needed to link open innovation to the broader literature on founders, including their motivations, influence and pre-launch preparation, as well as the interaction of serial entrepreneurship and founder succession upon open innovation choices.

JOEL WEST

References

Bianchi, M., Chiaroni, D., Chiesa, V. and Frattini, F. (2011), Organizing for external technology commercialization: evidence from a multiple case study in the pharmaceutical industry, *R&D Management*, **41**(2), 120–137.

Brunswicker, S. and van de Vrande, V. (2014), Exploring open innovation in small and medium-sized enterprises, in H. Chesbrough, W. Vanhaverbeke and J. West (eds), *New Frontiers in Open Innovation*, Oxford: Oxford University Press, pp. 135–156.

Chesbrough, H. (2003), *Open Innovation: The New Imperative for Creating and Profiting from Technology*, Boston: Harvard Business School Press.

Chesbrough, H. (2006), Open innovation: a new paradigm for understanding industrial innovation, in H. Chesbrough, W. Vanhaverbeke and J. West (eds), *Open Innovation: Researching a New Paradigm*, Oxford: Oxford University Press, pp. 1–12.

Colombo, M., Piva, E. and Rossi-Lamastra, C. (2014), Open innovation and within-industry diversification in small and medium enterprises: the case of open source software firms, *Research Policy*, **43**(5), 891–902.

Dahlander, L. (2007), Penguin in a new suit: a tale of how de novo entrants emerged to harness free and open source software communities, *Industrial and Corporate Change*, **16**(5), 913–943.

Dahlander, L. and Gann, D.M. (2010), How open is innovation?, *Research Policy*, **39**(6), 699–709.

Enkel, E., Gassmann, O. and Chesbrough, H. (2009), Open R&D and open innovation: exploring the phenomenon, *R&D Management*, **39**(4), 311–316.

Gruber, M. and Henkel, J. (2006), New ventures based on open innovation – an empirical analysis of start-up firms in embedded Linux, *International Journal of Technology Management*, **33**(4), 356–372.

Lee, S., Park, G., Yoon, B. and Park, J. (2010), Open innovations in SMEs – an intermediated network model, *Research Policy*, **39**(2), 290–300.

Parida, V., Westerberg, M. and Frishammar, J. (2012), Inbound open innovation activities in high-tech SMEs: the impact on innovation performance, *Journal of Small Business Management*, **50**(2), 283–309.

Spithoven, A., Clarysse, B. and Knockaert, M. (2011), Building absorptive capacity to organise inbound open innovation in traditional industries, *Technovation*, **31**(1), 10–21.

Teece, D. (1986), Profiting from technological innovation: implications for integration, collaboration, licensing and public policy, *Research Policy*, **15**(6), 285–305.

van de Vrande, V., De Jong, J., Vanhaverbeke, W. and de Rochemont, M. (2009), Open innovation in SMEs: trends, motives and management challenges, *Technovation*, **29**(6), 423–437.

Vanhaverbeke, W. and Cloodt, M. (2006), Open innovation in value networks, in H. Chesbrough, W. Vanhaverbeke and J. West (eds), *Open Innovation: Researching a New Paradigm*, Oxford: Oxford University Press, pp. 258–281.

Vanhaverbeke, W., Chesbrough, H. and West, J. (2014), Surfing the new wave of open innovation research, in H. Chesbrough, W. Vanhaverbeke and J. West (eds), *New Frontiers in Open Innovation*, Oxford: Oxford University Press, pp. 281–294.

West, J. (2014), Challenges of funding open innovation platforms: lessons from Symbian Ltd., in H. Chesbrough, W. Vanhaverbeke and J. West (eds), *New Frontiers in Open Innovation*, Oxford: Oxford University Press, pp. 71–93.

West, J. and Bogers, M. (2014), Leveraging external sources of innovation: a review of research on open innovation, *Journal of Product Innovation Management*, **31**(4), 814–831.

West, J. and Kuk, G. (2014), *Proprietary Benefits from Open Communities: How MakerBot Leveraged Thingiverse in 3D Printing*, paper presented at the Academy of Management Conference, Philadelphia, http://ssrn.com/abstract=2544970.

25 Proof of Concept Centers

Introduction
Policymakers increasingly expect research universities to make significant contributions to regional economic development. Several institutions have responded over the past ten years, establishing a new organizational innovation: the Proof of Concept Center (PoCC). A PoCC is a collection of services designed to encourage and support the commercialization of new technology stemming from university research.

Focus of Proof of Concept Centers
Within the context of university economic development, the primary focus of PoCCs is the *maturation* of new technology. The technology focus of PoCCs is driven by what Maia and Claro (2013: 641), building on Auerswald and Branscomb (2003), deem as the most critical phase of commercialization:

> occurs between invention and product development, when commercial concepts are created and verified, appropriate markets are identified, and protectable Intellectual Property (IP) may have to be developed. This Proof of Concept ... phase has a funding gap, caused by information and motivation asymmetries and institutional gaps between the Science and Technology and Business enterprises.

PoCCs are typically viewed as a complementary component of a larger university technology development strategy. Compared to the PoCC, technology transfer offices generally focus on processes associated with the disclosure, patenting and licensing of intellectual property mandated by the Bayh-Dole Act of 1980. Science parks are relatively large physical spaces designed to encourage both large and small companies to locate in close proximity to research universities. Accelerators or incubators are relatively small physical spaces that offer a wide range of services designed to promote entrepreneurship. And many technology funds typically provide financial resources for later-stage commercialization efforts.

These infrastructure elements have traditionally framed university economic development primarily in terms of resources: faculty researchers require discretionary funds and physical space to develop new technologies. Many PoCCs also provide early-stage seed funding and physical space but, in contrast, conceptualize commercialization in terms of culture and social networks.

This is a critical nuance. A robust empirical literature shows that faculty researchers typically lack the skills and experiences important for commercialization (Nicolaou and Birley, 2003; Franklin et al.,

2001; Radosevich, 1995). Conversely, faculty who have connections to industry – through consulting, sponsored research and joint research projects – have a higher propensity to patent, license and establish a company (O'Gorman et al., 2008; Dietz and Bozeman, 2005; Gulbrandsen and Smeby, 2005; Roberts, 1991). Recent research also finds that high social capital levels among university faculty can constrain commercialization success, while network connections to contacts outside of academia are critical sources of advice, technical assistance, and funding (Hayter, 2013, 2015; Johansson et al., 2005). In other words, if a university technology development infrastructure does not take into account network dynamics within an academic research environment, then it is unlikely to succeed.

PoCCs employ specific programs to account for commercialization challenges associated with academic social networks. For example, Gulbranson and Audretsch (2008) find that, in addition to early-stage seed funding and education programs, the von Liebig Center at the University of California San Diego and the Deshpande Center at the Massachusetts Institute of Technology both provide access to experienced advisors and volunteers. These individuals possess relevant technical and business background and, importantly, connect faculty researchers to technologists, service providers, investors and professional managers within the surrounding communities who can assist faculty researchers as their technologies (and subsequent spinoffs) mature.

According to Bradley et al. (2013), at least 32 PoCCs have been established over the past 15 years in the United States. Much of this growth, however, has occurred in the past five years: half of the existing PoCCs were established from 2010 to 2012 and at least six more have been established (or are planned) since the most recent empirical analysis. While individual universities have established most PoCCs, recent initiatives by New York State and the federal government illustrate growing interest in PoCCs as a multijurisdictional tool to promote university-based economic development and job growth.

PoCCs have also made it into the lexicon of state and national policymakers. For example, the National Governor's Association (Sparks, 2013: 7–8) recently reported that Colorado's Governor Hickenlooper supported the Advanced Industries Accelerator Act to promote 'technology commercialization, entrepreneurship and manufacturing in the advanced industries through proof-of-concept grants.'

At a national level, US Representative Collins from the state of New York introduced the Technology and Research Accelerating National Security and Future Economic Resiliency Act of 2013 (HR 2981). The Act proposed that each federal agency with a Small Business Technology Transfer (STTR) program establish a grants program to provide 'early-stage proof of concept funding for translational research' at universities.

Despite the growth in PoCCs and high-level policy interest, systematic empirical research relating to the establishment, structure, operations and impact of PoCCs is nearly 'non-existent' (Bradley et al., 2013). Anecdotal evidence shows that PoCCs help researchers understand the commercial value of their technology, bolstering the overall entrepreneurial culture of a university. Further, early PoCCs have a well-defined organizational structure that, through a variety of mechanisms, including technology evaluations, commercialization plans, educational courses and, as mentioned above, advisory services, help 'legitimize' a university researcher's technology for outside investors and companies (Gulbranson and Audretsch, 2008).

A recent exploratory analysis also finds that universities that have established a PoCC enjoy a positive and statistically significant increase in the number of spinoffs established each year after adoption (Hayter and Link, 2015a, 2015b). However, variations in the mean number of startups, including observable declines among individual universities in their sample, suggest that other structural, cultural and policy factors may affect the impact of PoCCs, a point reinforced by Maia and Claro (2013).

Conclusion

Beyond these modest contributions, more research is clearly needed to understand the establishment, structure and impact of PoCCs worldwide. The broader point is that there is suggestive evidence, at least in the United States, that PoCCs are growing in importance as a policy tool to encourage commercialization of university research. As such, PoCCs have the potential to become an important infrastructural element of a university's innovation system and perhaps that of a region or even a nation.

CHRISTOPHER S. HAYTER

References

Auerswald, P. and Branscomb, L. (2003), Valleys of death and Darwinian seas: financing the invention to innovation transition in the United States, *Journal of Technology Transfer*, **28**(3–4), 227–239.

Bradley, S.B., Hayter, C.S. and Link, A.N. (2013), Proof of concept centers in the United States: an exploratory look, *Journal of Technology Transfer*, **38**, 349–381.

Dietz, J. and Bozeman, B. (2005), Academic careers, patents, and productivity: industry experience as scientific and technical human capital, *Research Policy*, **34**(3), 349–367.

Franklin, S., Wright, M. and Lockett, A. (2001), Academic and surrogate entrepreneurs in university spin-out companies, *Journal of Technology Transfer*, **26**(1–2), 127–141.

Gulbrandsen, M. and Smeby, J. (2005), Industry funding and university professors' research performance, *Research Policy*, **34**(6), 932–950.

Gulbranson, C. and Audretsch, D. (2008), Proof of concept centers: accelerating the commercialization of university innovation, *Journal of Technology Transfer*, **33**(1), 249–258.

Hayter, C. (2013), Harnessing university entrepreneurship for economic growth: factors of success among university spinoffs, *Economic Development Quarterly*, **27**(1): 18–28.

Hayter, C. (2015), Social networks and the success of university spinoffs: toward an agenda for regional growth, *Economic Development Quarterly*, **29**(1), 3–13.

Hayter, C.S. and Link, A.N. (2015a), On the economic impact of university proof of concept centers, *Journal of Technology Transfer*, **40**(1), 178–83.

Hayter, C.S. and Link, A.N. (2015b), University proof of concept centers: empowering faculty to capitalize on their research, *ISSUES in Science and Technology*, Winter, 32–35.

Johansson, M., Jacob, M. and Hellstrom, T. (2005), The strength of strong ties: university spin-offs and the significance of historical relations, *Journal of Technology Transfer*, **30**(3), 271–286.

Maia, C. and Claro, J. (2013), The role of a proof of concept center in a university ecosystem: an exploratory study, *Journal of Technology Transfer*, **38**(5), 641–650.

Nicolaou, N. and Birley, S. (2003), Academic networks in a trichotomous categorisation of university spinouts, *Journal of Business Venturing*, **18**(3), 333–359.

O'Gorman, C., Byrne, O. and Pandya, D. (2008), How scientists commercialize new knowledge via entrepreneurship, *Journal of Technology Transfer*, **33**(1), 23–43.

Radosevich, R. (1995), A model for entrepreneurial spin-offs from public technology sources, *International Journal of Technology Management*, **10**(7–8), 879–893.

Roberts, E. (1991), *Entrepreneurs in High Technology: Lessons from MIT and Beyond*, New York: Oxford University Press.

Sparks, E. (2013), *Top Trends in State Economic Development*, National Governor's Association Policy Paper, August.

26 Protecting University Patents while Pursuing the Public Good

Introduction

Universities active in technology transfer face new challenges as they work to keep pace in the rapidly developing world of patent law. Time and again, federal courts have denied universities' attempts to be treated as special players within the patent system, as entities for whom the typically restrictive rules of patent eligibility and enforcement should be softened.[1] Instead, as courts continue to reject calls for university exceptionalism, an implicit message has been transmitted to the higher education community: institutions intending to capitalize on their patent portfolios must adopt the practices that have led commercial firms to success in this space (Lee, 2013).

The university's dilemma

The university's dilemma lies in maintaining its historic allegiance to the public good through research and technology transfer as it otherwise becomes more deeply entwined with the market and explores market-influenced approaches to patent protection, licensing and enforcement. Many policymakers expect that technology transfer involvement will generate substantial revenues for universities (McDevitt et al., 2014).

These often unrealistic expectations only further complicate the difficult position universities find themselves in. Harnessing the full power of patents – which, by definition, provide their holders with exclusionary powers – requires steely resolve, access to sophisticated legal counsel, and a seemingly limitless supply of money to use in furtherance of patent protection and enforcement efforts. The traditional notion that university involvement in technology transfer should further the public good to the greatest extent possible may seem secondary or even unachievable for some universities in the face of these powerful forces (Winickoff, 2013). Simply put, legal and business considerations are driving universities to be protective and guarded about their intellectual property in ways that challenge traditional societal conceptions of universities working openly in the public interest to broadly disseminate new knowledge.

For example, under recent changes to patent law included in the 2011 America Invents Act, those who wish to challenge the validity of patents have more options at their disposal than ever before. Third parties now may submit, during a patent application's pendency, prior art references that can be used to jeopardize the scope or eligibility of the application. University applicants can expect to face increased legal fees and delays in obtaining patents as a result. Additionally, and quite importantly, the US patent system now is a 'first-inventor-to-file' system, meaning that the consequences of faculty researchers failing to promptly disclose their inventions to university administrators can be devastating. Another inventor, later in time, may receive a patent on the invention, provided the second inventor is the first to file for protection (and the first inventor did not publicly disclose her invention before the second inventor filed for protection). While firms have the ability to monitor laboratory notebooks and prod employee behavior, universities are not as competitively positioned to ensure that all potentially lucrative intellectual property is claimed and treated as such due to academic freedom, faculty publishing expectations and the norms of the academy (Brandon and Solberg, 2014). The factual situation that led to *Stanford v. Roche* (131 S. Ct. 2188 (2011)), and higher education's structural difficulties in obtaining effective invention assignments from tenured faculty in the years since the decision, only further illustrate this problem.

Presenting even trickier challenges for university patent owners is the introduction of the post-grant review process, which can be used against patents that issue from applications filed on or after March 16, 2013 (Nickla and Harris, 2014). Once a patent application matures to registration, third parties now have a nine-month window in which to initiate a post-grant review of the patent at the United States Patent and Trademark Office (USPTO). A cheaper and quicker venue than federal court litigation, the USPTO's post-grant review proceeding allows third parties to attempt to invalidate a patent's claims on any basis that could have supported a refusal during the patent's prosecution. While no post-grant proceeding had been initiated as of winter 2014, the potential use of this mechanism to invalidate patents issuing in the future means that patents no longer are presumed valid until nine months and one day after issuance. This added uncertainty will likely wreak special havoc on universities, which typically lack the capital or access to capital enjoyed by other patentees.

The additional financial pressure of potentially having to defend newly issued patents is likely to reduce the instances where a university does not license technology until a patent issues, or at least may prolong the time from patent issuance to license execution. Prospective licensees, acting from a rational economic perspective, may prefer to take a bet that the patent will be deemed invalid in a post-grant review proceeding, rather than willingly enter into a license without first challenging the patent.

A related likelihood – and one that some in the university technology transfer community are touting as a positive development – is that the expense and uncertainty that post-grant proceedings create for universities will cause them to identify and partner with prospective licensees much earlier in the lifecycle of a technology's development than they previously have done. Yet this change, to the extent it materializes, could endanger the public good: exclusive licenses – long deemed risky, in part because they can hamstring universities' ability to disseminate new technology as widely and cost-effectively as possible – may soon become preferred over non-exclusive deals, which require universities to take a more active role in protecting and enforcing the patent, for reasons influenced both by law and policy (Rooksby, 2013a).

By engaging in exclusive licenses before patents issue, universities effectively acquire a funded ally to share in the risk of possible patent invalidation challenges. Even though licensees enjoy wide discretion to challenge the validity of licensed patents under the Supreme Court's ruling in *MedImmune v. Genentech* (549 US 118 (2007)), the prospect of such a challenge diminishes if universities seek to build lasting, long-term relationships with industry sponsors by entering into early-stage deals that convey tacit knowledge and knowhow, beyond what may be disclosed in the patent itself, as many are doing (Lee, 2012). Additional benefits to the innovation system may flow from strengthening academic–industry partnerships. For example, one recent study of the University of California system found that sponsored research – long an insignificant total of overall research funding in higher education – led to inventions that were licensed and cited more often than federally sponsored inventions, suggesting that innovation boosts can come from these alliances (Wright et al., 2014).

Universities shoulder more burdens, such as having to pay escalating patent maintenance fees, for technology that universities are unable to team with others to protect and develop. These financial burdens can lead to temptations for universities the longer they pursue commercialization without a partner. For example, issued patents that universities are unable to license often are attractive for their enforcement value on the secondary market; however, some view university activity in that market as inconsistent with the public-serving goals of university patent ownership (Ledford, 2013). Regardless, several institutions have sold or licensed portions of their portfolios to entities such as Intellectual Ventures, which specializes in monetizing patents, often through litigation that some call (with aspersive intent) 'patent trolling' (Feldman and Ewing, 2012). Confronting the same problem using a different approach, Pennsylvania State University held a public auction of its unlicensed patents in 2013. Although the event attracted much attention, the university received only one bid (Blumenstyk, 2014).

Amid this complex legal and business landscape, universities seeking patents while also pursuing the public good face difficult choices. On the one hand, few have the resources to thrive in a space whose laws and norms seem to favor firms over nonprofit entities. On the other hand, continuing rhetorical and historical pressures push universities of all sizes and statures to seek prominence in technology transfer (Rooksby and Pusser, 2014). Some authors have argued that universities need more agency – for example, to take title to federally funded inventions without the obligation to patent the invention (Vertinsky, 2012), or to decline to become involved in patent infringement litigation when an exclusive licensee exists (Rooksby, 2013b) – while others have suggested that the role of the university in technology transfer should cede to the entrepreneurial spirit of faculty inventors (Litan and Cook-Deegan, 2011), or even should be scaled back considerably (Love, 2012). Unsurprisingly, the established university technology transfer community strongly opposes proposals that would weaken the professional influence of their membership, which has grown considerably since 1980.

Conclusion

Whatever the ultimate resolution on any given campus, the university's dilemma reflects its precarious perch between government and industry, and the evolving struggle for guardians of academic science to simultaneously use and pursue private rights in furtherance of the public good.

JACOB H. ROOKSBY

Note

1. See *Griffith v. Kanamaru* (816 F.2d 624 (Fed. Cir. 1987)), *Madey v. Duke* (307 F. 3d 1351 (Fed. Cir. 2002)), *University of Rochester v. G.D. Searle & Co.* (358 F.3d 916 (Fed. Cir. 2004)), *Ariad Pharmaceuticals v. Eli Lilly* (598 F.3d 1336 (Fed. Cir. 2010)), and *Stanford v. Roche* (131 S. Ct. 2188 (2011)) for examples of university attempts to obtain special treatment under the patent laws.

References

Blumenstyk, G. (2014), Penn State's patent auction produces more lessons than revenue, http://chronicle.com/blogs/bottomline/penn-states-patent-auction-produces-more-lessons-than-revenue.

Brandon, R. and Solberg, S.D. (2014), Changes to the patent laws, in E. Rodriguez and S.D. Solberg (eds), *The Technology Transfer Law Handbook*, Chicago, IL: American Bar Association, pp. 1–32.

Feldman, R. and Ewing, T. (2012), The giants among us, *Stanford Technology Law Review*, **2012**, 1–61.

Ledford, H. (2013), Universities struggle to make patents pay, *Nature*, **501**, 471–472.

Lee, P. (2012), Transcending the tacit dimension: patents, relationships, and organizational integration in technology transfer, *California Law Review*, **100**, 1503–1571.

Lee, P. (2013), Patents and the university, *Duke Law Journal*, **63**, 1–87.

Litan, R.E. and Cook-Deegan, R. (2011), Universities and economic growth: the importance of academic entrepreneurship, in *Rules for Growth: Promoting Innovation and Growth through Legal Reform*, Kansas City, MO: Ewing Marion Kauffman Foundation, pp. 55–82.

Love, B.J. (2012), Subsidizing 'patent roulette,' *Indianapolis Star*, March 5, A13.

McDevitt, V.L., Mendez-Hinds, J., Winwood, D., Nijhawan, V., Sherer, T., Ritter, J.F. and Sanberg, P.R. (2014), More than money: the exponential impact of academic technology transfer, *Technology and Innovation*, **16**, 75–84.

Nickla, J.T. and Harris, E. (2014), Post-grant proceedings under AIA: impact on university technology transfer, in E. Rodriguez and S.D. Solberg (eds), *The Technology Transfer Law Handbook*, Chicago, IL: American Bar Association, pp. 65–80.

Rooksby, J.H. (2013a), When tigers bare teeth: a qualitative study of university patent enforcement, *Akron Law Review*, **46**(1), 169–205.

Rooksby, J.H. (2013b), Innovation and litigation: tensions between universities and patents and how to fix them, *Yale Journal of Law and Technology*, **15**, 312–404.

Rooksby, J.H. and Pusser, B. (2014), Learning to litigate: university patents in the knowledge economy, in B. Cantwell and I. Kauppinen (eds), *Academic Capitalism in the Age of Globalization*, Baltimore, MD: Johns Hopkins University Press, pp. 74–93.

Vertinsky, L. (2012), Universities as guardians of their inventions, *Utah Law Review*, **2012**, 1949–2021.

Winickoff, D.E. (2013), Private assets, public mission: the politics of technology transfer and the new American university, *Jurimetrics*, **54**(1), 1–42.

Wright, D., Drivas, K., Lei, Z. and Merrill, S. (2014), Technology transfer: industry-funded academic inventions boost innovation, *Nature*, **507**, 297–299.

27 Public Sector Entrepreneurship

Introduction

Our conceptualization of public sector entrepreneurship is derived from the fundamental characteristics of the private sector entrepreneur applied to the institutional context of the public sector.[1] In comparison to private sector entrepreneurship, the notion of public sector entrepreneurship is more controversial with some calling into question its desirability or value. It is our view that there are significant benefits from public sector entrepreneurship that contribute to the general economy's growth and prosperity.

Entrepreneurship versus public sector entrepreneurship
As Hébert and Link (2009) have discussed, there is a long history of thinking about entrepreneurship in purely private sector terms: who the entrepreneur is and what he does within a private sector setting. In any given circumstance, the entrepreneur may play a variety of roles (industrial leader, capitalist, contractor, decision-maker, etc.). However, most of these roles are not essentially entrepreneurial; they are often associated with general business activity and can be delegated to others. What is essential is the role of innovator who bears the special type of risk associated with uncertainty. The entrepreneur is one who recognizes an opportunity heretofore unexploited and who acts on that opportunity (Leyden and Link, 2015).[2]

Given that public sector actors rarely, if ever, operate primarily within a private sector market environment or have the possibility of earning personal profit through the activities that they pursue, one might logically ask: is there room for the notion of entrepreneurship within a public sector context? That question is reasonable; however, asking the question confuses – or so we contend (Leyden and Link, 2015) – the specific context in which the entrepreneur operates with the fundamental characteristics of the entrepreneur. And what are those fundamental characteristics? They are opportunity recognition and the pursuit of those opportunities (Leyden et al., 2014).

As Leyden (forthcoming) observes, what makes public sector entrepreneurship different is the institutional environment in which it operates, and this has implications for the nature of the public sector entrepreneur's motivations and reward, access to capital and the ability to act. While the desire for personal benefits may be the same for the public and private sector entrepreneur, benefits for the public sector entrepreneur typically manifest themselves in terms of recognition and career enhancement rather than monetary profits. But the desire to create and to achieve is the same as for the private sector entrepreneur, although perhaps associated more with the satisfaction that comes from contributing to the common weal than a private sector entrepreneur would have.

When it comes to access to capital and the ability to act, there are more significant differences. Constitutional and legal constraints may reduce access to funding as well as restrict the ability to act by precluding activities, exposing efforts to public scrutiny and slowing down the entrepreneurial process. There are also political constraints that function much the same way and that are due to the public having little taste for the chance of failure associated with entrepreneurial activity.

Despite such constraints, however, the range of public sector entrepreneurial activities is broad. Such activities can be categorized as either direct or indirect public sector entrepreneurship. Direct public sector entrepreneurship operates inside the public sector environment and is manifest in the innovative manipulation of that environment (particularly the expenditure, management and service mechanisms of government) for the public good. By contrast, indirect public sector entrepreneurship operates by innovatively altering the private sector economic environment to induce desirable behaviors on the part of private sector entrepreneurs, again for the public good.

Classifying policy as public sector entrepreneurship

Examples of direct public sector entrepreneurship include production innovations (providing the same goods and services at lower cost) and output innovations (improving the quality or range of goods and services).[3] Public sector production innovations can take a variety of forms – changes in management structures, changes in physical production processes and changes in delivery systems. In recent years, for example, much emphasis has been placed on digitization (that is, eGovernment) throughout the public sector with respect to record-keeping, making information available to the public and 'customer' service (for example, voting, voter registration, paying taxes and issuing licenses). Public sector output innovations, while often desirable, are more problematic because they deal with the fundamental decision of what goods and services are to be provided by the public sector, a decision that in a democratic society typically rests ultimately with the legislature. As a result, such innovations often must come directly from the legislature itself.

Given the typical size of a nation's public sector, direct public sector entrepreneurship has significant potential benefits. However, that potential is likely to be much smaller than the benefits of indirect public sector entrepreneurship. Indirect 'public sector entrepreneurship refers to innovative public policy initiatives that generate greater economic prosperity by transforming a status quo economic environment into one that is more conducive to economic units engaging in creative activities in the face of uncertainty' (Leyden and Link, 2015: 14). Such initiatives typically are manifest in innovative changes in private sector rules of the game (that is, changes in laws, regulations, etc.) that focus on increasing private sector economic growth. While such innovations can be promulgated by either the executive or legislative branches of government, history suggests that legislative action is often crucial.

Most nations have a portfolio of technology and innovation policies that their economic growth strategy is built upon. For many of these nations, these policies were promulgated in the late 1970s and early 1980s in response to the global slowdown in productivity growth. But not all technology and innovation policies meet the criteria for being considered public sector entrepreneurship. What makes such policies entrepreneurial is their ability to make the private sector economic environment more conducive to private sector entrepreneurial action. We contend, in an effort to forge the concept and attendant literature on public sector entrepreneurship toward policy evaluation, that the following are characteristics of a policy to consider when attempting to classify a policy as an example of public sector entrepreneurship or not.

- Advancement of knowledge: does the public policy advance the state of knowledge, and if so by how much?
- Impact on technology and innovation: does the public policy advance the state of existing technology or innovation, and if so how and by how much?
- Targeted parties: what are the targeted parties in the policy initiative? Are they parties that are a part of a national innovation system?
- Heterogeneity of experiential ties: does the public policy enhance the targeted parties' ties to external networks of knowledge, and if so how and how extensively?

Conclusions

Public sector entrepreneurship is the innovative manipulation of the instruments of government for the public good. While the potential benefits of direct public sector entrepreneurship – that is, the improvement of the output and productivity of the public sector – is large, the most significant benefits are with regard to indirect public sector entrepreneurship, that is, the use of innovative public policies that transform the private sector status quo economic environment into one that is more conducive to generating new technologies and innovations. When the public sector acts in such a manner, the effectiveness of knowledge networks is enhanced through an increase in the heterogeneity of experiential ties. Economic growth and development then follow.

DENNIS PATRICK LEYDEN AND ALBERT N. LINK

Notes

1. This chapter draws heavily from Leyden and Link (2015).
2. This characterization can be traced to the work of Schumpeter (1926/1934) and Knight (1921).
3. Revenue enhancements can be added as a third type of direct public sector entrepreneurial activity. However, such innovations are of limited interest in the context of the discussions here because they don't result in qualitative or quantitative productivity improvements in government except in the narrow domain of revenue collection.

References

Hébert, R.F. and Link, A.N. (2009), *A History of Entrepreneurship*, London: Routledge.

Knight, F.H. (1921), *Risk, Uncertainty, and Profit*, Boston: Houghton Mifflin.

Leyden, D.P. (forthcoming), A theory of public-sector innovation policy, in R. Heinrich (ed.), *Innovation in the Public Sector* (tentative title), Geneva: United Nations Economic Commission for Europe.

Leyden, D.P. and Link, A.N. (2015), *Public Sector Entrepreneurship: US Technology and Innovation Policy*, New York: Oxford University Press.

Leyden, D.P., Link, A.N. and Siegel, D.S. (2014), A theoretical analysis of the role of social networks in entrepreneurship, *Research Policy*, **43**, 1157–1163.

Schumpeter, J.A. (1926/1934), *The Theory of Economic Development*, 2nd edn, trans. R. Opie, Cambridge, MA: Harvard University Press.

28 Research and Technology Alliances

Introduction

The term 'strategic alliance' describes the multitude of forms of agreements between firms, universities and other research organizations whereby two or more partners share the commitment to reach a common goal by pooling their resources together and coordinating their activities (Teece and Jorde, 1992; Hagedoorn, 1993). Alliances denote some degree of strategic and operational coordination and may involve equity investments. They can occur vertically across the value chain, from the provision of raw materials and other factors of production, through research, design, production and assembly of parts, components and systems, to product/service distribution and servicing. They can also occur horizontally between partners at the same level of the value chain. An alliance can have both horizontal and vertical elements. Alliances may also be dispersed in several countries, thus establishing an international alliance.

A subset of alliances can be characterized as innovation-based, focusing primarily on the generation, exchange, adaptation and exploitation of technical advances. These are called herein *strategic technology alliances*. These encompass several ways in which collaboration can occur: various legal arrangements, different degrees of resources commitment, different levels and directions of technological flows, different coordination mechanisms and different time horizons may characterize strategic technological alliances. Such alliances can also involve cooperation among firms and other organizations, notably universities (Cunningham and Link, 2014; Mowery and Sampat, 2005). Examples include:

- research and development (R&D) joint ventures, where two or more organizations constitute a new legal entity in order to perform R&D activities;
- joint R&D agreements, where organizations share resources to undertake joint R&D projects;
- licensing and cross-licensing agreements;
- research contracts, where one partner undertakes research for another organization.

Incentives to partner

The theoretical and empirical literature has, over the years, tried to identify the most prevalent motives for the establishment of strategic alliances (Link and Zmud, 1984; Hagedoorn, 1993; Hagedoorn et al., 2000; Caloghirou et al., 2003; Colombo et al., 2006; Kim and Vonortas, 2014).

While differences among sectors exist (Zirulia, 2009), the main motives are the following (Williams and Vonortas, 2015):

1. Access product and financial markets.
2. Share costs and risk of large investments such as R&D.
3. Access complementary resources and skills of partners and benefit from synergies.
4. Accelerate return on investments through more rapid diffusion of assets.
5. Deploy resources efficiently to create economies of scale, specialization and/or rationalization.
6. Increase strategic flexibility through the creation and optimal exploitation of new investment options.
7. Co-opt competition and gain market power.
8. Increase revenues for public research organizations, and universities in particular.

Antecedents of partnering
The factors affecting the likelihood that firms participate in collaborative agreements can be firm-specific, dyad-specific or industry-specific.

A positive association between firm size and propensity to form strategic alliances is one of the most recurrent results in the literature. It is found, for example, in Link and Bauer (1987), Kleinknecht and Reijen (1992), Hagedoorn and Schakenraad (1994), Colombo (1995), Colombo and Garrone (1998), Vonortas (1997), Ahuja (2000), Tether (2002), Veugelers and Cassiman (2002), Becker and Dietz (2004). The positive effect of firm size shows also for university–industry relations (Stuart et al. 2007; Fontana et al., 2006). There are several possible explanations for this result. Large firms can spread the gain from innovation over a larger base of economic activity, increasing their incentives towards cooperative agreements, as a form of R&D investment (Cohen and Klepper, 1996). Some forms of cooperative agreements (for instance R&D joint ventures) entail high physical and legal setup costs for which small firms lack financial resources. Finally, large firms can have significant bargaining power in contracting with their partners.

When the analysis focuses on new firms only, however, the results of the effect of size are somewhat different and mixed. Shan (1990), for instance, find a negative relationship between size and network participation in biotech; Shan et al. (1994) do not find a significant relationship; Colombo et al. (2006) find an inverted U shape for a sample of Italian new technology-based firms. Some authors (Colombo et al., 2006) have tried to explain this result as the net effect of two forces: a positive effect of size, related to the 'spreading' of managerial and transaction cost; and a negative effect of size, as long as size is correlated with the control of significant commercial assets that make alliances less needed.

The positive relation between R&D intensity and technological capabilities, on the one side, and network participation, on the other, is also a common result (Tether, 2002; Link and Bauer, 1987; Sakakibara, 2002; Stuart, 1998). Exploratory internal R&D also increases the probability that firms collaborate with universities (Bercovitz and Feldman, 2007). This suggests that internal and cooperative R&D should be seen as complementary rather than substitutive, which in turn points at the role of absorptive capacity (Zhao and Anand, 2009). Conversely, firms lacking technological capabilities are not in a position to reap the benefits from cooperation (Rothaermel and Hess, 2007). For startups, another explanation may hold. In many cases, their attractiveness as partners is related to specific technological competences and knowledge to which large incumbents want to have access. Frequently this knowledge is embodied and signalled by patents: holding valuable patents allows startup firms to be active in networks and to attract prominent incumbents (Rothaermel, 2002; Stuart et al., 1999).

Finally, the finding that firms with more experience in managing collaborative ties are more likely to enter further collaborative agreements is also quite robust (Gulati, 1995; Powell et al., 1996; Ahuja, 2000; Sakakibara, 2002; Vonortas and Okamura, 2009). Three main explanations have been proposed. The first relates to the notion of 'cooperative capability' (Gulati, 1998). With experience, firms learn how to manage their collaborative ties, to develop inter-firm knowledge-sharing routines, to govern contractual arrangements characterized by moral hazard and incompleteness, and to initiate the necessary changes in the partnership as it evolves over time. Experience, then, increases the returns from strategic technological alliances, and consequently their formation rates. A second explanation points at the role of previous partners as sources of information about new opportunities for alliances and new partners (Gulati and Gargiulo, 1999). The third explanation is of particular relevance to new firms and it is related to a reputation effect. Stuart et al. (1999) show that biotechnology startups aim at entering alliances with prominent partners because this is likely to provide significant advantages in terms of both performance and of subsequent ties. Connecting to a prestigious incumbent does not only provide access to superior quality resources but also entails strong reputational benefits.

Regarding dyad-specific factors, Vonortas and Okamura (2009) find that firms are more likely to collaborate the closer they are in terms of technological and market profiles, the higher the expected knowledge spillovers among them and the more familiar they are with each other through past interaction. The effect of technological proximity can be interpreted in light of the role of absorptive capacity. In order to learn, firms need pre-existing knowledge in the partner's field of expertise, and cognitive proximity is required for effective communication to occur. Similar results were obtained by Stuart (1998). However, excessive similarity may harm cooperation, limiting the opportunity for complementarities to be exploited. Along these lines, Mowery et al. (1998) find evidence of an inverted U relationship between partners' technological overlap and the probability of alliance formation. Evidence of a nonlinear effect is provided in Vonortas and Okamura (2009). Through repeated interactions (developing familiarity), firms can build trust, lowering transaction costs and limiting the risk of opportunistic behavior (Gulati, 1995), although prior alliances with the same partners may also create disincentives through the anticipation of reduced additional benefits from the new R&D alliance (Hoang and Rothaermel, 2005) or potential lock-in (Molina-Morales and Martínez-Fernández, 2009). Finally, there is evidence that the relative importance of dyadic factors may vary in different types of agreements (Garcez and Sbragia, 2013).

Environmental conditions also affect the intensity of strategic technological alliances. Link and Bauer (1987), Sakakibara (2002) and Hernan et al. (2003) find that R&D cooperation is more likely to occur in concentrated industries. Recently, Yu et al. (2013) showed that the global competitive intensity between two rival multinationals in the automobile industry positively affects the likelihood that they will ally in any host country. A number of possible explanations exist. In oligopolistic markets it is easier to find appropriate partners or to reach agreement towards cooperation. In addition, market power associated with such structures allows firms to appropriate the return from the alliance. Once again, it is worth mentioning that mixed results are found for startups. While Colombo et al. (2006) find that alliances are less frequent in more competitive sectors, negative relation between concentration and the rate of formation of strategic alliances is found by Eisenhardt and Shooven (1996) based on a sample of 102 US new firms in the semiconductor sector. In particular, these authors find that the number of competitors in the segment in which the firm operates positively affects the rate of alliance formation. They relate this result to the gains of accessing external resources when market conditions are difficult.

Conclusions

In parallel to strategic alliances, an extensive literature on networks has emerged in several related fields such as economics, management, sociology and organization theory. An important area of research has focused on networks arising from strategic technology alliances (Ozman, 2009; Malerba and Vonortas, 2009). This approach reflects the widespread acceptance of the argument that innovation must be understood looking also at the webs of the various relationships occurring among firms (Powell and Grodal, 2004). This literature has explored a host of interesting questions such as the contribution of overall networking activity on the rate and direction of technological change. Strategic technology alliances can be considered as resource economizing instruments that assist participants to hedge their bets. In turbulent technological environments characterized by significant levels of uncertainty, firms engage in exploratory activities in order to cope with environmental discontinuities. If, in addition to uncertainty, one considers that R&D investments are at least partially irreversible, a real option approach becomes plausible (Kogut, 1991; Bajeux-Besnainou et al., 2010). It is only a small step then to imagine the network operating as a *search engine* for alliance participants (Hemphill and Vonortas, 2003).

This is a wholly open field for future research. It closely relates to the role of strategic technology alliances in the management of risk and uncertainty by small and large firms alike. And it relates to the broader issue of evolution and dynamics of networks.

NICHOLAS S. VONORTAS

References

Ahuja, G. (2000), The duality of collaboration: inducements and opportunities in the formation of interfirm linkages, *Strategic Management Journal*, **21**(3), 317–343.

Bajeux-Besnainou, I., Joshi, S. and Vonortas, N. (2010), Uncertainty, networks and real options, *Journal of Economic Behavior and Organization*, **75**(3), 523–541.

Becker, W. and Dietz, J. (2004), R&D cooperation and innovation activities of firms – evidence for the German manufacturing industry, *Research Policy*, **33**(2), 209–223.

Bercovitz, J. and Feldman, M.P. (2007), Fishing upstream: firm innovation strategy and university research alliances, *Research Policy*, **36**(7), 930–948.

Caloghirou, Y., Hondroyiannis, G. and Vonortas, N.S. (2003), The performance of research partnerships, *Managerial and Decision Economics*, **24**(2–3), 85–99.

Cohen, W.M. and Klepper, S. (1996), A reprise of size and R&D, *The Economic Journal*, **106**(437), 925–951.

Colombo, M.G. (1995), Firm size and cooperation: the determinants of cooperative agreements in information technology industries, *International Journal of the Economics of Business*, **2**(1), 3–30.

Colombo, M.G. and Garrone, P. (1998), A simultaneous equation model of technological agreements and inframural R&D, in M.G. Colombo (ed.), *The Changing Boundaries of the Firm*, London: Routledge.

Colombo, M.G., Grilli, L. and Piva, E. (2006), In search of complementary assets: the determinants of alliance formation of high-tech start-ups, *Research Policy*, **35**(8), 1166–1199.

Cunningham, J.A. and Link, A.N. (2014), Fostering university–industry collaborations in European Union countries, *International Entrepreneurship and Management Journal*, http://link.springer.com/article/10.1007%2Fs11365-014-0317-4.

Eisenhardt, K.M. and Schoonhoven, C.B. (1996), Resource-based view of strategic alliance formation: strategic and social effects in entrepreneurial firms, *Organization Science*, 7(2), 136–150.

Fontana, R., Geuna, A.and Matt, M. (2006), Factors affecting university–industry R&D projects: the importance of searching, screening and signalling, *Research Policy*, 35(2), 309–323.

Garcez, M.P. and Sbragia, R. (2013), The selection of partners in technological alliances projects, *Journal of Technology Management and Innovation*, 8, 219–232.

Gulati, R. (1995), Social structure and alliance formation patterns: a longitudinal analysis, *Administrative Science Quarterly*, 40(4), 619–652.

Gulati, R. (1998), Alliances and networks, *Strategic Management Journal*, 19, 293–317.

Gulati, R. and Gargiulo, M. (1999), Where do interorganizational networks come from? *American Journal of Sociology*, 104(5), 1439–1493.

Hagedoorn, J. (1993), Understanding the rationale of strategic technology partnering: interorganizational modes of cooperation and sectoral differences, *Strategic Management Journal*, 14, 371–385.

Hagedoorn, J. and Schakenraad, J. (1994), The effect of strategic technology alliances on company performance, *Strategic Management Journal*, 15(4), 291–309.

Hagedoorn, J., Link, A. and Vonortas, N.S. (2000), Research partnerships, *Research Policy*, 29(4–5), 567–586.

Hemphill, T. and Vonortas, N. (2003), Strategic research partnerships: a managerial perspective, *Technology Analysis & Strategic Management*, 15(2), 255–271.

Hernan, R., Marin, P.L. and Siotis, G. (2003), An empirical evaluation of the determinants of research joint venture formation, *Journal of Industrial Economics*, 51(1), 75–89.

Hoang, H. and Rothaermel, F.T. (2005), The effect of general and partner-specific alliance experience on joint R&D project performance, *Academy of Management Journal*, 48(2), 332–345.

Kim, Y. and Vonortas, N.S. (2014), Cooperation in the formative years: evidence from small enterprises in Europe, *European Management Journal*, 32(5), 795–805.

Kleinknecht, A. and Reijnen, J. (1992), Why do firms cooperate on R&D? An empirical study, *Research Policy*, 21(4), 347–360.

Kogut, B. (1991), Joint ventures and the option to expand and acquire, *Management Science*, 37(1), 19–33.

Link, A.N. and Bauer, L.L. (1987), An economic analysis of cooperative research, *Technovation*, 6, 246–260.

Link, A.N. and Zmud, R. (1984), R&D patterns in the video display terminal industry, *Journal of Product Innovation Management*, 1(2), 106–115.

Malerba, F. and Vonortas, N. (eds) (2009), *Innovation Networks in Industries*, Cheltenham, UK and Northampton, MA: Edward Elgar Publishing.

Molina-Morales, F.X. and Martínez-Fernández, M.T. (2009), Research notes and commentaries: too much love in the neighborhood can hurt: how an excess of intensity and trust in relationships may produce negative effects on firms, *Strategic Management Journal*, 30(9), 1013–1023.

Mowery, D.C. and Sampat, B.N. (2005), The Bayh-Dole Act of 1980 and university–industry transfer: a model for other OECD governments?, *Journal of Technology Transfer*, 30(1–2), 115–127.

Mowery, D.C., Oxley, J.E. and Silverman, B.S. (1998), Technological overlap and interfirm cooperation: implications for the resource-based view of the firm, *Research Policy*, 27(5), 507–523.

Ozman, M. (2009), Inter-firm networks and innovation: a survey of literature, *Economics of Innovation and New Technology*, 18(1), 39–67.

Powell, W.W. and Grodal, S. (2004), Networks of innovators, in J. Fagerberg, D.C. Mowery and R. Nelson (eds), *The Oxford Handbook of Innovation*, Oxford: Oxford University Press.

Powell, W.W., Koput, K.W. and Smith-Doerr, L. (1996), Interorganizational collaboration and the locus of innovation: networks of learning in biotechnology, *Administrative Science Quarterly*, **41**(1), 116–145.

Rothaermel, F.T. (2002), Technological discontinuities and interfirm cooperation: what determines a startup's attractiveness as alliance partner?, *IEEE Transactions on Engineering Management*, **49**(4), 388–397.

Rothaermel, F.T. and Hess, A.M. (2007), Building dynamic capabilities: innovation driven by individual-, firm-, and network-level effects, *Organization Science*, **18**(6), 898–921.

Sakakibara, M. (2002), Formation of R&D consortia: industry and company effects, *Strategic Management Journal*, **23**(11), 1033–1050.

Shan, W. (1990), An empirical analysis of organizational strategies by entrepreneurial high-technology firms, *Strategic Management Journal*, **11**(2), 129–139.

Shan, W., Walker, G. and Kogut, B. (1994), Interfirm cooperation and startup innovation in the biotechnology industry, *Strategic Management Journal*, **15**(5), 387–394.

Stuart, T.E. (1998), Network positions and propensities to collaborate: an investigation of strategic alliance formation in a high-technology industry, *Administrative Science Quarterly*, **43**(3), 668–698.

Stuart, T.E., Hoang, H. and Hybels, R.C. (1999), Interorganizational endorsements and the performance of entrepreneurial ventures, *Administrative Science Quarterly*, **44**(2), 315–349.

Stuart, T.E., Ozdemir, S.Z. and Ding, W.W. (2007), Vertical alliance networks: the case of university-biotechnology-pharmaceutical alliance chains, *Research Policy*, **36**(4), 477–498.

Teece, D.J. and Jorde, T.M. (eds) (1992), *Antitrust, Innovation, and Competitiveness*, New York: Oxford University Press.

Tether, B.S. (2002), Who co-operates for innovation, and why: an empirical analysis, *Research Policy*, **31**(6), 947–967.

Veugelers, R. and Cassiman, B. (2002), R&D cooperation and spillovers: some empirical evidence from Belgium, *American Economic Review*, **92**(4), 1169–1184.

Vonortas, N.S. (1997), *Cooperation in Research and Development*, Boston, MA: Kluwer Academic Publishers.

Vonortas, N.S. and Okamura, K. (2009), Research partners, *International Journal of Technology Management*, **46**(3–4), 280–306.

Williams, T. and Vonortas, N. (2015), Strategic alliances/knowledge-intensive partnerships, in N.S. Vonortas, P.C Rouge and A. Aridi (eds), *Innovation Policy: A Practical Introduction*, New York: Springer, pp. 47–64.

Yu, T., Subramaniam, M. and Cannella, A.A. (2013), Competing globally, allying locally: alliances between global rivals and host-country factors, *Journal of International Business Studies*, **44**, 117–137.

Zhao, Z.J. and Anand, J. (2009), A multilevel perspective on knowledge transfer: evidence from the Chinese automotive industry, *Strategic Management Journal*, **30**(9), 959–983.

Zirulia, L. (2009), The dynamics of networks and the evolution of industries: a survey of the empirical literature, in F. Malerba and N. Vonortas (eds), *Innovation Networks in Industries*, Cambridge: Cambridge University Press.

29 Returnee Entrepreneurs

Introduction

Returnee entrepreneurs are defined as skilled personnel, including students and scientists, who have returned to their home country to start a new venture after several years of education and/or business experience in developed countries or OECD countries (Filatotchev et al., 2009; Liu et al., 2010a; Wright et al., 2008). Returnee entrepreneurs, as an increasingly important phenomenon in emerging economies, have stimulated research interest that has resulted in a growing number of studies on this topic (Dai and Liu, 2009; Filatotchev et al., 2009; Lin et al., 2015; Liu et al., 2010b, 2014; Pruthi, 2014; Wright et al., 2008). This chapter provides an overview of the extant literature on returnee entrepreneurs in emerging economies.

Literature review
Existing academic research has found that returnee entrepreneurs have a number of unique characteristics compared with their local counterparts. First, returnee entrepreneurs have acquired advanced technology and knowhow due to their exposure to developed host countries and such knowledge can be transferred to their home emerging country. This knowledge may be academic knowledge from general education (Liu et al., 2010a). Alternatively, it may involve scientific and technical training together with practical business human capital as a result of working in a commercial environment or from starting a business in a developed economy (Wright et al., 2008). Second, returnee entrepreneurs are simultaneously exposed to the country where they studied/worked and their home country. Such dual exposure to both the home and host countries provides returnee entrepreneurs with an opportunity to identify cross-country knowledge gaps and draw upon sources of advanced knowledge and new ideas for their entrepreneurship (Dai and Liu, 2009). Finally, returnee entrepreneurs may develop international networks through social relationships in developed host countries where they worked/studied (Filatotchev et al., 2009; Liu et al., 2010b; Pruthi, 2014). They may be able to continue updating technology and gaining new ideas through personal and professional ties in the host country even after they have returned to their home country. In particular, such networks help returnee entrepreneurs to identify business opportunities in their home country and they act as knowledge brokers across national borders.

The existing literature on returnee entrepreneurs has systematically examined a number of issues, including the factors affecting their entrepreneurial decisions, the location choices of returnee entrepreneurs for starting their businesses, firm performance, as well as the impact of returnee entrepreneurs on other local firms (Dai and Liu, 2009; Filatotchev et al., 2009; Lin et al., 2015; Liu et al., 2010b, 2014; Pruthi, 2014; Wright et al., 2008; Zhou and Hsu, 2011). These studies can be categorized into four groups.

One group of studies focuses on factors affecting returnees' entrepreneurial decisions. Pruthi (2014) examined the role of social ties in venture creation by Indian returnee entrepreneurs based on qualitative analysis, and explored the structure of returnee entrepreneurs' social ties as they return home and create new ventures. The findings suggest that local ties are crucial for venture creation by returnee entrepreneurs. Her study enhances our understanding of the role of returnees' networks in upgrading domestic entrepreneurial capability and fills a research gap on what affects returnees' entrepreneurial decisions in the first place. Lin et al. (2015) conducted a comparative multi-case study on returnee entrepreneurs and local entrepreneurs in China. They found that returnee entrepreneurs' prior exposure to different institutional contexts shapes their new ventures' formal–informal balance at an early stage and returnee entrepreneurs emphasize formality more than informality compared with local entrepreneurs. However, over time, the formality and informality balance of both types of entrepreneurs converges in line with the institutional transition in China.

A second type of studies investigated how returnees choose locations for starting their new venture and how their location choices subsequently affect firm performance (Wright et al., 2008). The findings indicate that returnee entrepreneurs with academic knowledge in the form of patents transferred from abroad tend to locate in non-university science parks, while those with previous startup experience abroad choose university science parks to set up their businesses. In addition, the firms set up by returnee entrepreneurs in non-university science parks enjoy stronger employment growth, and those with commercial experience abroad perform better in university science parks. The empirical evidence confirms the view that returnee entrepreneurs seek complementarity concerning their location choices in the home country.

A third group of studies examined the relationship between the characteristics of returnee entrepreneurs and firm performance compared with non-returnee firms (Dai and Liu, 2009; Filatotchev et al., 2009; Liu et al., 2014). Some studies have compared whether the firms set up by returnee entrepreneurs are more export-orientated, more innovative and have better performance than non-returnee firms. The findings based on these studies suggest that the unique characteristics of returnee entrepreneurs have a positive association with firm performance in terms of exporting, innovation and employment growth. Liu et al. (2014) adopted the learning perspective and investigated the impact of the learning capabilities of returnee entrepreneurs on firm performance. They found that experiential and vicarious learning help boost perceptual performance, whereas vicarious learning is positively associated with employment growth. Firm age weakens the impact of experiential learning, especially on perceptual performance, and reduces the impact of vicarious learning on employment growth. By examining the interrelationship between returnee entrepreneurs' learning capabilities and firm age, their research revealed that the impact of entrepreneurial learning depends on organizational contexts.

However, some scholars have suggested that returnee entrepreneurs have disadvantages due to their absence from the home-country environment for a period of time when living in foreign countries. Returnee entrepreneurs may suffer from the liability of 'outsiderness' and a lack of local connections as well as difficulties in cultural readjustment (Li et al., 2012; Obukhova et al., 2013; Lin et al., 2015). Zhou and Hsu (2011) found that returnee entrepreneurs in China encounter culture shock and face considerable difficulties in adjusting to China's developing domestic market. They call for more studies taking account of both the advantages and disadvantages of returnee entrepreneurs.

Finally, the existing research has examined whether returnee entrepreneurs are a new channel for international knowledge spillovers (Liu et al., 2010a, 2010b). The findings from these studies suggest that the firms set up by returnee entrepreneurs positively affect the innovative activities of other local firms through knowledge spillovers, and the presence of returnee-owned firms helps to enhance the technological capabilities of other local firms (Filatotchev et al., 2011). The greater the technology gap experienced by the non-returnee firm in relation to international developed economy industry standards, the greater the effect of returnee-owned firms (Liu et al., 2010a, 2010b). These studies suggest that returnee entrepreneurs act as an alternative mechanism in resolving the deficit of entrepreneurship and stimulate innovation in emerging economies due to their dual exposure to the home and host countries.

Conclusion

Returnee entrepreneurs have become an emerging theme within the entrepreneurship field due to increasing human mobility across national borders. The existing literature on returnee entrepreneurs has investigated a wide range of issues in terms of entrepreneurial decisions, firm performance and the impact of returnee-owned firms. While the findings from existing studies have enhanced our understanding of this phenomenon, there remains a need to further advance research in this area. In particular, the impact of returnee entrepreneurs on host countries is missing. In addition, the existing literature has predominantly focused on Chinese and Indian returnee entrepreneurs. Future research should be extended to other emerging economies, especially African countries. Such an extension will enable scholars to obtain generalizable findings.

XIAOHUI LIU

References

Dai, O. and Liu, X. (2009), Returnee entrepreneurs and firm performance in emerging economies, *International Business Review*, **18**(4), 373–386.

Filatotchev, I., Liu, X., Buck, T. and Wright, M. (2009), The export orientation and export performance of high-technology SMEs in emerging markets: the effects of knowledge transfer by returnee entrepreneurs, *Journal of International Business Studies*, **40**(6), 1005–1021.

Filatotchev, I., Liu, X., Lu, J. and Wright, M. (2011), Knowledge spillovers through human mobility across national borders: evidence from Zhongguancun science park in China, *Research Policy*, **40**(3), 453–462.

Li, H., Zhang, Y., Li, Y., Zhou, L. and Zhang, W. (2012), Returnees versus locals: who performs better in China's technology entrepreneurship?, *Strategic Entrepreneurship Journal*, **6**(3), 257–272.

Lin, D., Lu, J., Li, P. and Liu, X. (2015), Balancing formality and informality in business exchanges as a duality: a comparative case study of returnee and local entrepreneurs in China, *Management and Organization Review*, **11**(2), 315–42.

Liu, X., Lu, J., Filatotchev, I., Buck, T. and M. Wright (2010a), Returnee entrepreneurs, knowledge spillovers and innovation in high-tech firms in emerging economies, *Journal of International Business Studies*, **41**(7), 1183–1197.

Liu, X., Wright, M., Filatotchev, I., Dai, O. and Lu, J. (2010b), Human mobility and international knowledge spillovers: evidence from high-tech small and medium enterprises in an emerging market, *Strategic Entrepreneurship Journal*, **4**(4), 340–355.

Liu, X., Wright, M. and Filatotchev, I. (2014), Learning, firm age and performance: an investigation of returnee entrepreneurs in Chinese high-tech industries, *International Small Business Journal*, http://isb.sagepub.com/content/early/2013/12/10/0266242613508147.

Obukhova, E., Wang, Y. and Li, J. (2012), *The Power of Local Networks: Returnee Entrepreneurs, School Ties, and Firm Performance*, working paper, MIT Sloan School of Management.

Pruthi, S. (2014), Social ties and venture creation by returnee entrepreneurs, *International Business Review*, **23**(6), 1139–1152.

Wright, M., Liu, X., Buck, T. and Filatotchev, I. (2008), Returnee entrepreneurs, science park location choice and performance: an analysis of high technology SMEs in China, *Entrepreneurship Theory and Practice*, **32**(1), 131–156.

Zhou, Y. and Hsu, J.Y. (2011), Divergent engagements: roles and strategies of Taiwanese and mainland Chinese returnee entrepreneurs in the IT industry, *Global Networks*, **11**(3), 398–419.

30 Risk Funding

Introduction

Since the work of Schumpeter (1911), an extensive literature has emphasized the positive influence of the development of a country's financial system on the level of its economy. It is indeed commonly believed that there is a positive relation between the development of stock markets and economic progress (Black and Gilson, 1998; Kortum and Lerner, 2000; Jeng and Wells, 2000). There are many reasons why the depth of financial sector development can promote economic growth, but the microeconomic rationale for financial systems is essentially based on the existence of frictions in the trading system. In a world in which writing, issuing and enforcing contracts consume resources and in which information is not symmetric and its acquisition costly, properly functioning financial systems can reduce these information and transactions costs.

The argument lies in the fact that the services granted by an efficient financial sector (e.g., reallocating capital, diversifying risk, mobilizing savings, monitoring the allocations of managers) may limit frictional costs and provide an important catalyst of economic growth (Pagano, 1993). The development of an efficient financial system facilitates indeed the interactions between savers and investors and, ultimately, stimulates economic growth. Rajan and Zingales (2001) argue that industries that are more dependent on external finance benefit from a competitive advantage in countries where the financial market is well-developed. Similarly, they suggest that financial development may play a particularly beneficial role in the rise of new firms, and thus enhance growth and innovation in indirect ways.

The existence of asymmetric information in capital markets means that financial institutions might not adequately assess risky projects. This effect is most important in the case of small and innovative businesses, owing to a lack of reliable information about their real status and performance. In order to alleviate the risk of market failure due to the lemon's problem (Akerlof, 1970; Spence, 1973; Stiglitz, 2000), firms often have to provide credible (and therefore costly) signals that convey the quality of their innovation projects. Risk funding is therefore a hard task for entrepreneurial firms. Nevertheless, access to financing is a key determinant of their growth.

The debate over financing is centered on understanding, evaluating and improving the external funding environment confronting innovative startups, in the absence of sufficient internally generated cash flows. Many discussions have revolved around the unsuitability of debt for early-stage financing (Stiglitz and Weiss, 1981). This is mainly due to the fact that debt-holders bear the downside risk, but do not share the upside of successful innovation (Berger and Udell, 1998). Prospects for contractual funding, such as securing collateral loans against appropriate assets, are severely limited for entrepreneurial firms, since most of their resources are intangible and tend to have limited salvage value because of their highly specific nature (Hubbard, 1998). Entrepreneurial firms typically seek external equity investors willing to bear risk and bet on future value creation opportunities (Carpenter and Petersen, 2002). For these firms, equity has a number of advantages over debt: it does not require the firm to post collaterals, the investors' positive returns are not bounded and managers are not encouraged to undertake excessively risky projects. Last but not least, external equity does not increase the probability of financial distress.

Even though debt and equity may be seen as substitute sources of corporate finance, there is strong evidence suggesting that this belief is misguided and that debt and equity act more as complements to each other (e.g., Demirgüç-Kunt and Levine, 1996; Demirgüç-Kunt and Maksimovic, 1996, 1998). In this chapter, therefore, we consider both debt and equity as forms of risk funding, although we clearly devote more attention to the second. With this aim, we first describe how firms can raise capital, and then focus on the risk funding for entrepreneurial firms. Finally, we conclude with an attempt to identify recent trends in entrepreneurial finance.

Raising capital

In the world of Modigliani and Miller (1958) – without taxes, bankruptcy costs, informational asymmetries or agency costs – capital structure is irrelevant to total firm value. But in a world with taxes and bankruptcy costs, capital structure matters, and an important question facing companies in need of new finance is whether to raise capital internally or externally, and whether to raise debt or equity. The academic debate on the optimal capital structure is extensive both theoretically and empirically.

The source of capital for an entrepreneur that may allow him to escape the costs arising from the presence of information asymmetries is self-financing: entrepreneurs draw upon their own money. In the presence of limited resources, however, the ability to grow rapidly will be constrained if external sources of capital are not used. When internal financing becomes insufficient, a firm must gain access to capital markets and make a decision about the type of funds to raise. There are two options: debt or equity.

Equity capital is represented by funds that are raised by a business in exchange for a share of ownership in the company. Equity financing allows a business to obtain funds without having to repay a specific amount of money at a particular time. On the contrary, debt capital is represented by funds borrowed by a business that must be repaid over a period of time, usually with interest. Debt financing can be either short-term, with full repayment due in less than one year, or long-term, with repayment due over a period greater than one year. The lender does not gain an ownership interest in the business and debt obligations are typically limited to repaying the loan with interest. Loans are often secured by some or all the assets of the company.

To summarize, the main difference between debt and equity is that debt-holders have a contract specifying that their claims must be paid in full before the firm can make payments to its equity-holders. This is the main reason why equity is often referred to as risky capital. The second distinction is that the cost of debt financing is generally viewed as a tax-deductible expense of the firm. The possibility to deduct interest expenses generates a 'tax shield,' which is one of the major advantages of issuing debt instead of equity. However, as leverage increases, the tax advantage of debt eventually will be offset by an increased cost of debt, reflecting the greater likelihood for the firm to incur financial distress (Jensen and Meckling, 1976). Excessive debt financing may indeed impair a firm's credit rating and its future ability to raise further capital. In addition, an excessive gearing may make the firm unable to weather unanticipated business downturns, credit shortages or interest rate increases. With a few exceptions, such as the recent development of a market for mini-bonds through crowdfunding platforms, it is therefore not surprising that debt is not a suitable source of risk funding.

Risk capital for entrepreneurial firms

Equity capital markets have two basic functions. The first function is accomplished by the primary market, which provides new capital for business, usually in the form of share issues or loans, while the second function is accomplished by the secondary market, where existing securities are traded. This chapter mainly focuses on the primary market and considers the processes that a firm would have to go through to raise fresh finance. By doing so, the present study is positioned in the panorama of the corporate finance literature. It first describes the main features of the process of raising external equity and distinguishes between private and public sources of risk funding.

Both private (e.g., venture capital) and public (stock exchanges) equity can be raised by firms. The essential features of private share issues are that they may be made only to limited numbers and categories of people and that they do not require the issue of any formal sales document or prospectus. There is no general rule about the documents required to attest a private share issue, but the main contractual obligation is usually associated with a subscription and a shareholder agreement covering the issue of shares itself. Private and public equity are strictly interconnected, as venture capitalists are more likely to invest when there is an active equity market that permits them to exit by selling their shares without incurring considerable transaction costs (Black and Gilson, 1998). For instance, a large number of public policies (especially in the European Union) have been designed with the explicit goal of developing risk capital markets capable of sustaining entrepreneurship and facilitating the expansion of existing small firms.

The activity of financing entrepreneurs has naturally existed almost as long as entrepreneurs themselves. While debt financing could satisfy the demand of capital at later stages of a firm's business, new, high-growth, high-risk ventures that expect several years of negative earnings have typically been forced to seek alternative sources of money. To this extent, venture capital represents one established solution to financing high-risk, high-reward ventures.

Venture capitalists (VCs) raise finance from outside investors and iden-tify investment opportunities and projects. The returns flow as capital gains upon completion of the project. Seed capital is the first type of financing a newly founded company might want to secure, in order to fund R&D and commercial expenditures; startup investments are targeted at companies gearing up to produce and market their products. Finally, in the expansion stage investing, the company has to fund growth oppor-tunities, enlarging its manufacturing and distribution capacity as well as engaging in external acquisitions.

Venture funding is believed to have a positive impact on creating jobs, boosting capital markets, and fostering innovation (Hellmann and Puri, 2000). Given the key role played by innovative young firms in the economy, and the importance of external financing for these firms, the crucial role played by VCs in fostering entrepreneurship is evident and has been documented by numerous studies (e.g., Colombo and Grilli, 2010; Chemmanur et al., 2011; Puri and Zarutskie, 2012; Croce et al., 2013). VCs provide portfolio companies with bundles of value-added activities, including direct coaching and indirect benefits, such as a certification effect to third parties (e.g., customers, skilled workers, alliance partners and financial intermediaries) (Gompers and Lerner, 2001).

However, for reasons that will be discussed in detail in the next section, the equity gap faced by young innovative firms cannot be entirely filled by the private VC market. Many governments have tried to face this issue by setting up programs aimed at fostering VC financing through the establishment of government VC funds (Cumming and Johan, 2009). Besides addressing the financial gap problem, this type of VC can pursue investments that will ultimately yield social payoffs and positive externali-ties for society as a whole. The drawback of these instruments, however, is that they may crowd out rather than stimulate private investments. The rationale and appropriateness of these programs are at the center of a controversial academic debate, reviewed in Colombo et al. (2014).

Yet, the presence of efficient stock exchanges dedicated to startups and growth firms is necessary to provide investors with an exit. The possibility to monetize investments by conducting an initial public offering (IPO) has indeed been mentioned as one of the most important factors that posi-tively influence the raising of new venture capital funds (Black and Gilson, 1998; Berlin, 1998; Gompers and Lerner, 1998; Jeng and Wells, 2000). As Black and Gilson (1998) point out, the existence of a well-developed stock market that permits exits through an IPO is critical to the exist-ence of a vibrant venture capital market. In fact, they found a significant relationship between the number of venture-backed IPOs and new capital commitments to venture capital funds in the following year.

The financial economics literature has notably focused on examining IPOs, potentially because they are an ideal setting in which to investigate the application of the IPO anomaly and efficient market hypotheses, and because share price data are easily available from the IPO onwards. The challenge of assessing for the first time the value of a new venture in a competitive marketplace is accomplished at the time of the IPO. Barry et al. (1990), Megginson and Weiss (1991), Lerner (1994), Gompers (1996), Gompers and Lerner (1998) and Lin and Smith (1998) have published papers concerning IPO underpricing and the VC-backed IPO as an event. VC-backed IPOs suffer from smaller underpricing because of the certification effect, and their mitigating role on adverse selection and moral hazard problems (Bruton et al., 2009). Similarly, VC-backed IPOs perform better in the long run than non-VC-backed IPOs, with the general long-term underperformance of IPOs mainly resulting from small non-VC-backed IPOs (Brav and Gompers, 1997). The presence of venture capitalists also improves the survival probability of IPO issuing firms (Jain and Kini, 2000).

Only public companies may offer shares to the public, and in doing so they must issue a prospectus complying with detailed regulations concerning the disclosure of information about the company, its business and its prospects. If a company's shares are to be listed on any stock exchange or are subject to any off-exchange dealing facility, the rules of the relevant exchange or dealing body will need to be complied with. These rules vary substantially according to the type of listing or dealing facility. Usually, there is a detailed set of listing rules covering financial and other information to be provided to shareholders and the market, how material transactions and transactions involving directors must be notified and approved, and corporate governance. The timescale for floating a company on a stock exchange tends to be significantly longer than that for a private issue. The main document associated with a public offer of shares is the prospectus, which is accompanied by a variety of agreements that will include an arrangement with the sponsor setting out the responsibilities of the company and its directors for the prospectus, and the responsibilities of the sponsor for sponsoring and, in the case of an underwritten offer, underwriting the offer. As a result, the process of raising equity from public rather than private investors tends to be more costly for firms, with auditing, legal, printing, exchange listing and investment banking fees being the main direct costs typically associated with an IPO (e.g., Ritter, 1987).

The valuation of an IPO company is determined by many factors.

Country-specific institutional characteristics, such as listing standards (Johan, 2010) and the quality and enforcement of securities laws (La Porta et al., 2006; Jackson and Roe, 2009), are found to affect the valuation obtained by the issuing firm. Firm-specific characteristics are also found to play a role, such as the listing firm's fundamentals (Aggarwal et al., 2009; Kim and Ritter, 1999), its ownership structure (Meoli et al., 2009; Yeh et al., 2008), insider ownership (Certo et al., 2003), the prestige of its top management team (Cohen and Dean, 2005; Pollock and Gulati, 2007) and its academic affiliation (Bonardo et al., 2011). Finally, a very important factor influencing the valuation of companies at the IPO stage is the quality of their corporate governance (Bell et al., 2012; Certo, 2003). Overall, the empirical evidence is supportive of the existence of a positive link between corporate governance quality and the valuation of IPO firms (Bertoni et al., 2014).

Conclusions

An intense debate has recently focused on the way in which a firm's existing shareholders are able to exit from their investment, as in the case of venture capitalists that look for the most convenient way to cash out. Part of the reason for the above interest is due to the fact that, in recent years, a private firm has been much more likely to be acquired than to go public: see, for example, Gao et al. (2013) who show the significant decline in the number of IPOs in the US over the past decade. This suggests an increased preference for acquisitions rather than IPOs as an exit mechanism. Existing empirical analyses of IPOs versus acquisitions treat private firms' exit decisions as a one-time choice between the two (Brau et al., 2003; Poulsen and Stegemoller, 2008; Chemmanur et al., 2012). However, in reality, a significant proportion of firms first go public and are acquired shortly thereafter. IPOs and acquisitions can therefore be seen not only as substitutes but also as complementary steps in a firm's exit process.

Chemmanur et al. (2014) are the first to take a dynamic approach and analyze how explicitly accounting for dynamic considerations, such as the benefits arising from being acquired after going public at higher valuations relative to a direct acquisition, or the costs arising from being delisted at lower valuations, alters the initial IPO versus acquisition trade-off. One crucial factor driving this choice is the product market. They find that firms that are more viable against product market competition, characterized by larger private benefits of control and lower information asymmetry, are more likely to choose an IPO over a direct acquisition as an initial exit mechanism. Then, firms that are more viable in the product market and are able to reduce information asymmetry to a greater extent by going public are more likely to be acquired post-IPO.

The IPO market and the merger and acquisition (M&A) market are therefore not as independent as often assumed. The fresh capital raised through an IPO could make available the funds needed to fuel the firm's external growth (Hovakimian and Hutton, 2010). Besides cash acquisitions, the IPO may also facilitate stock deals, as the establishment of a market price and the creation of public shares allows stocks to be used as currency to participate in M&As (Celikyurt et al., 2010). Indeed, the prospects of future deals grow as valuation challenges for would-be investors are alleviated with the IPO placing a price on the firm. Forming a currency of stock for future M&A deals is actually one of the most important motivations for going public (Brau and Fawcett, 2006).

The IPO may also mitigate inefficiencies in the M&A market in another way. IPOs can be part of a larger process of transferring control rights, where owner-managers of private firms use the IPO as part of a divestiture strategy (Reuer and Shen, 2004). In order to identify potential acquirers and to increase a firm's visibility, shareholders of private firms could decide to use sequential divestitures through IPOs rather than outright sales. The process of going public would therefore be responsive to adverse selection problems by increasing the amount of information available on the firm (Reuer and Shen, 2003). The IPO and the contextual move from the private to the public domain increases the level of a firm's disclosure and of investors' monitoring. The consequent decrease in information asymmetries may, in turn, raise the profile of the firm and increase its bargaining power vis-à-vis potential acquirers (Zingales, 1995). To the extent that the process of going public credibly reveals information on a firm's value, the IPO market can enhance the efficiency of the M&A market, which would otherwise be characterized by lengthier negotiations and less favorable bids for targets (Coff, 1999). An important role in certifying the quality of the company going public is played by the affiliation with reputable investment banks involved in the IPO process (Carter and Manaster, 1990). These financial intermediaries are expected to credibly certify the quality of firms because of the repeated nature of their business (Beatty and Ritter, 1986), which encourages them to preserve their reputational capital and to desist from opportunism (Paleari and Vismara, 2007). As a consequence, existing shareholders of private firms can maximize their firm's value by adopting the strategy of divesting after taking the company public, rather than directly selling a still-private firm at value limited by illiquidity (lack of marketability) discount (Silber, 1991).

Going public in an organized stock market does not represent any more the only possibility to raise public equity. A recent legislative initiative in the US, the Jumpstart Our Business Startups (JOBS) Act of 2012, was passed to stimulate economic growth by improving access to the public capital markets. Amongst others (e.g., the CROWDFUND Act), the JOBS Act defines the framework for crowdfunding in the US. Crowdfunding is concerned with raising funds (and advice) from a large pool of backers (crowd) collected online by means of a web platform. Crowdfunding has started making its way into entrepreneurial finance. Reward-based crowdfunding allows proponents of innovative projects to raise money from a crowd of backers before delivering to them a product or service. Equity crowdfunding will essentially allow unsophisticated investors to invest directly in young innovative firms. This means that crowdfunding platforms will need to cope with collective-action problems, since crowd-investors have neither the ability nor the incentive, due to small investment sizes, to devote substantial resources to due diligence. For this reason, crowdfunding will hardly offer high-average returns to investors (Ritter, 2014).

SILVIO VISMARA

References

Aggarwal, R., Bhagat, S. and Rangan, S. (2009), The impact of fundamentals on IPO valuation, *Financial Management*, **38**(2), 253–284.

Akerlof, G.A. (1970), The market for 'lemons': quality uncertainty and the market mechanism, *Quarterly Journal of Economics*, **84**(3), 488–500.

Barry, C.B., Muscarella, C.J., Peavy, J.W. and Vetsuypens, M.R. (1990), The role of venture capital in the creation of public companies: evidence from the going-public process, *Journal of Financial Economics*, **27**(2), 447–471.

Beatty, R.P. and Ritter, J.R. (1986), Investment banking, reputation, and the underpricing of initial public offerings, *Journal of Financial Economics*, **15**(1–2), 213–232.

Bell, R.G., Moore, C.B. and Filatotchev, I. (2012), Strategic and institutional effects on foreign IPO performance: examining the impact of country of origin, corporate governance, and host country effects, *Journal of Business Venturing*, **27**(2), 197–216.

Berger, A.N. and Udell, G.F. (1998), The economics of small business finance: the roles of private equity and debt markets in the financial growth cycle, *Journal of Banking and Finance*, **22**(6–8), 613–673.

Berlin, M. (1998), That thing venture capitalists do, *Federal Reserve Bank of Philadelphia Business Review*, **1**, 15–26.

Bertoni, F., Meoli, M. and Vismara, S. (2014), Board independence, ownership structure and the valuation of IPOs in Continental Europe, *Corporate Governance: An International Review*, **22**(2), 116–131.

Black, B.S. and Gilson, R.J. (1998), Venture capital and the structure of capital markets: banks versus stock markets, *Journal of Financial Economics*, **47**(3), 243–277.

Bonardo, D., Paleari, S. and Vismara, S. (2011), Valuing university-based firms: the effects of academic affiliation on IPO performance, *Entrepreneurship Theory and Practice*, **35**(4), 755–776.

Brau, J.C. and Fawcett, S.E. (2006), Initial public offerings: an analysis of theory and practice, *Journal of Finance*, **61**(1), 399–436.

Brau, J.C., Francis, B. and Kohers, N. (2003), The choice of IPO versus takeover: empirical evidence, *Journal of Business*, **76**(4), 583–612.

Brav, A. and Gompers, P.A. (1997), Myth or reality? The long-run underperformance of initial public offerings: evidence from venture and non-venture capital-backed companies, *Journal of Finance*, **52**(5), 1791–1821.

Bruton, G.D., Chahine, S. and Filatotchev, I. (2009), Founders, private equity investors, and underpricing in entrepreneurial IPOs, *Entrepreneurship Theory and Practice*, **33**(4), 909–928.

Carpenter, R.E. and Petersen, B.C. (2002), Capital market imperfections, high-tech investment, and new equity financing, *Economic Journal*, **112**(477), F54–F72.

Carter, R. and Manaster, S. (1990), Initial public offerings and underwriter reputation, *Journal of Finance*, **45**(4), 1045–1067.

Celikyurt, U., Sevilir, M. and Shivdasani, A. (2010), Going public to acquire? The acquisition motive in IPOs, *Journal of Financial Economics*, **96**(3), 345–363.

Certo, S.T. (2003), Influencing initial public offering investors with prestige: signaling with board structures, *Academy of Management Review*, **28**(3), 432–446.

Certo, S.T., Daily, C.M., Cannella, A.A. and Dalton, D.R. (2003), Giving money to get money: how CEO stock options and CEO equity enhance IPO valuations, *Academy of Management Journal*, **46**(5), 643–653.

Chemmanur, T.J., Krishnan, K. and Nandy, D.K. (2011), How does venture capital financing improve efficiency in private firms? A look beneath the surface, *Review of Financial Studies*, **24**(12), 4037–4090.

Chemmanur, T.J., He, J., He, S. and Nandy, D. (2012), *The Exit Choices of Entrepreneurial Firms*, unpublished working paper, Boston College.

Chemmanur, T.J., Signori, A. and Vismara, S. (2014), *Two Stage Exits: An Empirical Analysis of the Dynamic Choice between IPOs and Acquisitions by European Private Firms*, unpublished working paper, Boston College.

Coff, R.W. (1999), How buyers cope with uncertainty when acquiring firms in knowledge-intensive industries: caveat emptor, *Organization Science*, **10**(2), 144–161.

Cohen, B.D. and Dean, T.J. (2005), Information asymmetry and investor valuation of IPOs: top management team legitimacy as a capital market signal, *Strategic Management Journal*, **26**(7), 683–690.

Colombo, M.G. and Grilli, L. (2010), On growth drivers of high-tech start-ups: exploring the role of founders' human capital and venture capital, *Journal of Business Venturing*, **25**(6), 610–626.

Colombo, M.G., Cumming, D.J. and Vismara, S. (2014), Governmental venture capital for innovative young firms, *Journal of Technology Transfer*.

Croce, A., Martí, J. and Murtinu, S. (2013), The impact of venture capital on the productivity growth of European entrepreneurial firms: 'screening' or 'value added' effect? *Journal of Business Venturing*, **28**(4), 489–510.

Cumming, D. and Johan, S. (2009), Pre-seed government venture capital funds, *Journal of International Entrepreneurship*, **7**(1), 26–56.

Demirgüç-Kunt, A. and Levine, R. (1996), Stock market development and financial intermediaries: stylized facts, *The World Bank Economic Review*, **10**(2), 291–321.

Demirgüç-Kunt, A. and Maksimovic, V. (1996), Stock market development and financing choices of firms, *The World Bank Economic Review*, **10**(2), 341–369.

Demirgüç-Kunt, A. and Maksimovic, V. (1998), Law, finance, and firm growth, *The Journal of Finance*, **53**(6), 2107–2137.

Gao, X., Ritter, J.R. and Zhu, Z. (2013), Where have all the IPOs gone? *Journal of Financial and Quantitative Analysis*, **48**(6), 1663–1692.

Gompers, P. (1996), Grandstanding in the venture capital industry, *Journal of Financial Economics*, **42**(1), 133–156.

Gompers, P. and Lerner, J. (1998), Venture capital distributions: short-run and long-run reactions, *Journal of Finance*, **53**(6), 2161–2183.

Gompers, P. and Lerner, J. (2001), The venture capital revolution, *Journal of Economic Perspectives*, **15**(2), 145–168.

Hellman, T. and Puri, M. (2000), The interaction between product market and financing strategy: the role of venture capital, *Review of Financial Studies*, **13**(4), 959–984.

Hovakimian, A. and Hutton, I. (2010), Merger motivated IPOs, *Financial Management*, **39**(4), 1547–1573.

Hubbard, R.G. (1998), Capital-market imperfections and investment, *Journal of Economic Literature*, **36**(1), 193–225.

Jackson, H.E. and Roe, M.J. (2009), Public and private enforcement of securities laws: resource-based evidence, *Journal of Financial Economics*, **93**(2), 207–238.

Jain, B.A. and Kini, O. (2000), Does the presence of venture capitalists improve the survival profile of IPO firms? *Journal of Business Finance & Accounting*, **27**(9–10), 1139–1183.

Jeng, L.A. and Wells, P.C. (2000), The determinants of venture capital funding: evidence across countries, *Journal of Corporate Finance*, **6**(3), 241–289.

Jensen, M.C. and Meckling, W.H. (1976), Theory of the firm: managerial behavior, agency costs and ownership structure, *Journal of Financial Economics*, **3**(4), 305–360.

Johan, S.A. (2010), Listing standards as a signal of IPO preparedness and quality, *International Review of Law and Economics*, **30**(2), 128–144.

Kim, M. and Ritter, J.R. (1999), Valuing IPOs, *Journal of Financial Economics*, **53**(3), 409–438.

Kortum, S. and Lerner, J. (2000), Assessing the contribution of venture capital to innovation, *RAND Journal of Economics*, **31**(4), 674–692.

La Porta, R., Lopez-De-Silanes, F. and Shleifer, A. (2006), What works in securities laws? *Journal of Finance*, **61**(1), 1–32.

Lerner, J. (1994), Venture capitalists and the decision to go public, *Journal of Financial Economics*, **35**(3), 293–316.

Lin, T.H. and Smith, R.L. (1998), Insider reputation and selling decisions: the unwinding of venture capital investments during equity IPOs, *Journal of Corporate Finance*, **4**(3), 241–263.

Megginson, W.L. and Weiss, K.A. (1991), Venture capitalist certification in initial public offerings, *Journal of Finance*, **46**(3), 879–903.

Meoli, M., Paleari S. and Vismara, S. (2009), IPO valuation of European pyramidal groups, *Banking and Finance Review*, **1**(1), 17–34.

Modigliani, F. and Miller, M.H. (1958), The cost of capital, corporation finance and the theory of investment, *The American Economic Review*, **48**(3), 261–297.

Pagano, M. (1993), The flotation of companies on the stock market: a coordination failure model, *European Economic Review*, **37**(5), 1101–1125.

Paleari, S. and Vismara, S. (2007), Over-optimism when pricing IPOs, *Managerial Finance*, **33**(6), 352–367.

Pollock, T.G. and Gulati, R. (2007), Standing out from the crowd: the visibility-enhancing effects of IPO-related signals on alliance formation by entrepreneurial firms, *Strategic Organization*, **5**(4), 339–372.

Poulsen, A.B. and Stegemoller, M. (2008), Moving from private to public ownership: selling out to public firms versus initial public offerings, *Financial Management*, **37**(1), 81–101.

Puri, M. and Zarutskie, R. (2012), On the life cycle dynamics of venture-capital- and non-venture-capital-financed firms, *Journal of Finance*, **67**(6), 2247–2293.

Rajan, R.G. and Zingales, L. (2001), Financial systems, industrial structure, and growth, *Oxford Review of Economic Policy*, **17**(4), 467–482.

Reuer, J. and Shen, J.C. (2003), The extended merger and acquisition process: understanding the role of IPOs in corporate strategy, *European Management Journal*, **21**(2), 192–198.

Reuer, J.J. and Shen, J.C. (2004), Sequential divestiture through initial public offerings, *Journal of Economic Behavior and Organization*, **54**(2), 249–266.

Ritter, J.R. (1987), The costs of going public, *Journal of Financial Economics*, **19**(2), 269–281.

Ritter, J.R. (2014), Reenergizing the IPO market, *Journal of Applied Finance*, **24**, 37–48.

Schumpeter, J.A. (1911), *The Theory of Economic Development*, Cambridge, MA: Harvard University Press.

Silber, W.L. (1991), Discounts on restricted stock: the impact of illiquidity on stock prices, *Financial Analysts Journal*, **47**(4), 60–64.

Spence, M. (1973), Job market signaling, *Quarterly Journal of Economics*, **87**(3), 355–374.

Stiglitz, J.E. (2000), The contributions of the economics of information to twentieth century economics, *Quarterly Journal of Economics*, **115**(4), 1441–1478.

Stiglitz, J.E. and Weiss, A. (1981), Credit rationing in markets with imperfect information, *American Economic Review*, **71**(3), 393–410.

Yeh, Y.-H., Shu, P.-G. and Guo, R.-J. (2008), Ownership structure and IPO valuation – evidence from Taiwan, *Financial Management*, **37**(1), 141–161.

Zingales, L. (1995), Insider ownership and the decision to go public, *Review of Economic Studies*, **62**(3), 425–448.

31 Seed and Venture Capital

Introduction

Proper financial management is one of the key factors shaping innovative, high-growth-oriented ventures (Vanacker et al., 2014). The financing of these ventures, however, is more challenging compared to the financing of traditional small and medium-sized enterprises (SMEs) (Vanacker and Manigart, 2010). Innovative, growth-oriented ventures are typically characterized by (a) a need for external financing due to a lack of internal cash flow; (b) intangible investments in highly speculative R&D projects and market development; (c) a high probability of failure and uncertain performance prospects; and (d) high levels of information asymmetry between entrepreneurs and financiers (e.g., Aldrich and Ruef, 2006; Amit et al., 1998). These characteristics explain why traditional financing sources, such as bank debt, are often unavailable and may even be inappropriate for the financing of innovative, growth-oriented ventures (Carpenter and Petersen, 2002).

Seed and venture capital investors are professional financial intermediaries that specialize in investing in young, innovative ventures and providing them with the necessary financial resources to develop and grow. Venture capital specifically refers to equity or equity-linked investments made for the launch, early growth or expansion of innovative, growth-oriented ventures (Vanacker and Manigart, 2013). Seed funding can be considered as a subset of venture capital and focuses specifically upon a venture's pre-startup and startup phase. Money is invested to develop an intellectual property (IP) portfolio, build a prototype, to test initial concepts with the market, to develop a business plan or to assemble a strong team. All these activities should allow a seed-funded venture to enable further fundraising with larger, somewhat later-stage-oriented venture capital investors.

The venture capital process

Seed and venture capital investors have developed processes to cope with the high levels of uncertainty and information asymmetry they are confronted with when dealing with young ventures (Amit et al., 1998). Core processes, which have become largely institutionalized in the investment industry, pertain to the extensive pre-investment due diligence, the writing of contracts and the use of sophisticated financial instruments, the active monitoring and governance of the venture post-investment and the exit once the major value-creation is finished (Manigart and Wright, 2013a). We will expand on each of these processes hereafter.

When selecting their targets, early stage investors hold less information about the opportunity compared to the entrepreneurs. To decrease pre-investment information asymmetries and the ensuing risk of adverse selection, venture capital investors engage in information collection in the due diligence phase, which is more extensive compared to traditional investors who rely predominantly on historical achievements and collateral to deal with information problems (Berger and Udell, 1998).

Information asymmetries and goal misalignment may further lead to post-investment moral hazard problems, in that entrepreneurs may shirk effort or invest in their favorite projects to achieve private benefits at the expense of outside investors. Venture capital investors therefore typically write complex contracts that mainly serve to align the goals of entrepreneurs and investors (Kaplan and Strömberg, 2004; Cumming, 2008). Two features are common in early stage investment contracts: the use of convertible securities and staged financing. Convertible securities include financial instruments such as convertible preferred equity, warrants or convertible debt. The use of convertible securities optimizes an entrepreneur's effort incentives (Schmidt, 2003). Which securities are used to achieve that goal depends on the institutional context (Zambelli, 2014). Staged financing refers to the process by which early stage investors commit themselves to further invest if predefined milestones are met. Staging gives venture capital investors an option to abandon companies if they do not perform as expected. This gives them one of the strongest control mechanisms as it provides a powerful incentive for entrepreneurs to perform well (Sahlman, 1990).

A third process used by venture capital investors to reduce agency risk is to strongly engage with their portfolio companies after the investment. This allows them to reduce information asymmetries and ensuing moral hazard and hidden action problems (Gorman and Sahlman, 1989). Monitoring is mainly performed by holding seats on the board of directors, which also aims to improve the governance of the ventures (Fried et al., 1998). Next to managing uncertainty and information asymmetries, seed and venture capital investors are also instrumental in mobilizing resources for their portfolio companies. Young ventures lack legitimacy, making it difficult to attract external resources needed for their development. The reputation, professional network and experience of their venture capital investors hence not only facilitates further fundraising, but also helps to strengthen entrepreneurial teams and interactions with other stakeholders, such as prospective employees (Davila et al., 2003). Venture capital investors' active involvement also allows them to professionalize their portfolio companies, for example by the development of human resource policies, the adoption of stock option plans (Hellmann and Puri, 2002), or the adoption of professional management accounting systems (Davila and Foster, 2005).

A final crucial step in the venture capital investment process is the exit. Early stage investors typically do not get a financial return from their investment while invested, but aim for capital gains when selling their investment some three to seven years after the initial investment (Gompers and Lerner, 2001). Consistent with the idea that venture capital investors operate in environments characterized by high informational asymmetries, exits are most likely to occur through sales to informed investors, including other companies in the industry (as a trade sale) or the company's own management team (Amit et al., 1998). Trade sales may include very successful exits, but typically also include less successful exits (Puri and Zarutskie, 2012). Initial public offerings (IPOs) are only available for the most successful portfolio companies, providing (on average) the highest returns. Lately, 'secondary' transactions or sales to other financial investors like private equity investors have become more prevalent. Finally, given the highly risky nature of the investments, failures and liquidations are also an important exit route (Puri and Zarutskie, 2012).

The outcome of the venture capital process
With few exceptions, research reveals a positive association between venture capital funding and portfolio company success (Manigart and Wright, 2013a). Compared to non-venture capital backed ventures, venture capital backed ventures have, on average, a lower failure rate (Puri and Zarutskie, 2012), bring products faster to the market (Hellmann and Puri, 2000), experience higher employment growth (Davila et al., 2003) and invest at higher rates (Bertoni et al., 2011). However, recent research has acknowledged the diversity in venture capital and its ability to create value (Manigart and Wright, 2013b). Investors with higher levels of social capital (networks in their industry), human capital (investment managers with relevant education and experience) and experience disproportionally contribute to the development of their portfolio companies (Bertoni et al., 2011; Dimov and Shepherd, 2005; Sorenson, 2007).

While it is widely acknowledged that receiving seed or venture capital on average benefits portfolio companies, returns to investors in seed and venture capital funds do not seem to compensate them for the risk they take (Kaplan and Schoar, 2005; Phalippou and Gottschalg, 2009). This is especially the case for funds focusing on the very early stage of development, including seed capital. Interestingly, both studies show that returns persist strongly across subsequent funds of a partnership, with the best partnerships having a higher probability to continue to outperform. Given the failure to generate appropriate long-term returns for investors in early stage investment funds, independent venture capital investors largely refrain from investing in very young, small, seed-stage ventures (Cumming et al., 2009; Bertoni et al., 2012), favoring later-stage private equity and buyout investments. It hence is not surprising that most governments have actively intervened by setting up publicly funded schemes that either invest *directly* in young ventures, or *indirectly* as co-investors with private venture capital firms (Cumming et al., 2014; Brander et al., 2010; Brander et al., 2014; Bertoni and Tykvová, 2015; Grilli and Murtinu, 2014).

Conclusions

Seed and venture capital still holds an important position as a financial intermediary for the funding of young, growth-oriented ventures, despite the fact that new types of funding, including business angels and crowdfunding, have recently emerged. The professional approach of seed and venture capital investors and their strongly institutionalized investment processes, now serve as a reference for other types of investors. Nevertheless, investing in seed ventures remains challenging given the high levels of technology, business and agency risk. This continues to put pressures on the traditional venture capital model for seed investments.

SOPHIE MANIGART, THOMAS STANDAERT AND TOM VANACKER

References

Aldrich, H.E. and Ruef, M. (eds) (2006), *Organizations Evolving*, 2nd edn, Thousand Oaks, CA: Sage Publications.

Amit, R., Brander, J. and Zott, C. (1998), Why do venture capital firms exist? Theory and Canadian evidence, *Journal of Business Venturing*, **13**(6), 441–466.

Berger, A.N. and Udell, G.F. (1998), The economics of small business finance: the roles of private equity and debt markets in the financial growth cycle, *Journal of Banking and Finance*, **22**(6–8), 613–673.

Bertoni, F. and Tykvová, T. (2015), Does governmental venture capital spur invention and innovation? Evidence from young European biotech companies, *Research Policy*, **44**(4), 925–935.

Bertoni, F., Colombo, M.G. and Grilli, L. (2011), Venture capital financing and the growth of high-tech start-ups: disentangling treatment from selection effects, *Research Policy*, **40**(7), 1028–1043.

Bertoni, F., Colombo, M.G. and Quas, A. (2012), Patterns of venture capital investments in Europe, http://ssrn.com/abstract=1920351.

Brander, J.A., Du, Q. and Hellmann, T. (2014), The effects of government-sponsored venture capital: international evidence, *Review of Finance*, 1–48.

Brander, J.A., Egan, E.J. and Hellmann, T.F. (2010), Government sponsored versus private venture capital: Canadian evidence, in J. Lerner and A. Schoar (eds), *International Differences in Entrepreneurship*, Chicago, IL: University of Chicago Press, pp. 275–320.

Carpenter, R.E. and Petersen, B. (2002), Capital market imperfections, high-tech investment, and new equity financing, *The Economic Journal*, **112**(477), 54–72.

Cumming, D. (2008), Contracts and exits in venture capital finance, *Review of Financial Studies*, **21**(5), 1947–1982.

Cumming, D., Fleming, G. and Schwienbacher, A. (2009), Style drift in private equity, *Journal of Business Finance and Accounting*, **36**(5–6), 645–678.

Cumming, D., Grilli, L. and Murtinu, S. (2014), Governmental and independent venture capital investments in Europe: a firm-level performance analysis, *Journal of Corporate Finance*.

Davila, A. and Foster, G. (2005), Management accounting systems adoption decisions: evidence and performance implications from early-stage/startup companies, *Accounting Review*, **80**(4), 1039–1068.

Davila, A., Foster, G. and Gupta, M. (2003), Venture capital financing and the growth of startup firms, *Journal of Business Venturing*, **18**(6), 689–708.

Dimov, D.P. and Shepherd, D.A. (2005), Human capital theory and venture capital firms: exploring 'home runs' and 'strike outs,' *Journal of Business Venturing*, **20**(1), 1–21.

Fried, V.H., Bruton, G.D. and Hisrich, R.D. (1998), Strategy and the board of directors in venture capital backed firms, *Journal of Business Venturing*, **13**(6), 493–503.

Gompers, P. and Lerner, J. (2001), The venture capital revolution, *Journal of Economic Perspectives*, **15**(2), 145–168.

Gorman, M. and Sahlman, W.A. (1989), What do venture capitalists do? *Journal of Business Venturing*, **4**(4), 231–248.

Grilli, L. and Murtinu, S. (2014), Government, venture capital and the growth of European high-tech entrepreneurial firms, *Research Policy*, **43**(9), 1523–1543.

Hellmann, T. and Puri, M. (2000), The interaction between product market and financing strategy: the role of venture capital, *Review of Financial Studies*, **13**(4), 959–984.

Hellmann, T. and Puri, M. (2002), Venture capital and the professionalization of start-up firms: empirical evidence, *Journal of Finance*, **57**(1), 169–197.

Kaplan, S.N. and Schoar, A. (2005), Private equity performance: returns, persistence, and capital flows, *Journal of Finance*, **60**(4), 1791–1823.

Kaplan, S.N. and Strömberg, P. (2004), Characteristics, contracts, and actions: evidence from venture capitalist analyses, *Journal of Finance*, **59**(5), 2177–2210.

Manigart, S. and Wright, M. (2013a), Venture capital investors and portfolio firms, in Z. Acs (ed.), *Foundations and Trends in Entrepreneurship*, Boston, MA: NOW Publishers, pp. 365–570.

Manigart, S. and Wright, M. (2013b), Reassessing the relationships between private equity investors and their portfolio companies, *Small Business Economics*, **40**(3), 479–492.

Phalippou, L. and Gottschalg, O. (2009), The performance of private equity funds, *Review of Financial Studies*, **22**(4), 1747–1776.

Puri, M. and Zarutskie, R. (2012), On the life cycle dynamics of venture-capital- and non-venture-capital-financed firms, *Journal of Finance*, **67**(6), 2247–2293.

Sahlman, W.A. (1990), The structure and governance of venture-capital organizations, *Journal of Financial Economics*, **27**(2), 473–521.

Schmidt, K.M. (2003), Convertible securities and venture capital finance, *Journal of Finance*, **58**(3), 1139–1166.

Sorenson, M. (2007), How smart is smart money? A two-sided matching model of venture capital, *Journal of Finance*, **62**(6), 2725–2762.

Vanacker, T. and Manigart, S. (2010), Pecking order and debt capacity considerations for high-growth companies seeking financing, *Small Business Economics*, **35**(1), 53–69.

Vanacker, T. and Manigart, S. (2013), Venture capital, in H.K. Baker and G. Filbeck (eds), *Alternative Investments: Balancing Opportunity and Risk*, Hoboken, NJ: John Wiley & Sons, Inc., pp. 241–264.

Vanacker, T., Manigart, S. and Meuleman, M. (2014), Path-dependent evolution versus intentional management of investment ties in science-based entrepreneurial firms, *Entrepreneurship Theory and Practice*, **38**(3), 671–690.

Zambelli, S. (2014), If the facts don't fit the theory . . . the security design puzzle in venture finance, *International Journal of Management Review*, **16**(4), 500–520.

32 Serial Entrepreneurship

Introduction

'Serial entrepreneurship' refers to individuals who have two or more different episodes of entrepreneurship in their working career. It is important to distinguish between the terms 'serial entrepreneur' – that refers only to owner-manager roles – and the more inclusive 'serial entrepreneurship', which also involves a wider diversity of entrepreneurial forms including freelance entrepreneurs, corporate entrepreneurs and hands-on entrepreneurial investors. So, for example, a typical career path evolving from corporate entrepreneur to owner-manager and then on to exit and using the capital gain to become a business angel classifies as serial entrepreneurship. Only if this career path includes more than one episode as an owner-manager would this person be simultaneously classified as a serial entrepreneur.

Scholars of entrepreneurship have devoted much more attention to serial entrepreneurs than serial entrepreneurship. They have sought to use serial entrepreneurs as a means of exploring a number of wider questions about an individual's propensity for spending time as an entrepreneur throughout their working career, entrepreneurial ability, scale of learning and capital accumulation as well as being conduits for innovation. With such a list of potent entrepreneurial attributes, it is perhaps no surprise that serial entrepreneurs are typically assigned a position of prestige and mystique in the popular media. Scholars have discovered that the reality is somewhat different.

Most analyses of serial entrepreneurship are based on models of career choice dating back to the seminal work of Kihlstrom and Laffont (1979), where individuals choose to become entrepreneurs if they value the expected income from self-employment more than a less risky wage in employment. This model has subsequently been amended to account for the role of finance constraints (Evans and Jovanovic, 1989); satisfaction from being your own boss (Blanchflower and Oswald, 1998); as well as the role of education and the cost of effort (Burke et al., 2000). This literature points to a conceptual flaw in research seeking to focus on serial entrepreneurs as a proxy for an 'intense form' entrepreneurship. Of course, *ceteris paribus*, individuals with high entrepreneurial ability (and hence greater scope to earn more in self-employment) and/or those who attach a high value to being their own boss/independent are likely to be drawn back into another business venture once they exit their current enterprise. But there is a problem as at the other end of the ability spectrum, push factors – such as low human capital – reduce employment prospects forcing people into self-employment. Burke et al. (2000) show that more educated people with university degrees are less likely to choose to become self-employed because education brings good employment prospects and yet if they do become self-employed they perform better than their less educated counterparts. Foreman-Peck (1985) used the terms 'seedcorn and chaff' to refer to the varied quality of business startups that results from the coexistence of push and pull effects.

Thus, it becomes clear that serial entrepreneurs are not a good proxy for both entrepreneurial ability and a propensity to spend more of a career as an entrepreneur. Burke et al. (2008) tackled this problem noting that over a ten-year period nearly 43 per cent of the self-employed in their sample were continuously self-employed in the same business, i.e., persistent but nevertheless not serial entrepreneurs. To overcome the limitations of using serial entrepreneurs as the focal point to study entrepreneurial ability and propensity, Burke et al. take advantage of the common career choice theoretical model and develop the concept of 'entrepreneurial persistence' measured as the number of months (either continuous or discontinuous) spent in self-employment across the working life of the individual. In this empirical analysis they find that more persistent entrepreneurs are not driven by unemployment push effects but mainly driven by pull effects such as having a university education and a role model or mentor parent with a career background in self-employment, i.e., more likely to be seedcorn than chaff. The research also reveals path dependence in a career so that an early career spell in self-employment tends to cause entrepreneurial persistence across the working career.

This leads onto another area of exploration that has driven research on serial entrepreneurship that is motivated by a desire to get an insight into the importance of learning by serial entrepreneurs as they move from one venture to the next. By comparing serial to novice entrepreneurs, scholars have been able to assess the value of having prior entrepreneurial experience as a driver of a venture's performance. The results are not what many expected. Westhead and Wright (1998) find that, *ceteris paribus*, there is no difference in the performance of serial and novice entrepreneurs. Parker (2013) finds that there are some positive learning effects from one venture to the next but that the performance-enhancing effects are short-lived, i.e., fade away over time. Part of the weak or absent evidence of learning effects across ventures are likely to reside in the diversity of types of serial entrepreneurs that is caused by the contrasting nature of the push and pull effects that create them. Wright et al. (1997) show that this is a view shared by venture capitalists who, while preferring to invest in ventures with serial entrepreneurs, find them to have a mixed influence on business performance. Wright et al. (1997) find that venture capitalists believe that serial entrepreneurs have a greater tendency for hubris and over-optimism that negatively affects the performance of ventures. Worryingly, Ucbasaran et al. (2010) find that serial entrepreneurs who have experienced failure in an earlier business do not subsequently adjust their degree of over-optimism.

   Closely related to learning from previous venturing is the issue of capital accumulation. This takes us beyond the realm of serial entrepreneurs and into the relatively novel research area of serial entrepreneurship. Burke et al. (2010) show that previous career experience as an owner-manager raises the probability that an individual will subsequently become an informal investor in new ventures. As a result, serial entrepreneurship entails a virtuous circle effect where more entrepreneurs (who raise the demand for venture finance in the short run) eventually cause an increase the supply of venture finance in the longer run. Burke et al. (2014) shows that this result is bolstered as the amount of finance invested by informal investors is positively related to prior experience as an entrepreneur, which they attribute to capital accumulation from business venturing. Burke (2012) investigates a different dimension of serial entrepreneurship and highlights the post-business exit evolution from owner-manager to freelance serial entrepreneur who provides innovation and manages entrepreneurial projects for other businesses. This study finds evidence that serial freelance entrepreneurs can activate many more of their entrepreneurial ideas as freelance entrepreneurs than they could as owner-managers.

Conclusions

In summary, we highlight some of the challenges of using serial entrepreneurship as a means of measuring the propensity for being an entrepreneur. We show that a career as a serial entrepreneur can be caused by diverse contrasting push and pull influences, which creates challenges for scholars seeking to explore entrepreneurial ability, learning by doing and over-optimism through diverse serial entrepreneurs. Finally, the chapter closes by highlighting some initial findings from the relatively unexplored research area of serial entrepreneurship.

ANDREW BURKE

References

Blanchflower, D. and Oswald, A. (1998), What makes an entrepreneur? *Journal of Labor Economics*, **16**, 26–60.

Burke, A. (2012), *The Role of Freelancers in the 21st Century British Economy*, PCG Report, London: PCG.

Burke, A., FitzRoy, F.R. and Nolan, M. (2000), When less is more: distinguishing between entrepreneurial choice and performance, *Oxford Bulletin of Economics and Statistics*, **62**(5), 565–587.

Burke, A., FitzRoy, F.R. and Nolan, M. (2008), What makes a die-hard entrepreneur? Beyond the employee or entrepreneur dichotomy, *Small Business Economics*, **31**(2), 93–115.

Burke, A., Hartog, C., van Stel, A. and Suddle, K. (2010), How does entrepreneurial activity affect the supply of informal investors?, *Venture Capital*, **12**(1), 21–47.

Burke, A., van Stel, A., Hartog, C. and Ichou, A. (2014), What determines the level of informal venture finance investment? Market clearing forces and gender effects, *Small Business Economics*, **42**(3), 467–484.

Evans, D. and Jovanovic, B. (1989), An estimated model of entrepreneurial choice under liquidity constraints, *Journal of Political Economy*, **97**, 519–535.

Foreman-Peck, J.S. (1985), Seedcorn or chaff? New firm performance in the interwar economy, *Economic History Review*, **38**(3), 402–422.

Kihlstrom, R. and Laffont, J.J. (1979), A general equilibrium entrepreneurial theory of the firm formation based on risk aversion, *Journal of Political Economy*, **87**, 719–748.

Parker, S.C. (2013), Do serial entrepreneurs run successively better-performing businesses? *Journal of Business Venturing*, **28**(5), 652–666.

Ucbasaran, D.A., Westhead, P., Wright, M. and Flores, M. (2010), The nature of entrepreneurial experience, business failure and comparative optimism, *Journal of Business Venturing*, **25**, 541–555.

Westhead, P. and Wright. M. (1998), Novice, portfolio and serial founders: are they different?, *Journal of Business Venturing*, **13**, 173–204.

Wright, M., Robbie, K. and Ennew, C. (1997), Venture capitalists and serial entrepreneurs, *Journal of Business Venturing*, **12**(3), 227–249.

33   Social Entrepreneurship

Introduction

'Social entrepreneurship' refers to opportunity-driven activity with the aim of creating social change. It is a discrete and observable process that spans civil society, government and commerce, consisting of recognizing and acting on an opportunity to produce social change. Technology plays an increasingly vital role in social entrepreneurship in scaling initiatives, spreading issue awareness, opening participation and creating funding structures.

The process of social entrepreneurship begins with any sort of actor – be it a politician, civil servant, interest group, a citizen activist or anyone with an interest in producing social change – being alert to an opportunity to influence social welfare for a community, then seizing that opportunity. The recognized opportunity must be acted on; simply being aware of an opportunity is not by itself sufficient to constitute social entrepreneurship. While there is little empirical evidence that social entrepreneurs comprise a select group with observable personality traits or characteristics (e.g., risk tolerance, creativity, intellectual capacity), there remains a tendency to celebrate or even heroicize individual social entrepreneurs (see Bornstein, 2007). Rather, social entrepreneurship might be more usefully characterized as a universal behavior that can be carried out by anyone, any organization or any network in a limitless variety of contexts and situations (Light, 2006). The nature of the opportunity to produce social change can be 'objective' – for example, becoming aware of new needs of a community or demands from a constituency – or 'subjective' – for example, anticipating deficiencies or weaknesses in a community before a crisis erupts. Two signature examples of social entrepreneurship are 2006 Nobel Peace Laureate Muhammad Yunus and his Grameen family of social businesses (Yunus and Weber, 2007; www.grameenfoundation.org) and Fazle Abed and his organization BRAC (www.brac.net). Ashoka: Innovators for the Public and its founder Bill Drayton (www.ashoka.org) have championed the idea of social entrepreneurship across the globe since the 1980s.

The modern conception of entrepreneurship in economics

The modern conception of entrepreneurship in economics principally derives from the work of three economists: Joseph Schumpeter, Ludwig von Mises and Israel Kirzner. In his two major works, *The Theory of Economic Development* (1934) and *Capitalism, Socialism, and Democracy* (1950), Schumpeter conceives of 'creative destruction,' in which entrepreneurship consists of new combinations of existing resources that drive economic development, such as the introduction of a new good, technology or method of production; the opening of a new market; the conquest of a new source of supply of raw materials or half-manufactured goods; and the carrying out of the new organization of any industry.

The other two economists – von Mises and Kirzner – belong to what is usually referred to as the Austrian school of economics. In his magnum opus *Human Action* (1949), von Mises identifies entrepreneurship as a behavior universal to all activity. Entrepreneurship, he writes, 'is not the particular feature of a special group or class of men; it is inherent in every action and burdens every actor.' Consciously expanding on von Mises' conception, Kirzner in his primary works on entrepreneurship theory, such as *Competition and Entrepreneurship* (1973), locates entrepreneurship as the driver of all market processes in that entrepreneurial market participants acquire 'more and more accurate and complete mutual knowledge of potential demand and supply attitudes,' thus 'equilibrating' or stabilizing a market by moving it closer to equilibrium between supply and demand. Some contemporary social scientists (for example, Bielefeld, 2008; Shockley and Frank, 2011; Swedberg, 2006, 2009) have made efforts to establish a theoretical foundation of social entrepreneurship based on the modern conception of entrepreneurship in economics. In fact, social entrepreneurship might be a growing subfield in 'non-market entrepreneurship' (Shockley et al., 2008).

The role of technology in social entrepreneurship

Technology plays an increasingly vital role in social entrepreneurship in scaling initiatives, spreading issue awareness, expanding participation opportunities to contribute and creating funding structures. Internet technology enables each social entrepreneurship initiative to customize platforms for its unique needs. It also allows for a delivery of services that go beyond the constraints of a basic informational website. Technology also supports the formation of social capital by facilitating connections among people and organizations by expanding the reach and opening access to a geographically diverse set of participants or target populations (Coleman, 1988). Social capital also fosters mutual trust, reciprocity, collective identity, a sense of a shared future and other forms of cooperation (Putnam, 1996).

Crowdfunding and crowdsourcing are two recent innovations enabled by technology. Crowdsourcing allows dispersed individuals and organizations to contribute their nonfinancial time and talents to social entrepreneurship initiatives. Two examples of crowdsourcing demonstrate two different volunteer recruitment strategies. The first, www.volunteermatch. org, helps nonprofit organizations fill volunteer positions through job postings. The system works by taking potential volunteers directly to a large list of openings based primarily on geographic region. The website sets itself apart when users complete a profile that intuitively selects volunteer positions based on the individual's interests. The second, the Taproot Foundation (www.taprootfoundation.org), seeks to attract white-collar professionals and encourages them to use their time and talent to perform pro bono work for nonprofit organizations. The Taproot Foundation developed from the need for professionals with specialized skills and expertise to provide services to underfunded organizations. Both examples of crowdsourcing depend crucially on technology to link social entrepreneurship initiatives with volunteers.

Crowdfunding is a mirror image to crowdsourcing in that it allows a dispersed set of individuals and organizations to contribute financially to non-localized social entrepreneurship initiatives. Securing financial resources is fundamental to the success to any activity, including social entrepreneurship. Financial resources are necessary to invest in community capacity-building, underwrite businesses creation, stimulate civic engagement and develop community wealth. The classic method of funding a project is through garnering donations; www.donorschoose.org uses technology to enhance the classic method. Created by Charles Best, an elementary school teacher from New York, the website allows teachers to post funding requests for specific school projects. Potential donors can view listings and decide which projects to support and how much to donate. The website also tracks performance and measures impact in several ways. Kiva (www.kiva.org) operates in a very similar manner, in that it allows people with small projects in need of funds to market their project. Potential contributors can then select which projects they want to support and in what increment. A crucial difference, however, is that Kiva contributors are investors expecting some sort of return on their contrition, even if the return is suboptimal. As in the two crowdsourcing examples, the two crowdfunding examples depend crucially on technology to link projects with donors and investors. Technology thus undergirds the effectiveness of both crowdfunding and crowdsourcing in social entrepreneurship initiatives. In the parlance of the modern conception of entrepreneurship in economics, each instance of introducing a new technology to the field of social entrepreneurship constitutes a Schumpeterian new combination.

Conclusion

History is replete with social entrepreneurship. Insofar as there have been individuals who have been both alert to an opportunity to influence social welfare for a community and who have seized that opportunity, social change has occurred. The theoretical edifice to describe and explain social entrepreneurship, however, did not develop until the modern conception of entrepreneurship in economics in the twentieth century. Technology plays an increasingly vital role in social entrepreneurship in scaling initiatives, spreading issue awareness, expanding participation and opportunities to contribute and creating funding structures, such as in crowdsourcing and crowdfunding.

GORDON E. SHOCKLEY AND ANTHONY TALARICO

References

Bielefeld, W. (2008), Social entrepreneurship and social enterprise, in C. Wankel (ed.), *21st Century Management: A Reference Handbook*, Thousand Oaks, CA: Sage Publications, pp. 22–31.

Bornstein, D. (2007), *How to Change the World: Social Entrepreneurs and the Power of New Ideas*, updated edn, New York: Oxford University Press.

Coleman, J.S. (1988), Social capital in the creation of human capital, *American Journal of Sociology*, **94**, S95–S120.

Kirzner, I.M. (1973), *Competition and Entrepreneurship*, Chicago, IL: University of Chicago Press.

Light, P. (2006), Searching for social entrepreneurs: who they might be, where they might be found, what they do, in R. Mosher-Williams (ed.), *Research on Social Entrepreneurship: Understanding and Contributing to an Emerging Field*, ARNOVA Occasional Paper Series, Volume 1, Number 3, Indianapolis, IN: Association for Research on Nonprofit Organizations and Voluntary Action, pp. 13–38.

Putnam, R.D. (1996), Bowling alone: America's declining social capital, in L. Diamond and M.F. Plattner (eds), *The Global Resurgence of Democracy*, Baltimore: Johns Hopkins University Press, pp. 290–306.

Schumpeter, J.A. (1934/2002), *The Theory of Economic Development: An Inquiry into Profits, Capital, Credit, Interest, and the Business Cycle*, New Brunswick, NJ: Transaction Publishers.
Schumpeter, J.A. (1950), *Capitalism, Socialism, and Democracy*, New York: Harper & Row Publishers.
Shockley, G.E. and Frank, P.F. (2011), Schumpeter, Kirzner, and the field of social entrepreneurship, *Journal of Social Entrepreneurship*, **2**(1), 6–26.
Shockley, G.E., Frank, P.F. and Stough, R.R. (2008), Introduction: the emerging field of non-market entrepreneurship, in G.E. Shockley, P.F. Frank and R.R. Stough (eds), *Non-market Entrepreneurship: Interdisciplinary Approaches*, Cheltenham, UK and Northampton, MA: Edward Elgar Publishing, pp. 3–9.
Swedberg, R. (2006), Social entrepreneurship: the view of the young Schumpeter, in D. Hjorth and C. Steyaert (eds), *Entrepreneurship and Social Change*, Cheltenham, UK and Northampton, MA: Edward Elgar Publishing, pp. 21–34.
Swedberg, R. (2009), Schumpeter's full model of entrepreneurship: economic, non-economic and social entrepreneurship, in R. Ziegler (ed.), *An Introduction to Social Entrepreneurship: Voices, Preconditions, Contexts*, Cheltenham, UK and Northampton, MA: Edward Elgar Publishing, pp. 155–175.
von Mises, L. (1949/1996), *Human Action: A Treatise on Economics*, 4th edn, San Francisco: Fox & Wilkes.
Yunus, M. and Weber, K. (2007), *Creating a World without Poverty: Social Business and the Future of Capitalism*, New York: Public Affairs.

34 Spatial Elements of Innovation

Introduction

Geography matters for innovation and entrepreneurship. This statement is especially relevant when we consider the evolution and the success of innovative regions such as Silicon Valley. Silicon Valley emerged as one of the world's most eminent high-technology regions because entrepreneurs and innovators were able to harness the benefits of proximity to each other and to different kinds of support organizations such as universities, networking groups, venture capitalists, etc. (Braunerhjelm and Feldmann, 2006; Kenney, 2000; Saxenian, 1994). The interactions that resulted from these proximities contributed in substantial ways to the development of new ideas and innovations.

Take, for example, the case of the high-technology firm Hewlett-Packard: Hewlett-Packard was founded by two engineers who were supported by the dean of engineering at Stanford University. Not only did the founders' education at Stanford influence the direction Hewlett-Packard took, but also the ways in which Stanford supported the fledgling firm financially. The story of how Intel emerged as one of the most important semiconductor firms also sheds light on how geography matters when it comes to innovation and entrepreneurship. Intel was founded by former employees of Fairchild Semiconductors, a Silicon Valley firm that, in turn, was started by employees of Shockley Transistor, also a Silicon Valley firm (Kenney and von Burg, 2001). Many Silicon Valley-based firms have such traceable genealogies and new startups benefit from the region's unique innovative and entrepreneurial ecosystem.

Why geography matters

But why does geography matter when we consider innovation and entre-preneurship? There are several reasons why this is the case. First, geography or the spatial context in which new firms and ideas emerge plays an important role because of so-called localization economies. Localization economies are benefits that arise to firms, entrepreneurs and innovators because they are located in a region with other similar firms, entrepreneurs, innovators, etc. The co-presence of firms in the same sector, for example, facilitates – among other processes – the exchange of relevant information, the ways in which competition might unfold and in turn may trigger innovations, etc. Localization economies play an important role in specialized regions such as Silicon Valley. Second, face-to-face contacts are important for the creation of new ideas because often innovation depends on a certain type of knowledge, which is called tacit knowledge. In con-trast to codified knowledge, tacit knowledge is hard to put into writing and transfer from one part of the world to another, and therefore it is dif-ficult to transfer this kind of knowledge over long geographical distances. Proximity between innovators or entrepreneurs facilitates the exchange of tacit knowledge and helps them solve problems, come up with new ideas, etc. A third reason why geography matters is related to the ways in which knowledge is created and new ideas emerge. Here the concept of so-called knowledge spillovers is relevant. Knowledge spillovers emerge because employees move from one of the region's companies to another or former employees commercialize new ideas in a new startup in the same region as their former employer is located. Thus, these knowledge spillovers are mediated through geography (Audretsch and Feldmann, 1996; Feldman, 2000).

It was not just Silicon Valley that was able to harness the benefits for proximity for its economic development. Research has shown that regions outside of Silicon Valley, so-called 'second-tier regions,' are able to benefit from localized innovation and entrepreneurship processes even though they do not have the typical prerequisites such as large amounts of venture capital, a world-class university, etc. in place (Mayer, 2009, 2011). Second-tier regions such as Portland (Oregon), Boise (Idaho) or Kansas City (Kansas-Missouri) compensated the lack of a world-class research univer-sity through the presence of large, innovative firms that, in turn, helped foster an innovative and entrepreneurial milieu. These firms functioned like surrogate universities in that they attracted and retained technological talent that built the foundation for a specialized labor pool; they also invested in research and development efforts that helped create knowledge spillovers to the region; and they functioned as incubators of numerous spinoff companies. Geography played a role in the development of these regions inasmuch as the knowledge spillovers created in part by firms and spinoffs helped foster an innovative economy.

Economic geographers and scholars of regional development have focused on the territorial dimensions of innovation for a long time. To explain the phenomenon of Silicon Valley and other regions alike, they have developed concepts that help shed light on the various geographic mechanisms responsible for regional economic development. Today, the tool box of regional development scholars contains concepts such as regional innovation systems (Braczyk et al., 1998), industrial districts (Harrison, 1992) or clusters (Porter, 2000). These so-called territorial innovation models (Moulaert and Sekia, 2003) help us understand the spatial nature of economic development. In contrast to mainstream economics, which traditionally has not accounted for the territorial dimensions of innovation, the models consider the ways in which firms, entrepreneurs and other types of economic actors utilize and benefit from their environment and the proximities that result from co-location.

Geographic proximity is one important element when we want to explain why certain regions are more innovative and entrepreneurial than others. However, being close to each other is not the only success factor for entrepreneurs and innovators. Globalization and the associated dispersal of economic activity (Dicken, 2007) have significantly changed the ways in which regional economies function nowadays. Places such as Silicon Valley, Portland, Boise or Kansas City are integrated into global production networks through their firms' activities. These worldwide connections resemble something like global pipelines (Bathelt et al., 2004) through which new ideas and knowledge are brought into the regions. A region's ability to sustain innovation and translate new ideas into new firms depends, however, on the ways in which actors in these regions are able to process this knowledge. To process a certain local buzz (Bathelt et al., 2004) or regional milieu is necessary, which enables the region to absorb new ideas resulting from global interactions.

Conclusions
Given the globalized nature of today's economy and its influence on innovation processes, territorial dimensions of innovation have to be considered within their localized but also within their globalized contexts.

Heike Mayer

References

Audretsch, D. and Feldmann, M. (1996), R&D spillovers and the geography of innovation and production, *American Economic Review*, **86**(1), 630–640.

Bathelt, H., Malmberg, A. and Maskell, P. (2004), Clusters and knowledge: local buzz, global pipelines and the process of knowledge creation, *Progress in Human Geography*, **28**(1), 31–56.

Braczyk, H.-J., Cooke, P. and Heidenreich, M. (eds) (1998), *Regional Innovation Systems: The Role of Governance in a Globalized World*, London: UCL Press.

Braunerhjelm, P. and Feldmann, M. (eds) (2006), *Cluster Genesis: Technology-based Industrial Development*, Oxford: Oxford University Press.

Dicken, P. (2007), *Global Shift: Mapping the Changing Countours of the World Economy*, New York: Guilford Press.

Feldman, M. (2000), Location and innovation: the new economic geography of innovation, spillovers and agglomeration, in M. Feldman and M. Gertler (eds), *Handbook of Economic Geography*, Oxford: Oxford University Press, pp. 373–394.

Harrison, B. (1992), Industrial districts: old wine in new bottles? *Regional Studies*, **26**(5), 469–483.

Kenney, M. (ed.) (2000), *Understanding Silicon Valley: The Anatomy of an Entrepreneurial Region*, Stanford: Stanford University Press.

Kenney, M. and von Burg, U. (2001), Paths and regions: the creation and growth of Silicon Valley, in R. Garud and P. Karnoe (eds), *Path Dependence and Path Creation*, New York: Lawrence Erlbaum and Associates, pp. 127–148.

Mayer, H. (2009), *Bootstrapping High-tech: Evidence from Three Emerging High Technology Metropolitan Areas*, www.brookings.edu/research/reports/2009/06/metro-hightech-mayer.

Mayer, H. (2011), *Entrepreneurship and Innovation in Second Tier Regions*, Cheltenham: Edward Elgar Publishing.

Moulaert, F. and Sekia, F. (2003), Territorial innovation models: a critical survey, *Regional Studies*, **37**(3), 289–302.

Porter, M. (2000), Location, competition, and economic development: local clusters in a global economy, *Economic Development Quarterly*, **14**(1), 15–34.

Saxenian, A. (1994), *Regional Advantage: Culture and Competition in Silicon Valley and Route 128*, Cambridge, MA: Harvard University Press.

35   Student Entrepreneurship

Introduction

For at least the past 25 years, academic entrepreneurship has been defined as the establishment of a new spinoff company based on intellectual property generated by individual faculty researchers (Doutriaux, 1987; Shane, 2004; Hayter, 2013). Recent, albeit limited empirical research finds, however, that university students play a critical, often overlooked role within academic entrepreneurship. This paper explores the modest extant student entrepreneurship literature and advances one simple, yet important recommendation: scholars and policymakers would do well to reconceptualize academic entrepreneurship to include the realized and latent economic contributions of university students.

Academic entrepreneurship and regional growth

Contemporary economic theories typically embrace Romer's (1986) view that new knowledge – created through research and development (R&D) – is a critical ingredient for innovation and economic growth. However, recent scholarship takes exception to neoclassical assumptions that new knowledge spills over to other organizations automatically and is instead subject to various cultural, institutional and policy constraints (Braunerhjelm et al., 2010; Acs et al., 2009).

Accordingly, individual knowledge agents represent the vehicle through which new knowledge is diffused and transformed into useful applications. A well-developed literature explores the contributions of faculty entrepreneurs to technology commercialization and regional economic growth (Pressman, 2002; Shane, 2004; Hayter, 2013, 2015). Although empirical investigations of the economic impact of student entrepreneurship are rare, Roberts (1991) and Roberts and Easley (2009) find, for example, that student and alumni, especially from the Massachusetts Institute of Technology (MIT), play a critical role in the entrepreneurial economy of the Boston metropolitan region.

The emergence of student entrepreneurship

Policymakers increasingly acknowledge the role of students in the transfer of new knowledge generated within universities and, thus, regional economic development (e.g., Bok, 2003; Stephan, 2009). Beyond employment, the contributions of students are typically linked to post-graduation entrepreneurship activities. For example, Åstebro et al. (2012) find that recent university graduates are, in general, more likely to start new businesses than university faculty by a factor of 24.3 to 1.

Within a university context, student entrepreneurship research typically focuses on entrepreneurship education: higher education institutions are responding to increasing student demands for entrepreneurship courses and programs. According to Katz (2003, 2004), the number of entrepreneurship education programs established within universities has grown exponentially since the early 1980s. Further, Pittaway and Cope (2007) posit that a 'critical mass' of related empirical research exists on student propensity to establish new companies, entrepreneurship course pedagogy, entrepreneurial management education and the role of universities in entrepreneurship education.

Student entrepreneur motivations and characteristics[1]

A sizable literature exists relating to the personal characteristics and motivations of student entrepreneurs. More than 20 years ago, Roberts (1991) found that entrepreneurs within the Boston Metropolitan area were most likely to establish their first company in their late twenties or early thirties. However, a more recent analysis of MIT students and alumni finds that first-time entrepreneurs are not only younger but that early exposure to entrepreneurial ideas and networks helps form long-lasting entrepreneurial perspectives (Hsu et al., 2007; Roberts and Easley, 2009).

Student entrepreneurs are more likely to come from engineering, scientific or management fields (Hsu et al., 2007; Roberts, 1991). Recent evidence shows, however, that universities are expanding into so-called 'non-traditional' entrepreneurial fields, such as agriculture, psychology, nursing, music, education and history (Nelson, 2012; Mars et al., 2008; Mangan, 2004). Students also view entrepreneurship as a vehicle for issue activism and social problem-solving (Mars and Rhoades, 2012; Mars and Lounsbury, 2009).

Student entrepreneurship programs

University culture and entrepreneurship programs can positively impact the entrepreneurial motivations and attitudes of students (Pittaway and Cope, 2007). How students are initially exposed to entrepreneurship matters: Bailetti (2011) and Barr et al. (2009) compare traditional lecture format and hands-on entrepreneurial education, and find the latter is critical for enabling entrepreneurial skills important to success. Further, facilitated student interactions with entrepreneurs and small business owners provide students with role models, practical skills and expanded networks (Fukugawa, 2005; Wani et al., 2004; Ridder and van der Sijde, 2003; Brindley and Ritchie, 2000). Complementary to formal entrepreneurship programs, business plan competitions also provide a venue (and motivation) to develop relevant skills and work in teams (Hsu et al., 2007).

Limited evidence finds that entrepreneurship programs do not necessarily increase the likelihood that a student will establish a new company. Oosterbeek et al. (2010) find, for example, that entrepreneurship programs can moderate entrepreneurial intentions by providing students with a more realistic perspective on the lifestyle and skills needed for successful entrepreneurship. Further, Berggren and Lindholm Dahlstrand (2009) find that regional policies and networks may have a disproportionate impact on entrepreneurial motivations and success among students and faculty compared to internal university factors.

Entrepreneurial graduate students and postdocs

Recent research suggests that graduate students and postdoctoral fellows play a critical role in the establishment and operation of university spin-offs. For example, Boh et al. (2012) find that among 41 university spinoffs, graduate students were involved in their establishment and management

83 percent of the time. Similarly, Lubynsky (2012) finds evidence of substantial graduate student involvement in new companies spun off of MIT. Compared to university faculty who have invested a great deal of time and effort in their academic career, graduate students and postdocs are better positioned to accept the risks associated with the establishment of a new spinoff company. Further, university faculties are subject to limited leave policies, conflict of interest rules and intellectual property policies that typically do not apply to students (Nelson and Byers, 2005).

Graduate students and postdocs typically work closely with faculty researchers and may, in many cases, have a better understanding of core technologies resulting from university research. Thus, students are often in a better position to work with university's technology transfer offices and outside technology development contacts (Nelson and Byers, 2005, 2014). According to Boh et al. (2012), business school students may possess management, accounting, and fundraising capabilities complementary to the technical skills of science and engineering students and faculty. Recent research finds that graduate students often convince faculty researchers to establish a spinoff company, serve as co-founder, and – in some cases – serve as CEO (Hayter 2014). Lubynsky (2012) and Boh et al. (2012) not only find that students support faculty-established spinoffs, they also find several spinoffs with little or no faculty involvement. Related IP ownership, strategy and management issues may result in faculty–student conflict, resulting in legal disputes or student withdrawal from their academic program (Lubynsky, 2012).

Conclusion

Although not intended as a comprehensive review of the literature, this paper finds that – at a minimum – student entrepreneurship is a growing phenomenon with potential consequences for regional economic and social development. As mentioned, a relatively well-developed literature exists that relates to the establishment, structure and short-term efficacy of student entrepreneurship education programs. Another modest strain of literature discusses the contributions of student and alumni within the broader context of regional economic development. Finally, a few recent studies examine the role of graduate students within technology-based university spinoffs.

Despite these research contributions, large conceptual and empirical holes exist within the literature. More data is needed to follow students through their entrepreneurial experiences, from motivations for startup decisions or factors associated with entrepreneurial success. Further, a robust conceptual lens is needed to link and expand upon the disparate perspectives outlined above. This framework would enable scholars to examine the entrepreneurial development of students while enrolled within an institution and – perhaps most importantly – their contributions after graduation and beyond.

Scholars and policymakers can begin to address this conceptual gap by broadening the definition of academic entrepreneurship to include students and postdocs. Knowledge-based conceptual lenses, such as the knowledge spillover theory of entrepreneurship (Acs et al., 2009) and S&T human capital (Bozeman et al., 2001), offer frameworks useful for examining the entrepreneurial role and contributions of students compared to, for example, faculty researchers.

While space limits a more developed discussion of potential research questions and agenda, a number of additional policy-relevant issues and questions stem from this work. For example, what are the implications of student loan debt to entrepreneurial potential and success? How do student entrepreneurs compensate for their relatively underdeveloped social networks? And how does undergraduate entrepreneurship, a topic nearly nonexistent in the literature, differ from other forms of student entrepreneurship?

CHRISTOPHER S. HAYTER

Acknowledgement

Special thanks to Andrew Nelson, University of Oregon, for his helpful comments and suggestions.

Note

1. A handful of scholars have examined student propensity to take entrepreneurial risk (Lüthje and Franke, 2003; Koh, 1996; Hatten and Ruhland, 1995). Alternatively, Gartner (1988) posits that despite decades of research, we are yet unable to accurately predict who will become an entrepreneur, despite better understanding individual risk propensity.

References

Acs, Z., Braunerhjelm, P., Audretsch, D. and Carlsson, B. (2009), The knowledge spillover theory of entrepreneurship, *Small Business Economics*, **32**(1), 15–30.
Åstebro, T., Bazzazian, N. and Braguinsky, S. (2012), Startups by recent university graduates and their faculty: implications for university entrepreneurship policy, *Research Policy*, **41**(4), 663–677.
Bailetti, T. (2011), Fostering student entrepreneurship and university spinoff companies, *Technology Innovation Management Review*, October.
Barr, S., Baker, T., Markham, S. and Kingon, A. (2009), Bridging the valley of death: lessons learned from 14 years of commercialization of technology education, *Academy of Management Learning and Education*, **8**(3), 370–388.
Berggren, E. and Lindholm Dahlstrand, Å. (2009), Creating an entrepreneurial region: two waves of academic spin-offs from Halmstad University, *European Planning Studies*, **17**(8), 1171–1189.
Boh, W.F., De-Haan, U. and Strom, R. (2012), *University Technology Transfer through*

Entrepreneurship: Faculty and Students in Spinoffs, Kansas City: Ewing Marion Kauffman Foundation.

Bok, D. (2003), *Universities in the Marketplace: The Commercialization of Higher Education*, Princeton, NJ: Princeton University Press.

Bozeman, B., Dietz, J. and Gaughan, M. (2001), Scientific and technical human capital: an alternative model for research evaluation, *International Journal of Technology Management*, **22**(8): 616–630.

Braunerhjelm, P., Acs, Z.J., Audretsch, D.B. and Carlsson, B. (2010), The missing link: knowledge diffusion and entrepreneurship in endogenous growth, *Small Business Economics*, **34**(2), 105–125.

Brindley, C. and Ritchie, B. (2000), Undergraduates and small and medium-sized enterprises: opportunities for a symbiotic partnership?, *Education & Training*, **42**(9), 509–517.

Doutriaux, J. (1987), Growth pattern of academic entrepreneurial firms, *Journal of Business Venturing*, **2**(4), 285–297.

Fukugawa, N. (2005), Characteristics of knowledge interactions between universities and small firms in Japan, *International Small Business Journal*, **23**(4), 379–401.

Gartner, W. (1988), 'Who is the entrepreneur?' is the wrong question, *American Journal of Small Business*, **12**(4), 11–32.

Hatten, T. and Ruhland, S. (1995), Student attitude toward entrepreneurship as affected by participation in an SBI program, *Journal of Education for Business*, **70**(4), 224–227.

Hayter, C. (2013), Harnessing university entrepreneurship for economic growth: factors of success among university spinoffs, *Economic Development Quarterly*, **27**, 18–28.

Hayter, C. (2014), *Network Composition and Commercialization Outcomes Among Faculty Entrepreneurs*, working paper, Arizona State University.

Hayter, C. (2015), Social networks and the success of university spinoffs: toward an agenda for regional growth, *Economic Development Quarterly*, **29**(1), 3–13.

Hsu, D., Roberts, E. and Eesley, C. (2007), Entrepreneurs from technology-based universities: evidence from MIT, *Research Policy*, **36**(5), 768–788.

Katz, J. (2003), The chronology and intellectual trajectory of American entrepreneurship education, *Journal of Business Venturing*, **18**(2), 283–300.

Katz, J. (2004), *Survey of Endowed Positions in Entrepreneurship and Related Fields in the United States*, Kansas City: Ewing Marion Kauffman Foundation.

Kezar, A., Chambers, T. and Burkhardt, J. (2004), *Higher Education for the Public Good: Emerging Voices from a National Movement*, San Francisco, CA: Jossey-Bass.

Koh, H. (1996), Testing hypotheses of entrepreneurial characteristics: a study of Hong Kong MBA students, *Journal of Managerial Psychology*, **11**(3), 12–25.

Lubynsky, R. (2012), *Critical Challenges to Nascent Academic Entrepreneurs: From Lab Bench to Innovation*, unpublished dissertation, University of Maryland.

Lüthje, C and Franke, N. (2003), The 'making' of an entrepreneur: testing a model of entrepreneurial intent among engineering students at MIT, *R&D Management*, **33**(2), 135–147.

Mangan, K. (2004), Entrepreneurs in every department, *Chronicle of Higher Education*, **50**, A10–A11.

Mars, M. and Lounsbury, M. (2009), Raging against or with the private marketplace? Logic hybridity and eco-entrepreneurship, *Journal of Management Inquiry*, **18**(1), 4–13.

Mars, M. and Rhoades, G. (2012), Socially oriented student entrepreneurship: a study of student change agency in the academic capitalism context, *Journal of Higher Education*, **83**(3), 435–459.

Mars, M., Slaughter, S. and Rhoades, G. (2008), The state-sponsored student entrepreneur, *Journal of Higher Education*, **79**(6), 638–670.

Nelson, A. (2012), Putting university research in context: assessing alternative measures of production and diffusion at Stanford, *Research Policy*, **41**, 678–691.

Nelson, A. and Byers, T. (2005), Organizational modularity and intra-university relationships between entrepreneurship education and technology transfer, in G. Libecap (ed.), *University Entrepreneurship and Technology Transfer: Process, Design, and Intellectual Property*, San Francisco, CA: Elsevier.

Nelson, A. and Byers, T. (2014), Challenges in university technology transfer and the promising role of entrepreneurship education, in A. Link, D. Siegel and M. Wright (eds), *The Chicago Handbook of University Technology Transfer*, Chicago: University of Chicago Press.

Oosterbeek, H., van Praag, M. and Ijsselstein, A. (2010), The impact of entrepreneurship education on entrepreneurship skills and motivation, *European Economic Review*, **54**(3), 442–454.

Pittaway, L. and Cope, J. (2007), Entrepreneurship education: a systematic review of the evidence, *International Small Business Journal*, **25**(5), 479–510.

Pressman, L. (2002), *AUTM Licensing Survey: FY 2002*, Northbrook, IL: Association of University Technology Managers.

Ridder, A. and van der Sijde, P. (2003), Raising awareness of entrepreneurship and e-commerce: a case study on student-entrepreneurship, *International Journal of Entrepreneurship and Innovation Management*, **3**(5), 609–620.

Roberts, E. (1991), *Entrepreneurs in High Technology*, New York: Oxford University Press.

Roberts, E. and C. Easley (2009), *Entrepreneurial Impact: The Role of MIT*, Kansas City: Ewing Marion Kauffman Foundation.

Romer, P. (1986), Increasing returns and long-run growth, *Journal of Political Economy*, **94**, 1002–1037.

Shane, S. (2004), *Academic Entrepreneurship: University Spinoffs and Wealth Creation*, Northampton, MA: Edward Elgar Publishing.

Stephan, P. (2009), Tracking the placement of students as a measure of technology transfer, in G. Libecap (ed.), *Measuring the Social Value of Innovation: A Link in the University Technology Transfer and Entrepreneurship Equation*, Bingley: Emerald Group Publishing Limited, pp.113–140.

Wani, V., Garg, T. and Sharma, S. (2004), Effective industry/institute interaction for developing entrepreneurial vision amongst engineers for the sustainable development of SMEs in India, *International Journal of Technology Transfer and Commercialization*, **3**(1), 38–55.

36 Technology Transfer and Cluster Interactions

Introduction

It has been widely acknowledged that innovation has become one of the keystones for success in the twenty-first century (Audretsch et al., 2014; Crespi and Zuniga, 2012; Fagerberg et al., 2005). Innovation is increasingly seen as the result of complex linkages and the product of an intricate set of relationships among actors in a system (Edquist, 2004; OECD, 1997). Allied to the emergence of the knowledge-based economy, we are now witnessing a reconceptualization regarding how knowledge is produced. The previous paradigm of technological development, entailing a sequential or linear movement from one economic unit (firm department, lab, firm or country) to another, has been questioned (Amesse and Cohendet, 2001) and a new more permeable boundary of the firm has been advanced (Chesborough, 2003). Several theses or models have been developed to help us understand the complex relationships that lead to innovation, such as national innovation systems (Lundvall, 1992), regional innovation systems (Cooke et al., 1997), Mode 1 and 2 knowledge production (Gibbons et al., 1994) and the triple helix of university–industry–government relations (Etzkowitz and Leydesdorff, 1997). Increased understanding of technology transfer and cooperation between institutional actors and partners holds huge potential to augment innovative efficacy (de Faria et al., 2010).

Technology transfer

Technology transfer brings definitional and conceptualization issues as it often holds contradictory meanings and demarcations (Bozeman, 2000). Disciplinarian variations include the following: in economics it is often thought of as properties of generic knowledge, in sociology it is linked to innovation and in anthropology it signifies the role of technology in the context of cultural evolution (Bozeman, 2000; Zhao and Reisman, 1992). A common definition of technology transfer is given by Decter et al. (2007) as the transfer of new knowledge, products or processes from one entity to another for business advantage. Technology transfer has become increasingly topical over the past few years for both scholars and practitioners. For example, since 1979, *The Journal of Technology Transfer*'s dedication to TT issues has acted as a catalyst for its popularity. Correspondingly, the advance of technology transfer is also echoed in the increased numbers of academic papers written on the topic; for example, according to Thompson Reuters' Web of Science, 266 journal articles were published in 2013 on the topic of 'technology transfer' compared to 141 articles in 2003, 106 in 1993 and six in 1973.

Economies of agglomeration and clusters

Fagerberg et al. (2005) emphasize that innovation tends to cluster in specific industries or areas and that these 'clusters' in turn grow more rapidly. The inference being that clusters promote structural changes in production and demand, eventually leading to organizational and institutional change. For innovation within the firm to take place, a favorable context outside the firm is also needed. Alfred Marshall was one of the first to highlight the importance of external economics in 1890. The sources of economies of agglomeration include: labor market pooling, access to specialized goods and services and technological spillovers (Marshall, 1920). Industrial agglomeration has been studied through a variety of different lenses, including: industrial districts; innovative milieu and the collective learning region; anchor tenant hypothesis; industrial complexes; and clusters.

Clusters specifically denote tight connections that bind certain firms or industries together in terms of their common behavior (Bergman and Feser, 1999). One can also look to cluster manifestations pertaining to: geographic location, sources of innovation, shared suppliers and factors of production (Bergman and Feser, 1999). Porter (1990) outlined that clusters influence the competitive landscape in three ways: they increase both the cluster and cluster firms' productivity; they drive innovation and productive growth for constituent firms; and they stimulate the formation of new businesses that support and expand the cluster. Universities can increasingly be viewed as a key component of cluster development and growth (Hershberg et al., 2007; Porter, 1998; Wonglimpiyarat, 2006). Similarly, Etzkowitz (2003) outlined that the 'national champion' view of economic success is beginning to rescind, opening up a reconceptualization centering on the importance of clusters of closely associated firms usually connected with a focal university or other research institute.

The central role of the university within clusters and technology transfer

The university institutional context has begun to evolve and advance from its more traditional roles of teaching and research to a fuller appreciation of its place in a knowledge-based economy (Etzkowitz, 2004; Etzkowitz et al., 2000; Rasmussen et al., 2011). The university boundaries for disciplinary knowledge are beginning to morph, creating new organizational and normative boundaries for the university system (Benner and Sandstrom, 2000). With this, the role of higher education institutions is changing to become more inclusive of commercial activities (Campbell et al., 2004; Owen-Smith and Powell, 2003; Siegel et al., 2007; Thursby and Kemp, 2002), which brings increased technology transfer challenges. The university is now increasingly perceived as an agent of regional and national economic development and not solely as a passive mechanism for education and research (Breznitz and Feldman, 2012; Breznitz et al., 2008).

Externally, regional context poses an interesting challenge for the university's technology transfer practices and cluster formation (Geoghegan et al., forthcoming). Bramwell and Wolfe (2008) argue that the contribution of universities to local and regional economic dynamism periodically yields a greater result than the generation of commercializable knowledge and qualified research scientists. They argue that universities produce other mechanisms of knowledge transfer, such as generating and attracting talent to the local economy and collaborating with local industry by providing formal and informal technical support to aid cluster formation and development.

Conclusion

We are now seeing increased technology transfer between entities previously perceived as passive mechanisms within the knowledge production landscape. University and firm boundaries are becoming more permeable and open to technology transfer. Within this paradigm shift we are also witnessing the increased prominence of cluster membership and formation.

WILL GEOGHEGAN

References

Amesse, F. and Cohendet, P. (2001), Technology transfer revisited from the perspective of the knowledge-based economy, *Research Policy*, **30**(9), 1459–1478.

Audretsch, D., Coad, A. and Segarra, A. (2014), Firm growth and innovation, *Small Business Economics*, **43**(4), 743–749.

Benner, M. and Sandstrom, U. (2000), Institutionalizing the triple helix: research funding and norms in the academic system, *Research Policy*, **29**(2), 291–301.

Bergman, E.M. and Feser, E.J. (1999), *Industrial and Regional Clusters: Concepts and Comparative Applications*, Morganton, WV: Regional Research Institute, West Virginia University.

Bozeman, B. (2000), Technology transfer and public policy: a review of research and theory, *Research Policy*, **29**(4–5), 627–655.

Bramwell, A. and Wolfe, D.A. (2008), Universities and regional economic development: the entrepreneurial University of Waterloo, *Research Policy*, **37**(8), 1175–1187.

Breznitz, S. and Feldman, M. (2012), The engaged university, *The Journal of Technology Transfer*, **37**(2), 139–157.

Breznitz, S., O'Shea, R.P. and Allen, T.J. (2008), University commercialization strategies in the development of regional bioclusters, *Journal of Product Innovation Management*, **25**(2), 129–142.

Campbell, E.G., Powers, J.B., Blumenthal, D. and Biles, B. (2004), Inside the triple helix: technology transfer and commercialization in the life sciences, *Health Affairs*, **23**(1), 64–76.

Chesborough, H.W. (2003), *Open Innovation: The New Imperative for Creating and Profiting from Technology*, Cambridge, MA: Harvard Business School Press.

Cooke, P., Gomez Uranga, M. and Etxebarria, G. (1997), Regional innovation systems: institutional and organisational dimensions, *Research Policy*, 26(4–5), 475–491.

Crespi, G. and Zuniga, P. (2012), Innovation and productivity: evidence from six Latin American countries, *World Development*, 40(2), 273–290.

Decter, M., Bennett, D. and Leseure, M. (2007), University to business technology transfer – UK and USA comparisons, *Technovation*, 27(3), 145–155.

de Faria, P., Lima, F. and Santos, R. (2010), Cooperation in innovation activities: the importance of partners, *Research Policy*, 39(8), 1082–1092.

Edquist, C. (2004), Systems of innovation: perspectives and challenges, in J. Faberberg, D. Mowery and R.R. Nelson (eds), *The Oxford Handbook of Innovation*, Oxford: Oxford University Press, pp. 181–209.

Etzkowitz, H. (2003), Research groups as 'quasi-firms': the invention of the entrepreneurial university, *Research Policy*, 32(1), 109–121.

Etzkowitz, H. (2004), The evolution of the entrepreneurial university, *International Journal of Technology and Globalisation*, 1(1), 64–77.

Etzkowitz, H. and Leydesdorff, L.A. (1997), *Universities and the Global Knowledge Economy: A Triple Helix of University–Industry–Government Relations*, London: Cassell Academic.

Etzkowitz, H., Webster, A., Gebhardt, C. and Terra, B.R.C. (2000), The future of the university and the university of the future: evolution of ivory tower to entrepreneurial paradigm, *Research Policy*, 29(2), 313–330.

Fagerberg, J., Mowery, D.C. and Nelson, R.R. (2005), *The Oxford Handbook of Innovation*, New York: Oxford University Press.

Geoghegan, W., O'Kane, C. and Fitzgerald, C. (forthcoming), Technology transfer offices as a nexus within the triple helix: the progression of the university's role, *International Journal of Technology Management*.

Gibbons, M., Limoges, C., Nowotny, H., Scott, P., Schwartzman, S. and Trow, M. (1994), *The New Production of Knowledge: The Dynamics of Science and Research in Contemporary Societies*, London: Sage Publications.

Hershberg, E., Nabeshima, K. and Yusuf, S. (2007), Opening the ivory tower to business: university–industry linkages and the development of knowledge-intensive clusters in Asian cities, *World Development*, 35(6), 931–940.

Lundvall, B.Å. (1992), *National Systems of Innovation: Towards a Theory of Innovation and Interactive Learning*, London: Pinter.

Marshall, A. (1920), *Principles of Economics*, Boston: Macmillan.

OECD (1997), *National Innovation Systems*, Paris: OECD Publications.

Owen-Smith, J. and Powell, W.W. (2003), The expanding role of university patenting in the life sciences: assessing the importance of experience and connectivity, *Research Policy*, 32(9), 1695–1711.

Porter, M. (1990), The competitive advantage of nations, *Harvard Business Review*, March–April.

Porter, M. (1998), Clusters and the new economics of competition, *Harvard Business Review*, 76(6), 77–90.

Rasmussen, E., Mosey, S. and Wright, M. (2011), The evolution of entrepreneurial competencies: a longitudinal study of university spin-off venture emergence, *Journal of Management Studies*, 48(6), 1314–1345.

Siegel, D.S., Veugelers, R. and Wright, M. (2007), Technology transfer offices and commercialization of university intellectual property: performance and policy implications, *Oxford Review of Economic Policy*, 23(4), 640–660.

Thursby, J.G. and Kemp, S. (2002), Growth and productive efficiency of university intellectual property licensing, *Research Policy*, 31(1), 109–124.

Wonglimpiyarat, J. (2006), The dynamic economic engine at Silicon Valley and US government programmes in financing innovations, *Technovation*, 26(9), 1081–1089.

Zhao, L. and Reisman, A. (1992), Toward meta research on technology transfer, *IEEE Transactions on Engineering Management*, 39(1), 13–21.

37 Technology Transfer from Public Institutions

Introduction

Public to private technology transfer is a thorny topic conceptually. For instance, there are a number of ways to define 'technology.' Each of the academic disciplines interested in developing a systematic understanding of technology transfer – predominantly economics, management science, and science and technology policy – uses distinct interpretations that have implications for knowledge and practice. In addition, demarcating public from private organizations is not so straightforward. Whether a private defense contractor receiving 100 percent of its budget from governmental sources is as 'private' as a company receiving no public funding is debatable.

Despite these difficulties, they are not the focus of this chapter. There are already reviews of the conceptual issues (see Bozeman, 2000, 2009, 2014). Instead the focus here is, first, on 'active' mechanisms, such as laws and organizational forms implemented explicitly to facilitate the transfer of technology, however defined, from government and from public and private universities to private companies no matter their respective levels of public funding. (In contrast, 'passive' mechanisms are those that may indeed facilitate public to private transfer, but not necessarily as a primary function, e.g., the open scientific literature.) The second focus of this chapter is on what we know about the effectiveness of active mechanisms for public to private transfer – well, so far anyway.

First a brief explanation of why we are (or should be) interested in public to private transfer is in order. There are historical accounts (see Smith, 1990; Guston, 2007), but in short we are interested in public to private transfer to ensure accountability in and return-on-investment from publicly funded research and development (R&D). Whereas the overarching assumption for the first few decades after World War II was that the knowledge and technology developed in government agencies and universities with federal support would 'trickle down' to companies, today we have a number of active mechanisms designed to ensure – or at least increase the likelihood of – public to private transfer.

Mechanisms

Most of the active mechanisms for public to private transfer are enabled by a series of legislation and policies beginning in the early 1980s and continuing to date. The laws are detailed elsewhere, most notably in the 'Green Book,' which is updated regularly by the Federal Laboratory Consortium for Technology Transfer (see www.federallabs.org). The most studied of these laws are the 1980 Bayh-Dole Act allowing universities and small businesses to patent and license inventions funded by the federal government and the 1986 Federal Technology Transfer Act authorizing federal labs to enter into cooperative R&D agreements, or CRADAs as they are commonly known, with companies.

While the laws are many – the Green Book (currently in its fifth edition) details 53 sections of the US Code on public to private transfer, not to mention that additionally there are numerous state-level policies enabling public to private transfer – the mechanisms set in motion by these laws are fewer. For all intents and purposes, transfer-enabling laws and policies at any level of government are intended to do one or more of the following three things:

1. Economically incent public to private transfer; for example, by allowing inventions funded by government to be patented and licensed.
2. Require government agencies, and at the state-level universities, to develop internal processes for transfer; for example, by establishing technology transfer offices (TTOs).
3. Enable cooperative R&D between public and private entities; for example, CRADAs at the federal level and any number of comparable arrangements at the state level.

From an entrepreneurship perspective, the third category is the most important, because it is the entrepreneur's job to acquire the resources necessary to make any new technology venture innovative, which increasingly entails R&D involving companies working with government and/or universities (Block and Miller, 2008). Although intellectual property rights laws and technology transfer offices (the first two categories above) are important as well, information about each of these mechanisms is readily attainable online (see www.uspto.gov and www.federallabs.org, respectively) and is not manipulable in any direct sense by the entrepreneur. In contrast, cooperative R&D is the transfer mechanism that is most difficult for the entrepreneur to understand yet also is the mechanism over which the entrepreneur may exercise the most discretion.

Cooperative R&D as a mechanism for public to private transfer can be divided into two general types: legal and organizational. Among the first type is the CRADA. With the CRADA, federal labs may enter into cooperative research agreements and negotiate licenses with companies and nonprofits. Moreover, companies participating in CRADAs may patent technologies developed cooperatively with federal labs. But the CRADA is not simply government contracting in reverse. Unlike contractors' arm's-length supplier–buyer relationships with government, companies using CRADAs to work with federal labs benefit predominantly from the intellectual capacity of the labs and, in turn, from the enhancement of their own absorptive capacity rather than from any single product or process (Ham and Mowery, 1998).

One of the biggest problems with CRADAs has been the clash between the organizational cultures of federal labs and companies (Rogers et al., 1998). For example, companies view federal labs as taking too long to carry out projects (Eto et al., 1995) and labs view companies as myopic and overly concerned with intellectual property (Berman, 1994). But the CRADA, as a mode of cooperative R&D, is not the culprit. The unit of observation for the CRADA is the project, not the organization. Now, almost every federal lab has its own handbook of procedures for cir-cumventing 'culture clash' between labs and companies participating in CRADAs. Perhaps the most important element common across the hand-books is advice for determining when CRADAs are (and are not) appro-priate: CRADAs are generally recommended when both asset specificity and ease of measurement are 'high.'

Unlike the CRADA, most other modes of cooperative R&D for public to private transfer are explicit exercises in organizational design. These organizations are generally referred to as 'bridging institutions' because their generic function is to bridge the gap between publicly funded R&D and private sector commercialization. Bridging institutions include a number of forms that should be familiar to the entrepreneur: science parks, technology incubators, university research centers, industry con-sortia, proof-of-concept centers and innovation networks. This list is not conclusive; as new gaps for public to private transfer are discovered, new organizations will form to bridge those gaps. But as of this entry the list is more or less comprehensive. For example, most of the well-known National Science Foundation (NSF) research centers and newer Department of Energy (DOE) research centers fit the university research center mold (for a review, see Boardman et al., 2013).

The challenge for the entrepreneur is to understand which type of bridg-ing institution is relevant to a particular technology venture. Starting at the basic research end of the innovation continuum, cooperative R&D in some university research centers entails 'incremental' product and process improvements for mature industries like auto manufacturing, whereas other such centers emphasize relatively 'radical' R&D for the creation of new fields of inquiry and, with them, new industries (Boardman, 2012). Moving towards the middle of the continuum and thusly closer to market, proof-of-concept centers and technology incubators focus on business model development and venture capital in addition to cooperative R&D (well, mostly development) between universities and companies. Arriving at the commercialization end of the innovation continuum, science parks co-locate startups with one another and also with universities and federal labs (Boardman, 2014).

As of this entry, a new mechanism for cooperative R&D for public to private transfer has emerged, one that focuses on entrepreneurship directly. Entrepreneurs have always been fundamental to innovation systems (Nelson, 1993), but historically it has been more or less assumed that market forces were enough to guide the entrepreneur in her endeavors. In contrast, the I-Corps program at NSF (the 'I' stands for 'innovation') characterizes entrepreneurs as human capital to be developed. The program provides researchers from universities and federal labs with training in entrepreneurship. Rather than creating new bridging institutions to span the gaps in the continuum from basic research to commercialization, I-Corps emphasizes the use of extant university labs, federal labs, companies and bridging institutions. The idea is that the gaps for some fields of inquiry are now small enough for researchers to leap across given the appropriate training.

Conclusions

I conclude this chapter with a few caveats. First, I do not discuss academic contracting because this entails companies making a 'buy' (versus 'make') decision, not cooperative R&D. Contracting is an effective mechanism for public to private transfer, but it is not difficult for the entrepreneur to understand and requires no elucidation here. I also do not discuss industry consortia because when these involve public sector participants, the information exchanges that result are essentially those accomplished by the open scientific literature (Boardman et al., 2013). Last, I have not discussed the effectiveness of bridging institutions beyond CRADAs. The jury is still out for the different types of bridging institutions, not because not enough time has passed to evaluate some of them, but because of research design difficulties and measurement validity issues (Boardman, 2014).

CRAIG BOARDMAN

References

Berman, E.M. (1994), Technology transfer and the federal laboratories – a midterm assessment of cooperative research, *Policy Studies Journal*, **22**(2), 338–348.

Block, F. and Miller, M.R. (2008), Where do innovations come from? Transformations in the US national innovation system, 1970–2006, www.itif.org/index.php?s=policy_issues&c=Science-and-R38D-Policy.

Boardman, C. (2012), Organizational capital in boundary-spanning collaborations: internal and external approaches to organizational structure and personnel authority, *Journal of Public Administration Research and Theory*, **22**, 497–526.

Boardman, C. (2014), The new visible hand: understanding today's R&D management, *Issues in Science and Technology*, April.

Boardman, C., Gray, D. and Rivers, D. (eds) (2013), *Cooperative Research Centers and Technical Innovation: Policies, Strategies, and Organizational Dynamics of the New Science and Engineering Management*, New York: Springer.

Bozeman, B. (2000), Technology transfer and public policy: a review of research and theory, *Research Policy*, **29**, 627–655.

Bozeman, B. (2009), *All Organizations Are Public: Comparing Public and Private Organizations*, Washington, DC: Beard Books.

Bozeman, B., Rimes, H. and Youtie, J. (2015), The evolving state-of-the-art in technology transfer research: revisiting the contingent effectiveness model, *Research Policy*, **44**(1), 34–49.

Eto, M., Rogers, E.M., Wierengo, D., Byrnes, P. and Allbritton, M. (1995), *Technology Transfer from Government R&D Laboratories in the United States and Japan*, Albuquerque, NM: University of New Mexico Press.

Guston, D. (2007), *Between Politics and Science: Assuring the Integrity and Productivity of Research*, Cambridge: Cambridge University Press.

Ham, R.M. and Mowery, D.C. (1998), Improving the effectiveness of public–private R&D collaboration: case studies at a US weapons laboratory, *Research Policy*, **26**, 661–675.

Nelson, R.R. (ed.) (1993), *National Innovation Systems: A Comparative Analysis*, Oxford: Oxford University Press.

Rogers, E.M., Carayannis, E., Kurihara, K. and Allbritton, M. (1998), Cooperatibe research and development agreements (CRADAs) as technology transfer mechanisms, *R&D Management*, **28**(2), 79–88.

Smith, B.L.R. (1990), *American Science Policy Since World War II*, Washington, DC: The Brookings Institution.

38 Technology Transfer from Universities

Introduction

Technology transfer from universities is one of the key drivers of economic growth and scientific entrepreneurship (Grimaldi et al, 2011; Alridge and Audretsch, 2011). Technology transfer from universities to industry has shaped new industries and industrial sectors based on scientific excellence. It has also led to the creation of new products and services that we as individual citizens use and consume on a daily basis.

The role of technology transfer offices

To support technology transfer universities have established technology transfer offices (TTOs) with a core remit, as Fassin (2000: 37) notes, to be the 'guardian of the university's intellectual property'. The role of TTOs is more than protecting intellectual property (IP). TTOs are involved in the exploiting of IP through different technology transfer mechanisms. These include patents, licences, material transfer agreements, spin-out and spin-in firms. When TTOs receive invention disclosures from scientists, they decide if the intellectual property or creative works is worth protecting and exploiting. TTOs are involved in negotiating contracts regarding how IP is used or revealed.

TTOs' roles also includes the promotion of technology transfer within their institutional setting and to industry, as well as securing additional research funding through sponsored research agreements with industry partners (Cunningham and Harney, 2006). Some TTOs are involved in the provision and management of incubators and provision of incubator services that support new venture creation. Incubators provide opportunities, particularly for technology entrepreneurs, to build relational intellectual capital. A study of an Irish third-level incubation found that technology entrepreneurs build relational intellectual capital through the development of networks and contacts, relationship-building, accessing and leveraging knowledge experts and members of associations (Gately and Cunningham, 2014a). Incubator structured new venture creation programmes also support entrepreneurs to write their business plan. This structured business plan support contributes to the startup process for technology entrepreneurs in terms of financial resource appropriation, preliminary business and industry intelligence, market feedback, network mapping and development (Gately and Cunningham, 2014b).

Barriers to technology transfer
Technology transfer from universities can be complex and involve multiple academic and industry partners. Institutional barriers to technology transfer include TTO organization structure and supports, resources constraints and deficiencies, lack of clarity over IP ownership, perceived conflicts of interest, exaggerated IP valuations, partner trust and the lack of support for SME technology transfers (see Cunningham and Harney, 2006: 119–121). Cultural barriers can impede technology transfer from universities. Significant culture and mission differences exist between academia and industry. Typically, universities' values are focused on advancement of knowledge, new inventions and have a long-term focus. Industry typically values new applications, seeks to add value and has a short-term focus based on financial returns (see Cunningham and Harney, 2006: 123–124). This leads to mutual incomprehension between academia and industry. Cultural barriers to technology transfer can include departmental and faculty attitudes, lack of awareness, lack of soft skills and the perceived non-challenging nature of technology transfer (Cunningham and Harney, 2006).

Stimulating technology transfer from universities
So what stimulates technology transfer from universities? There are a number of factors that influence technology transfer from universities at macro and micro levels. Macro-level factors that stimulate technology transfer include the level of business investment in R&D in the region, proximity to industrial clusters, support of development agencies and research councils, government support and investment and cost-effective

patenting processes (see Evers et al., 2014: 46–48). Several micro-level factors can stimulate technology transfer from universities. These include research traditions, quality of the TTO, scope of commercialization activities, documented policies and inventor involvement (see Evers et al., 2014: 48–50). Previous studies have shown that involving the inventor – the scientist or scientific team – is important for effective technology transfer (see Goldfarb and Henrekson, 2003; Meseri and Maital, 2001). Furthermore, Jensen and Thursby (2001) found that at least 71 per cent of inventions require further involvement by the academic researcher if they are to be successfully commercialized.

Role of scientists in technology transfer

Scientists play a significant role in technology transfer from universities by creating the intellectual property from their research, which can be protected and exploited by industry with the involvement of TTOs. To advance knowledge scientists compete for public funding to support their research activities. In leading such large-scale research programmes, they take on the role of principal investigator (PI). Becoming a PI is seen as prestigious and a significant career milestone.

In the PI role, scientists are bridging between academia, TTOs, firms, regulators, society and policymakers. These large-scale public research programmes where scientists take on the role of PI include technology transfer activities. This technology transfer requirement is now commonplace in publicly funded research programmes. This in turn requires scientists as PIs to engage with industry partners and TTOs. As Mangematin et al. (2014) note: 'PIs are the linchpin of the transformation, shaping research avenues, articulating actors within programs, bridging academia and industry.' By responding, interpreting and articulating scientific trajectories in response to public research programmes, scientists as PIs are in a central position to shape science and markets through technology transfer (see Mangematin et al., 2014). PIs have become knowledge and technology transfer agents and brokers of science (Cunningham et al., 2015).

When it comes to technology transfer from universities, scientists in the role of PIs experience two main categories of inhibiting factors – political and environmental and institution-based (Cunningham et al., 2014). Inhibiting factors in relation to technology transfer for the political and environmental category include balancing the research delivery against funding agency expectations, dealing with the competing interests of industry partners and funders as research projects roll out in relation to research commercialization, as well as excessive IP valuations by TTOs. These inhibitors create a core tension for PIs, whether to focus on research and academic outputs, or pursue technology transfer opportunities. In relation to the institutional inhibitors category, the level of dedicated technology transfer support available to PIs was a major issue. TTOs focus on IP protection not technology marketing, the lack of technology push by TTOs and the narrow focus on legal aspects of commercialization were inhibiting factors experienced by PIs in relation to technology transfer.

Sustaining technology transfer from universities
For national economies, universities, TTOs, firms and scientific communities, creating effective sustainable technology transfer can benefit all. The entrepreneurial university is the latest reconceptualization of defining the role of universities in the twenty-first century. The reconceptualization emphasizes the pivotal role universities play in shaping economies and societies as Guerrero et al. (2014) note: 'An entrepreneurial university is a natural incubator that tries to provide a supportive environment in which the university community can explore, evaluate and exploit ideas that could be transformed into social and economic entrepreneurial initiatives.' Universities remain at the core of technology transfer and have growing importance and impact on economies and societies.

A recent study of the economic impact of 147 entrepreneurial universities in the UK reveals the positive and significant economic impact of teaching, research and entrepreneurial activities (Guerrero et al., 2015). The higher economic impact of the UK's entrepreneurial universities (the Russell Group) is explained by entrepreneurial spinoff. For the rest of the country's universities, the highest impact is associated with knowledge transfer (knowledge capital). This reinforces the important and economic benefit of technology transfer and of knowledge capital.

Conclusions
Sustaining effective technology transfer from universities requires fostering closer university–industry R&D collaborations. Such close collaboration has synergistic benefits for academia and industry. Involving academic partners for industry R&D projects enhances the probability of R&D realization (Link and Ruhm, 2009). Consequently, public R&D programmes in their design and implementation should encourage the development of long-term mutually beneficial R&D collaborations. Furthermore, based on a small sample of European data Cunningham and Link (2014) found that the extent to which access to business sector R&D facilities facilitates university cooperation with business was positive and statistically significant. Further research needs to be undertaken into university–industry R&D collaborations. These findings suggest the need for a more system-wide technology transfer harmonization of activities to enhance technology transfer from universities. Finally, open innovation

and open science offer new ways of sustaining technology transfer from universities, but require further research to establish the economic, societal and knowledge advancement impacts. Nevertheless, universities, TTOs, scientists as PIs, firms, funders and policymakers should not be afraid to experiment with new structures and approaches that enhance and disrupt conventional approaches to technology transfer from universities. This ultimately benefits society.

JAMES A. CUNNINGHAM

References

Aldridge, T.T. and Audretsch, D. (2011), The Bayh-Dole Act, and scientist entrepreneurship, *Research Policy*, **40**(8), 1058–1067.

Cunningham, J.A. and Harney, B. (2006), *Strategic Management of Technology Transfer: The New Challenge on Campus*, Cork, Ireland: Oak Tree Press.

Cunningham, J.A. and Link, A.N. (2014), Fostering university-industry R&D collaborations in European Union countries, *International Entrepreneurship and Management Journal*, http://link.springer.com/article/10.1007%2Fs11365-014-0317-4.

Cunningham, J., O'Reilly, P., O'Kane, C. and Mangematin, V. (2014), The inhibiting factors that principal investigators experience in leading publicly funded research, *Journal of Technology Transfer*, **39**(1), 93–110.

Cunningham, J.A., O'Reilly, P., O'Kane, C. and Mangematin, V. (2015), Managerial challenges of publicly funded principal investigators, *International Journal of Technology Management*, **68**(3/4), 176–202.

Evers, N., Cunningham, J. and Hoholm, T. (2014), *Technology Entrepreneurship: Bringing Innovation to the Marketplace*, Basingstoke: Palgrave Macmillan.

Fassin, Y. (2000), The strategic role of university Industry Liaison Offices, *Journal of Research Administration*, 1(2), 31–41.

Gately, C. and Cunningham, J. (2014a), Building intellectual capital in incubated technology firms, *Journal of Intellectual Capital*, **15**(4), 516–536.

Gately, C. and Cunningham, J. (2014b), The contribution and disconnection between writing business plans and the start-up process for technology entrepreneurs in an incubation programme, in A.C. Corbett, D.S. Siegel and J.A. Katz (eds), *Advances in Entrepreneurship, Firm Emergence and Growth*, Bingley: Emerald Group Publishing, pp. 197–241.

Goldfarb, B. and Henrekson, M. (2003), Bottom-up versus top-down policies towards the commercialization of university intellectual property, *Research Policy*, **32**(4), 639–658.

Grimaldi, R., Kenney, M., Siegel, D.S. and Wright, M. (2011), 30 years after Bayh-Dole: reassessing academic entrepreneurship, *Research Policy*, **40**(8), 1045–1057.

Guerrero, M., Urbano, D., Cunningham, J. and Organ, D. (2014), Entrepreneurial universities in two European regions: a case study comparision of their conditioning factors, outcomes and outputs, *Journal of Technology Transfer*, **39**(3), 415–434.

Guerrero, M., Cunningham, J.A. and Urbano, D. (2015), Economic impact of entrepreneurial universities' activities: an exploratory study of the United Kingdom, *Research Policy*, **44**(3), 748–764.

Jensen, R. and Thursby, M. (2001), Proofs and prototypes for sale: the tale of university licensing, *American Economic Review*, **91**(1), 240–259.

Link, A.N. and Ruhm, C.J. (2009), Bringing science to market: commercializing from NIH SBIR awards, *Economics of Innovation and New Technology*, **18**, 381–402.

Mangematin, V., O'Reilly, P. and Cunningham, J. (2014), PIs as boundary spanners, science and market shapers, *Journal of Technology Transfer*, **39**(1), 1–10.

Meseri, O. and Maital, S. (2001), A survey analysis of university-technology transfer in Israel: evaluation of projects and determinants of success, *Journal of Technology Transfer*, **26**(1), 115–125.

39 Technology Transfer Models

Introduction

Universities have amplified their entrepreneurial activities over the past few decades, especially as innovations derived from university–industry collaborations are increasingly recognized for their contributions to firm innovation and regional economic growth. There is a growing emphasis on formalizing technology transfer in universities.

Several existing paradigms have been useful in crafting the traditional model of technology transfer presented here. Miller and Acs (2013) characterize traditional technology transfer as an organization-centric model that combines Etzkowitz's (2003) triple helix model and Kerr's (2001) concept of the multiversity. Under the triple helix model of university–industry–government relations, reciprocal relationships are formed among the three institutions in which each attempts to enhance the performance of others. The multiversity is a modular institution centered on undergraduate and graduate schools with multiple activities and organizations, including science parks and research institutes, integrated or released depending on the needs of the students, faculty and regional communities. Miller and Acs' organization-centric model extends the path from Bush's implicit linear model (1945) to the Bayh-Dole Act, and achieves technology transfer through connections between university researchers and both federal funding and potential commercial opportunities.

The traditional model

The catalyst for starting the technology transfer process may come from the research support of the federal government or industry (Bozeman, 2000). Commonly, the university scientist receives a federal research grant. The scientist uses the grant to conduct research and purposely or serendipitously discovers a new product or process technology that might have market potential, thus beginning the technology transfer process. Alternatively, sometimes industry might initiate a partnership with a university.

The traditional model of the technology transfer process in Figure 39.1 is illustrated as a linear model and it begins with the process of discovery by a university scientist (Siegel et al., 2004). The scientist discloses the invention to the university's technology transfer office (TTO). The TTO then evaluates the invention and decides whether or not to pursue acquiring a patent. The TTO must consider the commercial potential of the invention and prospective interest from the public or private sector (Siegel et al., 2003). If the TTO decides to invest in the invention, the next step is the patent application process. If the patent is awarded, the TTO markets

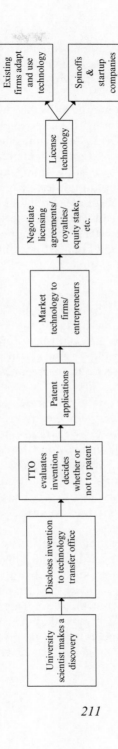

Source: Bradley et al. (2013)

Figure 39.1 Traditional model of university technology transfer

the technology to organizations and entrepreneurs. The goal of this marketing effort is to match the technology with an organization or entrepreneur to best utilize the technology and provide opportunity for revenues to the university.

When a suitable partner is found, the university works with the organization or entrepreneur to negotiate a licensing agreement. The licensing agreement typically includes a royalty to the university, an equity stake in the startup or other such compensation. When an agreement is reached, the technology is officially licensed. In the final stage of the process, the organization or entrepreneur adapts and uses the technology.

As universities become more entrepreneurial and look toward technology transfer in nontraditional fields, there is a need for alternative conceptualizations of technology transfer that are more accurate and realistic than the traditional linear model and that are generalizable to the nuances of the university to which they are applied.

Limitations of the traditional model

Although characteristic of the path to market for some innovations, the traditional model in Figure 39.1 has a number of limitations. Simply, the traditional model documented in the extant literature does not accurately capture the complexities of technology transfer in practice. The inaccuracies in the traditional model relate to discrepancies between academic postulations and how technology transfer is practiced in universities. The traditional model binds technology transfer to a rigid linear path and it oversimplifies the underlying, subtle complexities of the process. A one-size-fits-all traditional model does not accurately depict differences in technology transfer across disciplines, and forcing all disclosures to follow the traditional model's linear path to commercialization will likely ensure that many inventions fail. Finally, the traditional model places too much emphasis on patents as the primary output in the technology transfer process, overlooking other mechanisms for profitability and commercialization.

The inadequacies in the traditional model relate to processes that it fails to address. The traditional linear model fails to acknowledge the importance of informal mechanisms of technology transfer. The organizational cultures of the university and of the firm impact the majority of the technology transfer process, but these elements are not addressed in the traditional model. The types of reward systems in place in universities can greatly facilitate or impede faculty involvement in technology transfer activities, yet the traditional model has no representation of their influence.

An alternative model of technology transfer

The following alternative conceptualizations are intended to more accurately represent technology transfer in practice and to emphasize concepts of academic entrepreneurship and open innovation.

Figure 39.2 illustrates an alternative view of university technology transfer. The solid black arrows indicate processes of technology transfer, while the gray dashed arrows indicate factors that influence these processes.

This alternative view begins with a scientific discovery, as does the traditional model in Figure 39.1, but distinguishes between different inventors – university scientists, graduate students and research teams – that exist in practice. Also indicated are possible funding sources including federal contracts, federal grants, private grants, corporate contracts, donations and venture capital funds.

Once a discovery is made, the technology transfer process follows one of two paths:

- The inventor can choose to disclose his/her invention to the university's TTO – process 1 in Figure 39.2.
- The inventor can choose not to disclose his/her invention, bypassing the TTO – process 2 in Figure 39.2.

The inventor's decision to disclose is influenced by the university's reward systems and culture, as noted by the gray dashed arrows. If the university has a reward system in place that provides incentives for faculty to engage in commercialization activities, the inventor might be more likely to disclose and participate in the formal mechanisms of technology transfer. If there are too many perceived barriers and disadvantages to going through official channels, the inventor might circumvent disclosure and adopt informal mechanisms of technology transfer.

Once the inventor discloses to the TTO, the office evaluates the invention's commercialization potential, including the time it will take to bring the invention to market and its market potential. For private sources of funding (i.e., private grants, corporate contracts and donations), the university automatically holds title to the invention. Thus, the technology transfer process would move from the TTO to the decision on how to commercialize the invention (process 6 in Figure 39.2).

When the discovery results from a federally funded research project, one of two paths may be followed:

- The university can decline to retain title; the federal funding agency can then request title to the invention – process 3 in Figure 39.2.

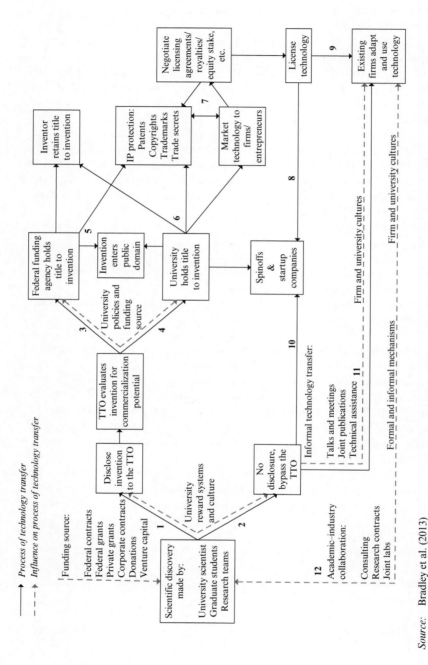

Source: Bradley et al. (2013)

Figure 39.2   Alternative model of university technology transfer

- The university can retain title to the invention – process 4 in Figure 39.2.

If the university declines to retain title to the invention, the responsibility goes to the federal agency that funded the discovery. The federal funding agency has the three following options (process 5 in Figure 39.2):

- Request the title to the invention and let it enter the public domain, effectively ending the technology transfer process.
- Allow the inventor(s) to retain title to the invention, as long as the university approves. The inventor is then free to file their own application for intellectual property (IP) protection.
- Request the title to the invention and file an application for IP protection, typically a patent.

Or, the university can choose to hold title to the invention and decide how to proceed with commercialization (process 6 in Figure 39.2):

- In some cases, it is decided early on that a spinoff or startup is the best way to develop the invention.
- In other cases, the university markets the technology to firms or entrepreneurs that can develop the technology.
- The university may also begin the process of acquiring IP protection in the form of patents, copyrights, trademarks, trade secrets, etc.
- The university may, with the funding agency's approval, allow the inventor(s) to retain title to the invention.
- If the invention is not federally funded, it may be allowed to enter the public domain if the invention is unlikely to have significant commercial value or there is no market interest in the invention.

The processes of marketing the invention, acquiring IP protection and negotiating licensing agreements and pecuniary returns can overlap and occur simultaneously (process 7 in Figure 39.2):

- The invention can be marketed before IP protection is acquired; that is, if the university wants to gauge market interest before investing significant time and resources to protecting the invention. Or, if the invention seems especially promising, the university might choose to apply for patents, copyrights, etc. before or even as they are marketing it to potential investors. The university could successfully market the invention, lock in an interested firm or entrepreneur, and begin licensing negotiations before the IP protection process is completed.

- If the federal funding agency holds title to the invention, its next step is to file patent applications.
- Similarly, if the inventor is permitted to retain title, he/she will likely seek IP protection before taking further steps to develop his/her invention.

Once the technology has been protected and successfully marketed, and a licensing agreement is concluded, the technology is officially licensed to a firm, organization or entrepreneur.

- If the technology has been licensed to an entrepreneur, such as the inventing faculty member or an outside party, a spinoff or startup company is established around the invention – process 8 in Figure 39.2.
- If the technology has been licensed to an existing firm, the firm adapts and uses the technology. Such technology typically requires significant further development before reaching the market – process 9 in Figure 39.2.

If the inventor bypasses the TTO (process 2 in Figure 39.2), the technology transfer process is carried out through informal mechanisms, including consulting, joint publications, presentations and conferences, and other communication processes between and among faculty members and industry contacts.

Similar to the path of formal technology transfer, the ideas and knowledge that are passed along through informal mechanisms can also result in:

- a spinoff or a startup company being established that utilizes the knowledge passed on from the university scientist – process 10 in Figure 39.2;
- the scientist's discovery, idea, or knowledge being adapted and used by an existing firm – process 11 in Figure 39.2; and/or
- other forms of knowledge dissemination, including the disclosure of the invention into the public domain.

Finally, the university scientist and the firm developing the invention often maintain a working relationship by means of academic–industry collaboration, which involves consulting, research contracts, the establishment of joint labs and other partnerships between the university and the firm

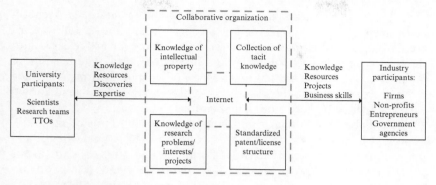

Source: Bradley et al. (2013)

Figure 39.3   *Collaborative model of university knowledge and technology transfer*

(process 12 in Figure 39.2). These collaborations can involve both formal and informal mechanisms of technology transfer.

A collaborative model of technology transfer

Another identifiable, and somewhat more experimental, method of technology transfer is referred to here as the collaborative view of knowledge and technology transfer. Building off the concept of open innovation (Chesbrough, 2003; Hayter, 2009), a new method of technology transfer is gaining popularity that is characterized by low-cost, streamlined, transparent collaboration between participants. The collaborative model is better suited to the transfer of knowledge than of physical inventions, although both can be accomplished within the model.

Figure 39.3 presents a collaborative view of knowledge and technology transfer. In this model, academia and industry are able to connect directly through the internet by means of a collaborative organization. The collaborative organization serves as a platform for matching innovators with the partners and resources they need to develop their product. They host, maintain and promote their web-based organization as an alternative to traditional methods of knowledge and technology transfer. The collaborative organization facilitates the academic–industry connection by gathering data from all participating institutions, often cataloguing it into databases. Examples of collected data include intellectual property owned by the institutions, tacit knowledge available from university or industry participants, research interests or projects, and a standardized patent and/or license structure such as Creative Commons.

Practices that emulate the collaborative view facilitate the technology transfer process by making knowledge transfer simple. Innovations are developed and commercialized as a joint effort, or are released into the public domain to be used by any interested party. The benefits of organizations utilizing a collaborative view of technology transfer include reduced costs of technology transfer activities, a freer exchange of knowledge and ideas, and accelerating innovations to market.

The collaborative model is in many ways the antithesis of the traditional linear model; it is fluid and continual, and allows knowledge and innovation to flow among participants with few limitations of structure or bureaucracy. In today's digital age, it seems advantageous to take advantage of the global connection the internet provides and to formulate a method of technology transfer that is equally global and connective.

SAMANTHA R. BRADLEY

References

Bozeman, B. (2000), Technology transfer and public policy: a review of research and theory, *Research Policy*, **29**(4–5), 627–655.

Bradley, S.R., Hayter, C.S. and Link, A.N. (2013), Models and methods of university technology transfer, *Foundations and Trends in Entrepreneurship*, **9**(6), 571–650.

Bush, V. (1945), *Science – the Endless Frontier: A Report to the President on a Program for Postwar Scientific Research*, Washington, DC: National Science Foundation.

Chesbrough, H. (2003), *Open Innovation: The New Imperative for Creating and Profiting from Technology*, Boston: Harvard Business School Press.

Etzkowitz, H. (2003), Research groups as 'quasi-firms': the invention of the entrepreneurial university, *Research Policy*, **32**(1), 109–121.

Hayter, C. (2009), *The Open Innovation Imperative: Perspectives on Success from Faculty Entrepreneurs*, PhD dissertation, George Washington University.

Kerr, C. (2001), *The Uses of the University*, Cambridge, MA: Harvard University Press.

Miller, D.J. and Acs, Z.J. (2013), Technology commercialization on campus: twentieth century frameworks and twenty-first century blind spots, *Annals of Regional Science*, **50**(2), 407–423.

Siegel, D.S., Waldman, D.A. and Link, A.N. (2003), Assessing the impact of organizational practices on the productivity of university technology transfer offices: an exploratory study, *Research Policy*, **32**(1), 27–48.

Siegel, D.S., Waldman, D.A., Atwater, L. and Link, A.N. (2004), Toward a model of the effective transfer of scientific knowledge from academicians to practitioners: qualitative evidence from the commercialization of university technologies, *Journal of Engineering and Technology Management*, **21**(1–2), 115–142.

40 Underexplored Issues in Entrepreneurial Finance

Introduction
In this chapter, we start by summarizing modern theorizing on entrepreneurial finance as depicted in the financial growth cycle paradigm (Berger and Udell, 1998). We then propose three areas for future research that may advance our current theoretical and practical understanding of entrepreneurial finance. While we do not intend to minimize the importance of the thousands of research papers in the entrepreneurial finance field published over the past decades, in this chapter we emphasize some key issues.

Financial growth cycle
Modern theories on the evolution of entrepreneurial financing are appealingly summarized in the financial growth cycle paradigm (Berger and Udell, 1998). In this paradigm, the optimal financial structure and availability of financing sources change as firms grow, age and become less informationally opaque. Startup firms are expected to primarily finance themselves with funds from founders (family or friends), trade credit and, if growth ambitions are high, angel financing. As firms develop a track record, generate steady cash flows and have high-quality collateral, they may also obtain access to bank debt. Firms with no or limited access to bank debt to finance their early growth can raise venture capital financing, but only when their growth ambitions are very high. Eventually, if firms reach a critical scale, they may gain access to public equity and debt markets to finance their continued growth.

The financial growth cycle paradigm gives an idea of the sources of financing that become important at different points in the firm lifecycle. However, firms do not necessarily move through all stages in the financial growth cycle due to supply-side and demand-side constraints. Specifically, many entrepreneurial finance scholars indicate that young entrepreneurial ventures with high growth potential face constraints in obtaining external financing, including bank debt and external equity financing, due to asymmetric information, transaction costs and other market imperfections, which may hamper firm growth and even threaten firm survival (Carpenter and Petersen, 2002a, 2002b; Cassar, 2004; Holtz-Eakin et al., 1994). Others indicate that entrepreneurs' self-determination motive may make them unwilling to raise certain sources of external financing (Sapienza et al., 2003).

Underexplored issues
The critical role of bank debt (and, more broadly, external debt financing) in startups and growing firms is currently not sufficiently recognized and is

hence under-researched: recent evidence suggests that contrary to common wisdom, bank debt plays a central role in the financing of startups (Cassar, 2004; Robb and Robinson, 2014). Vanacker and Deloof (2014), using a sample that covers the population of Belgian startups founded between 2006 and 2009, report that 73 percent of startup firms raise bank debt, and that bank debt represents, on average, 30 percent of the total amount of finance raised in the initial year of operation. Surprisingly, bank debt is the single most important source of financing, even for startups founded during the height of the recent financial crisis — which represented an unexpected negative shock to the supply of credit. This evidence is surprising in view of extant theories, which argue that startups will mainly rely on personal sources of financing and trade debt, because bank debt will often not be available as a consequence of market imperfections such as asymmetric information (Berger and Udell, 1998; Stiglitz and Weiss, 1981).

Recent evidence also shows that high growth ventures (Vanacker and Manigart, 2010) and venture capital backed startups (Robb and Robinson, 2014) rely heavily on debt financing. Vanacker, Seghers and Manigart (2012), for instance, using a sample of Belgian venture capital backed firms, show that after the initial venture capital investment, the majority of financing events involve attracting operational debt (34 percent) and financial debt (31 percent). Again, the heavy reliance on debt financing by venture capital backed firms is surprising in view of modern finance theory and prior empirical research that suggests that debt financing is unavailable, undesirable and/or expensive for young and innovative ventures with high growth ambitions (Carpenter and Petersen, 2002b). New equity issues represent only 22 percent of the total number of finance events in venture capital backed firms, although the amount of equity financing raised tends to be larger than the amount of debt financing raised. Nevertheless, Vanacker et al. (2012) show that the combined amount of operational and financial debt raised in the five years after the initial venture capital investment represents some 60 percent of the amount of equity finance that is raised over the same period. Hence, the vast majority of studies focusing exclusively on follow-on equity finance in venture capital backed firms (e.g., Gompers, 1995) seem to miss a significant part of the financial decisions taken within venture capital backed firms. Overall, we need a better theoretical and empirical understanding of the role of distinct sources of outside debt financing in entrepreneurial ventures.

We lack longitudinal evidence on the dynamics of a broad set of financing policies in early stage entrepreneurial firms: Hanssens, Deloof and Vanacker (2014) indicate that initial differences in leverage, debt maturity and debt specialization are largely persistent for up to 15 years after startup. For instance, very low (high) leveraged startups remain very low (high) leveraged for up to 15 years after startup. Such findings are difficult to reconcile with modern theories on the evolution of entrepreneurial financing, which suggest substantial changes will occur in a firm's financial policies over time (Berger and Udell, 1998). Moreover, recent research suggests that early financing decisions may also influence the extent to which subsequent financing decisions become more amenable to intentional management or become more path-dependent. Vanacker, Manigart and Meuleman (2014), for instance, show that ventures that raise early financing from experienced venture capital investors can subsequently raise financing from a broader set of investors and have more options to choose between investors, while ventures that raise early financing from inexperienced venture capital investors are typically forced to raise financing from other inexperienced investors or can only raise additional financing from the existing inexperienced investors. In sum, we need additional work that provides a deeper understanding of the factors that drive the dynamics in financial decision-making in entrepreneurial ventures.

The entrepreneurial finance literature is largely segmented by the source of financing, while we lack research that incorporates and compares multiple sources of financing: we have a relatively good understanding of different sources of financing in isolation, including venture capital (e.g., Cumming, 2006; Dimov and Shepherd, 2005; Vanacker and Manigart, 2013), angel financing (e.g., Collewaert, 2012; Mason and Harrison, 1996) and financial bootstrapping (e.g., Vanacker et al., 2011; Winborg and Landström, 2001). Recently scholars have embarked on understanding crowdfunding better as a relatively new phenomenon in the financing of entrepreneurial ventures (e.g., Mollick, 2014) and suggested that bank debt plays a more central role in the financing of entrepreneurial ventures, relative to what is commonly appreciated (e.g., Robb and Robinson, 2014). Unfortunately, to date, we have a comparatively limited understanding of how different sources of financing interact with one another, how entrepreneurs choose between different sources of financing (beyond the simple distinction between equity and debt financing) and the unique consequences of different sources of financing.

In a recent study, Cosh, Cumming and Hughes (2009) studied a broad set of financing sources available to entrepreneurs. Contrary to the view that entrepreneurial ventures are financially constrained, they found that entrepreneurs seeking financing are typically able to secure the requisite financing, although it may not be available in the form that they would like. Overall, we need more studies capturing different sources of financing because (smart) entrepreneurs are unlikely to make decisions with respect to one particular financing source in a vacuum without considering other financing sources.

In addition, recent research is just beginning to explore the differential performance consequences of distinct sources of entrepreneurial financing. For instance, while we know that both venture capital investors and angel investors *select* promising firms and *influence* the development of their portfolio firms, very little research has compared the differential impact of venture capital and angel investors on firm-level performance. Vanacker, Collewaert and Paeleman (2013) show, among other things, that venture capital and angel investors differently impact the performance consequences of a given set of resources in entrepreneurial ventures. Dutta and Folta (2014) recently focused on the differential impact of venture capital and angel investors for venture innovation and value creation. Understanding the differential real effects of distinct sources of entrepreneurial financing can advance the entrepreneurial finance field. However, such studies will require natural experiments (e.g., policy changes or the recent financial crisis) or more advanced econometric techniques to provide causal evidence because of the inherently endogenous nature of financial decision-making (Vanacker and Deloof, 2014).

Conclusions

In this chapter, we identify three wide-ranging gaps in the entrepreneurial finance literature and present recent empirical evidence that is counterintuitive and difficult to reconcile with modern theoretical paradigms, such as the financial growth cycle.

JÜRGEN HANSSENS, MARC DELOOF AND TOM VANACKER

References

Berger, A. and Udell, G. (1998), The economics of small business finance: the roles of private equity and debt markets in the financial growth cycle, *Journal of Banking and Finance*, **22**(6), 613–673.

Carpenter, R.E. and Petersen, B.C. (2002a), Is the growth of small firms constrained by internal finance?, *Review of Economics and Statistics*, **84**(2), 298–309.

Carpenter, R.E. and Petersen, B.C. (2002b), Capital market imperfections, high-tech investment, and new equity financing, *The Economic Journal*, **112**(477), F54–F72.

Cassar, G. (2004), The financing of business start-ups, *Journal of Business Venturing*, **19**(2), 261–283.

Collewaert, V. (2012), Angel investors' and entrepreneurs' intentions to exit their ventures: a conflict perspective, *Entrepreneurship Theory and Practice*, **36**(4), 753–779.

Cosh, A., Cumming, D. and Hughes, A. (2009), Outside entrepreneurial capital, *The Economic Journal*, **119**(540), 1494–1533.

Cumming, D. (2006), Adverse selection and capital structure: evidence from venture capital, *Entrepreneurship Theory and Practice*, **30**(2), 155–183.

Dimov, D.P. and Shepherd, D.A. (2005), Human capital theory and venture capital firms: exploring 'home runs' and 'strike outs,' *Journal of Business Venturing*, **20**(1), 1–21.

Dutta, S. and Folta, T.B. (2014), *A Comparison of the Effect of Angels and Venture Capitalists on Innovation and Value Creation*, working paper, Purdue University.

Gompers, P.A. (1995), Optimal investment, monitoring, and the staging of venture capital, *Journal of Finance*, **50**(5), 1461–1489.

Hanssens, J., Deloof, M. and Vanacker, T. (2014), *Dynamics of Debt Policies: Evidence from New Firms*, working paper, Ghent University.

Holtz-Eakin, D., Joulfaian, D. and Rosen, H.S. (1994), Sticking it out: entrepreneurial survival and liquidity constraints, *Journal of Political Economy*, **102**(1), 53–75.

Mason, C.M. and Harrison, R.T. (1996), Informal venture capital: a study of the investment process, the post-investment experience and investment performance, *Entrepreneurship and Regional Development*, **8**(2), 105–126.

Mollick, E. (2014), The dynamics of crowdfunding: an exploratory study, *Journal of Business Venturing*, **29**(1), 1–16.

Robb, A.M. and Robinson, D.T. (2014), The capital structure decisions of new firms, *Review of Financial Studies*, **27**(1), 153–179.

Sapienza, H.J., Korsgaard, M.A. and Forbes, D.P. (2003), The self-determination motive and entrepreneurs' choice of financing, in J.A. Katz and D.A. Shepherd (eds), *Cognitive Approaches to Entrepreneurship Research. Advances in Entrepreneurship, Firm Emergence, and Growth*, Oxford: Elsevier/JAI Press, pp. 107–140.

Stiglitz, J.E. and Weiss, A. (1981), Credit rationing in markets with imperfect information, *American Economic Review*, **71**(3), 393–410.

Vanacker, T. and Deloof, M. (2014), *The Financial and Real Effects of Credit Availability for Startup Firms: Evidence from the Recent Financial Crisis*, working paper, Ghent University.

Vanacker, T. and Manigart, S. (2010), Pecking order and debt capacity considerations for high-growth companies seeking financing, *Small Business Economics*, **35**(1), 53–69.

Vanacker, T. and Manigart, S. (2013), Venture capital, in K. Baker and G. Filbeck (eds), *Alternative Investments: Instruments, Performance, Benchmarks, and Strategies*, Hoboken, NJ: John Wiley & Sons, Inc, pp. 241–262.

Vanacker, T., Manigart, S., Meuleman, M. and Sels, L. (2011), A longitudinal study on the relationship between financial bootstrapping and new venture growth, *Entrepreneurship and Regional Development*, **23**(9–10), 681–705.

Vanacker, T., Seghers, A. and Manigart, S. (2012), Follow-on financing of venture capital backed companies, in D. Cumming (ed.), *The Oxford Handbook of Venture Capital*, Oxford: Oxford University Press, pp. 373–400.

Vanacker, T., Collewaert, V. and Paeleman, I. (2013), The relationship between slack resources and the performance of entrepreneurial firms: the role of venture capital and angel investors, *Journal of Management Studies*, **50**(6), 1070–1096.

Vanacker, T., Manigart, S. and Meuleman, M. (2014), Path-dependent evolution versus intentional management of investment ties in science-based entrepreneurial firms, *Entrepreneurship Theory and Practice*, **38**(3), 671–690.

Winborg, J. and Landström, H. (2001), Financial bootstrapping in small businesses: examining small business managers' resource acquisition behaviors, *Journal of Business Venturing*, **16**(3), 235–254.

41 University-derived Entrepreneurship

University-derived entrepreneurship (also known as 'academic entrepreneurship') has a long, little-appreciated history. For example, while a professor at the University of Padua, Galileo built telescopes that he presented to various European notables in his quest for patronage; in effect, building a small university knowledge-based enterprise (Biagioli, 2007). In 1907, Frederick Cottrell, a University of California, Berkeley chemistry professor, while undertaking research in his laboratory invented, patented and commercialized an electrostatic precipitator (Mowery et al., 2004). The practice of university personnel forming firms to commercialize research inventions persists. The roster of technology-based firms that have at least one founder who was affiliated with a university while funding a firm – or immediately prior to doing so – is impressive. For example, listing only the most prominent, graduate or undergraduate students were founders of Dell, Facebook, Google, Microsoft, Netscape, Sun Microsystems and Yahoo! Faculty members or professional researchers established Biogen, Broadcom, Chiron, Cisco, Digital Equipment Corporation, Genentech and Silicon Graphics. It is no exaggeration to say that the biotechnology industry was substantially formed by direct university spinoffs.

Scholarly research on academic entrepreneurship is relatively recent. It was sparked in the early 1980s by two different but not entirely separate phenomena. The first phenomenon was the recognition that local universities played an important role in the development of the high-technology regions of Silicon Valley and Route 128 (Cooper and Bruno, 1977; Etzkowitz, 2003). The second phenomenon was the commercialization of university biological research with the formation of the biotechnology industry beginning in the mid-1970s (Kenney, 1986). These two phenomena highlighted the significance of university-developed technology for economic growth and interest in understanding university entrepreneurship expanded immensely (e.g., Grimaldi et al., 2011; Rothaermel et al., 2007; Shane, 2004).

Since the mid-1990s, there has been increased interest in university entrepreneurship in Europe and Asia (Wright et al., 2007; Wong, 2011). It is difficult to make any blanket statements about the academic entrepreneurship in such a diverse set of political economies. What is certain is that governments in all nations have implemented policies to create incentives for entrepreneurship. Specific European universities such as the University of Cambridge in the United Kingdom have had significant histories of academic entrepreneurship. In East Asia the record is more mixed, but some universities, such as Tsinghua University in China, have experienced success.

There are vexing methodological issues in studies of university entrepreneurship. The first issue concerns the definition of what should be considered a university spinoff. This problem has a number of dimensions, the first of which concerns what types of firms should be included. If the definition is meant to include only research-based startups, in the US context, almost invariably the firms analyzed by scholars are those identified by having disclosed an invention to the university technology licensing office. Limiting study to the licensed startups eliminates research-based start-ups that are established outside official channels, leading to a significant underestimate of the number of spinoffs and biased results that cannot be generalized to the entire population of university faculty spinoffs (Aldridge and Audretsch, 2011; Fini et al., 2010). Many of these spinoffs are sole proprietorships through which professors consult and do other compensated activities. In a few cases, such as SAS and Quintiles, these activities can become significant firms. However, it is likely that most of these firms are, for lack of a better term, 'lifestyle' spinoffs. The definition of university entrepreneurship is further complicated when one considers the firms that are established by undergraduates – including Dell, Facebook and Microsoft – and graduate students – including Yahoo!, Google and Sun Microsystems.

Research universities are producers and disseminators of knowledge, and this knowledge is transmitted to the economy through multiple channels. The most common channel is through the university's role as educator. Universities also produce knowledge that is transmitted through publications in professional and academic journals, hosting conferences and professional consulting. Specific inventions that result from university research may be transmitted through two channels under the purview of the university's technology transfer office: patents and university spinoffs.

University spinoffs are typically founded in the city in which the university is located. This is due to both faculty founders wanting to retain their position with the university and the value in keeping the new firm close to the source of its technology. There is a large literature on the role of proximity in the transmission of tacit information in a university setting (Audretsch and Stephan, 1996; Zucker et al., 1998). The role of Stanford University spinoff firms in seeding Silicon Valley and the importance of the University of California, San Diego in building the San Diego biotech cluster are well-known, but the establishment of biotech firms in Madison, Wisconsin that spun off from the University of Wisconsin or information technology firms and Waterloo University in Canada provide other less well-known examples of universities being vital for the development of entrepreneurial clusters (Kenney et al., 2009; Wolfe, 2009).

The determinants of university entrepreneurship as manifested by university spinoffs have been the subject of much study (for a review, see Lockett et al., 2005). The foci of these studies have been directed at a variety of aspects of university spinoffs, some of which are unique to university spinoffs, such as the importance of a university's competence in certain academic disciplines including engineering and the life sciences

(O'Shea et al., 2005), the role of departmental cultures (Bercovitz and Feldman, 2008), the attributes of the university (Di Gregorio and Shane, 2003; Kenney and Goe, 2004), and the overall quality of the university (Wright et al., 2008). Other studies focus on issues common to all startups, such as the role of the functional position of the founder of the new firm (e.g., student, faculty, research staff) or the success of different spinoff business models (Stankiewicz, 1994). Finally, there is an extensive literature on the role of the technology licensing office (Siegel et al., 2003) in establishing and promoting successful university spinoffs.

During the past decade, the interest by both policymakers and scholars in academic entrepreneurship has flourished. This interest has been accompanied by the use of larger databases that have been collected by national governments and university licensing associations. This research is leading to improved understanding of the academic entrepreneurship process.

MARTIN KENNEY

References

Aldridge, T.T. and Audretsch, D. (2011), The Bayh-Dole act and scientist entrepreneurship, *Research Policy*, **40**(8), 1058–1067.

Audretsch, D. and Stephan, P. (1996), Company-scientist locational links: the case of bio-technology, *American Economic Review*, **86**(3), 641–652.

Bercovitz, J. and Feldman, M. (2008), Academic entrepreneurs: organizational change at the individual level, *Organization Science*, **19**(1), 69–89.

Biagioli, M. (2007), *Galileo's Instruments of Credit: Telescopes, Images, Secrecy*, Chicago: University of Chicago Press.

Cooper, A.C. and Bruno, A.V. (1977), Success among high-technology firms, *Business Horizons*, **20**, 16–22.

Di Gregorio, D. and Shane, S. (2003), Why do some universities generate more start-ups than others?, *Research Policy*, **32**(2), 209–227.

Etzkowitz, H. (2003), *MIT and the Rise of Entrepreneurial Science*, London: Routledge.

Fini, R., Lacetera, N. and Shane, S. (2010), Inside or outside the IP system? Business creation in academia, *Research Policy*, **39**(8), 1060–1069.

Grimaldi, R., Kenney, M., Siegel, D.S. and Wright, M. (2011), 30 years after Bayh–Dole: reassessing academic entrepreneurship, *Research Policy*, **40**(8), 1045–1057.

Kenney, M. (1986), *Bio-technology: The University–Industrial Complex*, New Haven: Yale University Press.

Kenney, M. and Goe, R.W. (2004), The role of social embeddedness in professorial entrepreneurship: a comparison of electrical engineering and computer science at UC Berkeley and Stanford, *Research Policy*, **33**(5), 691–707.

Kenney, M., Nelson, A. and Patton, D. (2009), The university-centric high-tech cluster of Madison, United States, in J. Potter and G. Miranda (eds), *Clusters, Innovation and Entrepreneurship*, Paris: OECD Publications, pp. 167–192.

Lockett, A., Siegel, D., Wright, M. and Ensley, M.D. (2005), The creation of spin-off firms at public research institutions: managerial and policy implications, *Research Policy*, **34**(7), 981–993.

Mowery, D.C., Nelson, R.R., Sampat, B.N. and Ziedonis, A.A. (2004), *Ivory Tower and Industrial Innovation University-Industry Technology Transfer Before and After the Bayh-Dole Act*, Stanford: Stanford University Press.

O'Shea, R.P., Allen, T.J., Chevalier, A. and Roche, F. (2005), Entrepreneurial orientation, technology transfer and spinoff performance of US universities, *Research Policy*, **34**(7), 994–1009.

Rothaermel, F.T., Agung, S. and Jiang, L. (2007), University entrepreneurship: a taxonomy of the literature, *Industrial and Corporate Change*, **16**(4), 691–791.

Shane, S.A. (2004), *Academic Entrepreneurship: University Spinoffs and Wealth Creation*, Cheltenham: Edward Elgar Publishing.

Siegel, D.S., Waldman, D. and Link, A. (2003), Assessing the impact of organizational practices on the relative productivity of university technology transfer offices: an exploratory study, *Research Policy*, **32**(1), 27–48.

Stankiewicz, R. (1994), University firms: spin-off companies from universities, *Science and Public Policy*, **21**(2), 99–107.

Wolfe, D.A. (2009), The Waterloo ICT cluster, in J. Potter and G. Miranda (eds), *Clusters, Innovation and Entrepreneurship*, Paris: OECD Publishing, pp.193–216.

Wong, P.K. (ed.) (2011), *Academic Entrepreneurship in Asia: The Role and Impact of Universities in National Innovation Systems*, Cheltenham: Edward Elgar Publishing.

Wright, M., Clarysse, B., Mustar, P. and Lockett, A. (2007), *Academic Entrepreneurship in Europe*, Cheltenham: Edward Elgar Publishing.

Wright, M., Clarysse, B., Lockett, A. and Knockert, M. (2008), Mid-range universities in Europe linkages with industry: knowledge types and the role of intermediaries, *Research Policy*, **37**(8), 1205–1223.

Zucker, L., Darby, M. and Brewer, M. (1998), Intellectual human capital and the birth of US biotechnology enterprises, *American Economic Review*, **88**(1), 290–306.

42 University–Industry Relations

Introduction

'University–industry relations' is an umbrella term to describe two types of interaction between universities and firms. The first is academic engagement, which refers to collaboration between academics and 'users' of academic science, such as firms or public sector organizations. The second is commercialization, which is the exploitation of university-generated intellectual property. In this chapter, I focus primarily on academic engagement involving universities and firms but I also address how academic engagement is related to commercialization.

The scope of relations

Academic engagement comprises a whole spectrum of collaborative links between universities and firms, including sponsored research, contract research, consulting, personnel exchange and informal interaction (Cohen et al., 2002; Link et al., 2007; Perkmann and Walsh, 2008; Perkmann et al., 2013). Academic engagement has a long tradition, particularly at universities that emphasize practical and technical relevance as part of their mission (Mowery and Nelson, 2004; Mowery, 2009). Dense network relationships between university laboratories and chemical firms enabled the rise of the German synthetic dye industry (Murmann, 2003) and the creation of firms in the Bay area (Lenoir, 1997; Kenney, 1986), and, as early as the 1930s, universities developed policies for faculty consulting and licensing patents to industry (Etzkowitz, 2002).

High profile initiatives such as the Energy Biosciences Institute involving the University of California at Berkeley and BP, the global network of Rolls-Royce Research and University Technology Centres, and the Structural Genomics Consortium exemplify the significant scale at which academic engagement can take place. From a macro perspective, only approximately 6 per cent of university research conducted across the OECD countries is funded by industry,[1] yet this figure actually underplays the extent of academic engagement. Government research grants are often used to subsidize collaborative university–industry projects, and academic consulting may not be categorized as university research income. In fact, academic engagement is commonly practised among academics, especially in the technical and scientific disciplines (Perkmann et al., 2013). In the UK, almost half of government grant-holders in the physical sciences and engineering pursued collaborative research, contract research or consulting in a two-year period (D'Este and Perkmann, 2011). In the US, just under 20 per cent of academics across all disciplines at research-intensive universities obtained an industry grant or consulting assignment within a 12-month period (Bozeman and Gaughan, 2007), while in Germany 20 per cent of academics published with industrial partners and 17 per cent served as a consultant within a 12-month period (Grimpe and Fier, 2010).

The university perspective

What are the benefits and consequences of academic engagement for universities? Most academic scientists' primary motivation for working with industry is to further their own academic research agendas while the desire to commercialize technologies is important only to a minority (D'Este and Perkmann, 2011). Engagement tends to be regarded by academics as a natural extension of publication-driven public science, as it enables them to gain insights into technical problems, obtain data and materials, and raise funding (Rosenberg, 1994; Lee, 2000; Boardman and Ponomariov, 2009; Perkmann and Walsh, 2009).

In view of fears that close interaction with industry may have undesired effects, studies have explored the impact of university–industry relations on the evolution of science, with the following results. First, working with industry does not appear to have detrimental effects on an academic's research productivity, at least until a threshold of engagement is reached (Lin and Bozeman, 2006). In fact, most studies suggest that researchers' involvement with industry is positively correlated with their research productivity (Van Looy et al., 2006; Tartari et al., 2014). Second, while industry-funded research is more applied (Gulbrandsen and Smeby, 2005; Boardman and Corley, 2008), the evidence tends to indicate that involvement with industry does not shift academics' research agendas away from basic science (Godin and Gingras, 2000; Van Looy et al., 2004). These results reinforce the proposition that academic engagement is largely pursued as an activity complementary to academic research.

The firm perspective

Among the total population of firms only a minority work with universities. For instance, according to the UK Community Innovation Survey, only 2 per cent of firms report that universities represent a highly important source of innovation (Laursen and Salter, 2004). Among the US manufacturing firms sampled by the Carnegie Mellon Survey on industrial R&D, less than a third of firms reported using public science research findings and approximately 20 per cent practised contract research with public science institutions (Cohen et al., 2002). However, for R&D-intensive firms in specific sectors, such as pharmaceuticals and chemicals, interaction with universities plays an important role in their innovation efforts (Meyer-Krahmer and Schmoch, 1998; Cohen et al., 2002). Most firms consider academic engagement as relatively more valuable than mere access to university-generated intellectual property (Cohen et al., 2002; Agrawal and Henderson, 2002). This is reflected in the fact that, on an economy-wide level, universities' revenue from academic engagement exceeds income from intellectual property by an order of magnitude (Perkmann et al., 2011a).

Firms work with universities for several reasons (Perkmann et al., 2011b). First, doing so enables science-based firms to build and enhance their capabilities at the frontier of scientific developments and emerging technologies (Powell et al., 1996; Feller, 2005; Bercovitz and Feldman, 2007). In basic science focused collaborations, the generation of commercializable intellectual property is relatively less important than access to new knowledge even if the latter is publicly disclosed and becomes part of the industry commons (Perkmann and Schildt, 2015). Moreover, due to the availability of government and charitable grants, the cost of participating in such initiatives is usually only a fraction of comparable activities pursued in-house.

Second, some firms seek to access universities' problem-solving capabilities for their ongoing R&D programmes. Academics are engaged to run tests, contribute to technology development and provide feedback on intermediate outputs (Mansfield, 1995). Many firms see universities' role in 'contributing to project completion' as more important than 'suggesting new projects' (Cohen et al., 2002), implying that the role of universities is not limited to providing firms with access to frontier science.

Finally, there are also more generic benefits to collaborating with academics. These include access to a pool of highly skilled potential future employees. Moreover, working with universities can increase a firm's reputation within the open, barter-governed networks in academia, helping it access wider scientific and technical expertise (Hicks, 1995; Murray, 2002).

Academic engagement and firm performance

Collaborating with universities tends to be positively correlated with firms' performance. Jaffe's (1989) study showed that the innovativeness of firms in the areas of drugs and medical technology, electronics and optics is higher if universities are located nearby, suggesting there are spillover effects from academic research. Other studies investigated whether actual formal and information collaboration with universities has an impact on firms. A study of biotechnology firms, for instance, indicates that those with university connections (including licensing) were more innovative than those without (George et al., 2002). Similarly, collaboration with high-performing scientists, tracked via co-authorship of scientific papers, increases the value of patents generated by biotechnology companies (Zucker et al., 2002).

Studies using the European Community Innovation Survey data and similar data from other countries find a positive relationship between the extent of firms' collaboration with universities and their innovativeness or commercial performance (Belderbos et al., 2004; Faems et al., 2005; Rothaermel and Thursby, 2005; Eom and Lee, 2010). The same set of studies demonstrates that firms working with universities tend to launch more radical innovations than their non-collaborating counterparts (Belderbos et al., 2004). While they collaborate less frequently with universities, evidence also suggests that small firms benefit disproportionately from working with universities (Link and Rees, 1990).

A question related to the performance effects of university relations is whether there are synergies between academic engagement and commercialization. Agrawal's study (2006) suggests that 'engaging the inventor' increases the likelihood and degree of commercialization success. University of California data indicate that corporate-sponsored inventions are licensed more often, with many licences being granted to firms other than the original sponsor firm (Wright et al., 2014). However, to date we lack broader evidence on how academic engagement and commercialization are related. Future research should address whether and how academic engagement – for instance, via industry-sponsored research – enables academics to generate more valuable inventions. Related to this is the question of which intellectual property regimes are most suitable for exploiting university knowledge (Kenney and Patton, 2009). New models of collaboration in the wake of the Human Genome Project, using 'weak' intellectual property systems and loose large-scale coordination, in particular, may not only offer pathways for enhancing the overall societal impact of public science but also enable firms to advantageously shape the evolution of the knowledge commons in their sectors (Rhoten and Powell, 2008; Rai et al., 2008; Perkmann and Salter, 2012).

Conclusions

Academic engagement – collaborative interactions between academics and non-academic entities – is widely practised at universities and is more extensive than suggested by the measure of financial contributions from industry to university research alone. For many academic scientists, the motive underpinning their collaboration with industry is to advance their academic research agendas, suggesting a high degree of complementarity between industry-oriented projects and academic science. For firms, particularly in science-based sectors, collaborating with academics offers the opportunity to participate in the evolution of frontier science, but often also provides access to problem-solving capabilities for ongoing R&D programmes. Open questions in this area of research, however, pertain to how academic engagement is related to the creation and exploitation of university-generated intellectual property, and the relative importance of 'weak' and 'strong' intellectual property regimes as a means for firms to appropriate university-generated knowledge.

MARKUS PERKMANN

Note

1. OECD Main Science and Technology Indicators.

References

Agrawal, A. (2006), Engaging the inventor: exploring licensing strategies for university inventions and the role of latent knowledge, *Strategic Management Journal*, 27(1), 63–79.
Agrawal, A. and Henderson, R.M. (2002), Putting patents in context: exploring knowledge transfer from MIT, *Management Science*, 48(1), 44–60.
Belderbos, R., Carree, M. and Lokshin, B. (2004), Cooperative R&D and firm performance, *Research Policy*, 33(10), 1477–1492.
Bercovitz, J.E.L. and Feldman, M.P. (2007), Fishing upstream: firm innovation strategy and university research alliances, *Research Policy*, 36(7), 930–948.
Boardman, P.C. and Corley, E.A. (2008), University research centers and the composition of research collaborations, *Research Policy*, 37(5), 900–913.
Boardman, P.C. and Ponomariov, B.L. (2009), University researchers working with private companies, *Technovation*, 29(2), 142–153.
Bozeman, B. and Gaughan, M. (2007), Impacts of grants and contracts on academic researchers' interactions with industry, *Research Policy*, 36(5), 694–707.

Cohen, W.M., Nelson, R.R. and Walsh, J.P. (2002), Links and impacts: the influence of public research on industrial R&D, *Management Science*, **48**(1), 1–23.

D'Este, P. and Perkmann, M. (2011), Why do academics engage with industry? The entrepreneurial university and individual motivations, *The Journal of Technology Transfer*, **36**(3), 316–339.

Eom, B.-Y. and Lee, K. (2010), Determinants of industry–academy linkages and, their impact on firm performance: the case of Korea as a latecomer in knowledge industrialization, *Research Policy*, **39**(5), 625–639.

Etzkowitz, H. (2002), *MIT and the Rise of Entrepreneurial Science*, New York: Routledge.

Faems, D., Van Looy, B. and Debackere, K. (2005), Interorganizational collaboration and innovation: toward a portfolio approach, *Journal of Product Innovation Management*, **22**(3), 238–250.

Feller, I. (2005), A historical perspective on government-university partnerships to enhance entrepreneurship and economic development, in S. Shane (ed.), *Economic Development through Entrepreneurship: Government, University and Business Linkages*, Cheltenham: Edward Elgar Publishing, pp. 6–28.

George, G., Zahra, S.A. and Wood, D.R. (2002), The effects of business–university alliances on innovative output and financial performance: a study of publicly-traded biotechnology companies, *Journal of Business Venturing*, **17**(6), 577–609.

Godin, B. and Gingras, Y. (2000), Impact of collaborative research on academic science, *Science and Public Policy*, **27**, 65–73.

Grimpe, C. and Fier, H. (2010), Informal university technology transfer: a comparison between the United States and Germany, *The Journal of Technology Transfer*, **35**(6), 637–650.

Gulbrandsen, M. and Smeby, J.C. (2005), Industry funding and university professors' research performance, *Research Policy*, **34**(6), 932–950.

Hicks, D. (1995), Published papers, tacit competencies and corporate management of the public/private character of knowledge, *Industrial and Corporate Change*, **4**(2), 401–424.

Jaffe, A.B. (1989), Real effects of academic research, *The American Economic Review*, **79**(5), 957–970.

Kenney, M. (1986), *Biotechnology: The University–Industrial Complex*, New Haven: Yale University Press.

Kenney, M. and Patton, D. (2009), Reconsidering the Bayh-Dole Act and the current university invention ownership model, *Research Policy*, **38**(9), 1407–1422.

Laursen, K. and Salter, A. (2004), Searching high and low: what types of firms use universities as a source of innovation?, *Research Policy*, **33**(8), 1201–1215.

Lee, Y.S. (2000), The sustainability of university-industry research collaboration: an empirical assessment, *The Journal of Technology Transfer*, **25**(2), 111–133.

Lenoir, T. (1997), *Instituting Science: The Cultural Production of Scientific Disciplines*, Stanford, CA: Stanford University Press.

Lin, M.-W. and Bozeman, B. (2006), Researchers' industry experience and productivity in university–industry research centers: a 'scientific and technical human capital' explanation, *The Journal of Technology Transfer*, **31**(2), 269–290.

Link, A.N. and Rees, J. (1990), Firm size, university based research, and the returns to R&D, *Small Business Economics*, **2**(1), 25–31.

Link, A.N., Siegel, D.S. and Bozeman, B. (2007), An empirical analysis of the propensity of academics to engage in informal university technology transfer, *Industrial and Corporate Change*, **16**(4), 641–655.

Mansfield, E. (1995), Academic research underlying industrial innovations: sources, characteristics, and financing, *Review of Economics and Statistics*, **77**(1), 55–65.

Meyer-Krahmer, F. and Schmoch, U. (1998), Science-based technologies: university-industry interactions in four fields, *Research Policy*, **27**(8), 835–851.

Mowery, D.C. (2009), Plus ca change: industrial R&D in the 'third industrial revolution', *Industrial and Corporate Change*, **18**(1), 1–50.

Mowery, D.C. and Nelson, R.R. (eds) (2004), *Ivory Tower and Industrial Innovation:*

University–Industry Technology Before and After the Bayh-Dole Act, Stanford, CA: Stanford University Press.

Murmann, J.P. (2003), *Knowledge and Competitive Advantage: The Coevolution of Firms, Technology, and National Institutions*, Cambridge: Cambridge University Press.

Murray, F. (2002), Innovation as co-evolution of scientific and technological networks: exploring tissue engineering, *Research Policy*, **31**(8–9), 1389–1403.

Perkmann, M. and Salter, A. (2012), How to create productive partnerships with universities, *MIT Sloan Management Review*, **53**, 79–88.

Perkmann, M. and Schildt, H. (2015), *Open Data Partnerships Between Firms and Universities: The Role of Boundary Organizations*, Research Policy, **44**(5), 1133–1143.

Perkmann, M. and Walsh, K. (2008), Engaging the scholar: three forms of academic consulting and their impact on universities and industry, *Research Policy*, **37**(10), 1884–1891.

Perkmann, M. and Walsh, K. (2009), The two faces of collaboration: impacts of university-industry relations on public research, *Industrial and Corporate Change*, **18**(6), 1033–1065.

Perkmann, M., King, Z. and Pavelin, S. (2011a), Engaging excellence? Effects of faculty quality on university engagement with industry, *Research Policy*, **40**(4), 539–552.

Perkmann, M., Neely, A. and Walsh, K. (2011b), How should firms evaluate success in university-industry alliances? A performance measurement system, *R&D Management*, **41**(2), 202–216.

Perkmann, M., Tartari, V., McKelvey, M., Autio, E., Broström, A., D'Este, P., Fini, R., Geuna, A., Grimaldi, R., Hughes, A., Kitson, M., Krabel, S., Llerena, P., Lissoni, F., Salter, A. and Sobrero, M. (2013), Academic engagement and commercialization: a review of the literature on university–industry relations, *Research Policy*, **42**(2), 423–442.

Powell, W.W., Koput, K.W. and Smith-Doerr, L. (1996), Interorganizational collaboration and the locus of innovation: networks of learning in biotechnology, *Administrative Science Quarterly*, **41**(1), 116–145.

Rai, A.K., Reichman, J.H., Uhlir, P.F. and Crossman, C.R. (2008), Pathways across the valley of death: novel intellectual property strategies for accelerated drug discovery, *Yale Journal of Health Policy, Law, and Ethics*, **8**(1).

Rhoten, D. and Powell, W.W. (2008), The frontiers of intellectual property: expanded protection versus new models of open science, *Annual Review of Law and Social Science*, **3**, 345–373.

Rosenberg, N. (1994), *Exploring the Black Box: Technology, Economics, and History*, Cambridge: Cambridge University Press.

Rothaermel, F.T. and Thursby, M. (2005), University–incubator firm knowledge flows: assessing their impact on incubator firm performance, *Research Policy*, **34**(3), 305–320.

Tartari, V., Perkmann, M. and Salter, A. (2014), In good company: the influence of peers on industry engagement by academic scientists, *Research Policy*, **43**(7), 1189–1203.

Van Looy, B., Callaert, J. and Debackere, K. (2006), Publication and patent behavior of academic researchers: conflicting, reinforcing or merely co-existing? *Research Policy*, **35**(4), 596–608.

Van Looy, B., Ranga, M., Callaert, J., Debackere, K. and Zimmermann, E. (2004), Combining entrepreneurial and scientific performance in academia: towards a compounded and reciprocal Matthew-effect?, *Research Policy*, **33**(3), 425–441.

Wright, B.D., Drivas, K., Lei, Z. and Merrill, S.A. (2014), Technology transfer: industry-funded academic inventions boost innovation, *Nature*, **507**(7492), 297–299.

Zucker, L.G., Darby, M.R. and Armstrong, J.S. (2002), Commercializing knowledge: university science, knowledge capture, and firm performance in biotechnology, *Management Science*, **48**(1), 138–153.

43 University Research Parks

Introduction
University research parks (URPs) are a post-World War II phenomenon (Link and Scott, 2007). Studies in both the United States and in a
number of European countries show that the formation of URPs peaked
in the 1980s and early 1990s. This was perhaps due to a country-specific
saturation of parks at the major research universities and/or due to the
immediate growth in research and development (R&D) investments in the
aftermath of numerous technology and innovation policies promulgated
in the late 1970s and early 1980s to reverse the worldwide slowdown in
productivity growth.

Regardless of the primary motivation for the growth in URPs or the
decline (in absolute terms), what might be most relevant to the broader
study of entrepreneurship are the research questions that have been asked
within the academic literature and the answers that are currently known.
And, as Link and Link (2009) have argued, the study of URPs has academic and policy importance because it represents an example of government as entrepreneur.[1]

Research on university research parks
What are the factors that affect a firm's decisions to locate on a URP?

- Much of the empirical evidence seems to support the view that firms
  locate a park based on the potential spillover benefits (i.e., knowledge spillover benefits) that will exist among the other tenants of the
  park (Leyden et al., 2008).
- The key criterion for location on a park, from the perspective of a
  firm, is the linkage between itself and the university or, if generalizable, to other countries, the higher education institution (Goldstein
  and Luger, 1992).
- Firms locate on a park because of a need for social capital to
  facilitate entrepreneurial growth (Hansson et al., 2005).

How do firms perform once located on a URP?

- The research productivity (broadly defined) of on-park firms is
  greater than of off-park firms (Link and Scott, 2003; Siegel et al.,
  2003; Squicciarini, 2008).
- The average rate of growth of employment in a firm on a URP is
  greater the geographically closer the park is to the host university
  (Link and Scott, 2006).

- The survival rate of on-park firms is greater than of off-park firms (Westhead and Cowling, 1995).

Do URPs contribute to regional economic growth and development?

- Policies that include the formation of science parks are crucial for regional economic development (Huang et al., 2013).
- The most important for economic growth and development is the economic and cultural context in which park success is defined (Sofouli and Vonortas, 2007).
- URPs contribute to regional growth and development by leveraging new business startups (Goldstein and Luger, 1992).

Conclusions

While the questions about URPs addressed in the literature, as mentioned above, are the appropriate questions to have asked, from both an academic and policy perspective, the answers to date have been limited by the availability of data. This is especially true in the United States and in some developing nations. However, from our perspective, it is questionable that the public sector will support the development of such data bases in the absence of focused policy initiatives related to URPs. Such initiatives will be unlikely in nations that have shifted their policy focus from university infrastructures to other mechanisms to support regional economic growth and development. Traversing the policy landscape suggests to us that these other mechanisms might include public (at the federal and local level) support of the development of technology-focused clusters as well as innovation districts located in urban areas. While policymakers have discussed both of these mechanisms in detail, empirically based conclusions about their effectiveness is yet to come.

ALBERT N. LINK

Note

1. Link and Link (2009: 125) argue that the government's indirect support of URPs is based on the argument that parks serve as an environment conducive for industry/university research collaborations and academic entrepreneurship. 'Thus, the environment created by the park is a technology infrastructure that facilitates leveraging both public (i.e., the university or the public-sector tenants in the park) and private R&D.'

References

Goldstein, H.A. and Luger, M.I. (1992), University-based research parks as a rural development strategy, *Policy Studies Journal*, **20**(2), 249–263.

Hansson, F., Husted, K. and Vestergaard, J. (2005), Second generation science parks: from structural holes jockeys to social capital catalysts of the knowledge society, *Technovation*, **25**(9), 1039–1049.

Huang, Y., Audretsch, D.B. and Hewitt, M. (2013), Chinese technology transfer policy: the case of the national independent innovation demonstration zone of East Lake, *Journal of Technology Transfer*, **38**(6), 828–835.

Leyden, D.P., Link, A.N. and Siegel, D.S. (2008), A theoretical and empirical analysis of the decision to locate on a university research park, *IEEE Transactions on Engineering Management*, **55**, 23–28.

Link, A.N. and Link, J.R. (2009), *Government as Entrepreneur*, New York: Oxford University Press.

Link, A.N. and Scott, J.T. (2003), US science parks: the diffusion of an innovation and its effects on the academic mission of universities, *International Journal of Industrial Organization*, **21**(9), 1323–1356.

Link, A.N. and Scott, J.T. (2006), US university research parks, *Journal of Productivity Analysis*, **25**(1), 43–55.

Link, A.N. and Scott, J.T. (2007), The economics of university research parks, *Oxford Review of Economic Policy*, **23**(4), 661–674.

Siegel, D.S., Westhead, P. and Wright, M. (2003), Assessing the impact of science parks on research productivity: exploratory firm-level evidence from the United Kingdom, *International Journal of Industrial Organization*, **21**(9), 1357–1369.

Sofouli, E. and Vonortas, N.S. (2007), S&T parks and business incubators in middle-sized countries: the case of Greece, *Journal of Technology Transfer*, **32**(5), 525–544.

Squicciarini, M. (2008), Science parks' tenants versus out-of-park firms: who innovates more? A duration model, *Journal of Technology Transfer*, **33**(1), 45–71.

Westhead, P. and Cowling, M. (1995), Employment change in independent owner-managed high-technology firms in Great Britain, *Small Business Economics*, **7**(2), 111–140.

44   University Technology Transfer Offices

Introduction

Establishing legitimacy and a clear identity within the university is fundamentally important for technology transfer offices (TTOs).[1] Once legitimate, TTOs may have greater access to resources and encounter fewer barriers when promoting commercialization activities within the university. In contrast, a failure to establish legitimacy may result in disengagement, resource withdrawal and claims that their role is redundant. Therefore, how TTOs go about legitimizing their role and shaping their identity within the university is an issue of fundamental importance. Drawing directly on a paper in *Research Policy* (O'Kane et al., 2015), this chapter focuses on how TTOs manage this particular challenge. Specifically, this chapter proposes that TTOs' identity-shaping strategies are incomplete and, in order for them to improve their legitimacy within the university, they need to shift their attention to shaping a wholly distinctive identity.

The role of TTOs

TTOs are committed to protecting intellectual property disclosures and increasing and improving commercial forms of technology transfer from academia. TTO executives broker relationships between academia and industry (Phan and Siegel, 2006; Powers and McDougall, 2005) and help academics access critical resources, expertise and support in the commercialization process (Clarysse and Moray, 2004; Colombo and Delmastro, 2002; Siegel et al., 2003). However, in their role within the university, TTOs must operate as a dual agent for both academics and management.

When two principals exist in an agency relationship in this manner, conflicting expectations can arise. For TTOs, this conflict is reflected in their efforts to balance academic and commercial forces when shaping their identity. On the one hand, TTOs need to be sensitive to the fact that their host institutions and the academic profession are traditionally committed to scientific autonomy (Nelson, 2004) and guiding norms of skepticism, universalism, communism and disinterestedness (Merton, 1973). This can cause tensions given that the commercialization activities that TTOs promote are heavily characterized by market needs and economic returns (Haeussler and Colyvas, 2011; Nelson, 1959) and can reduce the accumulation of public knowledge (Toole and Czarnitzki, 2010). On the other hand, TTOs are of increasing strategic importance to universities committed to the commercialization of academic knowledge. TTOs are aware that university management holds a number of expectations with regard to their role.

With an increasingly constrained public funding environment, management realizes that an efficient TTO may generate earnings that protect existing research activities and help pursue future research breakthroughs (Bozeman, 2000). Proficiency in technology transfer can also enhance the reputation and prestige of the university, thus helping to recruit and retain leading researchers and increase student intake (Etzkowitz and Leydesdorff, 2000; Markman et al., 2009). Furthermore, university management has an interest in ensuring that their TTOs contribute to social development as well as regional and national competitiveness through the commercialization of university research (Etzkowitz, 1983; Feller, 1990; Mowery and Ziedonis, 2002; Sörlin, 2007).

The TTO challenge

It seems apparent, therefore, that university TTOs operate in a pluralistic context, characterized by competing strategic demands and potentially divergent stakeholder goals (Denis et al., 2007; Van Gestel and Hillebrand, 2011). These shared boundaries of science and business significantly complicate TTOs' efforts to build legitimacy and shape identity. Specifically, it is unlikely that one strategy or identity will be sufficient to legitimize the TTO with both academics and management. Although it is acknowledged that organizations can hold multiple identities (Albert and

Adams, 2002; Pratt and Foreman, 2000; Vora and Kostova, 2007) and that this can enhance responsiveness and resilience to diverging stake-holder needs (Albert and Whetten, 1985; Sillince and Brown, 2009), it is also reported that multiple identities can conflict and cause uncertainty within the organization (Pratt and Rafaeli, 1997), even resulting in legiti-macy discounts from interested stakeholders (Dutton and Dukerich, 1991; Zuckerman, 1999).

Illustrating this challenge, O'Kane et al. (2015) undertook a study of 63 TTO executives across 22 universities in Ireland, New Zealand and the United States and found that TTOs shape a dual identity, one scientific and the other business, with academics and management respectively. On the one hand, TTOs prioritize the key determinants of legitimacy with *academics* as scientific credibility. Therefore, when interacting with the research community TTOs shape a *scientific identity* that promotes homogeneousness with the dominant norms and expectations of aca-demia. For example, it is explained in the study that TTOs are careful to rationalize how their commercialization focus and activities fit with the core purpose of the university, namely the creation and dissemination of knowledge.

TTOs also initiate communication and dialogue with academics in an unthreatening contract or technology-free environment in order to broaden their reach and enhance the potential for future engagement. Furthermore, TTOs' executives explain how they very deliberately publi-cize the recruitment of personnel with doctorates and other such scientific credentials in shaping this identity. On the other hand, TTOs prioritize the key determinants of legitimacy with *management* as alignment with the university strategy.

TTOs proactively sense what they believe is required or anticipated from university management and then shape a *business identity* that cap-tures their ability to meet these expectations. For example, the findings reveal that TTOs convey a rigorous strategic planning process to clearly articulate their overarching purpose, daily activities and measures of performance to university management. Added to this, TTO executives explain how their presence and the commercialization activities they advo-cate promote entrepreneurial activities (e.g., patents, licenses, contract research, etc.) that can diversify university revenue streams for research funding; enhance the reputation of the university to industry, prospective students and staff globally; and contribute to the university's capacity to stimulate regional competiveness, foster closer connectivity with industry (e.g., joint research and startups), and positively impact local communi-ties and society (e.g., health benefits). However, O'Kane et al. find that this combination of identities is proving ineffective for legitimizing the

TTO within the university. It is reported that legitimacy discounts are compounded by TTOs misdiagnosing the *actual* determinants of legitimacy among the academic community (i.e., business expertise), as well as university management providing insufficient traction for TTOs to realize their strategic potential on behalf of the university.

Drawing on the idea of 'optimal distinctiveness' (Brewer, 1991), O'Kane et al. (2015) propose that, rather than being characterized as incorrect or ineffective, the identity-shaping strategies of TTOs are merely incomplete. Theory informs us that legitimacy is as dependent on being different as it is on being the same (Deephouse, 1999). Therefore, concentrating on fitting in with the expectations of stakeholders may be insufficient to build legitimacy. Legitimate distinctiveness refers to an identity form that contains both conformance to stakeholder expectations and institutionalized norms, as well as claims of distinctiveness that deviate the organization from these same forces (Navis and Glynn, 2011).

Therefore it is suggested that in shaping a scientific and business identity, TTOs are inadequately managing the challenging dilemma of sameness and uniqueness (Navis and Glynn, 2010). Solely borrowing from the identities of academics and management hinders TTO legitimacy as it engenders a confusing identity that is partially academic and partially business. It is proposed that in order to develop their legitimacy standing and become recognized as value-adding and unique actors in the university, TTOs need to shift their attention to shaping a distinctive and individual identity. TTOs may need to consider explicitly attending to the questions of 'Who are you?', 'What is your purpose and vision?' and 'Why are you the best option?', in addition to explaining how they fit in and how they can potentially help. Even if this individualistic identity is criticized, the attention will, at a very minimum, recognize and reinforce TTO distinctiveness.

Discussion

The findings and associated propositions from O'Kane et al.'s study (2015) are timely for a number of reasons. First, in a review of the services and business models of technology transfer organizations, Landry et al. (2013) report that university TTOs typically lack a distinct or differentiated business model when compared to other organizations involved in knowledge transfer activities, thus offering support for the propositions put forward by O'Kane et al. Second, the absence of a distinct identity offers an alternative perspective on why TTOs may only have marginal direct effects in stimulating academic entrepreneurship (Muscio, 2010), and why the academic community frequently refers to skills deficiencies among TTOs (Mustar et al., 2006; Swamidass and Vulasa, 2009) and/or chooses to sidestep the services of TTOs (Aldridge and Audretsch, 2011; Bodas-Freitas et al., 2013; Link et al., 2007; Shane, 2004). Finally, O'Kane et al.'s findings provide a possible extension to TTOs' widely accepted identity as neutral intermediaries or brokering actors between universities and industry (Clarysse and Moray, 2004; Phan and Siegel, 2006; Powers and McDougall, 2005). Specifically, the findings propose that TTOs consider progressing beyond balancing the expectations of their stakeholders and concentrate on developing their own unique identity as guided by their own distinctive values, beliefs and models.

In conclusion, it is suggested that, in order to have a legitimate presence within the university, scholars and management must recognize the identity of the TTO as being distinct from their own. Shaping a scientific and a business identity begins the process by which this distinctive identity is formed and recognized.

CONOR O'KANE

Note
1. This chapter presents a summary of O'Kane et al. (2015).

References

Albert, S. and Adams, E. (2002), The hybrid identity of law firms, in G. Soenen and B. Moingeon (eds), *Corporate and Organizational Identities: Integrating Strategy, Marketing, Communication and Organizational Perspectives*, New York: Routledge, pp. 35–50.

Albert, S. and Whetten, D.A. (1985), Organizational identity, *Research in Organizational Behavior*, **17**, 263–295.

Aldridge, T.T. and Audretsch, D. (2011), The Bayh-Dole Act and scientist entrepreneurship, *Research Policy*, **40**, 1058–1067.

Bodas Freitas, I.M., Geuna, A. and Rossi, F. (2013), The governance of university-industry knowledge transfer: why small firms do (not) develop institutional collaborations?, *Research Policy*, **42**, 50–62.

Bozeman, B. (2000), Technology transfer and public policy: a review of research and theory, *Research Policy*, **29**, 627–655.

Brewer, M.B. (1991), The social self: on being the same and different at the same time, *Personality and Social Psychology Bulletin*, **17**, 475–482.

Clarysse, B. and Moray, N. (2004), A process study of entrepreneurial team formation: the case of a research-based spin-off, *Journal of Business Venturing*, **19**, 55–79.

Colombo, M.G. and Delmastro, M. (2002), How effective are technology incubators? Evidence from Italy, *Research Policy*, **31**, 1103–1122.

Deephouse, D.L. (1999), To be different, or to be the same? It's a question (and theory) of strategic balance, *Strategic Management Journal*, **20**(2), 147–166.

Denis, J.L., Langley, A. and Rouleau, L. (2007), Strategizing in pluralistic contexts: rethinking theoretical frames, *Human Relations*, **60**, 179–215.

Dutton, J.E. and Dukerich, J.M. (1991), Keeping an eye on the mirror: image and identity in organizational adaptation, *Academy of Management Journal*, **34**, 517–554.

Etzkowitz, H. (1983), Entrepreneurial scientists and entrepreneurial universities in American academic science, *Minerva*, **21**, 198–233.

Etzkowitz, H. and Leydesdorff, L. (2000), The dynamics of innovation: from National Systems and "Mode 2" to a Triple Helix of university–industry–government relations, *Research Policy*, **29**, 109–123.

Feller, I. (1990), University patent and technology-licensing strategies, *Educational Policy*, **4**, 327–340.

Haeussler, C. and Colyvas, J.A. (2011), Breaking the ivory tower: academic entrepreneurship in the life sciences in UK and Germany, *Research Policy*, **40**, 41–54.

Landry, R., Amara, N., Cloutier, J.S. and Hailem, N. (2013), Technology transfer organizations: services and business models, *Technovation*, **33**, 431–449.

Link, A.N., Siegel, D.S. and Bozeman, B. (2007), An empirical analysis of the propensity of academics to engage in informal university technology transfer, *Industrial and Corporate Change*, **16**, 641–655.

Markman, G.D., Gianiodis, P. and Phan, P. (2009), Supply-side innovation and technology commercialization, *Journal of Management Studies*, **46**, 625–649.

Merton, R.K. (1973), *The Sociology of Science. Theoretical and Empirical Investigations*, Chicago: University of Chicago Press.

Mowery, D.C. and Ziedonis, A.A. (2002), Academic patent quality and quantity before and after the Bayh-Dole act in the United States, *Research Policy*, **31**, 399–418.

Muscio, A. (2010), What drives the university use of technology transfer offices? Evidence from Italy, *The Journal of Technology Transfer*, **35**(2), 181–202.

Mustar, P., Renault, M., Colombo, M.G., Piva, E., Fontes, M., Lockett, A., Wright, M., Clarysse, B. and Moray, N. (2006), Conceptualizing the heterogeneity of research-based spin-offs: a multi-dimensional taxonomy, *Research Policy*, **35**, 289–308.

Navis, C. and Glynn, M. (2010), How new market categories emerge: temporal dynamics of legitimacy, identity, and entrepreneurship in satellite radio, 1990–2005, *Administrative Science Quarterly*, **55**, 439–471.

Navis, C. and Glynn, M. (2011), Legitimate distinctiveness and the entrepreneurial identity: influence on investor judgments of new venture plausibility, *Academy of Management Review*, **36**, 479–499.

Nelson, R.R. (1959), The simple economics of basic scientific research, *Journal of Political Economy*, **67**(3), 297–306.

Nelson, R.R. (2004), The market economy, and the scientific commons, *Research Policy*, **33**(3), 455–471.

O'Kane, C., Mangematin, V., Geoghegan, W. and Fitzgerald, C. (2015), 'University technology transfer offices: the search for identity to build legitimacy', *Research Policy*, **44**(2), 421–437.

Phan, P. and Siegel, D.S. (2006), The effectiveness of university technology transfer: lessons learned, managerial and policy implications, and the road forward, *Foundations and Trends in Entrepreneurship*, **2**(2), 77–144.

Powers, J.B. and McDougall, P. (2005), University start-up formation and technology licensing with firms that go public: a resource-based view of academic entrepreneurship, *Journal of Business Venturing*, **20**(3), 291–311.

Pratt, M.G. and Foreman, P.O. (2000), Classifying managerial responses to multiple organizational identities, *Academy of Management Review*, **25**(1), 18–42.

Pratt, M.G. and Rafaeli, A. (1997), Organizational dress as a symbol of multilayered social identities, *Academy of Management Journal*, **40**, 862–898.

Shane, S. (2004), *Academic Entrepreneurship: University Spinoffs and Wealth Creation*, Cheltenham: Edward Elgar Publishing.

Siegel, D., Waldman, D. and Link, A. (2003), Assessing the impact of organizational practices on the relative productivity of university technology transfer offices: an exploratory study, *Research Policy*, **32**, 27–48.

Sillince, J.A. and Brown, A.D. (2009), Multiple organizational identities and legitimacy: the rhetoric of police websites, *Human Relations*, **62**, 1829–1856.

Sörlin, S. (2007), Funding diversity: performance-based funding regimes as drivers of differentiation in higher education systems, *Higher Education Policy*, **20**, 413–440.

Swamidass, P.M. and Vulasa, V. (2009), Why university inventions rarely produce income? Bottlenecks in university technology transfer, *The Journal of Technology Transfer*, **34**, 343–363.

Toole, A.A. and Czarnitzki, D. (2010), Commercializing science: is there a university brain drain from academic entrepreneurship?, *Management Science*, **56**, 1599–1614.

Van Gestel, N. and Hillebrand, B. (2011), Explaining stability and change: the rise and fall of logics in pluralistic fields, *Organization Studies*, **32**(2), 231–252.

Vora, D. and Kostova, T. (2007), A model of dual organizational identification in the context of the multinational enterprise, *Journal of Organizational Behavior*, **28**, 327–350.

Zuckerman, E.W. (1999), The categorical imperative: securities analysts and the illegitimacy discount, *American Journal of Sociology*, **104**, 1398–1438.

45 University Venture Funds

Introduction

University venture funds, or investment assets held by universities dedicated to backing university technology commercialization at the startup, early or growth stages, are a recent phenomenon. The first student-managed venture fund is the University of Utah's University Venture Fund, established in 2001, by an alumnus at the height of the internet boom. Since then, the growth of such funds has been slow, relative to the growth of university endowments (among the largest institutional investor class in the world) and student-managed portfolio funds trading in public equity and fixed income assets. However, the growth is noticeable because much of it has been recent and comes on the heels of a crisis in the public funding of academic research and development (Mowery, 1998). Except for the UK, this phenomenon is largely US-based and therefore shaped by the institutional structure of the US higher education system (cf., Groh et al., 2011), including the funding model for research and development, securities legislation and culture of risk-taking. In other countries, public venture capital comes from the government (Lerner, 2002; Chang et al., 2008).

The remainder of this chapter discusses the following: the likely reasons for university venture funds; the types of university venture funds and their characteristics; issues related to the management of such entities; and future directions university venture funds are likely to take. I will also discuss the research challenges and opportunities of the phenomenon and suggest some approaches.

The rationale for university venture funds

At first blush, the reason for university venture funds is not obvious. University endowment managers, except for the occasional fad such as internet equity and hedge funds, are generally governed by conservative investment philosophies. The Employee Retirement Income Security Act (ERISA) of 1974, under which some university investable funds may fall, further restricts the degree of risk that universities can take. State legislatures have their own rules and, in the case of public universities, may impose risk limiting restrictions to protect endowments.

The endowments of universities are primarily designed to support their teaching, research and public service missions. They are often managed to meet two objectives, namely to fund existing obligations and new strategic initiatives, many of which are long-term in nature – such as buildings, educational programs, professorial chairs and scholarships – and to comply with the wishes of donors, many of whom are trying to create legacies. Therefore, university endowment investment objectives tend to focus on wealth protection and generating predictable cash flows (Goetzmann et al., 2010). So investments in high-risk assets are uncommon and, if used, are kept to a minimum (generally less than 10 percent of portfolio value).

Having said this, we note that university ventures funds almost always invest in the seed and early stages of university startups. These are in the high-risk category of startup investments and are generally avoided by professional venture capital funds. Some university venture funding programs even provide non-dilutive direct grants, similar to the Small Business Innovation and Research (SBIR) program, to pre-startup ventures to help with technology exploration and concept proofing. The combination of very early stage investing, restricted (to university-related) investment targets and the lack of an exit (many funds are evergreen with returns recycled to the fund) mean that these funds are unlike typical venture capital funds. We know a lot about venture capital in the literature. We know little about university venture funds. Indeed, the relative newness of this phenomenon is illustrated by the lack of meaningful empirical research (except for Croce et al., 2014). Yet, the fact that a small number of universities have continued to invest in venture capital – indeed, that the University of California system announced in September 2014 the creation of the $250 million UC Ventures Fund – suggests a phenomenon that is not transitory and therefore worth exploring in the context of university entrepreneurship and innovation.

We know that startups in technology domains face the Valley of Death (Barr et al., 2009). This phenomenon refers to the financial and skills gaps in the conversion of a scientific discovery to the creation of a sustainable business (Marczewski, 1997) and is especially salient for university discoveries because they tend to be closer to the bench than the market (Christini, 2012). A detailed examination of the investment rationale for many university venture funds shows that bridging the Valley of Death so as to encourage more startup activity is a major reason they exist (cf., Fini et al., 2009). The University of Rochester's University Technology Seed Fund, for example, states that '[b]ecause of the many uncertainties and high risks inherent in very early stage investing, few venture funds make seed investments, particularly in this region,' and thus believes that the university's intellectual capital is more likely to be commercialized with support from internal risk capital. The president of the University of California, Janet Napolitano, states: 'In addition to any financial benefits, we see this fund as a potential vehicle for providing resources to support the basic research and talent – among both faculty and students – required to develop innovations that can benefit California and the world.'

The second reason for such funds, especially those managed by students, is educational (Mallett et al., 2010). The University of Pennsylvania's Wharton Social Venture Fund is a student-led organization with the express purpose of preparing 'students to become leaders in the impact investment community, where sound investment principles are applied to complex social and environmental problems.' At Pennsylvania State University, the $5 million Garber Venture Capital Fund was established in 1999 to provide 'MBA students with real-world experience' by bringing reality to 'the process of private equity investing in early stage technology-based companies.'

The third reason for the existence of university venture funds is to benefit the community in which the university operates and types of companies (green tech, socially conscious, energy, etc.) that exemplify the university's values. Here, the purpose of the fund is to improve regional economic growth by bringing the university's intellectual and human capital to bear on wealth creation through high potential startups (Lawton-Smith, 2006; Grimaldi et al., 2011). The University of Michigan's Social Venture Fund, the first student-run (MBA) impact investment fund in the US, and Cornell University's BR Venture Fund, managed by MBAs at the Johnson Graduate School, are examples of university venture funds developed to directly have impact on their surrounding communities. Portland Development Commission, the economic development agency for the city of Portland, says of the University Venture Development Fund at Portland State University, that 'a research university [presents] exciting opportunities to develop catalytic projects and create jobs. PSU's Venture Development Fund is one of the most efficient mechanisms to grow the economy in Oregon.'

Types of university venture funds
University venture funds fall into two general categories. Those that involve students and those that do not. There is some overlap between the two categories because some funds that do not involve students in the active management of the assets may allow students to observe the process as a learning experience.

The first category of university venture funds do not directly involve students and appear to have three subcategories. One consists of those in which the university treats a venture capital fund as another professionally managed asset class but that invests in university-originated discoveries. For example, Stanford University invested $3.6 million into StartX, an accelerator/venture fund dedicated to commercializing the university's discoveries. The University of Rochester, in addition to its own student-managed venture fund, partnered with the Trillium Group to create the $6.5million University Technology Seed Fund in 2002. That fund includes such limited partners as accredited investors, educational institutions, corporations, trusts and others in the community.

The second subcategory consists of independent private funds that partner with universities to source and invest in their technologies. Osage University Partners, for example, is a $100 million venture fund that works exclusively with more than 50 universities and research labs to provide seed-stage funding for their commercialization efforts. IllinoisVENTURES, launched by the University of Illinois, Chicago, is a seed and early-stage technology investment firm focused on information technology, green technology, life and physical sciences startups from Midwest universities and federal laboratories. At the University of Pennsylvania, MentorTech Ventures is a privately owned and operated, seed and early-stage venture capital fund that invests in startups from the Penn ecosystem.

In the third subcategory are funds directly managed by the university that may be run out of the office of technology transfer or the university central administration under the auspices of the provost or president. For example, the University of Oregon Venture Development Fund is overseen by the vice-president for research and innovation, who is also the dean of the Graduate School. At the University of Kansas, the KUIC Venture Fund is disbursed by the president who is advised by an Expert Advisory Group consisting of alumni and friends who are business and scientific technology professionals. The President's Venture Fund, which is non-dilutive to the entrepreneur, at the University of Georgia is managed by the President's Office and is designed to bridge the gap between research grants and seed-stage funding. At New York University, the $20 million NYU Innovation Venture Fund was created in 2010 through the sale of a company spun out of NYU. It exclusively invests in seed-stage startups founded by students, faculty and researchers. The KUIC Venture Fund at the University of Kansas does a similar thing, as does Indiana University's $10 million Innovate Indiana Fund. The Indiana University fund divides its investment into pre-seed and seed stage, in order to deepen its assistance to inventors.

The second type of university venture funds are those that involve students. Andrews and Tichenor (2014) report three subcategories of student-related university venture funds. Student-managed funds are those in which students make the investment decisions and are accountable for the results. Examples include: the $7 million University of Michigan Wolverine Venture Fund, among the first of its kind in the world; the $18 million University of Utah University Venture Fund, the biggest by investments in the world; Cornell University's BR Venture Fund; and the Wharton Social Venture Fund at the University of Pennsylvania. Perhaps the most comprehensive fund of this type, focused on all stages of the venturing process, is Northeastern University's student-founded IDEA organization. IDEA provides coaching, connections and funding to entrepreneurs from the university. On the funding side, the organization provides direct, non-educational grants called the Gap Fund, as well as seed capital to develop prototypes of ideas that could be evaluated for marketability. The funds are provided in the form of non-dilutive grants to help Northeastern entrepreneurs get a head start on their ideas.

Student-observed funds are those managed by professionals but include students as 'eavesdroppers' in the process. Students participate in sourcing and structuring deals, business analysis and portfolio monitoring, with the professionals making the final investment decision. These internship experiences are part of the students' educational curriculum but because the investment decision is not made, do not carry the same degree of responsibility and potential liability as student-managed funds (Meyer et al., 2011; Peng et al., 2009). Examples include Stanford University's StartX and Oregon State University's Venture Development Fund.

The third type of student-involved university venture funds are angel alumni networks, which are not strictly funds, but syndicates of angels with association to the university, usually as alumni who are entrepreneurs or former entrepreneurs with an interest in fostering entrepreneurship on campus. An example is Columbia University's Columbia Technology Ventures, which is Columbia's office of technology transfer with a strong focus on startups. CTV fosters startups by networking industry partners with inventors and students and arranges for the seed funding of its startups through the Columbia alumni network. This category of student-involved funds is less common and, because it does not directly involve the university endowment, tends to be less organized.

Structure of university venture funds

Although the specific structure of university venture funds is varied, there are some common elements that one can detect from the literature. Those funds that directly invest in startups are organized like for-profit venture capital funds. There is a general partner (the university or the student management team) and limited partners (accredited investors, alumni and friends, or other investment funds). Among those funds that invest in other funds (i.e., funds of funds), the structure is unitary, consisting of the endowment manager with an advisory board and the university endowment as the sole client. In the case of student-managed funds, the structure can be more varied but is generally unitary and consists of the student management team with an advisory board consisting of technology experts and faculty. Many university venture funds, such as the NYU Innovation Venture Fund and UC Ventures, are legally separate from the university in order to limit liability and comply with securities regulations involving the management of other people's money.

Unlike standard venture capital, university venture funds tend to be evergreen. This means that they invest the cash flows from exits back into the fund to be redirected to other investment opportunities. While such funds can pay dividends, mostly to private investors, the real value for non-university affiliates to be involved is in the opportunity to better understand the university's research programs to find technologies for licensing, as well as to be 'in on the ground floor' in the case of breakthrough innovations. The sources of university venture funds tend to be more varied than those of for-profit venture capital funds. In the examples given in this chapter, the funds almost always have a component of philanthropic support from alumni and individuals (faculty and staff) who have benefited from their entrepreneurial activities at the university. Generally, funds of this type are dedicated to the development activities surrounding venture capital and used to provide pre-seed grants for concept proofing or prototyping. They are non-dilutive. Another source of funds comes from the university endowment. These funds might form a very small component of the university's total endowment (not more than 10 percent) but are nonetheless critical because they demonstrate the university's commitment to its social enterprise mission. They are often the seed funds to create the venture fund and therefore can be significant in size. More importantly, such funds serve as magnets for other syndicated investors. The third source of funds, which is dilutive, comes from limited partners and other investment managers seeking to access cutting-edge university technologies. This source is relatively small compared to the contributions from donors and the university. However, they are also critical in that they expose university venture fund management to market forces and practices. From the standpoint of the educational benefit of having a university venture fund, the inclusion of for-profit institutional investors provides an opportunity for students and faculty to network directly with venture capital professionals – a learning experience that is very difficult to replicate in the classroom.

The varied sources of funds make the management of a university venture fund a complicated matter. This is particularly true for standards of performance. Unlike for-profit venture capital funds, where the return on investment is a clear and often sole criterion for follow-on investments and managerial discipline, university ventures funds serve a number of purposes (as discussed earlier in the chapter). Therefore, the rate of start-ups and deal flow are often more important than the exit values. Because they are evergreen, sustainability of the fund may be more important than profitability. These criteria are dissimilar to for-profit venture capital funds. The latter do not generate deal flow per se (although deal flow is a criterion for judging the health of a fund's investment potential), and are willing to take more risk on individual deals because the lifespan of a fund is typically delimited by an exit event (they do not have similar capital preservation constraints as the evergreen university venture fund). Second, university venture funds are mission-driven (as distinct from strategy-driven). This is especially true for social venture funds of the type earlier described. These funds restrict themselves to specific investment criteria and impact goals. While this may be similar to impact investment funds, because the range of potential ventures is restricted by the requirement to invest in university derived ideas, the rate of growth of such funds is naturally attenuated. As can be seen from the data presented earlier, university venture funds, especially the student-managed variety, tend to be small in size. Therefore, the impact that they might have on regional economic development is yet to be fully understood.

Discussion and future directions
Given the emergent nature of this phenomenon, the topic of university venture funds deserves more research. Beginning with building good theory, this phenomenon offers the researcher an opportunity to extend agency theory in new directions. In standard agency theory, the interests of the investor are relatively clear, even if the types of investors (hedge funds, pension funds, individuals, corporate venture funds, insurance funds and so on) differ. The standard approach to modeling the variation of investor interests is to construct a portfolio of investment horizons over which the investment syndicate optimizes its returns on investment or over which the investment syndicate writes claims of various durations, risk/return profiles and priorities. In university venture funds, the philanthropic component adds an investment objective that is not strictly financial. Hence, how this is treated in the model is yet to be properly specified and can be the subject of creative theorizing.

Except for Croce et al. (2014), Andrews and Tichenor (2014) and Peng et al. (2009) there have been few attempts at empirically studying university venture funds. This is an area rich for further work, although the data collection would be challenging. First, specifying the sampling frame, given the heterogeneity of funds described in this chapter, is challenging. Technically, the selection of a sampling framework should proceed by identifying a dependent variable (with the appropriate variations) that the sample cases have in common. Because the sources of funds vary among university venture funds, their performance objectives and standards of performance will systematically vary. Although this can be statistically accounted for by the use of control variables (or fixed effects models), the construction of the survey questionnaire (which is the only way that one can obtain data at this stage of development) would be challenging. The appropriate constructs to operationalize and the theoretical relationships hypothesized are likely to be systematically heterogeneous. This will render the saliency and valence of the questions in the survey systematically different for different types of respondents. Nonetheless, in spite of these challenges, this topic is worth expending resources to be better understood, if for no other reason than that the role of the university in venture creation and economic wealth creation continues to increase in importance, as the role of governments continues to decline in developed economies.

PHILLIP H. PHAN

References

Andrews, W.A. and Tichenor, J.M. (2014), Considering a student managed venture capital fund? Approaches, benefits, and performance, *Journal of Applied Business and Economics*, **16**(4): 22–30.

Barr, S.H., Baker, T., Markham, S.K. and Kingon, A.I. (2009), Bridging the Valley of Death: lessons learned from 14 years of commercialization of technology education, *Academy of Management Learning and Education*, **8**(3), 370–388.

Chang, Y.-C., Chen, M.-H., Yang, P.Y. and Hua, M. (2008), Universities as patent- and licensing income-generating institutions: a survey in Taiwan, *International Journal of Technology Management*, **42**(3), 290–309.

Christini, A. (2012), Why universities should step up in venture investing, *Nature Biotechnology*, **30**(10), 933–936.

Croce, A., Grilli, L. and Murtinu, S. (2014), Venture capital enters academia: an analysis of university-managed funds, *Journal of Technology Transfer*, **39**(5), 688–715.

Fini, R., Grimaldi, R. and Sobrero, M. (2009), Factors fostering academics to start up new ventures: an assessment of Italian founders' incentives, *Journal of Technology Transfer*, **34**(4), 380–402.

Goetzmann, W.N., Griswold, J. and Tseng, Y.F. (2010), Educational endowments in crises, *The Journal of Portfolio Management*, **36**(4), 112–123.

Grimaldi, R., Kenney, M., Siegel, D.S., and Wright, M. (2011), 30 years after Bayh–Dole: reassessing academic entrepreneurship, *Research Policy*, **40**(8), 1045–1057.

Groh, A.P., Liechtenstein, H. and Lieser, K. (2011), The European venture capital and private equity country attractiveness indices, *Journal of Corporate Finance*, **16**, 205–224.

Lawton-Smith, H. (2006), *Universities, Innovation and the Economy*, London: Routledge.

Lerner, J. (2002), When bureaucrats meet entrepreneurs: the design of effective 'public venture capital' programmes, *The Economic Journal*, **112**(477), F73–F84.

Mallett, J.E., Belcher, L.J. and Boyd, G.M. (2010), Experiment no more: the long-term effectiveness of a student-managed investments program, *Journal of Financial Education*, **36**(3/4): 1–15.

Marczewski, R.W. (1997), Bridging the virtual valley of death for technology, *R&D Scientist*, **11**(2), 11–12.

Meyer, A.D., Aten, K., Krause, A.J., Metzger, M.L. and Holloway, S.S. (2011), Creating a university technology commercialisation programme: confronting conflicts between learning, discovery and commercialisation goals, *International Journal of Entrepreneurship and Innovation Management*, **13**(2), 179–198.

Mowery, D.C. (1998), The changing structure of the US national innovation system: implications for international conflict and cooperation in R&D policy, *Research Policy*, **27**(6), 639–654.

Peng, Z., Dukes, W. and Bremer, R. (2009), Evidence on student-managed funds: a survey of US universities, *Business Education and Accreditation*, **1**(1), 55–64.

46 Valuing an Entrepreneurial Enterprise

Introduction

Why does one company have a greater value than another? Placing a value on companies has long been one of the most important concerns to scholars as well as thought leaders in business and policy. Not surprisingly, given the importance of this issue, a large and compelling literature has emerged that provides both frameworks and guidance to practitioners as to how valuing companies can best be approached and undertaken. These frameworks and approaches have provided insights and guidance to generations of practitioners in understanding both how to value companies as well as the reasons underlying why some companies are valued more highly than others.

However, more recently a new type of company has emerged – the high-technology-based enterprise. These companies differ from earlier generations and forms of businesses in many dimensions. For example, technology-based startups typically may not yet have a viable product that is a proven commercial success in the market. They may not yet have made their first sale. This throws the more traditional approaches to company valuation into disarray, and raises a number of questions and issues that were not relevant for the more traditional approaches to valuing traditional businesses.

The purpose of this chapter is to provide a brief and succinct overview about the most recent and compelling new approaches that are emerging to value technology-based entrepreneurial companies. In particular, this chapter addresses questions such as how does one value a technology-based entrepreneurial enterprise; a company that is nascent, embryonic or even young and has yet to commercialize any technology? As best we can estimate, there is a steady state of about 100,000 such new technology-based enterprises that are in need of valuation in the United States, and globally the number is in the millions.[1] Traditional valuation tools are based either on a projection from past earnings or on marketable assets. The problem is that a nascent or young entrepreneurial enterprise rarely has either.

This chapter identifies and explains the central problem inherent with traditional valuation methods and then provides a discussion for new models of valuation.

The problem with traditional valuation models

The most commonly used valuation model for a going concern is one that is based on a projection of past earnings. In Table 46.1 we set forth the steps that a valuation will normally take to arrive at a fair market value for

Table 46.1   Present value of adjusted future net earnings valuation method

Steps	Procedure	Comments about applicability for an entrepreneurial enterprise
1	Determine the expected life of the business – a limited life of n years or an indefinite life.	Given the nature of an entrepreneurial enterprise and its entrepreneur, it is impossible to determine the life of the enterprise.
2	Estimate an appropriate discount rate, r.	Because the discount rate reflects the resource and market risk of the enterprise, and because there are no comparable businesses, r cannot be estimated.
3	Normalize the income statement.	By definition, there are no revenues on the enterprise's income statement. Normalizing it for, say, owner's compensation could be done, but it would have no useful value.
4	Calculate a weighted average of adjusted future net earnings assuming that a weighted average of adjusted future net earnings is appropriate.	There are no net earnings to weigh.
5	Calculate the present value of the weighted average of adjusted future net earnings using either the limited life present value equation, to which a residual value for the business must then be added, or a capitalization equation.	Absent net earnings, no present value can be calculated.
6	Adjust for marketability as appropriate.	Absent a present value estimate, a marketability adjustment is meaningful.

Source: Audretsch and Link (2012: 135–136)

a going concern. And we annotate those steps to illustrate how this model is inappropriate for valuing an entrepreneurial enterprise.

While the academic and professional literature on the topic of how to value an entrepreneurial enterprise is nearly non-existent, we propose in this chapter that there is a systematic method through which one can approach the problem. The approach that we support can be summarized as follows. 'When valuing an entrepreneurial enterprise – a technology-based entrepreneurial enterprise in particular – the key to approaching the valuation is to focus on and understand the availability of alternative or complementary technologies rather than the existence of substitutable products' (Audretsch and Link, 2012: 3).[2]

Discussion

We are convinced that the general issue of valuing an entrepreneurial enterprise is of growing importance. In a globalized economy, creating and acting upon new ideas to generate valuable products and services has taken on a new significance. However, taking a domestic perspective, such products and services are being supplied by entrepreneurial overseas companies; creativity certainly is not geographically bound. Thus, it is reasonable to expect that, as technology lifecycles are shortening and forecasts for which new technologies will gain market acceptance are variable and uncertain, the need for a systematic valuation of an entrepreneurial enterprise is apparent.

In addition, the traditional methods of enterprise valuation are based on assessing the risks associated with various outcomes. However, such enterprise valuation is premised on the assumption that such risks can be assigned a reasonable level of probability and that the set of outcomes can be reasonably known. By contrast, a technology-based entrepreneurial enterprise is better characterized by uncertainty in that the outcomes may not even be known, so that no such associated risk assessments and probabilities can be linked to outcomes.

DAVID B. AUDRETSCH AND ALBERT N. LINK

Notes

1. This chapter draws heavily on Audretsch and Link (2012).
2. This approach is illustrated for a hypothetical entrepreneurial enterprise in Audretsch and Link (2012).

Reference

Audretsch, D.B. and Link, A.N. (2012), *Valuing an Entrepreneurial Enterprise*, New York: Oxford University Press.

Index